T0139912

Humanity Driven AI

Fang Chen · Jianlong Zhou
Editors

Humanity Driven AI

Productivity, Well-being, Sustainability and Partnership

Editors
Fang Chen
University of Technology Sydney
Sydney, NSW, Australia

Jianlong Zhou
University of Technology Sydney
Sydney, NSW, Australia

ISBN 978-3-030-72190-9 ISBN 978-3-030-72188-6 (eBook)
https://doi.org/10.1007/978-3-030-72188-6

This Springer imprint is published by the registered company Springer Nature Switzerland AG
The registered company address is: Gewerbestrasse 11, 6330 Cham, Switzerland

Preface

Artificial intelligence (AI) is changing the world around us dramatically. Along with the development of the digital age, AI technologies have been rapidly blossoming, advancing and maturing. Through AI, machines have exhibited human-like cognition, as they relieve workers of repetitive or dangerous tasks. AI is, therefore, claimed to be the driving force of the Fourth Industrial Revolution. When we look at the past 200 years, the previous industrial revolutions have radically improved the standards of living for humans. As AI becomes more sophisticated and gains the ability to perform more complex human tasks, we will only see more and more questions regarding what AI will be in decades—and what it means, not just for business, but for humanity as a whole, and for the future of humans and society. Ultimately, AI will change the way people are living, working and entertaining.

Let us draw our attention to how much human expertise revolves around data, how much knowledge can be encoded into data and how much knowledge can be formed via analysis of data. AI is uniquely situated for automating routine knowledge work and generating new insights from available data. Such AI abilities create different excellent smart systems to improve **productivity** for different purposes. For example, AI can continuously monitor the condition of critical infrastructures (e.g. bridges, water pipes) and predict their risks and failures automatically. AI-driven intelligent transport systems allow to monitor transport volumes to avoid heavy congestions and provide on-demand transport capabilities. Moreover, AI will play even more critical roles in dangerous fields like mining, firefighting and clearing mines for not only productivity but also human safety.

While we continuously find that AI benefits various aspects of human needs, increased human social and economic activity creates more opportunities for AI to achieve human goals. The addition of AI to existing world not only removes obstacles to human creativity, but also turbocharges human skills with the cognitive and processing power of AI. New opportunities are being created to enhance human **well-being**. For example, AI can be put to work in human services, enabling intelligent processes that improve service delivery speed, providing insight-driven services that optimise decision-making and offering proactive and personalised support at the right time, thereby delivering new and improved personalised services for citizens. AI is also changing the recruiting and hiring processing, matching job seekers to the most relevant open positions. Besides, AI plays tremendous roles in fighting COVID-19 pandemic to protect people from virus infections. AI can benefit human well-being significantly, in almost as many ways as it is possible to imagine.

Climate change and global warming are increasingly becoming major concerns of society, resulting in the growing awareness of the importance of sustainable activities. AI has the potential to greatly improve environmental **sustainability** by achieving better monitoring, understanding and prevention of damage and overuses on the Earth's land, air and water. For example, AI can help water and waste management systems to more efficiently monitor water loss (e.g. water leakage) and water quality. It can also more effectively manage sewer water processing such as by adding reasonable chemical dosing, as to lessen environmental impacts. Furthermore, AI can be used to better monitor air pollutions and identify sources of air quality issues faster and more accurately. Moving to the energy sector, AI can make renewable energy technology like solar panels and wind turbines more efficient and cost effective by optimising relevant parameters. AI enables to develop more efficient and greener systems for the more sustainable future—in the right applications, it can only lower our dependence on fossil fuels and move our paths towards sustainable use of land.

As varied as the applications of AI can be, the crux of the matter is the following: human and AI actively enhance each other's complementary strengths for a **partnership**. AI augments human capabilities and empowers individuals for better decisions, while humans assist AI in training models, explain the AI outcomes with domain knowledge and sustain the responsible use of AI, such as by preventing AI from harming humans. AI needs to follow a core principle that anything an AI does has to fit into a human-centred value system, not a machine-centred value system, by taking unique human abilities into account. Such human–AI collaboration, or partnership, can only be beneficial. AI does not exist without the human in partnership and, therefore, fundamentally needs to fit into value systems that are human in nature. As such, we only continue to advance our understanding of how AI functions as a facilitator to achieve and enhance human goals, from basic needs to high-level well-being. These understandings advance along with the development of AI technologies and grow as we realise the large and numerous impacts of AI on society.

The above observations and discussions motivate the editing of this book: *Humanity Driven AI*. The edited book makes a systematic investigation into how AI functions as a facilitator to achieve and enhance human needs in the digital age. We report the state-of-the-art advances in theories, techniques and applications of humanity-driven AI. The book specifically focuses on four aspects of humanity that AI can interact with: **productivity**, **well-being**, **sustainability** and **partnership**. The book consists of five parts.

The first part emphasises that to satisfy human needs are important aspects of the humanity and proposes that AI solutions can be categorised to meet various human needs in different levels of Maslow's hierarchy of needs. A concept of humanity-in-the-loop is presented to integrate human needs into every stage of AI life cycle. Other chapters in this book can be fit into this concept. During this process, ethics should be well maintained and assured by implementing AI ethical principles at every stage of the AI life cycle. Human needs must be met ethically.

The second part focuses on the aspects of AI that improve productivity to meet human needs. We move first to the fact that infrastructures such as water pipes are indispensable assets of a city. The efficiency of water infrastructure management plays significant roles in the smooth running of society. AI can help water utilities to maintain their distribution systems in a financially viable way. Next we consider a well-functioning urban transport networks and how such a network is crucial and essential for the free flow of people and freight. AI can predict the mobility of public transport and help to mitigate the impact of traffic congestion by providing timely information of bus arrival time to promote productivity in traffic congestion management. AI can also help the railway services to meet the performance metrics and recover from incidents with consideration of a range of impacting factors.

The third part introduces the attempts and efforts of the use of AI for improving human well-being. Privacy protection is an important issue in health-related organisations. AI can enable the development of an open health ecosystem by learning a shared model across users or organisations, without direct access to the data. We also show the use of AI for investigation of 3D neuron morphology in order to understand functions and activities in brain circuits, moving towards discovering the brain development process related to health and brain function modification to improve human well-being. More recently, AI has been playing significant roles in combating the battle against COVID-19 pandemic to protect human well-being. This part introduces case studies where AI plays a significant role and in an essential component from this perspective.

The fourth part features the use of AI for improving sustainability and environment protection. Taking the wastage of water as an example generated every moment in the earth because of various activities of humans, the safe delivery of wastewater through sewer pipes from its occurrence place to the treatment factory is a critical one that significantly affects the earth's land, air and clean water. Here we present the use of AI in inspecting the corrosion status of sewer pipes in order to improve efficiency and save costs in sewer pipe maintenance and rehabilitation. Air pollution is another issue that affects human health and environment sustainability. We also demonstrate the great potential for AI in improving knowledge and understanding about air pollution and environmental health. Furthermore, AI can help to protect the marine ecosystems by avoiding the use of human-made tools such as shark nets in coast regions while maintaining human safety at the same time.

The fifth part explores the AI–human relationships and reports on AI–human partnerships from different perspectives. From the educational perspective, AI has changed the human–machine interaction mode of online learning and helps to provide personalised teaching and guidance for online learners with a multi-channel interaction mechanism. AI can further examine and track learners' engagement in educational situations. Furthermore, AI can help people with disabilities by addressing practical problems that they encounter in a variety of domains. This part investigates opportunities and issues in order to enhance the partnership between AI and people with disabilities. In addition, AI explainability plays a significant role in building high trustworthiness of AI to humans. This part provides a common understanding of important aspects and factors involved in building a trustworthy AI for explainability and causability measures in medicine.

This edited book creates an important opportunity to not only promote AI techniques from the humanity's perspective, but also invent novel AI applications for better humanity. The book aims to serve as the dedicated source for the theories, methodologies and applications on humanity-driven AI, establishing state-of-the-art research and providing a ground-breaking textbook to graduate students, research professionals and AI practitioners.

Sydney, Australia
July 2021

Fang Chen
Jianlong Zhou

Contents

AI for Sustainability

AI + Human Partnership

Contributors

Colin Bellinger Digital Technologies, National Research Council of Canada, Ottawa, Canada

Michael Blumenstein School of Computer Science, Australian Artificial Intelligence Institute, University of Technology Sydney, Sydney, NSW, Australia

Luka Brcic Medical University Graz, Graz, ST, Austria

Weidong Cai School of Computer Science, University of Sydney, Sydney, NSW, Australia

Fang Chen Data Science Institute, University of Technology Sydney, Sydney, NSW, Australia

Allison Clarke Data and Analytics Branch, Health Economics and Research Division, Australian Department of Health, Canberra, NSW, Australia

Xuhui Fan The University of New South Wales, Sydney, Australia

Amir H. Gandomi Faculty of Engineering and Information Technology, University of Technology Sydney, Sydney, NSW, Australia

Christian Geißler DAI-Labor, Technical University Berlin, Berlin, Germany

Leah Gerrard Faculty of Engineering and Information Technology, Australian Artificial Intelligence Institute, University of Technology Sydney, Sydney, NSW, Australia

Guido Governatori CSIRO Data61, Eveleigh, NSW, Australia

Ting Guo Data Science Institute, University of Technology Sydney, Sydney, Australia

Andreas Holzinger Medical University Graz, Graz, ST, Austria

Mohomed Shazan Mohomed Jabbar Alberta Machine Intelligence Institute, Edmonton, Canada

Jing Jiang Faculty of Engineering and Information Technology, Australian Artificial Intelligence Institute, University of Technology Sydney, Sydney, NSW, Australia

Michaela Kargl Medical University Graz, Graz, ST, Austria

Bettina Kipperer Medical University Graz, Graz, ST, Austria

Tobias Küster DAI-Labor, Technical University Berlin, Berlin, Germany

Bin Li Fudan University, Shanghai, China

Boyu Li Data Science Institute, University of Technology Sydney, Sydney, Australia

Zhidong Li Data Science Institute, University of Technology Sydney, Sydney, Australia

Bin Liang Data Science Institute, University of Technology Sydney, Sydney, Australia

Dongnan Liu School of Computer Science, University of Sydney, Sydney, NSW, Australia

Jun Liu School of Computer Science and Technology, Xi'an Jiaotong University, Xi'an, China

Siqi Liu Digital Services, Digital Technology & Innovation, Paige AI, New York, NY, USA

Guodong Long Faculty of Engineering and Information Technology, Australian Artificial Intelligence Institute, University of Technology Sydney, Sydney, NSW, Australia

Qinghua Lu CSIRO Data61, Eveleigh, NSW, Australia

Ling Luo School of Computing and Information Systems, University of Melbourne, Melbourne, VIC, Australia

Heimo Müller Medical University Graz, Graz, ST, Austria

Charlene Nielsen School of Public Health, University of Alberta, Edmonton, Canada

Alvaro Osornio-Vargas Department of Pediatrics, University of Alberta, Edmonton, Canada

Yuming Ou Data Science Institute, University of Technology Sydney, Sydney, NSW, Australia

Markus Plass Medical University Graz, Graz, ST, Austria

Iman Rahimi Faculty of Engineering and Information Technology, University of Technology Sydney, Sydney, NSW, Australia

Peter Regitnig Medical University Graz, Graz, ST, Austria

Rohit Salgotra Department of Electronics and Communication Engineering, Thapar Institute of Engineering and Technology, Patiala, India

Muhammed Saqib School of Computer Science, Australian Artificial Intelligence Institute, University of Technology Sydney, Sydney, NSW, Australia

Paul Scully-Power Ripper Corporation Pty Ltd, South Brisbane, QLD, Australia

Jesus Serrano-Lomelin Department of Obstetrics and Gynecology, University of Alberta, Edmonton, Canada

Nabin Sharma School of Computer Science, Australian Artificial Intelligence Institute, University of Technology Sydney, Sydney, NSW, Australia

Tao Shen Faculty of Engineering and Information Technology, Australian Artificial Intelligence Institute, University of Technology Sydney, Sydney, NSW, Australia

Yang Song School of Computer Science and Engineering, University of New South Wales, Sydney, NSW, Australia

Yue Tan Faculty of Engineering and Information Technology, Australian Artificial Intelligence Institute, University of Technology Sydney, Sydney, NSW, Australia

Zihao Tang School of Computer Science, University of Sydney, Sydney, NSW, Australia

Heng Wang School of Computer Science, University of Sydney, Sydney, NSW, Australia

Yang Wang Data Science Institute, University of Technology Sydney, Sydney, Australia

Bifan Wei School of Continuing Education, Xi'an Jiaotong University, Xi'an, China

Jason J. G. White Educational Testing Service, Princeton, NJ, USA

Jon Whittle CSIRO Data61, Eveleigh, NSW, Australia

Osnat Wine Department of Pediatrics, University of Alberta, Edmonton, Canada

Jie Xu Data Science Institute, University of Technology Sydney, Sydney, NSW, Australia

Xiwei Xu CSIRO Data61, Eveleigh, NSW, Australia

Jianhui Yu School of Computer Science, University of Sydney, Sydney, NSW, Australia

Kun Yu Data Science Institute, University of Technology Sydney, Sydney, NSW, Australia

Osmar R. Zaïane Alberta Machine Intelligence Institute, Edmonton, Canada

Norman Zerbe Charité Universitätsmedizin Berlin, Berlin, Germany

Chaoyi Zhang School of Computer Science, University of Sydney, Sydney, NSW, Australia

Donghao Zhang Monash e-Research Centre, Monash University, Melbourne, VIC, Australia

Jianjia Zhang School of Biomedical Engineering, Sun Yat-sen University, Guangzhou, China

Lingling Zhang School of Computer Science and Technology, Xi'an Jiaotong University, Xi'an, China

Qinghua Zheng School of Computer Science and Technology, Xi'an Jiaotong University, Xi'an, China

Jianlong Zhou Data Science Institute, University of Technology Sydney, Sydney, Australia

Liming Zhu CSIRO Data61, Eveleigh, NSW, Australia

AI and Humanity

Towards Humanity-in-the-Loop in AI Lifecycle

Jianlong Zhou and Fang Chen

1 Humanity and Human Needs

According to Merriam Websters dictionary, humanity is the quality of being human, which includes different aspects such as human nature and human condition, from philosophy. Human needs are important aspects for the humanity. Maslow's hierarchy of needs [9, 12] is a commonly referenced model of human needs (see Fig. 1). From this theory, human needs are represented as a five-stage model of pyramid from the basic needs at the bottom to higher psychological needs on the top of the needs pyramid, which are physiological needs, safety needs, belongings and love needs, esteem needs, and self-actualisation. The needs that belong towards the bottom of the pyramid are basic needs (physiological and safety), the ones at the middle of the pyramid are psychological needs (belongingness and love and esteem), and the ones that belong to the top of the pyramid are growth needs (self-actualisation). One must satisfy lower-level basic needs before progressing on to meet higher level growth needs.

Furthermore, the progress of humanity is always driven by the advancement of technologies in meeting various human needs from ancient stone tools and bronze and iron tools, the eighteenth centuries' Industrial Revolution of water and steam power to mechanise production, to recent electric power to create mass production and more recent electronics and information technology to automate production. We are currently in the so-called the Fourth Industrial Revolution driven by big data and artificial intelligence (AI) [27]. It is therefore significant to understand how AI can benefit the humanity's progress effectively and how humanity can contribute to the advancement of AI technologies.

In this chapter, we firstly introduce powerful capabilities of AI and negative effects AI may cause to humans. It is shown that different levels of human needs based on the Maslow's hierarchy can be met by AI solutions. On the other hand, AI can be

J. Zhou (✉) · F. Chen
Data Science Institute, University of Technology Sydney, Sydney, Australia
e-mail: jianlong.zhou@uts.edu.au

F. Chen
e-mail: fang.chen@uts.edu.au

F. Chen and J. Zhou (eds.), *Humanity Driven AI*,
https://doi.org/10.1007/978-3-030-72188-6_1

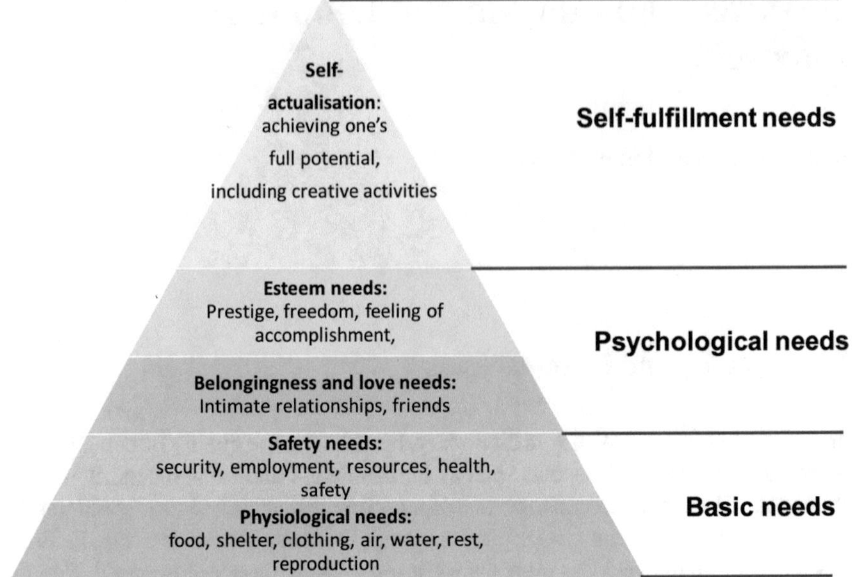

Fig. 1 Maslow's hierarchy of needs

implemented through various stages in a lifecycle. A concept of humanity-in-the-loop is proposed to integrate human needs into the AI lifecycle. We show how human needs can be met at the every stage of the AI lifecycle. Furthermore, AI ethics is integrated into this concept for meeting human needs ethically. We also demonstrate the challenges of humanity-in-the-loop of AI for meeting human needs.

2 Artificial Intelligence

AI is typically defined as an autonomous and self-learning agency with the ability to perform intelligent functions in contrast to the natural intelligence displayed by humans, such as learning from experience, reasoning, problem-solving [19, 27]. It is a computer system which performs tasks that are typically associated with human intelligence or expertise. It has powerful capabilities in prediction, automation, planning, targeting, and personalisation (see Fig. 2). It is transforming our world, our life, and our society and affects virtually every aspect of our modern lives [26].

The impressive performance of AI we have seen across a wide range of domains motivates extensive adoptions of AI in various sectors including public services, transport, health care, retail, education and others. For example, AI enables the monitoring of climate change and natural disasters [17], enhances the management of public health and safety [14], automates administration of government services [2],

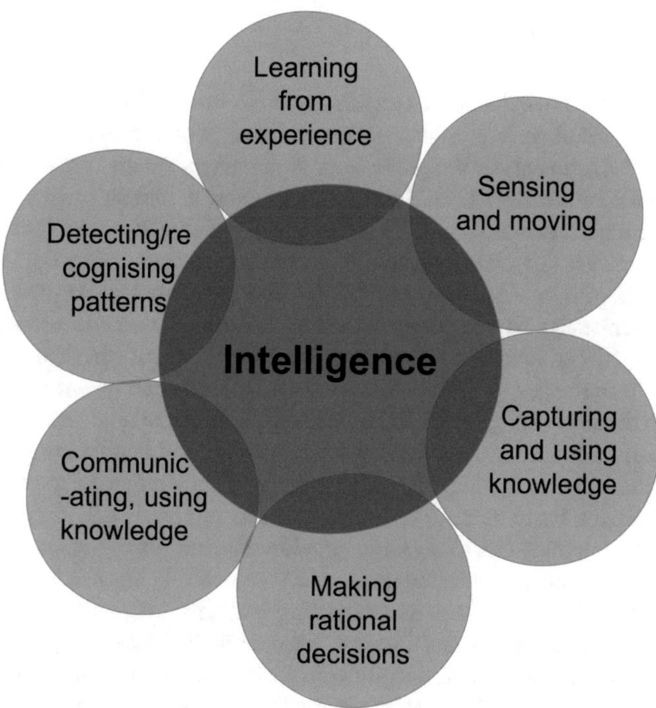

Fig. 2 AI can make things as smart as humans or even smarter

and promotes productivity for economic well-being of the country. AI also helps to enable efficient fraud detection (e.g. in welfare, tax, trading, credit card) [3] and enhances the protection of national security (e.g. with unauthorised network access and malicious email detection) [1] and others.

However, AI may cause negative effects to human beings. For example, AI may require huge volumes of personal data in some domains in order to learn and make decisions, and the concern of privacy becomes one of important issues in AI [6]. Because AI can do many repetitive work more efficiently than humans, people also worry about that their jobs will be replaced by AI and they will lose jobs. Furthermore, the highly developed AI algorithms such as generative adversarial networks (GANs) can generate high-quality and lifelike faces, voices, and other human expressions [16], which may also be used to do illegal things in the society. For example, GANs have been used to create fake videos by replacing the face of a person by the face of another person, which have harmful usages including fake news, hoaxes, and financial fraud [20].

3 AI for Human Needs

Generally, it is assumed that AI can enable machines to exhibit human-like cognition, and it is more efficient (e.g. higher accuracy, faster, working 24 h) than humans in various tasks. Claims about the promise of AI are abundant and growing related to different areas of our lives [27]. Some examples are: in human's everyday life, AI can recognise objects in images [29], it can transcribe speech to text, it can translate between languages [13], it can recognise emotions in images of faces or speech [11, 24, 25]; in travelling, AI makes self-driving cars possible [5], AI enables drones to fly autonomously, AI can predict parking difficulty by area in crowded cities; in medicine, AI can discover new uses for existing drugs, it can detect a range of conditions from images, it enables the personalised medicine; in agriculture, AI can detect crop disease, and spray pesticide to crops with pinpoint accuracy; in finance, AI can make stock trades without human intervention and handle insurance claims automatically; AI can identify potentially threatening weather in meteorology. In meeting human's basic needs, AI can be used to predict water pipe failures for reliable water supplies [23, 31] and to provide efficient energy management [22]. Furthermore, AI can promote human's safety and well-being needs by providing personalised medicine [18] and understanding human's emotions [11, 24, 25, 30] during decision-making. AI and robotics are able to simulate the emotional experience and consequences of physically being with another person, which is called artificial intimacy and could meet needs for tenderness and warmth, for romance, empathy, and friendship [7]. The applications of artificial intimacy may include a therapy-bot, a best-friend-for-your-child-bot, or a care-bot for grandma. Examples of self-esteem needs include fame, prestige, and self-confidence. AI can conduct various creative work, such as paint a van Gogh painting [8], write poems and music, write film scripts, design logos, recommend songs/films/books you like [4] for people's self-esteem needs. Furthermore, self-actualization sits highest on the pyramid of Maslow's hierarchy of needs. To utilise and develop talents are example for this level of needs. AI can help to conduct effective employee development and upskilling skills [10, 21].

These diverse and ambitious claims motivate wide adoptions of AI in various sectors including retail, education, health care, and others. All these adoptions will ultimately help to deliver a better quality of life with manageable cost of living, better environment, easy access of transport for time saving, etc. These diverse and ambitious claims of AI can be categorised to meet various levels of human needs in the Maslow's hierarchy of needs (see Fig. 1). Table 1 shows examples of AI solutions meeting different human needs in the Maslow's hierarchy (see Fig. 1).

Therefore, human needs play a significant role in and drive the AI development. However, it is not clear how human needs can be integrated with the AI development effectively so that AI can benefit humanity with high impact. This chapter introduces a concept of humanity-in-the-loop in AI lifecyle in the next section by considering human needs at every stage of the AI lifecyle.

Table 1 Human needs and AI

Human needs type	Needs examples	AI examples for needs
Physiological needs	Water, energy, food, health, sleep, clothes, shelter, sex	Water pipe failure prediction [31], energy management [22]
Safety needs	Personal security, emotional Security, financial security, Well-being	Personalised medicine [18], Recognise emotions [11, 24, 25, 30]
Belongingness and love needs	Family, friendship, intimacy	Artificial intimacy [7]
Esteem needs	Fame, prestige, Self-confidence	Paint a van Gogh painting [8], Write poems and music, recommend songs/films/books [4]
Self-actualisation upskilling needs	Utilising and developing talents and abilities, partner acquisition, pursuing goals, parenting	Employee development and skills [10, 21]

4 Humanity-in-the-loop in AI Lifecycle

In this section, we firstly present different stages of the AI application lifecycle. We then introduce the concept of humanity-in-the-loop and demonstrate how human needs can be integrated into the AI lifecycle to better meet human needs.

4.1 *AI Lifecycle*

A typical lifecycle for an AI application project development usually includes different stages from business and use case development, design phase, training and test data procurement, building AI application, testing the system, deployment of the system to monitoring performance of the system (see Fig. 3). The AI lifecycle delineates the role of every stage in data science initiatives ranging from business to engineering. It provides a high-level perspective of how an AI application project development should be organised for real and practical business value with the completion of every stages. In the AI lifecycle, the first stage is to identify a business and use case to tangibly improve operations, increase customer satisfaction, or otherwise create value. Based on the identified problems, the AI application is designed at least with the following information: (1) the objectives to be obtained in the AI application, (2) the data to be collected, and (3) machine learning algorithms to be used and formalised. The next stage is to collect and prepare all of the relevant data for use in machine learning. After this, the machine learning model is trained and tested with the collected data. The major objective is to get high performed and easily

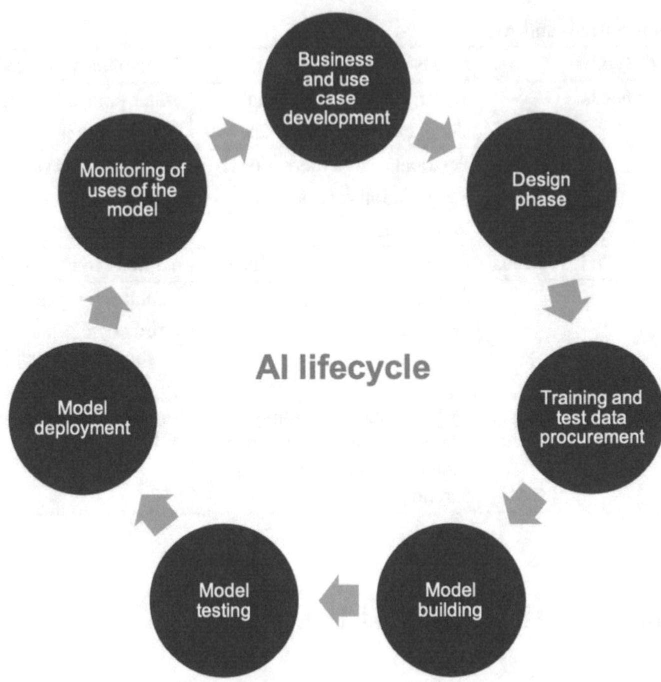

Fig. 3 Different stages of an AI lifecycle

generalised machine learning models. Then, the model is deployed in applications and monitored during the use to improve it iteratively if any problems are found.

4.2 Humanity-in-the-loop for Human Needs and AI Ethics Assurance

It is one of important objectives of AI solutions to meet various human needs. In this section, we introduce human needs into the AI lifecycle and propose a concept of humanity-in-the-loop. AI ethics can also be regarded as a special kind of human need. It is integrated into this concept as well for meeting human needs ethically. Based on this concept of humanity-in-the-loop, during the business and use case development stage in the AI lifecycle, the human needs that the AI solution aims to solve are clearly identified and well understood. These needs can be any types of needs ranging from physiological needs to self-actualisation needs presented in the previous section and should be reachable based on the current AI techniques and available data.

After human needs are identified, the AI solution is designed to decide what data will be used, what outcomes will be, who will use it, and what AI approaches will be used as well as others. During this stage, human needs are refined to make them implementable in AI. In the training and test data procurement stage, different data related to human needs are collected so that they are used to build AI models and test them in the followed stages, where AI models are required to meet human needs as accurately as possible.

In the model deployment stage, the AI model is deployed in practice to meet human needs. The use of the AI model is also monitored to find any possible problems of the AI model in meeting human needs. If any problems are found during this stage, the AI lifecycle will be iterated to solve problems. Therefore, in the whole AI lifecycle, human needs act as the core in driving the AI lifecycle for the successful AI solutions (see Fig. 4).

Furthermore, the AI lifecycle delineates the role of every stage in data science initiatives ranging from business to engineering. It provides a high-level perspective of how an AI project should be organised for real and practical business value with the completion of every stages. Morley et al. [15] constructed a typology by combining the ethical principles with the stages of the AI lifecycle to ensure that the AI system is designed, implemented and deployed in an ethical manner. The typology indicates that each ethical principle should be considered at every stage of the AI lifecycle.

In the AI ethics for the whole AI lifecycle, different stages of AI lifecycle may have different emphases on ethical principles. For example, in the data procurement stage,

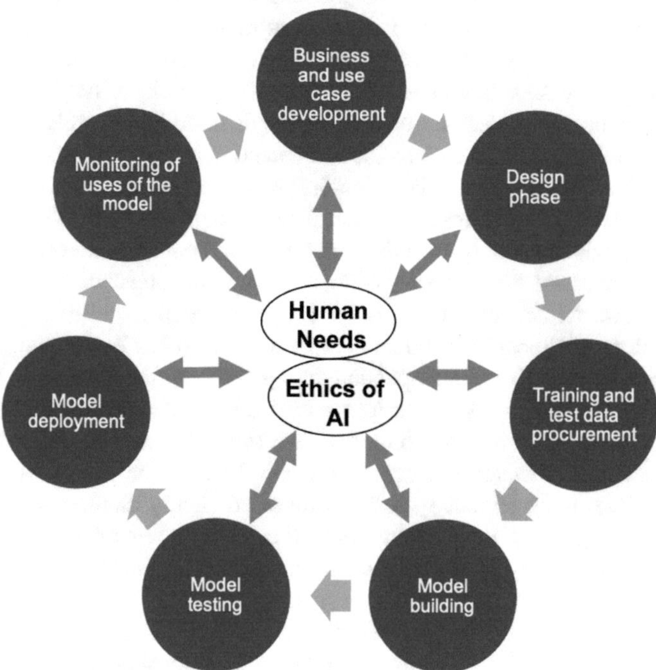

Fig. 4 Human needs and AI ethics assurance in the AI lifecycle

the data privacy is the core principle, while in the AI model building stage, stakeholders are more interested in the model transparency. Therefore, AI ethics plays as the key component in the AI lifecycle to control the development and use of AI models [28]. The concept of AI ethics assurance aims to ensure the compliance of whole AI lifecycle with ethical principles. Ethical principles should also be implemented at every stage of the AI lifecycle while also giving different emphases on different ethical principles at different stages of the AI lifecycle. From this perspective, the assurance of AI ethics is implemented at every stage of the AI lifecycle. Furthermore, we argue that AI ethics assurance should be combined with human needs in the AI lifecycle considering the effects of human needs on AI ethics assurance.

As a result, the humanity-in-the-loop provides a high-level framework to make sure that AI meets various levels of human needs ethically by considering requirements of human needs and integrating assurance of ethical AI at every stage of the AI lifecycle. Such concept of humanity-in-the-loop of AI not only guarantees that AI meets human needs effectively and ethically, but also provides high-level guidance for the development of AI solutions in meeting various human needs.

5 Discussion

Human needs are important aspects for the humanity. AI has the strong capacity to meet or promote various levels of human needs ranging from basics needs such as food and water needs to self-fulfilment needs such as creative activities. This chapter tried to encapsulate AI solutions into the Maslow's hierarchy of needs to show how different AI approaches meet various human needs in different levels. It was found that the most of current AI solutions focus on meeting human's basic needs with the use of AI-driven smart systems. For example, AI can continuously monitor the condition of critical infrastructures (e.g. water pipes) and predict their risks and failures automatically, which not only meets human needs for the stable water supply but also significantly improves the efficiency of infrastructure maintenance (see Chap. 3).

Furthermore, AI benefits humanity by enhancing human well-being in various aspects such as healthcare and human services. AI also has been playing tremendous roles in fighting COVID-19 pandemic to protect people from virus infections (see Chap. 8). In addition, AI can improve environmental sustainability by achieving better monitoring, understanding, and prevention of damage and overuses on Earth's land, air, and water. For example, Chap. 9 shows the use of AI in helping water and waste management systems to more efficiently monitor water wasting (e.g. water leakage) and water quality, as well as to more effectively manage sewer water processing (e.g. by adding reasonable chemical dosing to lessen environmental impacts).

AI can help humanity for the self-fulfilment needs by forming partnerships between human and AI. For example, AI can provide personalised education based on learner's personal background and learning experiences to augment learning capabilities and empower individuals for better learning performance to achieve individuals' full potential (see Chap. 13). AI can help to improve the employee development and upskilling skills based on personal expertise and experiences.

This chapter proposed humanity-in-the-loop approach to integrate humanity and ethics of AI into every stage of AI lifecycle in order to make sure that human needs are fully understood at the the beginning stage of business and use case development, enough data are collected for high-performance modelling to meet human needs, and human needs are met consistently by monitoring the use of the model after the model is deployed. During this process, ethics should be well maintained and implemented at every stage of the lifecycle to make sure that the use of AI is ethical and does not cause any harms to humans.

While AI meets human needs in different levels for the productivity, well-being, sustainability, and partnership, we are continuously seeing further challenges when AI is used for various human needs, and some of examples are:

- The conversion of human needs to applicable AI problems is a challenge. Some human needs are abstract and may be difficult to design effective corresponding AI problems because of data and evaluation issues;
- The collection of data for various level of human needs is a challenge because of availability, privacy, or other issues;
- The implementation of AI ethical principles at each stage of the AI lifecycle is still a challenge.

Therefore, the future work on humanity-in-the-loop of AI can focus on the set up of pipelines/frameworks to convert various human needs into AI problems that can be implementable. For a specific case of human need to AI problem conversion, innovative techniques such as sensor technologies can be used to collect data used for the model building. AI ethical principles should be implemented at each stage of the AI lifecycle.

6 Summary

This chapter proposed that AI solutions can be categorised to meet various levels of human needs in Marslow's hierarchy of needs. Based on the review of AI capabilities and the AI application lifecycle, a concept of humanity-in-the-loop was presented to integrate human needs into the AI lifecycle so that human needs are fully understood and met at each stage of the AI lifecycle. AI ethical principles were proposed to be implemented at each stage of the AI lifecycle to make sure that human needs are met ethically. The humanity-in-the-loop provides high-level guidance for the development of AI solutions in meeting various human needs. The future work on the humanity-in-the-loop of AI can focus on the effective setup of AI problems from various human needs, innovative approaches for data collection for building models as well as the implementation of ethical principles of AI at each stage of the AI lifecycle.

References

1. Amrollahi, M., et al.: Enhancing network security via machine learning: Opportunities and challenges. In: Handbook of Big Data Privacy, pp. 165–189. Springer (2020)
2. Anastasopoulos, L.J., Whitford, A.B.: Machine learning for public administration research, with application to organizational reputation. Journal of Public Administration Research and Theory **29**(3), 491–510 (2019)
3. Awoyemi, J.O., Adetunmbi, A.O., Oluwadare, S.A.: Credit card fraud detection using machine learning techniques: A comparative analysis. In: Proceedsing of 2017 ICCNI, pp. 1–9 (2017)
4. Batmaz, Z., Yurekli, A., Bilge, A., Kaleli, C.: A review on deep learning for recommender systems: challenges and remedies. Artificial Intelligence Review **52**(1), 1–37 (2019)
5. Bojarski, M., Del Testa, D., Dworakowski, D., Firner, B., Flepp, B., Goyal, P., Jackal, L.D., Monfort, M., Muller, U., Zhang, J., Zhang, X., Zhao, J., Zieba, K.: End to end learning for self-driving cars. arXiv:arXiv:1604.07316v1 [cs, CV] (2016). https://arxiv.org/abs/1604.07316v1
6. Deane, M.: AI and the future of privacy. https://towardsdatascience.com/ai-and-the-future-of-privacy-3d5f6552a7c4 (2018)
7. Essig, T.: Sleepwalking towards artificial intimacy: How psychotherapy is failing the future. https://www.forbes.com/sites/toddessig/2018/06/07/sleepwalking-towards-artificial-intimacy-how-psychotherapy-is-failing-the-future/ (2018). Forbes
8. Gao, X., Tian, Y., Qi, Z.: RPD-GAN: Learning to draw realistic paintings with generative adversarial network. IEEE Transactions on Image Processing **29**, 8706–8720 (2020)
9. Kenrick, D.T., Griskevicius, V., Neuberg, S.L., Schaller, M.: Renovating the pyramid of needs: Contemporary extensions built upon ancient foundations. Perspectives on psychological science **5**(3), 292–314 (2010)
10. Liu, J., Huang, J., Wang, T., Xing, L., He, R.: A data-driven analysis of employee development based on working expertise. IEEE Transactions on Computational Social Systems pp. 1–13 (2021)
11. Luo, S., Zhou, J., Duh, H.B.L., Chen, F.: BVP feature signal analysis for intelligent user interface. In: Proceedings of the 2017 CHI Conference on Human Factors in Computing Systems Extended Abstracts (2017)
12. McLeod, S.: Maslow's hierarchy of needs. Simply Psychology (2020)
13. Monroe, D.: Deep learning takes on translation. Communications of the ACM **60**(6), 12–14 (2017)
14. Mooney, S.J., Pejaver, V.: Big data in public health: Terminology, machine learning, and privacy. Annual Review of Public Health **39**(1), 95–112 (2018)
15. Morley, J., Floridi, L., Kinsey, L., Elhalal, A.: From what to how. an overview of AI ethics tools, methods and research to translate principles into practices. arXiv:1905.06876 [cs] (2019). http://arxiv.org/abs/1905.06876
16. Nguyen, T.T., et al.: Deep learning for deepfakes creation and detection: A survey. arXiv:1909.11573 [cs, eess] (2020). http://arxiv.org/abs/1909.11573
17. Rolnick, D., et al.: Tackling climate change with machine learning. arXiv:1906.05433 [cs, stat] (2019). http://arxiv.org/abs/1906.05433
18. Schork, N.J.: Artificial intelligence and personalized medicine. Cancer treatment and research **178**, 265–283 (2019)
19. Taddeo, M., Floridi, L.: How AI can be a force for good. Science **361**(6404), 751–752 (2018)
20. Tolosana, R., Vera-Rodriguez, R., Fierrez, J., Morales, A., Ortega-Garcia, J.: DeepFakes and beyond: A survey of face manipulation and fake detection. arXiv:2001.00179 [cs] (2020). http://arxiv.org/abs/2001.00179
21. Varshney, K.R., Chenthamarakshan, V., Fancher, S.W., Wang, J., Fang, D., Mojsilovic, A.: Predicting employee expertise for talent management in the enterprise. In: Proceedings of KDD 2014 (2014)
22. Xu, Y., Ahokangas, P., Louis, J.N., Pongrácz, E.: Electricity market empowered by artificial intelligence: A platform approach. Energies **12**(21) (2019)

23. Zhang, B., Guo, T., Zhang, L., Lin, P., Wang, Y., Zhou, J., Chen, F.: Water Pipe Failure Prediction: A Machine Learning Approach Enhanced By Domain Knowledge, pp. 363–383. Springer (2018)
24. Zhao, S., Gao, Y., Jiang, X., Yao, H., Chua, T.S., Sun, X.: Exploring principles-of-art features for image emotion recognition. In: Proceedings of the 22nd ACM international conference on Multimedia, pp. 47–56 (2014)
25. Zhou, J., Bridon, C., Chen, F., Khawaji, A., Wang, Y.: Be informed and be involved: Effects of uncertainty and correlation on users confidence in decision making. In: Proceedings of ACM SIGCHI Conference on Human Factors in Computing Systems (CHI2015) Works-in-Progress (2015)
26. Zhou, J., Chen, F.: Human and Machine Learning: Visible, Explainable, Trustworthy and Transparent. Springer (2018)
27. Zhou, J., Chen, F.: AI in the public interest. In: C. Bertram, A. Gibson, A. Nugent (eds.) Closer to the Machine: Technical, Social, and Legal Aspects of AI. Office of the Victorian Information Commissioner (2019)
28. Zhou, J., Chen, F., Berry, A., Reed, M., Zhang, S., Savage, S.: A survey on ethical principles of AI and implementations. In: Proceedings of 2020 IEEE SSCI (2020)
29. Zhou, J., Li, Z., Zhi, W., Liang, B., Moses, D., Dawes, L.: Using convolutional neural networks and transfer learning for bone age classification. In: Proceedings of 2017 International Conference on Digital Image Computing: Techniques and Applications (2017)
30. Zhou, J., Sun, J., Chen, F., Wang, Y., Taib, R., Khawaji, A., Li, Z.: Measurable decision making with gsr and pupillary analysis for intelligent user interface. ACM Transactions on Computer-Human Interaction **21**(6) (2015)
31. Zhou, J., Sun, J., Wang, Y., Chen, F.: Wrapping practical problems into a machine learning framework: using water pipe failure prediction as a case study. International Journal of Intelligent Systems Technologies and Applications **16**(3), 191–207 (2017)

AI and Ethics—Operationalizing Responsible AI

Liming Zhu, Xiwei Xu, Qinghua Lu, Guido Governatori, and Jon Whittle

1 Introduction

When it comes to AI and Ethics/Law,[1] there are two interrelated aspects of the topic. One is on how to design, develop, and validate AI technologies and systems responsibly (i.e., Responsible AI) so that we can adequately assure ethical and legal concerns, especially pertaining to human values. The other is the use of AI itself as a means to achieve the Responsible AI ends. In this chapter, we focus on the former issue.

In the last few years, AI continues demonstrating its positive impact on society while sometimes with ethically questionable consequences. Not doing AI responsibly is starting to have devastating effect on humanity, not only on data protection, privacy, and bias but also on labor rights and climate justice [1]. Building and maintaining public trust in AI has been identified as the key to successful and sustainable innovation [2]. Thus, the issue of ethical AI or responsible AI has gathered high-level attention. Nearly one hundred principles and guidelines for ethical AI have been issued by private companies, research institutions, and public organizations [3, 4] and some consensus around high-level principles has emerged [5]. On the other hand, principles

[1] Law is usually considered to set the minimum standards of behavior while ethics sets the maximum standards so we will use the word "ethics" throughout the chapter.

L. Zhu (✉) · X. Xu · Q. Lu · G. Governatori · J. Whittle
CSIRO Data61, 13 Garden Street, Eveleigh, NSW, Australia
e-mail: liming.zhu@data61.csiro.au

X. Xu
e-mail: xiwei.xu@data61.csiro.au

Q. Lu
e-mail: qinghua.lu@data61.csiro.au

G. Governatori
e-mail: guido.governatori@data61.csiro.au

J. Whittle
e-mail: jon.whittle@data61.csiro.au

F. Chen and J. Zhou (eds.), *Humanity Driven AI*,
https://doi.org/10.1007/978-3-030-72188-6_2

and guidelines are far from ensuring the trustworthiness of AI systems [6]. Complicating the issue further, humans and societies perceive trust in AI in intricate ways, which does not necessarily closely match the trustworthiness of a particular AI system [7–9].

The remainder of the paper is organized as follows: Sect. 2 discusses the challenges of existing works on ethical AI. The framework with an integrated view of three aspects of ethical AI is discussed in Sect. 3. Section 4 shares our experience and observations in a crop yield prediction project. Section 5 talks about the high-level ethical principles and their operationalization. Finally, Sect. 6 concludes the chapter.

2 Ethical AI Challenges

2.1 Classification of Existing Works on Ethical AI

Significant research has gone into addressing ethical AI challenges. In this section, we discuss the existing works, which fall into three large categories:

1. **High-level ethical principle frameworks**. A large number of high-level ethical principle frameworks [4] (e.g., Australian AI Ethics Principles[2]). They identify the important ethical and legal principles responsible AI technologies and systems are supposed to adhere to. Some effort, such as [10], further divides these high-level principles into guidelines at the team, organizational, and industry level. These high-level principles are hard to operationalize for many reasons [6] we will discuss later.
2. **Ethical algorithms**. Significant research has gone into ethical algorithms where the formulation of some ethical/legal properties is amenable to mathematical definitions, analysis, and theoretical guarantees. These include properties such as privacy [11] and fairness [12] or for specific types of AI systems [13]. This covers mechanisms that deal with preprocessing of data (to remove bias or individualistic characteristics), the learning process itself (to take into consideration of ethical constraints), learned models (to be further compliant with ethical constraints), and predictive results (to correct for residual bias or revealing individualistic information). However, these mechanisms are algorithm focused with limited theoretical heuristic, confined to a small number of quantification-amenable properties, and a small subset of ethical principles and human values [14]. Most of the time, these ethical-aware algorithms are too complicated to explain to less numeracy-equipped stakeholders and not connected to the broader decision-making process [2]. They are also not linked to the software development processes, especially system design methods, requirements engineering, or user-centered design (UCD) processes.

[2] https://www.industry.gov.au/data-and-publications/building-australias-artificial-intelligence-capability/ai-ethics-framework/ai-ethics-principles.

3. **Human values in software engineering and their operationalization**. Recently, there has been emerging research in human values in software engineering and their operationalization [15, 16], including:

   (a) Extension of value-based design methods (e.g., value-sensitive design—VSD) [17]
   (b) Extension of human factor research on productivity and usability into human values consideration but still limited to a small subset of human values [14]
   (c) Software engineering methods for embedding human values and ethical consideration throughout the software development life cycle (SDLC) [15, 18, 19]
   (d) Architecture and design patterns that can improve (qualitatively or quantitatively) [20] or assure (with strong mathematical guarantees), "by-design," certain ethical or human-value related quality attributes such as privacy and non-maleficence (e.g., security, safety, and integrity) [21, 22]

2.2 *Issues of Existing Works on Ethical AI*

We identify three issues in current research work regarding operationalizing ethical principles to achieve the ultimate trust from stakeholders.

2.2.1 Mixing Inherent Trustworthiness with Perceived Trust

The inherent and technical *"trustworthiness"* of an AI system can be directly reflected in technologies/**products** via code, algorithms, data, or system design or indirectly reflected via the software development **processes**). On the other hand, trust is a stakeholder's (i.e., truster's) subjective estimation of the trustworthiness of the AI system. This subjective estimation is based on a truster's expected and preferred future behavior of the AI system. Mixing the two in terms of identifying assurance mechanisms and presenting trustworthy evidence can overlook the additional and special mechanisms required to gain trust (different from the ones for gaining trustworthiness).

A highly technically trustworthy system may not be trusted by trusters for one reason or another, rationally or irrationally. This is because a truster's subjective estimation of the system's trustworthiness and expectations may have a significant gap compared to the system's inherent trustworthiness. It can also be the other way around when a truster overestimates a system's trustworthiness and puts undue trust into it.

The reasons for this gap may be related to several issues:

- a truster's numeracy (impacting the understanding of different types of trustworthiness evidence);
- a truster's prior beliefs and experiences;

- a truster's preferences and expectations on acceptable behaviors, types of evidence, and explanation[9];
- a system's observable behaviors to a truster.

2.2.2 Operationalizing Ethical Principles

There are many reasons why we still lack systematic methods to operationalize the high-level ethical principles. Some are due to the AI field's relatively short history (e.g., compared with the medical field) thus lacking professional norms, legal and professional accountability mechanisms, clear common aims, fiduciary duties, and importantly proven methods to translate principles into practices [6]. Others are due to the lack of consideration of a wider set of human values [23] such as political self-determination and data agency beyond technical dependencies [24].

We believe another important factor is due to the relatively narrow attempt to operationalize human values and ethical principles into verifiable "product" trustworthiness (via mathematical guarantees) without systematically exploring a wider variety of mechanisms in development processes to improve both **trustworthiness** and **trust**. Looking at process mechanisms can include highly tailored evidence gathering and communication mechanisms for different types of trusters. These will help close the gap between their subjective estimation and the system's more objective inherent trustworthiness.

2.2.3 Unique Characteristics of AI

Finally, many of the works do not actively consider the unique characteristics of AI during operationalization. Referring to one [25] of the many definitions of AI, AI is a collection of interrelated technologies used to **solve problems autonomously** and perform tasks to achieve defined objectives, in some cases **without explicit guidance from a human being**. AI has its own agency [3] reflected in its autonomy (i.e., acting independently), adaptability (i.e., learning in order to react flexibly to unforeseen changes in the environment), and interactivity (i.e., perceiving and interacting with other agencies, human or artificial). So by AI's definition and its inherent autonomy-related characteristics, it would be impossible (not simply hard) to accurately and completely specify all the goals, undesirable side-effects, and constraints (including ethical ones) at its finest level of details. This is known as the value alignment problem: given an optimization algorithm, how to make sure the optimization of its objective function results in outcomes that we actually want, *in all respects*? As one saying goes, "*It never does just what I want, but only what I tell it.*" This inherent under-specification issue is both a boon and a bane of AI. Thus, it is important not just to use guarantee mechanisms but to introduce a range of product and process-related risk mitigation mechanisms. This will include things like continuous validation and monitoring of systems [26] after deployment, broadening specifications, and real-world validation [27].

3 Our Solution

Although previous work has produced high-level ethical AI principles, general notions of trust vs trustworthiness and product vs process support, they have not been integrated into the context of responsible AI. The contribution of this book chapter is the integrated view of the three aspects and how they help improve both trust and trustworthiness of AI for a wider set of stakeholders. This integrated view includes three components:

- the difference between trust and trustworthiness in the context of ethical AI principles;
- how different product and process mechanisms can achieve trustworthiness for different ethical principles;
- how different product and process evidence can be presented to different types of trusters to improve the accuracy of their subjective estimation so they match the inherent trustworthiness of the systems.

Our work also takes into consideration of the autonomy characteristics of AI and its inherent under-specification challenges. Figure 1 gives a graphical representation of our framework.

For conceptualizing the relationship between trust and trustworthiness, we use the definitions and concepts from Bauer's work [28]:

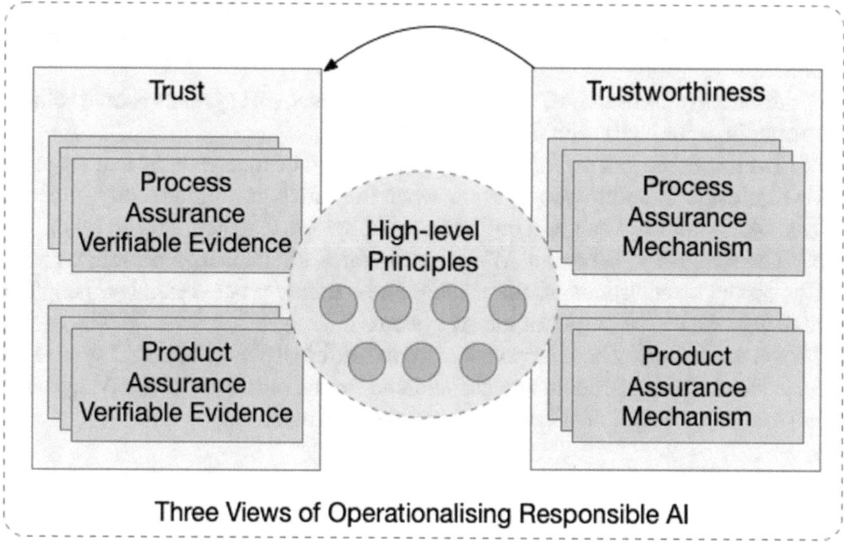

Fig. 1 Conceptual model

Trust $P_{A_{it_0}}$ is truster A_i's subjective estimate of the probability P_{b_j} that B_j will display A_i's preferred behavior X_{kt_1}, i.e., of B_j's trustworthiness.

In our work, B_j represents an AI system. The behaviors X_{kt_1} displayed by B_j can include functional behaviors, behaviors that handle ethical constraints (e.g., privacy, security, reliability, safety, and other human values and well-being) and metalevel behaviors (e.g., transparency, explainability [29], and accountability). A truster's subjective estimate at t_0 is about the AI system's future behavior at t_1. There are some arguments around the concept of trust being binary (rather than probabilistic) in reality as you either trust something or not. When you eventually decide to accept a system to be trusted, you then accept the associated harm if the trusted party fails. We believe this binary notion is consistent with the probabilistic notion if you introduce a threshold along the probability spectrum to discern trusted or not trusted.

We use Australia's ethical AI principles [25] and their definitions as a close-enough representation of the many similar ones [4, 5] around the world. Australia's ethical AI principles contain eight key principles.

- *P1: Human, social, and environmental well-being*: Throughout their life cycle, AI systems should benefit individuals, society, and the environment.
- *P2: Human-centered values*: Throughout their life cycle, AI systems should respect human rights, diversity, and the autonomy of individuals.
- *P3: Fairness:* Throughout their life cycle, AI systems should be inclusive and accessible and should not involve or result in unfair discrimination against individuals, communities, or groups.
- *P4: Privacy protection and security*: Throughout their life cycle, AI systems should respect and uphold privacy rights and data protection and ensure the security of data.
- *P5: Reliability and safety*: Throughout their life cycle, AI systems should reliably operate in accordance with their intended purpose.
- *P6: Transparency and explainability:* There should be transparency and responsible disclosure to ensure people know when they are being significantly impacted by an AI system and can find out when an AI system is engaging with them.
- *P7: Contestability:* When an AI system significantly impacts a person, community, group, or environment, there should be a timely process to allow people to challenge the use or output of the AI system.
- *P8: Accountability:* Those responsible for the different phases of the AI system life cycle should be identifiable and accountable for the outcomes of the AI systems, and human oversight of AI systems should be enabled.

3.1 The Difference Between Trust and Trustworthiness in the Context of Ethical Principles

We group the eight principles in two categories based on their nature and characteristics. The first group includes the first five principles (P1–P5), which are human values and ethical constraints similar to the non-functional software qualities [30] to be considered. The second group includes the last three principles (P6, P7, and P8), which are metalevel governance issues.

3.1.1 Principles as Software Qualities

These principles sometimes can be framed as functional requirements of a software system. If that is the case, in the context of software engineering, the methodology of requirement engineering could be adopted to ensure that the requirements captured are as accurate and complete as possible. It is worth noting again that AI systems cannot be fully specified and will try to solve the problems **autonomously** with a level of independence and agency. On the other hand, there will be conflicting requirements whereby tradeoff decisions need to be made.

Some principles, such as security, reliability, and safety, are the non-functional properties well studied in the dependability research community [31]. These principles can be captured as non-functional requirements and considered from the early stage of system design. There are technical mechanisms or reusable design fragments, like patterns and tactics, that could be applied to fulfill the quality requirements [32]. Privacy is not a standard software quality [30], but has been treated as an increasingly important property of a software system to realize regulatory requirements, like General Data Protection Regulation (GDPR)[3] and Australia Privacy Act, into technical artifacts. Reusable practices and patterns have been summarized in both industry and academia for privacy [20]. Fairness is a concern that the machine learning developers should consider from the early stage of the data processing pipeline. Similar to before, collections of best practice and mechanisms to remove bias at different stages of the pipeline have been compiled [12]. The reason to group these principles is that they can be handled and validated using a similar approach: the methodology of how non-functional properties is handled in software system design. Some principles can be validated in a quantifiable way, like reliability. Others could be validated against process-oriented best practices, methods, and widely used patterns.

3.1.2 Principles as Governance Issues

The principles within this group are largely governance issues and designed to improve truster's confidence in the AI system. They can be seen as clear requirements

[3] General Data Protection Regulation, https://gdpr-info.eu/.

for certain functionality provided by the software system or entities providing the system. For example, contestability requires a system or entity function that allows the trusters to challenge the output or use of the AI system. Transparency and explainability are similar in that the users can have access to the system, data, algorithms to understand it, including receiving an explanation of a decision or prediction.

3.1.3 Trust Versus Trustworthiness of Ethical AI Principles

Each principle can have different implications in terms of trust vs. trustworthiness. Essentially, the difference is between what an AI system can objectively perform (trustworthiness) and what a truster/stakeholder "prefers/wants" (trust expectation) and their subjective estimation of the behavior of the AI system. And it has been observed that human may have very different expectations of AI or human even their trustworthiness are similar [7]. We list these differences in Table 1.

As we can see, trust is about subjective estimation and perception and often not limited to the AI system's trustworthiness properties (whether via software artifacts or development processes). As identified in [8], multiple factors contributes to people's trust in an AI system, including factors not related to a specific AI system such as current society safeguards such as regulations, overall AI uncertainty, job impact, and familiarity of AI. Some factors may be related to the organizations that build the AI systems, use the AI system, or evaluate the AI system. The specific characteristic of the AI system only plays a minor role in trust.

3.2 Product and Process Mechanisms for Trustworthiness

We continue using the same grouping as the last section to analyze the eight principles to demonstrate different product and development process (including the people aspect) mechanisms to improve trustworthiness. This differentiation teases out a broader set of considerations to improve trustworthiness, which subsequently helps understand what are the different ways in which these mechanisms could be communicated to different stakeholders/trusters to improve trust.

For human, social, and environment well-being and human-centered values, we also consider organizational culture and SDLC methods including roles and agile practices. For quality attributes-related ethical principles, we apply architecture and design processes, patterns and tactics, and refer to a range of data, model [27], and algorithmic considerations. [34]. We consider design process ("in design"), design artifacts ("by-design"), and designers ("for designers"). [3] For governance issues, we build upon the principles in [3, 16, 24, 35].

We introduce some considerations and examples across the Product and Process/People dimension in Table 2. Many of the mechanisms presented in the table rely on industry-wide and society-wide work, in particular:

Table 1 Trust versus trustworthiness

	Trustworthiness	Trust
Human, social, and environmental well-being	Whether stakeholder requirements are captured accurately and completely and tradeoff are made in an informed and consultative way	Whether a truster perceives the entity, the process, and society safeguards [8] collecting requirements and making tradeoffs are trustworthy and whether a truster's requirements are addressed adequately
Human-centered values	Whether comprehensive sets of relevant values are considered [33] throughout the SDLC	Whether a truster perceives the entity, the process, and society safeguards [8] of developing, verifying, and validating the system are trustworthy
Fairness	Whether data, learning algorithms, learned models, decisions, predictive results, and overall designs are developed with quantifiable fairness, privacy, and security constraints in mind and satisfy the reliability and safety requirements	Whether a truster understands how these constraints are satisfied and perceives the entity, the process and society safeguards of developing, verifying and validating the system are trustworthy
Privacy protection and security		
Reliability and safety		
Transparency and explainability	Whether system requirements, specifications, data, algorithms, models, decisions, system designs, and source code, i.e., all related artifacts, are open for stakeholder inspection and understandable	Whether a truster perceives they can understand the artifacts and explanation associated or they can delegate such access and understanding to a trustworthy third party or society's safeguard regulations
Contestability	Whether there is a timely process specified for people to challenge the use or output of the AI system at an individual decision, group or society level	Whether a truster perceives there is a timely and trustworthy process run by trustworthy entities to challenge the use or output of the AI system at an individual decision, group or society level
Accountability	Whether there are entities and humans identified to be accountable for the outcomes of the AI systems	Whether a truster perceives the identified accountable entities and humans are the right ones and can bear proportionate responsibilities under adverse outcomes

Table 2 Product and process assurance mechanisms

	Product	**Process and people**
Human, social, and environmental well-being	Well-being metrics and associated requirements and subsequent design and continuous validation and monitoring features. Misuse cases and entities, undesirable side-effects	Stakeholder engagement, independent boards, and conflict/tradeoff resolution process. Roles, ceremonies, and organizational culture
Human-centered values	Digital sovereignty [24], culture norms, value statement and stories, value definition and explicit tradeoffs, value-aware training data, learning algorithms, models and decisions/predictions, continuous validation and monitoring	Value tradeoff processes (with accuracy, profit and among different conflicting values). Roles, ceremonies, and org culture
Fairness	Fairness definition and explicit tradeoffs, fairness-aware data, learning algorithms, models and decisions/predictions, continuous validation and monitoring, game-theoretical approach	Fairness tradeoff processes (with accuracy, profit, and among different conflicting fairness measures) roles, ceremonies, org culture, org-level boards, licensed developers
Privacy protection and security	Privacy and security requirements, privacy/security-by-design architectures (such as federated learning), privacy-enhancing data treatment and learning algorithms (such as differential privacy, secure-multiparty-computation), continuous validation and monitoring	Privacy and security definition and tradeoff processes (with accuracy, profit, and among different conflicting values). Roles, ceremonies, org culture
Reliability and safety	Reliability and safety requirements, reliability/safety architectures and designs patterns, reliability/safety-enhancing algorithms	Reliability and safety tradeoff processes (with other quality attributes). Roles, ceremonies, org culture
Transparency and explainability	Features that generate human understandable explanations tailored for different stakeholders. Registration and record keeping, provenance and documentation of all artifacts. Explanations of data, algorithm, models, and decisions. Adjust model complexity. Have "Why did you do that button"	Open process across SDLC including full access to artifacts from stakeholders or 3rd parties representing stakeholders. Processes for iterative exploration and explanation. Consider "no algorithm allowed"
Contestability	Features that allow human intervention of decisions ex ante and ex post	Contestability definition. Roles, ceremonies, org culture, process conformance to standard processes
Accountability	Features that allow provenance and traceability of artifacts and decisions that always have a clear accountable entity and human	Artifact-specific lifecycle management process (such as data accountability [16] and process creation)

- Multistakeholder sector-specific [2] and domain-specific guidelines (such as banned practices in digital platforms [36], regulating software-based medical devices [37], technical solutions, and empirical knowledge bases [6]).
- AI and data ethics board or other governance mechanisms at the organization level [35] to oversee the overall AI-driven decision-making processes (not just algorithms and products).
- Regulator levers that incentivize organizations and create a level playing field for ethical innovation [2] including validation and certification agencies.
- Technical and non-technical ethics and human rights training for different roles and organizational awareness.
- Incentives for employees to play a role in identifying AI ethical risks [35].
- Ongoing monitoring and engagement with stakeholders [26, 35].

Due to the under-specification and value alignment problem of AI, none of the assurance mechanisms can guarantee a desirable outcome alone. Each helps reduce the risk and the ongoing monitoring and engagement post-deployment plays a critical role in identifying and mitigating undesirable side-effects early.

3.3 How to Present Trustworthiness Evidence to Different Types of Trusters

It is important that we present trustworthiness evidence (e.g., product artifacts assurances and process/people assurances) to different types of trusters to help with their subjective estimation so the estimation matches the inherent trustworthiness of the AI systems. Here we have to take into considerations of two different aspects.

Truster Preference: Based on expectation and past experiences, different types of trusters, such as AI algorithm developers, AI system developers, professional users of AI systems, affected subjects (whereby AI systems have impacts on them), regulators and certifiers, or the general public may have different preferences of an AI system's behavior.

Truster-Specific Verifiable Evidence: Different types of trusters may expect different types of evidence for assuring the trustworthiness of an AI system. They may have different abilities to understand and assess the evidence and expect different types of explanations [9]. For example, an AI expert can assess the algorithms while a general public would have no use of the algorithms. A system developer may understand an AI algorithm and the data associated but have limited ability to evaluate the algorithm and bias in data.

When presenting evidence, such as assurance mechanisms in the last section, the following factors should be taken into consideration:

- Consider a stakeholder's technical abilities to understand the evidence.
- Consider a stakeholder's resources and time to assess the evidence.

- Allow both stakeholders and third parties who represent the stakeholders to examine the evidence.
- Allow broader ethical and legal “standing” so the evidence can be produced and examined at an individual decision, group, and society level by a wide range of stakeholders or their delegates.
- Present both process and product assurance mechanisms to the right stakeholders in the right ways.
- Focus more on process mechanisms when ethical principles cannot be easily defined and quantified.
- Focus more on the product mechanisms when ethical principles can be defined and quantified and technically assured.
- Improve overall awareness/familiarity of AI, and understanding of broader AI issues such as current society safeguards, AI’s overall uncertainty, and job impact.

4 Example: Crop Yield Prediction Project

In this section, we share our experience and observations in a crop yield prediction project. In the project, we applied a data-driven approach using machine learning algorithms to develop an improved version of a crop yield prediction model. The previous model was built using a domain model-driven approach and integrated into a commercialized software product. The project combines commercial satellite data and data collected from different farms, largely owned by individual farmers. The resulting machine learning model predicts future yields of farms in both the farm data collection region but also in new regions significantly different from the original regions. There are three types of stakeholders in the project: the technical team (a research organization playing the role of both AI system developer and operation-time learning coordinator), data contributor (i.e., participating farmers who provided the data), and model user (i.e., farmers who use the models for yield prediction). We used a federated machine learning approach to deal with the data ownership problems and the non-IID (independent and identically distributed) data distribution problem. The learning coordinator (i.e., the technical team) designs and operates the model training process on multiple, distributed data contributors. The model was first trained locally on a local server and then sent to a central server for aggregating and improving a global model. The model user performs inference using the aggregated global model. Trustworthiness and trust issues manifested differently for different stakeholders. We applied our approach retrospectively to the project and made the following observations in terms of trust and trustworthiness.

- **Human, social, and environmental well-being**
  - Positive well-being requirements were considered for the project itself but not for wider issues outside the project.
  - Potential misuse of data collected was considered but not for the predictive models.

  - Both data contributors and model users have high-level trust in the technical team as an entity but have very little trust in any third parties who may also use the data (even for claimed well-being improvement reasons).
  - Well-being requirements were specified as high-level goals, not quantifiable metrics.

- **Human-centered values**
  - Human factors on usability and accessibility were considered, consulted, and designed in the original prediction app.
  - No additional human-centered values were captured apart from the explicit ones below.

- **Fairness**
  - Fairness issues were considered at the training data, learning algorithm, and model level but not explicitly explained to data contributors and model users.
  - A range of product assurance mechanisms was used, such as:
    - Counterfactual analysis to discover potential hidden or proxy variables that lead to different yields.
    - Sensitive-variable-aware data preprocessing including random split crop separation (wheat vs. barley) and location separation (at paddock and region level). Each attribute may have associations, thus becoming a proxy variable regarding sensitive and protected attributes.
  - Two team members built fairness-aware models in parallel as a process assurance.
  - Used domain attributes that were understandable to farmers (data contributors and model users) in both training and explanation so farmers can have a higher-level trust in the model regarding fairness across groups (not just accuracy).

- **Privacy and Security**
  - The personal privacy of individual farmers and privacy/confidential info of farms were both identified as key requirements.
  - Potential misuses and harms of privacy info leakage were identified.
  - Both data contributors and model users have high-level trust in the technical team as an entity.
  - Federated learning, including strong privacy guarantees, was used as an architectural pattern fulfilling data privacy requirements.
  - The exchanged model updates were encrypted to improve model security. A model registry was established locally to maintain the mappings of encrypted models to the decrypted models.
  - The concept of federated learning, privacy guarantee, and security mechanisms was difficult to explain to farmers, but the high-level trust in the project team coupled with the notion that their data never left the local server and strong encryption was used gained adequate trust.

- **Transparency and Explainability**
  - Transparency and explainability requirements were identified in the project.
  - Although the farmers would not be able to evaluate data, code, and models directly, the project team nevertheless made all artifacts open to stakeholders (under privacy and confidentiality constraints).
  - Code, model, and data provenance were captured in Git and Bitbucket.
  - On the data contributor side, a data contributor registry was built to store and manage the information of the participating farmers and their paddocks that joined the learning process. Further, a model versioning registry was implemented to keep track of all local model versions of each data contributor and the corresponding global model. Both of the design mechanisms helped increase the trust of both model user and learning coordinator on the participating data contributors.
  - On the learning coordinator side, a decentralized aggregator was designed to replace the central server of the learning coordinator, which could be a possible single point of failure. This improved the trust of farmers (i.e., both data contributors and model users) on the learning coordinator.
- **Contestability**
  - Data contributors can always withdraw from the projects with their data deleted. However, the model trained by their data will not be immediately updated to remove the data.
  - Model users always have the right not to use the prediction or allow the prediction to be used by others.
- **Accountability**
  - The accountability was largely governed by the legal agreement between data contributors, model users, and the project team.
  - No role-level accountability was established, but the provenance of data, model, and code allowed accountability to be examined.

5 Discussion

5.1 Interpretation of High-Level Ethical Principles

Mappings of different ethical principles and guidelines have been recently studied in [4, 5]. Although a global consensus emerges on the core principles (e.g., privacy, transparency, fairness), there have been debates on the classification and definition of AI ethical principles. As we are using Australia's AI ethical principles, we discuss our interpretation and observations of these principles.

- **Autonomy**. Autonomy is not discussed explicitly in the framework. Instead, a broader principle about human-centered values is given, which covers human rights, diversity, and the autonomy of individuals. Autonomy refers to the freedom of AI system users to a range of activities, including self-sovereignty/determination, the establishment of relationships with others, selection of a preferred platform/technology, experimentation, surveillance, and manipulation [4]. This might conflict with AI systems' inherent autonomy which refers to independent actions without a human being. Further, users (i.e., data owners) expect to exert full control over their data and activities without having to rely on others. To ensure autonomy, a distributed ledger technology like blockchain can play a vital role in the design and implementation of a decentralized AI platform, in which secure and self-determined interactions between stakeholders are enabled without a central coordinator.
- **Explainability**. Explainability is listed together with transparency in Australia's AI ethical principles. Transparency refers to disclosure of all related AI artifacts, such as source code, data, algorithms, models, and documentation. Although transparency enables explainability, explainability is more than helping stakeholders understand how an AI system works through responsible disclosure. Stakeholders expect to understand the reasons for AI system behavior and insights about the causes of decisions. However, it is challenging to present the explanations (e.g., representation of data in a network—roles of layers/neurons) to gain the trust of stakeholders [9, 38] .
- **Accountability**. Accountability principles are covered by most of the ethical AI principles and guidelines, including Australia's AI ethical principles. Ethical AI is often present together with responsible AI. However, the difference between responsibility and accountability is rarely discussed. Responsibility refers to the duty to complete a task throughout the life cycle of an AI system. For example, a developer may be responsible for implementing an algorithm in an AI project. Accountability is the duty to be accountable for a task after it is completed, which happens after a situation occurs. For example, an AI startup company's CEO may be accountable for the inaccurate or biased decisions made by their AI system product and has to take the role to explain how the decision is made. Role-level accountable entities and humans should be clearly identified in AI projects. Product features and management processes that ensure provenance and traceability of AI artifacts and decisions can increase accountability of AI systems.

5.2 Operationalizing AI Ethics

AI ethics can be operationalized in a variety of different ways. There are more approaches and mechanisms beyond high-level principles and low-level algorithms.

- **Requirements**. In addition to conventional functional requirements and non-functional requirements, ethical principles can be defined as a subset of requirements of AI systems. As discussed in Sect. 3.1, the eight principles can be classified into three groups: 1) P1 and P2 principles as functional requirements, 2) P3, P4, and P5 as non-functional requirements (software qualities), and 3) P6, P7, and P8 as metalevel governance-related functional requirements to improve truster's confidence. However, it is hard to justify whether the P1 and P2 (i.e., human, social, and environmental well-being and human-centered values) are fulfilled adequately. Risk mitigation mechanism might be needed to deal with AI autonomy and ensure the fulfillment of P1 and P2.

- **Design**. Design patterns/mechanisms can be proposed to address the ethical principles. Existing principles intend to protect users and the external world of AI system users. In distributed learning systems, trust issues also exist in between participating nodes. For example, in federated learning systems, learning coordinator might become a single point of failure. Thus, all the stakeholders should be carefully considered in design patterns/mechanisms.
- **Operations**. Continuous validation and monitoring mechanisms are needed to check the ethical principles continuously. Engaged stakeholders need to identify the threshold for the significant impact which triggers the validation mechanisms.
- **Governance**.

  Ethical maturity certification. An AI ethics maturity certification scheme/system could be developed to assess an organization's ethical maturity of AI project management. Based on the review of AI projects, different levels of ethical maturity certificates could be issued to an organization. The level/type of certificate could be upgraded later.

  Ethics review. Internal and external reviews on ethical impact can be conducted to address ethical principles. Representatives of stakeholders are expected to join the reviews.

  Project team. When the development team is set up, team members' diversity (e.g., background, cultures, and disciplines) should be considered.

6 Summary

In this chapter, we explored the interaction of three issues related to humanity and AI: hard-to-operationalize ethical AI principles, general notion of trust vs trustworthiness, and product vs process support for trust/trustworthiness. We provided an integrated view of them in the context of AI ethical principles and responsible AI. It points to additional mechanisms especially process mechanisms and trust-enhancing mechanisms for different stakeholders. By using the example of crop yield prediction involving different types of data and stakeholders, we elicited the missing elements in operationalizing ethical AI principles and potential solutions. We envision some future directions in ethical AI such as quantifying trust and its link with trustworthiness and novel process mechanisms for improving trust and trustworthiness.

References

1. Crawford, K.: The hidden costs of ai. New Scientist **249**(3327), 46–49 (2021)
2. CDEI: Review into bias in algorithmic decision making. https://www.gov.uk/government/publications/cdei-publishes-review-into-bias-in-algorithmic-decision-making/main-report-cdei-review-into-bias-in-algorithmic-decision-making (2020). Accessed on 16 December 2020
3. Dignum, V.: Responsible Artificial Intelligence: How to Develop and Use AI in a Responsible Way. Springer International Publishing (2019)
4. Jobin, A., Ienca, M., Vayena, E.: The global landscape of ai ethics guidelines. Nature Machine Intelligence **1**(9), 389–399 (2019)
5. Fjeld, J., Achten, N., Hilligoss, H., Nagy, A., Srikumar, M.: Principled artificial intelligence: Mapping consensus in ethical and rights-based approaches to principles for ai. Berkman Klein Center Research Publication (2020-1) (2020)
6. Mittelstadt, B.: Principles alone cannot guarantee ethical ai. Nature Machine Intelligence **1**(11), 501–507 (2019). DOI 10.1038/s42256-019-0114-4
7. Hidalgo, C.A., Orghiain, D., Canals, J.A., De Almeida, F., Martín, N.: How Humans Judge Machines. MIT Press (2020)
8. Lockey, S., Gillespie, N., Curtis, C.: Trust in artificial intelligence: Australian insights. https://home.kpmg/au/en/home/insights/2020/10/artificial-intelligence-trust-ai.html (2020). DOI 10.14264/b32f129. Accessed on 16 December 2020
9. Miller, T.: Explanation in artificial intelligence: Insights from the social sciences. Artificial Intelligence **267**, 1 – 38 (2019). https://doi.org/10.1016/j.artint.2018.07.007. http://www.sciencedirect.com/science/article/pii/S0004370218305988
10. Shneiderman, B.: Bridging the gap between ethics and practice: Guidelines for reliable, safe, and trustworthy human-centered ai systems. ACM Trans. Interact. Intell. Syst. **10**(4) (2020). DOI 10.1145/3419764. https://doi.org/10.1145/3419764
11. Ji, Z., Lipton, Z.C., Elkan, C.: Differential privacy and machine learning: a survey and review (2014)
12. Mehrabi, N., Morstatter, F., Saxena, N., Lerman, K., Galstyan, A.: A survey on bias and fairness in machine learning (2019)
13. Dong, M., Yuan, F., Yao, L., Wang, X., Xu, X., Zhu, L.: Survey for trust-aware recommender systems: A deep learning perspective (2020)
14. Perera, H., Hussain, W., Whittle, J., Nurwidyantoro, A., Mougouei, D., Shams, R.A., Oliver, G.: A study on the prevalence of human values in software engineering publications, 2015 – 2018. In: Proceedings of the ACM/IEEE 42nd International Conference on Software Engineering, ICSE '20, p. 409–420. Association for Computing Machinery, New York, NY, USA (2020). DOI 10.1145/3377811.3380393. https://doi.org/10.1145/3377811.3380393
15. Hussain, W., Perera, H., Whittle, J., Nurwidyantoro, A., Hoda, R., Shams, R.A., Oliver, G.: Human values in software engineering: Contrasting case studies of practice. IEEE Transactions on Software Engineering pp. 1–1 (2020). https://doi.org/10.1109/TSE.2020.3038802
16. Hutchinson, B., Smart, A., Hanna, A., Denton, E., Greer, C., Kjartansson, O., Barnes, P., Mitchell, M.: Towards accountability for machine learning datasets: Practices from software engineering and infrastructure (2020)
17. van den Hoven, J., Vermaas, P.E., van de Poel, I.: Design for values: An introduction. In: J. van den Hoven, P.E. Vermaas, I. van de Poel (eds.) Handbook of Ethics, Values, and Technological Design: Sources, Theory, Values and Application Domains, pp. 1–7. Springer Netherlands, Dordrecht (2015)
18. Ferrario, M.A., Simm, W., Forshaw, S., Gradinar, A., Smith, M.T., Smith, I.: Values-first se: Research principles in practice. In: 2016 IEEE/ACM 38th International Conference on Software Engineering Companion (ICSE-C), pp. 553–562 (2016)
19. Thew, S., Sutcliffe, A.: Value-based requirements engineering: Method and experience. Requirements Engineering **23**(4), 443–464 (2018). DOI 10.1007/s00766-017-0273-y. https://doi.org/10.1007/s00766-017-0273-y

20. Chia, S.Y., Xu, X., Paik, H.Y., Zhu, L.: Analysing and extending privacy patterns with architectural context. In: Proceedings of the 36th Annual ACM Symposium on Applied Computing. Association for Computing Machinery, Virtual Event , Republic of Korea (2021)
21. Lo, S.K., Lu, Q., Wang, C., Paik, H.Y., Zhu, L.: A systematic literature review on federated machine learning: From a software engineering perspective (2020)
22. Zhang, W., Lu, Q., Yu, Q., Li, Z., Liu, Y., Lo, S.K., Chen, S., Xu, X., Zhu, L.: Blockchain-based federated learning for device failure detection in industrial iot. IEEE Internet of Things Journal pp. 1–1 (2020). DOI 10.1109/JIOT.2020.3032544
23. Mougouei, D., Perera, H., Hussain, W., Shams, R., Whittle, J.: Operationalizing human values in software: A research roadmap. In: Proceedings of the 2018 26th ACM Joint Meeting on European Software Engineering Conference and Symposium on the Foundations of Software Engineering, ESEC/FSE 2018, p. 780–784. Association for Computing Machinery, New York, NY, USA (2018)
24. IEEE SA: Ethically aligned design: A vision for prioritizing human well-being with autonomous and intelligent systems. https://standards.ieee.org/content/ieee-standards/en/industry-connections/ec/autonomous-systems.html (2019). Accessed on 16 December 2020
25. DISER: Australia's ai ethics principles. https://industry.gov.au/data-and-publications/building-australias-artificial-intelligence-capability/ai-ethics-framework/ai-ethics-principles (2020). Accessed on 16 December 2020
26. Staples, M., Zhu, L., Grundy, J.: Continuous validation for data analytics systems. In: Proceedings of the 38th International Conference on Software Engineering Companion, ICSE '16, p. 769–772. Association for Computing Machinery, New York, NY, USA (2016). DOI 10.1145/2889160.2889207. https://doi.org/10.1145/2889160.2889207
27. D'Amour, A., Heller, K., Moldovan, D., Adlam, B., Alipanahi, B., Beutel, A., Chen, C., Deaton, J., Eisenstein, J., Hoffman, M.D., Hormozdiari, F., Houlsby, N., Hou, S., Jerfel, G., Karthikesalingam, A., Lucic, M., Ma, Y., McLean, C., Mincu, D., Mitani, A., Montanari, A., Nado, Z., Natarajan, V., Nielson, C., Osborne, T.F., Raman, R., Ramasamy, K., Sayres, R., Schrouff, J., Seneviratne, M., Sequeira, S., Suresh, H., Veitch, V., Vladymyrov, M., Wang, X., Webster, K., Yadlowsky, S., Yun, T., Zhai, X., Sculley, D.: Underspecification presents challenges for credibility in modern machine learning (2020)
28. Bauer, P.C.: Conceptualizing trust and trustworthiness (2019)
29. Holzinger, A., Langs, G., Denk, H., Zatloukal, K., Müller, H.: Causability and explainability of artificial intelligence in medicine. Wiley Interdisciplinary Reviews: Data Mining and Knowledge Discovery **9**(4), e1312 (2019)
30. ISO: Iso/iec25010:2011 systems and software engineering–systems and software quality requirements and evaluation (square)–system and software quality models. International Organization for Standardization **34**, 2910 (2011)
31. Avizienis, A., Laprie, J.C., Randell, B., Landwehr, C.: Basic concepts and taxonomy of dependable and secure computing. IEEE Trans. Dependable Secur. Comput. **1**(1), 11–33 (2004). DOI 10.1109/TDSC.2004.2. https://doi.org/10.1109/TDSC.2004.2
32. Bass, L., Clements, P., Kazman, R.: Software architecture in practice. Addison-Wesley Professional (2003)
33. Whittle, J.: Is your software valueless? IEEE Software **36**(3), 112–115 (2019). DOI 10.1109/MS.2019.2897397
34. Kearns, M., Roth, A.: The Ethical Algorithm: The Science of Socially Aware Algorithm Design. Oxford University Press USA (2019)
35. Blackman, R.: A practical guide to building ethical ai. https://hbr.org/2020/10/a-practical-guide-to-building-ethical-ai (2020). Accessed on 16 December 2020
36. European Commission: The digital services act package. https://ec.europa.eu/digital-single-market/en/digital-services-act-package (2020). Accessed on 16 December 2020
37. Australian Government Department of Health: Regulation of software based medical devices. https://www.tga.gov.au/regulation-software-based-medical-devices (2021). Accessed on 11 April 2021

38. Gilpin, L.H., Bau, D., Yuan, B.Z., Bajwa, A., Specter, M., Kagal, L.: Explaining explanations: An overview of interpretability of machine learning. In: 2018 IEEE 5th International Conference on Data Science and Advanced Analytics (DSAA), pp. 80–89 (2018). DOI 10.1109/DSAA.2018.00018

AI for Productivity

Machine Learning for Efficient Water Infrastructure Management

Zhidong Li, Bin Liang, and Yang Wang

1 Introduction

AI has led to significant advances recently. Alpha GO [27], a Google-developed AI system, has won the board game GO versus the most famous player. It overcomes highly complicated challenges, including complex actions to take, variations of decisions, and enormous computing capability needed. Not just for games, AI has also deployed into many industrial areas. As one of the top industrial-collaboration data science institute, we have deployed many AI-based systems for industries across multiple sectors. The capability of AI has been approved. For example, it can provide services for a financial checking system, a maintenance support system for urban infrastructures, a scheduled optimisation system for transportation, and a customer-relation system for telecommunication. In this section, machine learning will be our main focus for productivity.

The machine learning systems are usually targeting two tasks. First, we hope to use the machine learning system to replace manual work that requires excessive labours. This type of work needs human to repeat their behaviours or to make decisions continuously for many times. For example, to detect track faults in railway infrastructures, millions of pictures or long videos are used by human to check. It takes unacceptable long time for humans to check them one by one. Another type of work is infeasible for human. For example, water pipes buried underground cannot be inspected without an acceptable budget. For such work, the machine learning system can help by creating new functions to make the task feasible, just like from zero to one.

For both tasks, the machine learning system has the capability to reduce the cost by boosting productivity. However, the AI researches usually emphasis the

Z. Li (✉) · B. Liang · Y. Wang
Data Science Institute, University of Technology Sydney, Sydney, Australia
e-mail: zhidong.li@uts.edu.au

B. Liang
e-mail: bin.liang@uts.edu.au

Y. Wang
e-mail: yang.wang@uts.edu.au

F. Chen and J. Zhou (eds.), *Humanity Driven AI*,
https://doi.org/10.1007/978-3-030-72188-6_3

algorithm and methods and validate them using public data sets. The validations do not distinguish the importance of practical needs and real impacts such as a social–economic consequence measurement. We will discuss how machine learning systems, particularly machine learning models, are used in real projects, where how it can improve productivity against the manual work, and even machine learning model themselves. We will also see the productivity in different measurements, such as the social effects and economic effects.

In this chapter, productivity-boosting scenarios for water network management will be discussed. As it is shown in Fig. 1, the traditional management of water network is mainly relying on experts. The experts are responsible for interpreting the observations, either from on-site or from laboratory environments, into the knowledge that will be used for management tasks. Such a strategy is inefficient, and the modern approaches based on machine learning can improve the efficiency by automatically discovering the patterns in the data using machine learning models. However, the model building is still time-consuming, even with machine learning experts, since the configuration of models is not straightforward. Another improvement for the modelling will be discussed as shown in the last branch (AI-powered machine learning) of Fig. 1. The improvement is to consider the model configuration itself as a machine learning task, so it uses a more generalised approach to learn models with machine learning techniques. This approach further reduces the labour of machine learning experts to increase productivity.

In Fig. 1, we also list possible tasks in water network management, including water supply prediction, demand prediction, network assets failures such as pipe break,

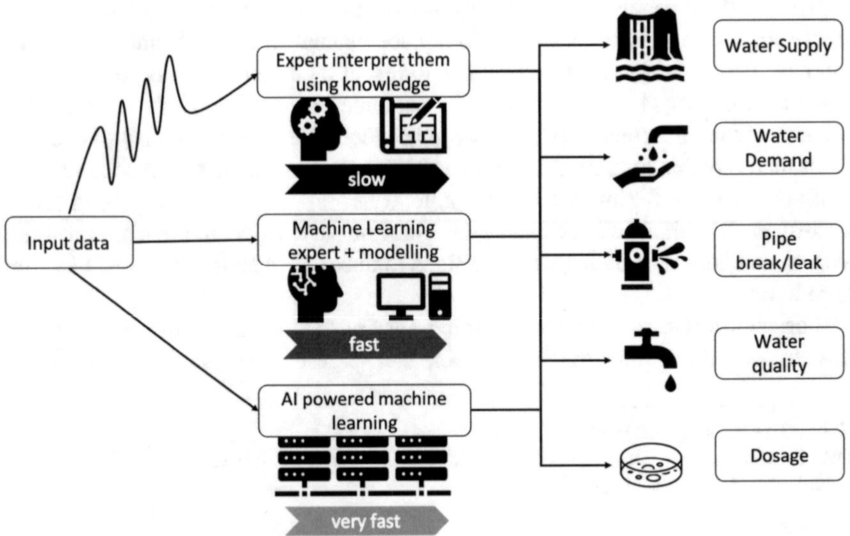

Fig. 1 General strategies to boost the productivity of possible tasks

water quality prediction, and dosage optimisation. We will focus on the following two tasks:

- **Water pipe failure prediction**: Drinking water supply networks are valuable urban infrastructure assets that are responsible for reliable water resource distributions. However, due to fast-growing demand and ageing assets, water utilities find it increasingly difficult to efficiently maintain their pipe networks. Pipe failures, especially the critical water pipe breaks, can cause high economic and social costs, and hence have become the primary challenge to water utilities. Identifying key influential factors, e.g. pipes' physical attributes, environmental features, is critical for understanding pipe failure behaviours.
- **Water quality prediction**: Monitoring drinking water quality in the entire water delivery network is a critical component of overall water supply management. The water quality can be quantified by a variety of indicators, but mainly the total chlorine. However, it is extremely difficult to collect sufficient total chlorine data from the network at customer sites(taps), which makes it sparse for comprehensive modelling.

This chapter will focus on the solutions based on the fastest approach in Fig. 1. We will discuss the technique branch for deploying an machine learning system. A common machine learning system can be composed of three steps: factor analysis, model design, and inference, as we have shown in Fig. 2. Using two piratical cases in water infrastructure management, we will discuss three aspects of each step:

- First, we will list potential challenges in each step. Two cases will be discussed: the water pipe failure prediction and water quality prediction.
- Second, we will discuss the solutions to the challenges. The methodologies of the solutions will be discussed in details; selected outcomes are illustrated based on the two cases.
- Third, the examples of potential risks of the solutions will also be included. We will also provide examples of our efforts against the risks.

There will be five sections after the Sect. 1. The two cases are discussed in Sect. 2. Then for each of the three steps, the challenges are discussed in Sect. 3. In Sect. 4, we examine the potential solutions to the challenges. These solutions are not only based on theories, but also the experiences from industrial projects. We further discussed the risk of deploying these solutions in Sect. 5. The conclusions are summarised in Sect. 6.

2 Two Case Studies

2.1 Background of Water Pipe Failure Prediction

The water utilities are responsible for providing an adequate and satisfactory supply of water to meet the demands of the territory and for maintaining a sound water supply system. To deliver water to end consumers, water utilities rely on the healthy condition of water pipes (most of them are buried underground). The network scale is also large; the decades of urbanisation accumulate the most water pipes in large cities to thousands of kilometres. The large territories may be maintaining network over ten thousand kilometres.

Most water pipes were constructed more than 100 years ago. In recent decades, conditions of more and more pipes are deteriorating, and maintenance is required. Given the poor condition of the water pipes, proactive maintenance, including replacement and rehabilitation, is the most effective solution. The proactive maintenance relies on the prediction of failures. Otherwise, the cost and time are extraordinarily high. This is an urgent necessity as the water mains will continue to age and deteriorate.

The proactive maintenance is based on the predictive prioritisation, which requires a good understanding of the failures and pipes. The mechanisms of water pipe failure have been studied for decades, and various physical and mechanical models, involving pipe wall thickness [8], material deterioration according to environmental conditions and quality of manufacturing [24], and hydraulic characteristics [20], have been developed to estimate the remaining pipe life. However, for non-intrusive technologies, based on condition assessment, the operators can drastically improve productivity. The water utilities are engaging with machine learning scientists for consulting water main failure analysis and prediction.

Machine learning techniques have their value in the aforementioned problem. Generally, there are two types of models for the prediction of water pipe failure: physical models and statistical models. Physical models [15] are significantly influenced by domain knowledge and usually designed to capture the mechanisms of failures due to certain causes, e.g. soil corrosion. Once the process is done with a correctly built physical model, the prediction is accurate. But they have significant limitations, e.g., budget restriction for experiments, when applying to a large water mains network with complex factors. In contrast, statistical models usually require fewer resources and can capture hidden statistical failure patterns caused by different physical reasons. Hence, they can be applied to large-scale water main networks for guiding proactive maintenance. The statistical machine learning models are trained by considering historical failure records, physical characteristics of pipes, and environmental factors.

2.2 Background for Water Quality Prediction

Ensuring the continuous supply of high-quality drinking water is a critical requirement for water supply networks management. The treatment process involves the removal of contaminants from raw water by filtering and chemical dosing to produce water that is pure enough for human consumption without any risk of adverse health effect. Chlorination is the most widely used method for disinfecting water supplies [6]. It relies on a balance between the dosing of new chlorine and the amount of residual chlorine that remains within the system until the treated water reaches the next dosing station or its destination. This is because the disinfected water may be polluted again when the water is being transported for a long time. Hence, given the chlorine at the outlet of reservoirs and unknown transportation time, accurate prediction of total chlorine of the customer taps can be significant and crucial to water supply management. However, it is extremely difficult to collect sufficient total chlorine data in residents and makes it sparse.

A data-driven solution can enhance productivity by providing total chlorine prediction within the whole delivery network. Such a system faces a series of challenges. First, the hydraulic system needs to capture the topology of the delivery network, so that the water travel time can be estimated using predicted water demand across the topology. The travel time links the upstream (e.g. reservoir) data to the downstream (e.g. tap or resident) data. Then, a two-step strategy is required for the determination of the crucial factors and construction of machine models for total chlorine decay to predict total chlorine with the travel time. At last, the issue of uncertainties of both data and the model is a concern. It should be analysed to indicate the confidence of prediction for better decision making. The proposed models will have capabilities to effectively predict water supply–demand and capture the variability in data with sparse samples. As the outcome, the quantification will output distributions, providing more information for decision making. The approach also provides the insight into which factors are important in predicting water demand and quality.

3 Productivity Challenges in Machine Learning for Water Network Management

The productivity challenge of water network management can be improved by applying the data-drive methodology. As it is shown in Fig. 2, the key steps of the data-driven methodology include data analytic for understanding the mechanism; model design for the task such as regression, classification, and prediction; and model computation to infer the parameters. As it is shown in Fig. 2, data will be input for factor analysis and used for model. Then, the model will be inferred. The model output will be used for the task, while the factor analysis outcomes are usually for explanation and proof of concepts. We will list the challenges of each component.

3.1 *Challenge of Data Analytics*

To improve the productivity, machine learning is leveraged to find possible correlations between the target (e.g. failure, water quality variation) and available set of factors. For example, pipe ageing can cause pipe breaks, and temperature can be the reason of variability of quality. It may not lead to significant amount of work for

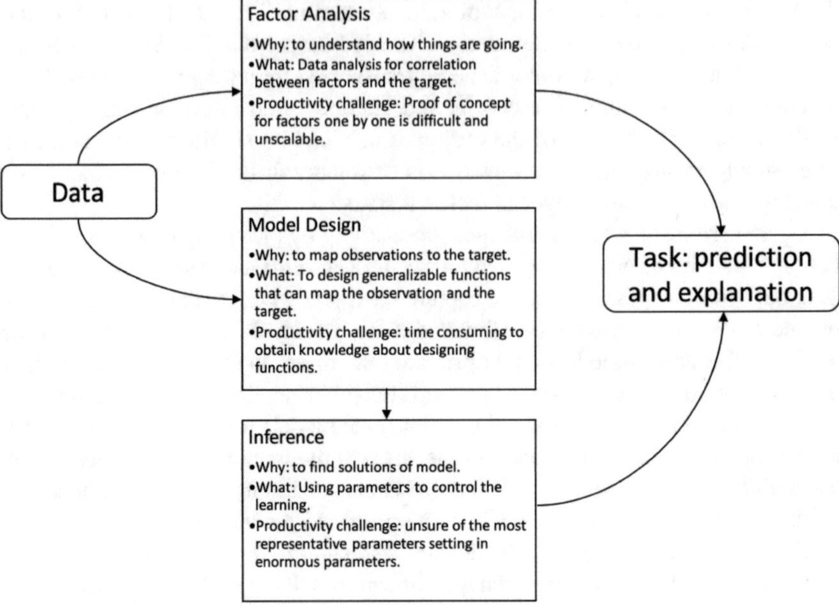

Fig. 2 Standard steps in a data-driven task.

experts when just a few factors take the major response and the response is certain. However, in reality, these factors are usually complex. Taking water pipe failure as an example, ageing is not the only factor that causes failures. There are other factors with unknown impacts. There factors usually include pipe materials, laid year, construction year, and diameter. All these factors or combinations of these factors can be part of the reason of failures. The combination of these factors can create at least hundreds of pipe categories that the their failures are different because of the joint impact. However, it is not easy for experts to interpret this. For example, it is uncertain to determine whether pipe with wall thickness of 10mm laid in 1960 (thin wall but new) is more risky than the pipe with wall thickness of 15mm laid in 1920 (thick but aged). Even with the same category of pipes, the performances are still different if they are buried in different locations.

Furthermore, using machine learning method, we can observe important correlation patterns that have not be noticed by experts. For example, the material used in many decades are not as strong as before so those pipes tend to experience more failures. An example is shown in Fig. 3 where more failures occurred for water pipes laid between 1950 and 1980, although these pipes are newer than pipes laid between 1920 and 1930. These factors are even unknown to domain experts, not mentioning the more complex factors or the joint impact from multiple factors.

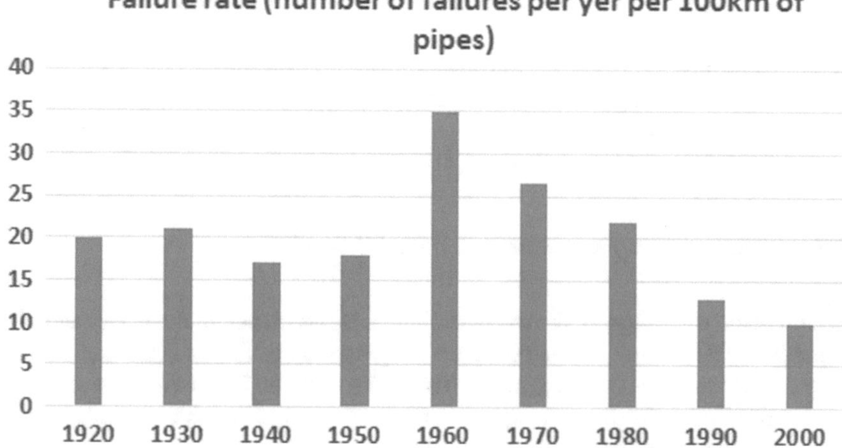

Fig. 3 Failure rate (the number of failures normalised by length) in different construction years. Generally, older pipes are more likely to fail, but the observation shows that pipes laid in 1960 have higher failure rate than pipes laid in 1920, which can only be discovered from the data

Therefore, our discussion is based on two questions for productivity:

- How can we use data-driven methodology to identify the importance of factors, for the proof of concept?
- How can we effectively quantify the importance of factors given massive factors?

3.2 *Challenges of Designing Machine Learning Models*

The main purpose of model design is to build up a system (or equations or optimisation objectives) to take the observed data in, to map the observations to the targeted events. Traditionally, the statisticians tried to model the physical mechanism using mathematical functions, such as stochastic differential equation. Then, necessary data are applied to the model to obtain the variables. However, in a complex system where the targeted events are significantly impacted by multiple factors, the physical modelling is severely restricted.

For data scientists, the industrial problems are usually in their unfamiliar domains. For example, hydraulic system of supply water is complex. Given nearly half million water pipes, buried undergrounds, it is impossible for experts to learn the complete knowledge about how fast the water is travelling inside. Since the travelling time is a key factor to understand the level of chlorine in the water, the lack of such knowledge makes the task difficult to estimate the water quality. The unfamiliarity then becomes obstacle to experts to design the appropriate model on data for the goal.

To improve the productivity, we will focus on the challenge of how the data scientist or machine learning experts can model data for solution, given the limitation of the domain knowledge. This also provides productivity boost for industrial users, without knowing how to set up physical systems, such as using experimental environments for simulation.

3.3 Challenges of Learning Model Variables

After models are designed, the major challenge is how to obtain the latent variables in models. The process is referred as learning/training/calibration/inference. There are many discussions on the process. The major solution is to take the process as an optimisation problem, as learning is to determine the variables by minimising a loss function or by maximising a likelihood function. The techniques are based on derivative, sampling, variational distribution, etc. Most of the models, if being applied from an on-shelf package, include the inference in the implementation.

However, the inference still requires inputs. This inputs are referred as model parameters (or hyperparameters). The parameters are usually manually set to control what and how the models should learn. The learning parameters configuration is also time-consuming. For example, the Bayesian model requires prior parameters, even the sophistic implementation [23] of random forest model requires more than 10 parameters to work. In the traditional practice, these parameters are configured by data scientists with solid background, but just to shrink a small part of the parameter space of a trial-and-error method. Such method is time-consuming, and there is a gap between data scientists who configure the model and domain experts who have the knowledge to the problem.

4 Productivity Boost Methodologies

4.1 Efficient Factor Analysis

Machine learning-based analysis can be categorised into two classes, and each one considers the correlation from a different end. One end is based on the assumption from expert's knowledge. The assumption provided by experts will be testified by data scientists. We refer this method as top-down factor analysis. The other end is the bottom-up factor analysis, starting from the data to the knowledge. In a bottom-up approach, using the data, we can obtain the correlation between the collected data features and the targeted label. This approach can be used to evaluate factors in a more automatic way. We will discuss both approaches when they are employed for productivity boost.

4.1.1 Top-Down Factor Analysis

The top-down analysis is based on concepts given by experts when the scientific analysis of concepts is complex. Here, we will study a top-down factor analysis case using water quality. The study is based on the knowledge that water temperature in reservoirs can affect the water quality which is represented by the chlorine level (Cl) of water users' taps.

Estimating the correlation is not trivial. Traditional approaches, such as correlation coefficient, are usually used to obtain simple correlations. However, complexity is one of the main challenges here. First, without being a simple correlation, such as linear or quadratic, the relation between temperature and Cl can be even non-monotonic. Second, the temperature does not stand out as the unique driving factor, and there are many other factors, such as travel time.

This is the typical case for top-down factor analysis. The proposed solution is using machine learning to surrogate the physical model by skipping the physical relationship between all factors and Cl. For example, a knowledge-free model, like the random forest [3] or SVR [5], can be used here. If we denote the model as f, we have $f : D \rightarrow Y$. Here $D = X, T_p$ is the generalised representation for input factors, including temperature T_p and other factors X. Y is the generalised representation for sample labels. The label is Cl in our case, given $Y \in \mathbb{R}^+$.

The machine learning model creates an extremely flexible possibility to be used for approximating complex mechanism. Therefore, it provides the capability of simulating the mechanism in selected segments of D. It is only for the chosen segments because of the data availability. For example, in Fig. 6b and c, we show such situation that the regression on segments around the observed data points is closer to the ground truth. By this approach, we will alter the temperature as input to see the variation of Cl.

The output Cl is then compared with ground truth. We listed examples in Fig. 4. These results indicate the complex correlation between temperature and Cl. For four regions, the temperature varies in each region, and the prediction is obtained for each tap under monitoring. The predicted Cl values are then compared with the median prediction for the normalisation purpose. Then, the distribution of the difference is plotted as box plots. We can see the complex correlation, and the correlations are different in various regions.

4.1.2 Bottom-Up Factor Analysis

We show another example for bottom-up factor analysis, on identifying the systematic characteristics that may affect Cl at downstream. The study is based on a dataset with multiple factors. All these factors are suggested by experts that they may be useful, but there is no sufficient information about which ones are the dominant factors. The integrated dataset has assembled the factors from both reservoirs and tap users, along with level sensors and water quality analysers at the reservoirs. The linking between the reservoirs and tap users is approximated by travel time estimation, using network

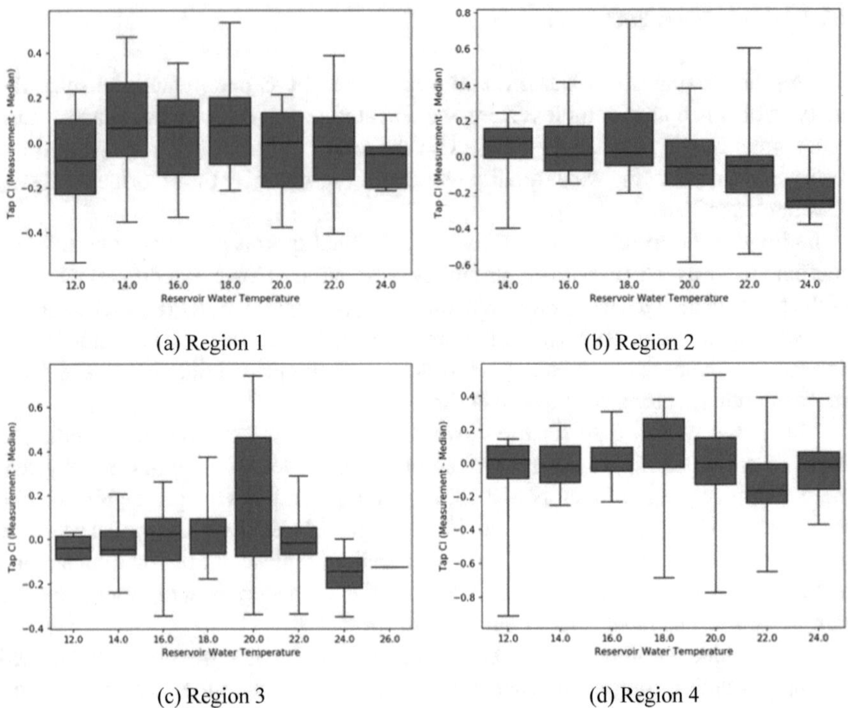

(a) Region 1 (b) Region 2

(c) Region 3 (d) Region 4

Fig. 4 Variation of predicted Cl (normalised by median) with changing temperatures

topology and water flow velocity. The dataset enables us to capture: (1) reservoir total chlorine (mg/L), (2) water temperature (°C), (3) total chlorine to ammonia ratio, (4) water pH balance, (5) water turbidity, (6) ammonia (mg/L), and (7) reservoir level in percentage.

It is difficult to determine the importance of factors for the quality among their complicated joint influence. This is even hard for domain experts. A nonparametric fashion analysis is used to extract the importance as the bottom-up manner, without imposing any assumptions on the relationship between the factors and Cl. The purpose is to rank the correlations, without making upfront assumptions on what chemical or physical processes are at work.

The analysis uses a machine learning model based on random forest algorithm [3]. A recursive learning/predicting is performed where, starting with all factors, each factor is considered in turn and the factor that produces the smallest reduction in predictive error is removed. Here, each time we train and test the data with selected factors with cross-validation to obtain the error. This recursive elimination is repeated until all features have been removed. After each elimination, the data will be reused to train and test for updated error. This enables the most critical predictive factors to be identified. The rank of the predictive factors indicates the importance of the factors.

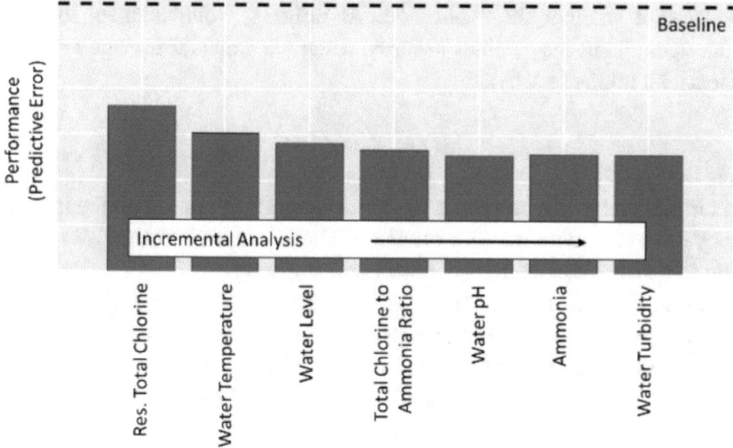

Fig. 5 Factor importance for water quality

The results are shown in Fig. 5, where the factors are ranked according to an incremental order. This means the performance shown for each factors is the combination of all factors to the left side of the one shown. The baseline error is obtained using the historical mean Cl as prediction, representing the removal of all factors, so it causes the largest error. The result shows that reservoir total chlorine and temperature at reservoirs capture over 90% of the variability in the downstream Cl (the error reduction for more factors is much less). Only these two factors can reduce about 50% of the total error. Other factors have a much smaller effect, while turbidity provides virtually no additional information.

4.2 *Machine Learning Models for Productivity*

Data modelling is the core part of tasks such as prediction, regress, classification, and forecast. There are two options: the parametric model and the nonparametric model. We will introduce and compare both options and discuss a case of applying nonparametric models to water pipe failure prediction.

4.2.1 Parametric Model Versus Nonparametric Models

Parametric models represent all information within parameters. The assumption is that the data distribution can be defied in terms of a finite set of parameters. By choosing a functional form with the fixed set of parameters, these methods are highly constrained to the specified form. We are using a popular parametric model, the Weibull process [28], in water pipe failure prediction as an example. Suppose we hope to predict whether the event, such as failures, would happen to pipes in a particular age. Using the Weibull process, when we consider the age t as input, we aim to learn an intensity λ by:

$$\lambda(t) = f(t) = at^b \tag{1}$$

which is in the shape of a power curve. The assumption is based on the truth that the frequency of events increase with time/age. Then, λ is different for all t, defined as $\lambda(t)$, and to be obtained from $f(t)$ based on the average of λ.

Algorithms that do not make strong assumptions about the form of the mapping function are called nonparametric machine learning algorithms. By not making assumptions, they are free to learn any functional form from the training data. The nonparametric models, such as random forest [3] and deep learning models [12], have been applied in various fields and used to solve many challenging machine learning tasks. In many scenarios, these models empirically outperform other traditional models with manual settings. The name of nonparametric models does not mean that no parameters are needed. On the contrary, it requires enormous parameters to construct. For the same problem, the nonparametric models do not assume any function like (1). The nonparametric model assumes a much more flexible function that the degree of freedom increases with data volume. Suppose we denote the model structure as $\mathscr{A}$, then a nonparametric has the ability to determine it by $\mathscr{A} \sim g(D)$, where D is the dataset. It is noticeable that the degree of freedom is high, so that the number of parameters is also larger than the parametric model. They must be fit by a growing number of data to obtain $\lambda(t)$. For models such as neural network [1], or random forest [3], the parameter size is usually fixed as a large number, so that it can model the flexibility of large data.

The differences between parametric model and nonparametric models are shown in Fig. 6. In Fig. 6(a), we show how the data points are fit by a parametric model. In the figure, we generate 5 points as D, and then, we generate each of corresponding Y with a deterministic function(a quadratic function), plus a random effect(Gaussian noise). Here, two parametric models, linear model and quadratic model, are applied to fit these data. We can see the fit functions are close to the points. However, the assumption of the linear model is wrong, so its fitting is less accurate. We then use two nonparametric models (decision tree and random forest regression) to fit those points. We can see that the results in Fig. 6(c) are less accurate. This comparison shows that the parametric model may present a more confident prediction when data are scarce, but the assumption of the model structure must be correct.

Another comparison is conducted between Fig. 6a, b. Here, we show that the data have been approximately fit in Fig. 6b using nonparametric methods (decision tree and random forest models). So its advantage here is that we do not acquire any domain knowledge to design such a model. Here, the noise is larger at the end of the fitted curve than the increase of uncertainty being observed. As a result, the model not only fits the data but also retains the noise when it is large.

In Fig. 6d, we employ the Bayesian nonparametric model which is the Gaussian process. The model can adjust its flexibility with data as well. The comparison

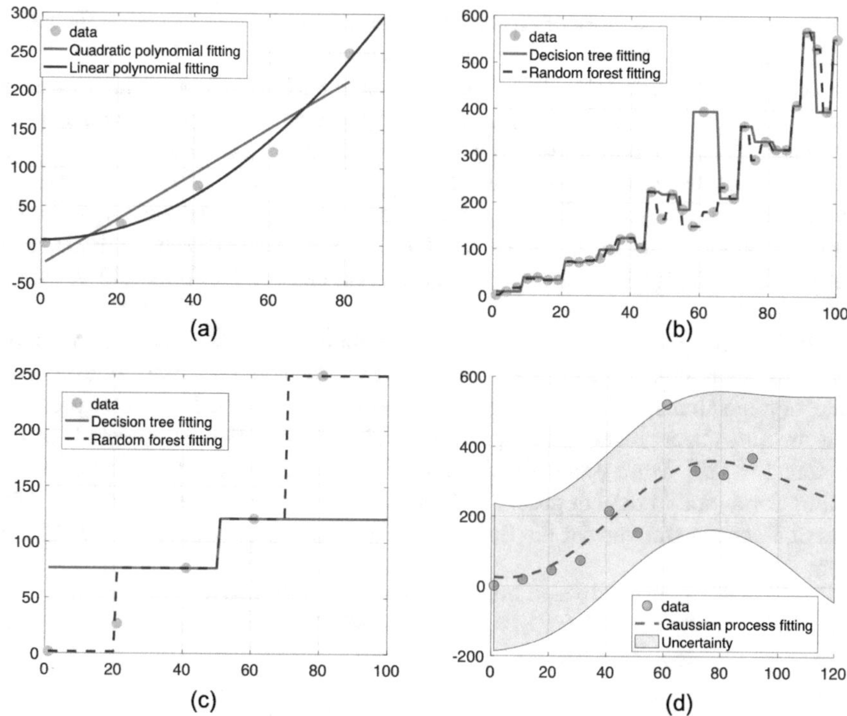

Fig. 6 Comparison between parametric model and nonparametric models. **a** is for parametric model. **b-d** are for nonparametric models

between Fig. 6b, d is that the noise has been almost cancelled out. The fitted curve (average value from the Gaussian process) is smooth and close to the quadratic function. Some of the significant noise has less impact on the fit curve. The fitting also shows the uncertainty area that is enlarged to acknowledge missing observations, such as the right part of the curve. In addition, less data are required by the models in Fig. 6d than Fig. 6b.

4.2.2 Modelling Water Pipe Failures with Bayesian Nonparametric Model

The Bayesian nonparametric approach can be used for water pipe failure prediction. The model to be discussed here is the hierarchical beta process model. The failure data are sparse, so Bayesian prior is required for the model. It makes the model invulnerable to wrong model structure assumptions and adaptable to various failure patterns, thereby leading to more accurate predictions.

The exampled model is developed in [19]. First, the model is based on the assumption that the failures are random events, complying with a Bernoulli distribution with parameter p_k for a category of pipe k. However, p_k will be unstable given the spare data. Therefore, a Bayesian prior will be applied to support p_k from drifting too far away from the true value. For a timely changing p_k, we use the beta process as the prior. a beta process, $B \sim BP(c, B_0)$, is a positive random measure on a space Ω, where c, the concentration is a positive value, and B_0, the base measure, is a fixed measure on Ω. If B_0 is discrete, $B_0 = \sum_k q_k \delta_{\omega_k}$, then B has atoms at the same locations $B = \sum_k p_k \delta_{\omega_k}$, where $p_k \sim Beta(cq_k, c(1 - q_k))$, and each $q_k \in [0, 1]$. Then, an observation data X could be modelled by a Bernoulli process with the measure B, $X \sim BeP(B)$, where $X = \sum_k z_k \delta_{\omega_k}$, and each z_k is a Bernoulli variable, $z_k \sim Ber(p_k)$.

Furthermore, when there exists a set of categories, and all data belong to one of them, the hierarchical beta process could be used to model the data. Within each category, the atoms and the associated atom usage are modelled by a beta process. Meanwhile, a beta process prior is shared by all the categories. More details could be found in [29]. For a water distribution system, denote π_{ki}, as the probability of failure for a pipe in the kth group, and the observation time interval (year) j. The hierarchical construction for the Bayesian nonparametric modelling can be written into:

$$\begin{aligned} q_k &\sim \text{Beta}(c_0 q_0, c_0(1 - q_0)), \text{ where } k = 1, 2, ..., K, \\ \pi_{k,i} &\sim \text{Beta}(c_k q_k, c_k(1 - q_k)), \text{ where } i = 1, ..., n_k, \\ z_{k,i,j} &\sim \text{Ber}(\pi_{k,i}) \end{aligned} \tag{2}$$

Here, q_k and c_k are the mean and concentration parameters for the kth group, q_0 and c_0 are hyperparameters for the hierarchical beta process, $z_{k,i} = \{z_{k,i,j} | j = 1, ..., m_{k,i}\}$ is the history of pipe failure across $m_{k,i}$ years, $z_{k,i,j} = 1$ means the pipe failed in jth year, otherwise $z_{k,i,j} = 0$.

For the hierarchical beta process, a set of $\{q_k\}$ are used to describe failure rates of different groups of pipes. For each pipe group, with fixed concentration parameter c_k, our goal is to find $\pi_{k,i}$ for pipe i in group k. This can be estimated from the observation, so we have:

$$p(\pi_{k,i} | z_{k,1:n_k}) = \int p(q_k, \pi_{k,i} | z_{k,1:n_k}) dq_k = \int p(\pi_{k,i} | q_k, z_{k,i}) p(q_k | z_{k,1:n_k}) dq_k \tag{3}$$

Each term in Eq. (3) can be represented by:

$$p(\pi_{k,i} | q_k, z_{k,i}) \sim Beta\left(c_k q_k + \sum_j z_{k,i,j},\ c_k(1 - q_k) + m_{k,i} - \sum_j z_{k,i,j}\right), \tag{4}$$

and

$$p(q_k|z_{k,1:n_k})(q_k, z_{k,1:n_k}) = p(q_k) \prod_i \left[\int p(\pi_{k,i}|q_k) p(z_{k,i}|\pi_{k,i}) d\pi_{k,i} \right]$$
$$\propto q_k^{c_0 q_0 - 1} (1 - q_k)^{c_0(1-q_0)-1} \prod_i \frac{\Gamma(c_k q_k + \sum_j z_{k,i,j}) \Gamma(c_k(1 - q_k) + m_{k,i} - \sum_j z_{k,i,j})}{\Gamma(c_k q_k) \Gamma(c_k(1 - q_k))} \tag{5}$$

In the model, we can see that the group failure rate is controlled by hierarchical level parameters c_0 and q_0. These two parameters are used to keep the learning stable, especially when data are sparse. This can help experts to understand the group performance without looking into all factors of an individual pipe.

4.3 Automatic Learning for Machine Learning

As we mentioned in Sect. 3.3, the hyperparameter setting is a key challenge. Every machine learning model has hyperparameters, and setting the such parameters is not a trivial task given that the enormous parameters to test without related knowledge.

To reduce these onerous development costs, a novel idea of automating the entire pipeline of machine learning (ML) has emerged, i.e. automated machine learning (AutoML). AutoML aims to automate any part of the process of building a machine learning model from raw data. The most basic task AutoML is to automatically set hyperparameters to optimise performance. There are various definitions of AutoML. According to [31], AutoML is designed to reduce the demand for data scientists and enable domain experts to automatically build ML applications without much requirement for statistical and ML knowledge. In [30], AutoML is defined as a combination of automation and ML. In a word, AutoML can be understood to involve the automated construction of an ML pipeline on the limited computational budget. With the exponential growth of computing power, AutoML has become a hot topic in both industry and academia. A complete AutoML system can make a dynamic combination of various techniques to form an easy-to-use end-to-end ML pipeline system (as shown in Fig. 1). The success of AutoML crucially relies on the following tasks: pre-process the data, select appropriate features, select an appropriate model family, optimise model hyperparameters, post-process machine learning models, and critically analyse the results obtained. Many machine learning companies have created and publicly shared such systems (e.g. Cloud AutoML by Google) to help people with little or no ML knowledge to build high-quality custom models.

Due to the immense potential of AutoML, many tools have been developed in this area. AutoML tools differ in their backends they rely on (e.g. WEKA or scikit-learn [23]), the combined algorithm selection, and hyperparameter optimisation (CASH) methods (e.g. Bayesian optimisation or genetic programming), the library of algorithms they select from, or whether they perform model ensembling (e.g. bagging or boosting). Table 1 shows a comparison of the popular AutoML tools. The first prominent AutoML tool is Auto-WEKA [16], which uses Bayesian optimisation to

Table 1 Comparison of popular AutoML tools

Tool	Back-end	CASH strategy	Model ensembling
Auto-WEKA	WEKA	Bayesian optimisation	Bagging, boosting, stacking, voting
Auto-sklearn	Scikit-learn	BayesOpt + Meta-learn	Ensemble selection
TPOT	Scikit-learn	Genetic programming	Stacking
H_2O AutoML	H_2O	Random search	Stacking + bagging
AutoGluon	Scikit-learn	Fixed defaults	Multi-layer stacking + repeated bagging

select and tune the algorithms in a machine learning pipeline based on WEKA. Auto-sklearn [9] does the same task using scikit-learn and adds meta learning to warm-start the search with the best pipelines on similar datasets, as well as ensemble construction. TPOT [21] optimises scikit-learn pipelines via genetic programming, starting with simple ones and evolving them over generations. H2O AutoML [22] optimises H2O components by stacking the best solutions found by a random search. Finally, AutoGluon [7] optimises scikit-learn models by multi-layer stacking and repeated bagging.

From the perspective of performance, the latest research [11] claims that there is no AutoML tool which consistently outperforms all the others. The researchers compared the popular AutoML systems across 39 datasets and cannot draw clear conclusions about which AutoML tool is suitable for what kind of datasets.

From the perspective of flexibility and implementation, we choose TPOT to implement AutoML framework for water pipe failure prediction. In order to investigate potential effects of AutoML in water industry, we have compared the pipe failure prediction results from TPOT [18] and a standard machine learning model (XGBoost [4]). The pipeline of the experiment is illustrated in Fig. 7.

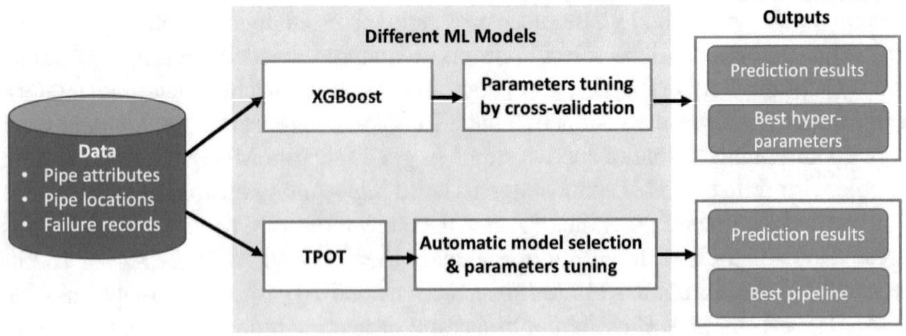

Fig. 7 Pipeline of comparison of AutoML and classic machine learning model

The boosting technique used in XGBoost consists in fitting sequentially multiple tree-based base learners in a very adaptive way: each model in the sequence is fitted giving more importance to observations in the high-dimensional features that were badly handled by the previous models in the sequence. Finally, the ensemble model is built based on a weighted sum of base learners. The model relies on hyperparameters tuning, so finding the right combination of values by cross-validation is critical to good prediction. However, a successful machine learning model is also dependent on feature engineering and model selection. In an effort to make machine learning more accessible, to reduce the human expertise required, and to improve model performance, AutoML emerged as an exciting new area of active research. With the water domain experience (the knowledge on availability of data streams, quality of data, resolution and type of data, physical models and expectations on outcomes, etc.), an AutoML can be designed and implemented. This will enable the automation on algorithm selection. TPOT is selected to implement AutoML pipeline, aiming to automate the most tedious part of machine learning by intelligently exploring thousands of possible pipelines to find the best one for the training set. Once TPOT is finished searching, it provides the best pipeline in addition to prediction results.

The training set used in the experiment includes 160,000 samples which cover 20 years of failure records. Two years (2018 and 2019) are selected for the pipe failure prediction. The prediction results are validated with actual ground truth data by calculating the percentage of detected failures with respect to the percentage of prioritised pipes (when pipes are ranked in descending order of the failure likelihoods). The failure detection rates are calculated when top 5, 10, 15, and 20% prioritised pipes are selected based on their predicted failure probabilities. The result of performance comparison is shown in Fig. 8. It can be seen that the overall performance of TPOT is slightly better than XGBoost. This is because TPOT not only optimises models, but also feature selectors and transformation operators. Compared with cross-validation used in XGBoost parameters tuning, AutoML requires less human efforts and is more efficient than classic machine learning model in terms of model selection and parameters tuning. In the experiment, each pipeline in AutoML needs 179s, while each pipeline in cross-validation for XGBoost needs 280s. This is because the pipelines in TPOT are optimised with genetic algorithm instead of iterations in cross-validation.

For the optimisation in TPOT, 32 operators are used including 13 ML algorithms (e.g. Gaussian NB, decision tree, random forest), 14 feature transformation operators (e.g. Min Max scaler, normaliser, PCA), and 5 feature selectors (e.g. Select Percentile, Variance Threshold, RFE). After 3 h training for each experiment on test year of 2018 and 2019, the optimal pipelines are obtained:

- 2018: MaxAbsScaler + XGBClassifier
- 2019: MinMaxScaler + XGBClassifier

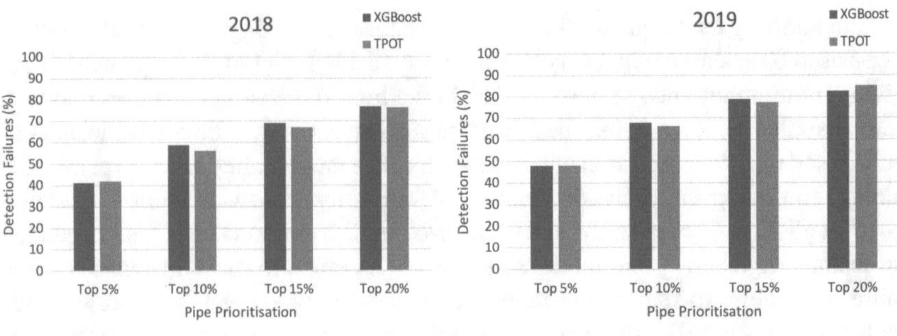

(a) Failure prediction evaluation in 2018 (b) Failure prediction evaluation in 2019

Fig. 8 Performance comparison of AutoML and standard machine learning model

5 Risks of Machine Learning Solution

The machine learning solution can drastically boost the productivity. However, they are not free lunch when applying them into the water network management. We list potential risks when deploying the solutions. They include:

- The factor analysis is correlation based rather than causality based, which may hinder the generalisation of analysis. The observation data may be imperfect which could also create issues.
- The designed model can provide prediction; however, the prediction is usually an individual value so it may be limited for delivering enough information. The value is also not 100% guaranteed to be correct. A certainty indicator will be useful for using the prediction.
- AutoML can boost the productivity significantly; however, the results are unstable, and it may create over confidence on prediction while the knowledge is ignored.

5.1 Risk of Factor Analytics

The purpose of factor analysis is to prove the concepts. However, there are still risks for the data-based evidence.

5.1.1 Correlation

The significant risk of factor analysis is essential to distinguish causality and correlation. The causality means the cause and effects and is used for the factor or event, which indeed contributes to the occurrence of the targeted label, while the correlation can only indicate the co-occurrence of them. The analysed factors with significant correlation may or may not be the cause of the target. The causality analysis is an extension of the factor analysis we have introduced. It can also improve productivity with more certainty.

5.1.2 Imperfect Data

The data used for analysis could be imperfect. In water pipe prediction, the critical failures are rare. Furthermore, the observation is not for the whole life of pipes, as the failures of new pipes are rare. For example, failure rate is defined as the number of failures per year of a 100 m pipe. With the definition, assuming that a 100 m pipe with 2 historical failures in 1 year, its failure rate is 2. However, if we consider a Poisson distribution, for a pipe with failure rate of 2, it has 13.5% probability that no failures can be observed, so the failure rate learned using this data is wrong. This will become an imperfect data issue when the failure rate is low.

An example is shown in Fig. 9. We compare the bias of samples using Poisson distribution. Different true failure rates are set as the parameters of Poisson distribution. For each failure rate, a number of samples, 10 or 100, are sampled from the distribution. The bias is calculated using the difference between the empirical mean and the true failure rate, and then normalised by the true failure rate. The trend of the results show that when failure rate is low, the bias can be higher. The bias also depends on the number of samples, where the imperial mean could be two times more than the true failure rate.

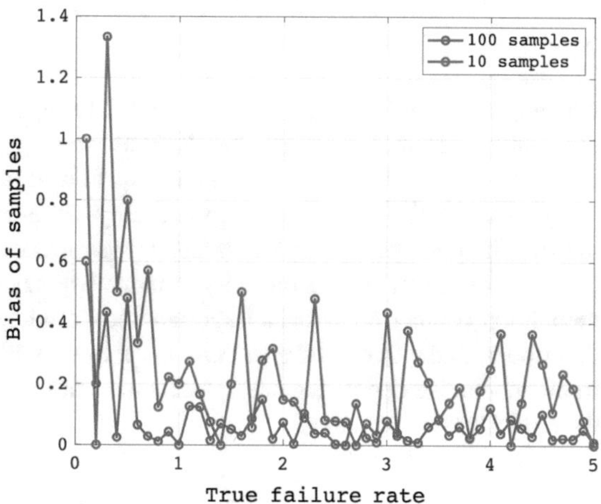

Fig. 9 Sample bias and failure rate

5.2 *Model Uncertainty*

One of the risks of designing machine leaning models is the uncertainty of the prediction. The source of uncertainty can be different, such as incompleteness of data and model setup. Uncertainty is a critical part which is usually required in decision making. Although the current machine learning models can be used to obtain the most possible predictions with surprisingly high accuracy [17], the model is yet to be 100% trusted, especially when the detection can easily be changed with minor modification on the data and model [13]. For deterministic models, uncertainty is not straightforward to model. For example, Yarin et al. [10] simulated uncertainty of deep neural networks by Gaussian process [2]. However, the uncertainties come from both the nature of data and the prediction model. Here, we will show two examples for dealing with the uncertainty from data (a.k.a. *Aleatory* uncertainty [14]) and model (a.k.a. *Epistemic* uncertainty) [14] respectively, using the water demand estimation case.

5.2.1 Modelling Epistemic Uncertainty

In the hydraulic model, to estimate the water travel duration τ from location u to location s, a model is created.

to estimate the volume $V_{u,s}$ from within the time τ until t_s. The model is:

$$V_{u,s} = \int_{t_s-\tau}^{t_s} f^s(t)\mathrm{d}t \tag{6}$$

where t_s is a given end time to be predicted for s, and $V_{u,s}$ is the network volume that can be obtained from the topology of water pipe connection, diameter size, and length. Here, $f^s(t)$ is the instantaneous flow at time t. However, it can only be sampled as the discrete observations in reality, our example is based on the flow data in every 15 min. Here, τ can be obtained by simple maths.

Here, the model ignores the daily change of demand, which creates uncertainty in modelling. We then construct a Bayesian linear model for its simplicity and ability to describe both the trend and *epistemic* uncertainty with a normal distribution $\mathcal{N}(\cdot)$. In the model, we denote the observed features at t in day n as $\mathbf{x}_{n,t} \in \mathbb{R}^d$. Therefore, the model can be written as

$$f_n(t) = \mathbf{x}_{n,t}^{\mathrm{T}}\mathbf{w} + \sigma_t\eta,\ \eta \sim \mathcal{N}(0, 1) \tag{7}$$

where T denotes the transpose operator, $\mathbf{w} \in \mathbb{R}^d$ and σ_t are the model parameters to be learned. $f_n^s(t)$ is used for customer connection s on day n. For the inference, the following posterior can be used:

$$P(\mathbf{w}, \sigma_{h=1...96}|\mathbf{f}, \mathbf{X}, \Theta) \propto \prod_{n\leq N} \prod_{h=1}^{96} \mathscr{N}(f_n(h); \mathbf{x}_{n,h}^{\mathrm{T}}\mathbf{w}, \sigma_h) \\ \mathscr{N}(\mathbf{w}; \Theta_1)\mathscr{G}(\sigma_h|\Theta_2) \quad (8)$$

where $\mathbf{X} = \{\mathbf{x}_{n,h}\}$ denotes the set of observed features, and $\mathbf{f} = \{f_n(h)|n \leq N, h = 1..96\}$ denotes the water flow at the hth 15 min on the nth day. This can be used to predict the flow for each 15 min in the next 24 h. During the training stage, historical records of $N = 2500$ days are used. In order to simplify the inference, two distributions (normal distribution and inverse gamma distribution) are used as they are conjugated priors. Θ_1 and Θ_2 are hyperparameters of the normal distribution $\mathscr{N}(\cdot)$ (multivariate normal with diagonal covariance matrix) and the inverse gamma distribution ($\mathscr{G}(\cdot)$), respectively. The implementation is based on sklearn-bayes [26] where a variational inference method is proposed.

5.2.2 Modelling Aleatory Uncertainty

The water consumption pattern varies for different hours, days, months, and years and also varies with different locations. For example, demand is high at weekends and hot months and is heavily dependent on the weather for gardening and lawn irrigation. Figure 10 depicts the observed daily water consumption pattern of one customer connection over three years. The blue line is median value, and shading areas are for 75th, 90th, and 99th percentile of the historical data. It can be seen that the variability of water consumed from time to time.

In the previous model, the explicit observation $f(t)$ is only for the flow of the whole residential zone, and each location in the zone is to be modelled independently. For individual location, the data is recorded for the total water usage in a month based on the bills. Therefore, it is intuitive to separate the flow for each location, which brings the issue of data uncertainty given that the individual usage is incomplete. Given a month m^* in the past, we can model the water flow to s on day n by

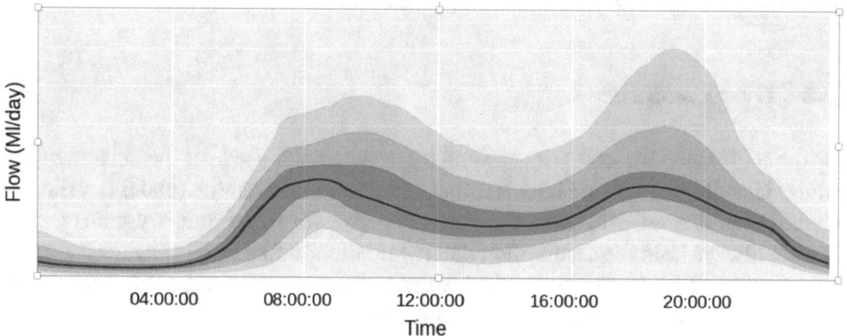

Fig. 10 Pattern and uncertainty of daily water consumption by one customer connection over three years.

$$\mathbf{f}_n^s = [r^s(m^*) f_n(h)], \tag{9}$$

where $r^s(m)$ is the proportion of the usage by s to the total usage in the zone. For any month m, the uncertainty of the separation is denoted as:

$$\mathbf{r^s(t)} = \mathbf{r^s(m)} = \frac{\boldsymbol{\mu}^\mathbf{s} + \boldsymbol{\eta}_\mathbf{d}}{2}, \boldsymbol{\eta}_\mathbf{d} \sim \mathscr{D}(\alpha). \tag{10}$$

Here, $\mathscr{D}$ is the Dirichlet distribution. α is the parameter of Dirichlet distribution. For the Dirichlet distribution, the summation of each element in a sampled vector η_d is always 1. Therefore, we also need to set $\sum_s \mu^s$ to 1. Then, the water flow in s can be obtained by

$$f^s(t) = (\frac{\boldsymbol{\mu}^\mathbf{s} + \boldsymbol{\eta}_\mathbf{d}}{2}) f(t) \tag{11}$$

5.3 *Risk of AutoML*

AutoML brings nearly grid search for the optimised parameters. It seems that the results given is flawless. However, the risk of using AutoML cannot be ignored. The risk of AutoML can be easily found with a quick search, and here, we will focus on the risks in our scenario.

5.3.1 Lack of Stability

Due to the randomness in the optimisation procedure, different optimal pipelines may be obtained when AutoML is conducted multiple times. In order to adress this issue, AutoML needs a long time (hours to days) to allow the optimisation to thoroughly search the pipeline space. However, the optimisation procedure is still more effective than human efforts in parameters tuning in standard ML algorithms.

5.3.2 Over Confidence

The model learned indicates the optimal hyperparameter used for the current model setting. Usually, we can see high training accuracy, and even the model is validated on additional dataset. However, the prediction task for water industry management does not always hold the assumption that the prediction function is always the same. For example, the failure pattern or the factor impact can change when pipes are getting older. Then, the best prediction does not last.

On the other hand, users may have high confidence over the AutoML model, and then decisions are made based on the model. However, such high confidence from accuracy cannot be guaranteed to generalise to new data, especially factors like time can change to prediction. The problem of such false confidence can cause the worst consequence that nothing to be prepared for the wrong decision.

The model explanation is critical for curing this issue. The aim of explanation is to help users understand the model mechanism. The most explanation take the machine learning experts as the audience, by showing a simpliefd model that can represent the learned model, or visualise the learned representatoin level in the model. Another type of exaplanation is factor based, which show the audience the importance of factors.

An important and well-accepted algorithm is LIME [25] (Local Interpretable Model-Agnostic Explanations). LIME generates the prediction on local neighbourhood of each data sample under investigation. Then, a simplified model (e.g. linear regression) is used to fit the local observation. The features weights are then obtained from the simplified mode. As a result, LIME can give each data a list of weights of factors to explain how the model is built.

6 Conclusion

This chapter has presented practical cases to illustrate how machine learning can be leveraged for improving the productivity, using the data-driven water main failure prediction and water quality prediction as examples. The water pipe failure problem is to predict the failure rate of water pipes buried underground, using the data including pipe properties, surrounding environment, and historical failures. The water quality prediction problem is to estimate the water quality, mainly the total chlorine level in customers' taps, based on the observation of chemical residuals in reservoir and temperature.

The discussion is based on three main steps in a standard machine learning system. The three steps include factor analysis, model design, and model inference. Here, model design and model learning must be used together for the prediction task, while the factor analysis can help users to understand the importance of factors. The automatic factor analysis and modelling can increase the level of productivity by replacing the manual work.

Furthermore, we have shown the challenges of all steps. In the challenges, the factor analysis must provide an automatic manner to extract the correlations among a large number of factors. For modelling, it is difficult to use physical knowledge when the situation is complex. Then, learning the machine learning model itself is also a challenge that hyperparameter setting requires resources to be feasible.

We discussed corresponding solutions to all challenges, and there are many other alternatives. Machine learning models are used for analysis to understand the correlations, and then, we discussed the difference between parametric model with nonparametric models. The studies on pipe failure prediction using Bayesian nonparametric models are illustrated. Then, we show examples using AutoMl to recursively learn models with different hyperparameter settings.

We also discussed potential risks when using these methods. The correlation is not the cause or effect so it is concerning when the analysis is conducted. In addition, imperfect data can be an issue, but it will be less problematic with substantial data. The uncertainty of data and model are also potential risks if they are ignored. At last, using AutoML can cause over confidence for users.

Because of the limitation of pages and our knowledge, this chapter cannot list all productivity work using AI. The future work on productivity enhancement will still be the aggregated effects from data, modelling, and inference. With the trend of increasing computational power, the machine learning algorithms will be applied into more industrial projects, further improving the productivity, but facing more practical issues. The applicable machine learning will then be the dominated research direction in AI.

References

1. Bengio, Y.: Learning deep architectures for AI. Now Publishers Inc (2009)
2. Bishop, C.M.: Pattern recognition and machine learning. springer (2006)
3. Breiman, L.: Random forests. Machine learning **45**(1), 5–32 (2001)
4. Chen, T., Guestrin, C.: XGBoost: A scalable tree boosting system. In: Proceedings of the 22nd ACM SIGKDD International Conference on Knowledge Discovery and Data Mining, KDD '16, pp. 785–794. ACM, New York, NY, USA (2016). DOI 10.1145/2939672.2939785. http://doi.acm.org/10.1145/2939672.2939785
5. Drucker, H., Burges, C.J., Kaufman, L., Smola, A., Vapnik, V.: Support vector regression machines. Advances in neural information processing systems **9**, 155–161 (1996)
6. Edition, F.: Guidelines for drinking-water quality. WHO chronicle **38**(4), 104–8 (2011)
7. Erickson, N., Mueller, J., Shirkov, A., Zhang, H., Larroy, P., Li, M., Smola, A.: Autogluon-tabular: Robust and accurate automl for structured data. arXiv preprint arXiv:2003.06505 (2020)
8. Ferguson, P., Heathcote, M., Moore, G., Russell, D.: Condition assessment of water mains using remote field technology. WATER-MELBOURNE THEN ARTARMON- **23**, 6–8 (1996)
9. Feurer, M., Klein, A., Eggensperger, K., Springenberg, J., Blum, M., Hutter, F.: Efficient and robust automated machine learning. In: Advances in neural information processing systems, pp. 2962–2970 (2015)
10. Gal, Y., Ghahramani, Z.: Dropout as a bayesian approximation: Representing model uncertainty in deep learning. In: international conference on machine learning, pp. 1050–1059 (2016)
11. Gijsbers, P., LeDell, E., Thomas, J., Poirier, S., Bischl, B., Vanschoren, J.: An open source automl benchmark. arXiv preprint arXiv:1907.00909 (2019)
12. Goodfellow, I., Bengio, Y., Courville, A., Bengio, Y.: Deep learning, vol. 1. MIT press Cambridge (2016)
13. Huang, L., Joseph, A.D., Nelson, B., Rubinstein, B.I., Tygar, J.: Adversarial machine learning. In: Proceedings of the 4th ACM workshop on Security and artificial intelligence, pp. 43–58. ACM (2011)
14. Kendall, A., Gal, Y.: What uncertainties do we need in bayesian deep learning for computer vision? In: Advances in neural information processing systems, pp. 5574–5584 (2017)
15. Kleiner, Y., Rajani, B.: Comprehensive review of structural deterioration of water mains: statistical models. Urban water **3**(3), 131–150 (2001)
16. Kotthoff, L., Thornton, C., Hoos, H.H., Hutter, F., Leyton-Brown, K.: Auto-weka 2.0: Automatic model selection and hyperparameter optimization in weka. The Journal of Machine Learning Research **18**(1), 826–830 (2017)

17. Krizhevsky, A., Sutskever, I., Hinton, G.E.: Imagenet classification with deep convolutional neural networks. In: Advances in neural information processing systems, pp. 1097–1105 (2012)
18. Le, T.T., Fu, W., Moore, J.H.: Scaling tree-based automated machine learning to biomedical big data with a feature set selector. Bioinformatics **36**(1), 250–256 (2020)
19. Li, Z., Zhang, B., Wang, Y., Chen, F., Taib, R., Whiffin, V., Wang, Y.: Water pipe condition assessment: a hierarchical beta process approach for sparse incident data. Machine learning **95**(1), 11–26 (2014)
20. Misiūnas, D.: Failure Monitoring and Asset Condition Asssessment in Water Supply Systems. Vilniaus Gedimino technikos universitetas (2008)
21. Olson, R.S., Moore, J.H.: Tpot: A tree-based pipeline optimization tool for automating machine learning. In: Workshop on automatic machine learning, pp. 66–74. PMLR (2016)
22. Pandey, P.: A deep dive into h2o's automl. Tech. rep., Technical report, 2019. http://www.h2o.ai/blog/a-deep-dive-into-h2os-automl (2019)
23. Pedregosa, F., Varoquaux, G., Gramfort, A., Michel, V., Thirion, B., Grisel, O., Blondel, M., Prettenhofer, P., Weiss, R., Dubourg, V., Vanderplas, J., Passos, A., Cournapeau, D., Brucher, M., Perrot, M., Duchesnay, E.: Scikit-learn: Machine learning in Python. Journal of Machine Learning Research **12**, 2825–2830 (2011)
24. Rajani, B., Kleiner, Y.: Comprehensive review of structural deterioration of water mains: physically based models. Urban water **3**(3), 151–164 (2001)
25. Ribeiro, M.T., Singh, S., Guestrin, C.: "why should i trust you?" explaining the predictions of any classifier. In: Proceedings of the 22nd ACM SIGKDD international conference on knowledge discovery and data mining, pp. 1135–1144 (2016)
26. Shaumyan, A.: Python package for bayesian machine learning with scikit-learn api (2017)
27. Silver, D., Schrittwieser, J., Simonyan, K., Antonoglou, I., Huang, A., Guez, A., Hubert, T., Baker, L., Lai, M., Bolton, A., et al.: Mastering the game of go without human knowledge. nature **550**(7676), 354–359 (2017)
28. Soland, R.M.: Bayesian analysis of the weibull process with unknown scale and shape parameters. IEEE Transactions on Reliability **18**(4), 181–184 (1969)
29. Thibaux, R., Jordan, M.I.: Hierarchical beta processes and the indian buffet process. In: International conference on artificial intelligence and statistics, pp. 564–571 (2007)
30. Yao, Q., Wang, M., Chen, Y., Dai, W., Yi-Qi, H., Yu-Feng, L., Wei-Wei, T., Qiang, Y., Yang, Y.: Taking human out of learning applications: A survey on automated machine learning. arXiv preprint arXiv:1810.13306 (2018)
31. Zöller, M.A., Huber, M.F.: Benchmark and survey of automated machine learning frameworks. arXiv preprint arXiv:1904.12054 (2019)

AI for Real-Time Bus Travel Time Prediction in Traffic Congestion Management

Yuming Ou

1 Introduction

1.1 Urbanization and Traffic Congestion

According to a report [37] by United Nations, in 1990 there were 2.3 billion people—43% of the world's population—living in urban area. In 2018, the urban population has increased to 4.2 billion, which was 55% of the world's population. This urbanization trend is expected to continue. In 2050, the global urban population is projected to 6.7 billion. In other words, in mid-century, about 68% of the world's population will be living in urban area. The rapid urbanization brings opportunities as well as challenges to us. If managing it well by improving productivity and allowing innovation, we can benefit from the urbanization and enjoy the sustainable growth as more than 80% of global GDP is generated in cities. However, the urbanization also imposes the challenges to meet the accelerated demands such as affordable housing, more jobs and efficient transport systems.

Transport is vital to urban development. Transport systems provide essential mobility for citizens to access to jobs, education, housing, services and recreational facilities. Transport systems also move goods in the cities and significantly contribute to the economic growth. Urban growth and transport are strongly related to each other. Transport has a big influence on urban development. Efficient transport systems can attract more people and boost the urbanization. On the other hand, population growth can cause an increase in travel demand and thereby an increase in the need for transport infrastructure.

With the rapid urbanization trend, one critical problem in transport systems is traffic congestion. Traffic congestion has significantly negative impact on economy. It imposes additional costs to the communities and businesses by longer and less predictable travel times, reduces economic opportunities and lowers quality of life.

Y. Ou (✉)
Data Science Institute, University of Technology Sydney, Sydney, Australia
e-mail: yuming.ou@uts.edu.au

F. Chen and J. Zhou (eds.), *Humanity Driven AI*,
https://doi.org/10.1007/978-3-030-72188-6_4

It is shown that traffic congestion has been increasing over the world in the past decades. Effectively and efficiently managing traffic congestion is a pressing need for many cities.

1.2 Significance of Bus Travel Time Prediction

In the modern cities, public transport systems play the key role of moving people, increasing business productivity and improving air quality. It is the most popular transport means for commuters who regularly travel to work in the rush hour. Public transport can help riders avoid the stress that results from the daily driving in highly congested areas. Conveying more people in much less space than individual cars, public transport also helps to lower traffic congestion and reduce harmful air emission. Public transport provides an economical and environmentally friendly way of travel in cities.

However, public transport is also impacted by the congestion and suffering from traffic delay. In order to enhance the satisfaction of transit users and attract more people to use public transport, it is significant to improve public transport services, for example, by reducing delays and timely updating passengers with useful information when delays happen.

Timely and accurate bus travel time prediction is important to the public transport operations. It helps the transit operators to plan effective and robust schedules resulting in less congestion and delay. Early knowing the delay can enable transit operators to promptly respond and take action to the unexpected events. For the transit users, this type of information is also of importance. By keeping the passengers well-informed, the impact of delay and the consequent anxieties are largely relieved. The travellers can optimize their travel plans, mitigate traffic delay, and avoid traffic congestion as much as possible based on the up-to-date information. Therefore, the overall quality of transit services can be improved by providing such information to the transit users.

1.3 Research Problem

The research problem of this study is to predict bus travel time in real time. Bus travel time is the time for a bus to travel from one place to another place, which usually means bus stops. Technically, travel time, arrival time and delay have the same meaning in the context of public transport as any of them can be easily inferred by others. In this chapter, we use these three terms, and they are interchangeable if not specified.

Bus travel time prediction has always been an active research topic over the past decades due to its importance to our real-life applications. With the advance of technologies, the methods for bus travel time prediction are progressing. Nowadays, automatic vehicle location (AVL) systems have been widely adopted by many transit agencies, which make use of the Global Positioning System (GPS) automatically determining and transmitting the geographic location of a vehicle in a real-time fashion. This technology advance provides the transit agencies with an effective way to track their transit vehicles. Thanks for the AVL systems, a wealth of real-time information about the movements of vehicles is available and can be used for travel time prediction.

Artificial intelligence (AI) particularly machine learning technologies can provide solutions to this problem. Utilizing machine learning technologies, we can build prediction models on the historical vehicle movement data collected by the AVL systems and then make predictions by feeding the latest data into the models.

In this chapter, we propose an AI-based approach to address the research problem. The proposed approach is an end-to-end solution including real-time data retrieving and parsing, GPS data map matching and travel time prediction. Our approach can be used in the systems that provide real-time bus arrival time and delay information.

1.4 Research Challenges

Accurately predicting bus travel time in real time is a very challenging task. Firstly, as the nature of transport systems, there are so many stochastic variables that can affect the travel time. For instance, travel speed fluctuates over time due to the ever change of traffic conditions. A broken vehicle or a major car incident can block a road and cause the congestion on the upstream road segments. Traffic signals can impact the traffic flow and cause intersection delays if they are not well configured. It is expected to take a longer travel time if the weather is bad.

Secondly, the dwell time depending on travel demand also affects the travel time. The unexpected surge of travel demand caused by events such as concerts and sports can largely increase the dwell time and result in delays. The stochastic passenger arrival at the the bus stops makes the prediction more difficult.

Thirdly, it requires a real-time prediction for providing timely bus arrival information. This means that the real-time data needs to be retrieved, processed and fed into the prediction model for quickly responding to the new situations within a short period of time window.

1.5 Organization of the Chapter

The rest of this chapter is organized as follows. The related work will be introduced in Sect. 2, in which five categories of methods for travel time prediction will be presented. Section 3 will propose the overall framework of bus travel time prediction. The data used in this study and the method to collect the data will be introduced in Sect. 4. Section 5 will present the problem formulation with a number of definitions, the approach to correct GPS location data and our proposed method for travel time prediction. The case study that we have applied our approach to predict bus travel time in an area of Sydney will be introduced in Sect. 6. The discussion about the implication of our proposed approach to the humanity will be given in Sect. 7. Finally, Sect. 8 will conclude this chapter.

2 Related Work

Over the past decades, many pieces of research have been conducted to address the problem of bus travel time prediction due to its significance. A variety of approaches have been proposed, which can be categorized into the following five types: (1) historical average methods, (2) time series methods, (3) regression methods, (4) Kalman filter methods and (5) machine learning methods. The five categories of approaches are introduced in the following subsections.

2.1 Historical Average Methods

As pointed out in [53], traffic conditions normally follow consistent daily and weekly patterns, which indicates that a reasonable forecast of future traffic conditions at a particular time of day and day of week can be given by the historical average of conditions at the same time of day and day of week. Based on this finding, historical average methods assume that the future traffic condition is consistent with previous journeys in the same time period and then predict the future travel time by observed historical travel time.

The basic idea of this type of methods is to find the previous journeys under similar traffic conditions and then use historical average travel time of previous journeys to predict the future travel time. The variation of this type of methods is the way to choose similar journeys. A naive approach is to simply use the journeys at the same location and in the same time period, which is usually used as a baseline method for benchmarking other methods. K-nearest neighbour (KNN) [8, 41, 44] is a popular approach to choose similar journeys, which select the K-nearest neighbours of previous journeys. However, determining the optimal size of nearest neighbours is very tricky. The size of nearest neighbours largely influences the prediction performance [8]. Apart from that, K-NN is computationally intensive if a large-scale number of historical journeys are present.

In general, the historical average methods are reliable only when the traffic patterns in the area of interest are relatively stable, such as the rural areas.

2.2 Time Series Methods

Time series methods [9, 43] assume that there is a pattern or a mixture of patterns in the historical time series data, and the patterns will remain the same in future time period. Based on the assumption, time series methods try to model the historical time series data by mathematical functions and use the mathematical functions to forecast the future.

In [9], a nonlinear time series model is used to predict the travel time on a highway section in Orlando, Florida. In this study, two models including single-variable model and multiple-variable model have been built and compared with each other. Interestingly, the results showed that the single-variable model based on speed time series data outperformed the multiple-variable model based on speed, occupancy and volume time series data.

The accuracy of this type of methods highly depends on the fitness of the mathematical functions to model the historical data and the similarity between historical and real-time traffic patterns. Both the variation of historical data and changes of real-time from historical traffic patterns can largely impact the accuracy of the prediction results.

2.3 Regression Methods

Regression methods assume that the bus arrival time is an output of a function of different variables such as traffic circumstances, number of passengers, number of bus stops and climate situations. Therefore, this type of methods uses a mathematical function to describe the relationship between the dependent variable—travel time—with a set of independent variables.

There were many studies [5, 24, 27, 36, 40] that used regression models for bus travel time prediction. The major difference is the independent variables used for building the regression models. One of the advantages of regression methods is that the importance of each independent variable to the dependent variable can be known by the built regression models. For example, in a study [36] a set of multiple linear regression models has been developed using independent variables including distance, number of stops, dwell time, boarding and alighting passengers and weather to predict bus arrival time. According to the results, weather is less important than other inputs in the models.

The major limit of regression methods is that variables in transport systems are likely to be inter-correlated rather than completely independent [6].

2.4 Kalman Filter Methods

Originated from the state-space representations in modern control theory, Kalman filter is a recursive procedure that estimates the future states of dependent variables. It is introduced to travel time prediction because of its advantage in continuously updating the state variable using new observations [6].

Many studies based on Kalman filter algorithm have been reported for travel time prediction [7, 26, 34, 47, 49]. For instance, Chu et al. [7] developed a method for travel time estimation based on Kalman filtering. The proposed method can dynamically estimate noise statistics of the system by adapting to the new observations. The Kalman filtering-based algorithm was evaluated under recurrent and non-recurrent traffic congestion conditions. The results showed that the proposed method outperformed the benchmark method for both situations. In Yang's study [26], a discrete time Kalman filter was used to predict arterial travel time in the scenarios of special events such as graduation ceremony.

2.5 Machine Learning Methods

Machine learning [31] is a branch of artificial intelligence which is based on the idea that systems can learn from data and make decisions. It focuses on studying computer algorithms that build models based on historical data and improve the models automatically through experience. Typically building a machine model consists of four phases including (1) preparing training data set, (2) choosing a candidate algorithm, (3) training a model by the selected algorithm on the training data set and (4) using and improving the model.

Support vector machine (SVM) is one of the popular machine learning algorithms that are reported in the literature of bus travel time prediction. SVM uses kernel functions to find a hyperplane or set of hyperplanes that can be used for classification, regression or outliers detection. Yu et al. [2, 56] used SVM to predict bus arrival time by considering the segment-level travel time and four traffic conditions including peak time and sunny day, off-peak time and sunny day, peak time and rainy day, and off-peak time and rainy day. The model used three inputs consisting of segment, travel time of current segment and the latest travel time of next segment, to output the predicted travel time.

Artificial neural network (ANN) [1] is also a popular machine learning algorithm for bus travel time prediction. ANN is inspired by biological neural networks, in which there are multiple layers of processing units called artificial neurons. Each neurons has an activation function and is connected with other neurons. The connection between two neurons means the output of a neuron as the input of another neuron. Each connection is assigned a weight which represents its importance. Through learning process, the initial weights are adjusted to capture the relationship between inputs and outputs usually by backpropagation algorithm [28]. ANN-based methods have gained popularity in predicting bus travel time because of their ability to solve complex nonlinear relationships [5, 6, 25, 38] . For example, Ramakrishna et al. [38] developed a multiple layer perceptron (MLP) for predicting bus travel time using vehicle speed data and passenger data, which achieved better performance over the linear regression approach. In the study of Jeong et al. [25], the ANN model outperformed both historical data model and regression model in predicting bus travel time using actual vehicle location data in Houston, Texas.

One advantage of machine learning methods is that they can deal with large volume of data sets. Another advantage is that they can discover the complex relationships between predictors, such as nonlinear relationships. The ability to tolerate noisy data is also an advantage of machine learning methods.

3 Proposed System Framework

The proposed system framework of bus travel time prediction is illustrated in Fig. 1, in which each parallelogram represents a function component, each rectangle is the output of each function component, solid line stands for the process of model training, and dashed line stands for the prediction process. There are four major function components which are described as follows.

- *Real-Time GTFS Data Collection*: the component to collect real-time GTFS data which will be introduced in Sect. 4 of this chapter.
- *GPS Data Correction*: the component to correct GPS data points and match them to road segments, which will be introduced in Sect. 5.2 of this chapter.
- *Model Training*: the component to train a prediction model using historical GPS data, which will be introduced in Sect. 5.3 of this chapter.
- *Model Prediction*: the component to predict bus travel time using the trained prediction model, which will be introduced in Sect. 5.3 of this chapter.

4 Real-Time Data Collection

This section introduces the data used for this research work and the workflow to collect the real-time data through RESTful data APIs.

4.1 GTFS Data

The General Transit Feed Specification(GTFS) [16] defines a common data format to allow public transit agencies to publish their transit data so that the data can be consumed by various applications. Generally, GTFS is divided into two streams

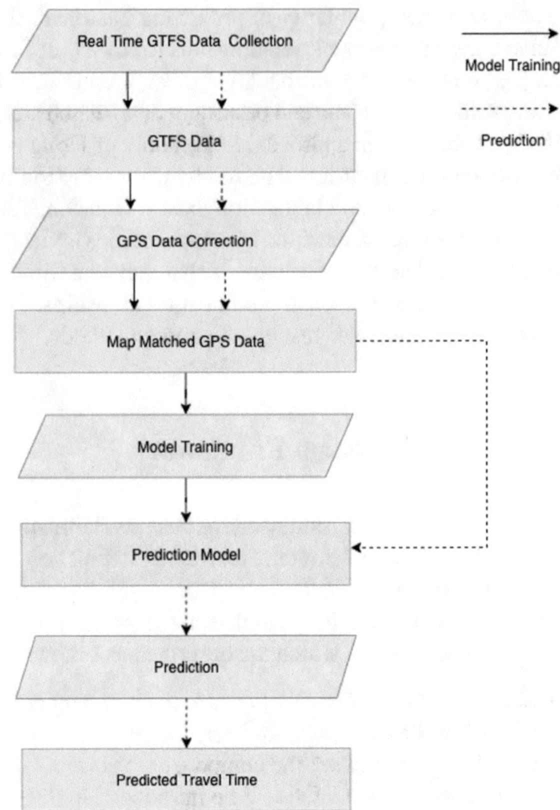

Fig. 1 *Framework of travel time prediction*: each parallelogram represents a function component, each rectangle is the output of each function component, solid line stands for the process of model training, and dashed line stands for the prediction process. Best viewed in colour

including GTFS static and GTFS real time. The former contains public transportation schedules and associated geographic information while the latter contains the real-time vehicle positions and all trip updates.

GTFS has been used as an industry standard for majority of transit agencies to publish their transit data around the world [17]. As GTFS data contains both scheduled and real-time information about transit operations, it has been actively used for many research problems such as transit accessibility [10, 11, 14, 19, 35], transit network analysis [20, 51], performance evaluation [4, 50], delay prediction [45, 46, 55] and transit trip inference [32, 57].

4.2 GTFS Data Collection

The data used for this study is the GTFS data published by the local transport agency: Transport for NSW [33]. We collect the following three data sets.

- *Real-Time Bus Position Data*: the real-time buses' movements with longitudes, latitudes and associated time stamps. The real-time bus positions are captured by the GPS devices mounted on the buses. There are always errors associated with the GPS data. We need to correct the GPS data by a map matching algorithm which we introduce in Sect. 5.2 of this chapter.
- *Bus Timetable Data*: containing the scheduled bus trips and scheduled arrival times at bus stops.
- *Bus Network Data*: containing the geolocations of all bus stops and the physical geometry of the bus routes.

As the bus position data is published in real time, we need to develop a data collection service for continuously collecting the data through RESTful data APIs. Figure 2 illustrates the workflow of data collection. To collect the real-time bus position data, the data collection service sends a data pulling request to the data APIs every 5 s. After receiving the data returned from the data API, the service then parses the data and checks whether it is exactly the same to the previous data points. If so, then it discards the data; otherwise, it appends the data to stored data files. The purpose of removing the duplicate records is to save space as well as to reduce the computation cost in the following step of data processing. In the entire Sydney metropolitan region, there are around 24,000 bus stops, and more than 25,000 bus trips are being

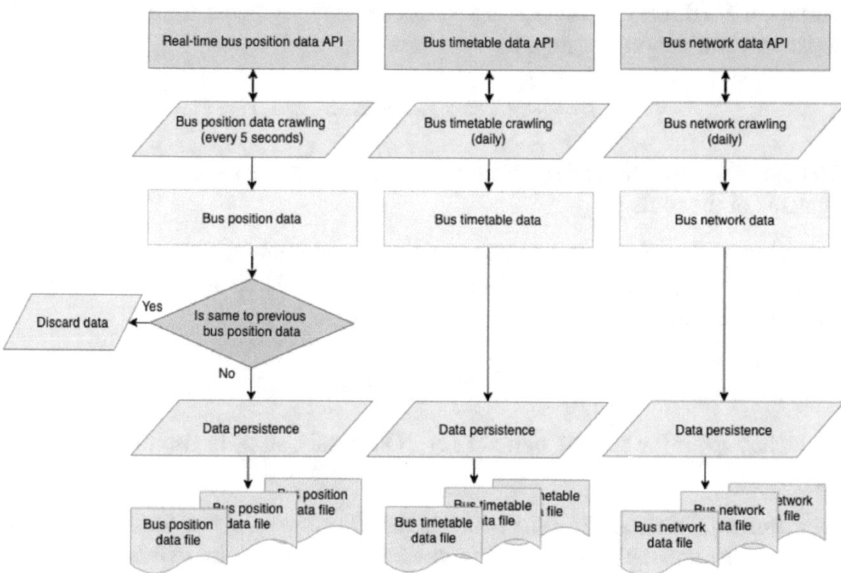

Fig. 2 *Workflow of data collection service*: the data collection service sends a data pulling request to the real-time bus position data API every 5 s. After receiving the data returned from the data API, the service then parses the data and checks whether it is exactly the same to the previous data points. If so, then it discards the data; otherwise, it appends the data to stored data files. Apart from the bus position data, the data collection service also collects timetable and network data daily in a similar fashion

scheduled during a 24-h day, which leads to more than 3GB of real-time bus position data being collected every day. Apart from the bus position data, the data collection service also collects timetable and network data daily in a similar fashion, in order to have up-to-date timetable and network data.

5 Methodology

5.1 Problem Formulation

In this subsection, we first give the definitions of *Road Segment*, *Route*, *Bus Stop* and *Trip*. On top of the definitions, we then propose the equation to calculate the travel time between two bus stops. Finally, we formulize the research problem of travel time prediction.

Definition 1 (Road Segment): A road segment seg is a portion of the road between two consecutive bus stops, which is represented by a tuple consisting of segment ID id and its length l.

$$\text{seg} = (id, l) \tag{1}$$

Definition 2 (Route): A route r is a vector of road segments from the origin bus stop to the destination bus stop,

$$r = [\text{seg}_1, \text{seg}_2, ..., \text{seg}_i, ..., \text{seg}_n] \tag{2}$$

in which seg_i is the ith road segment of the route r and n is the total number of road segments of the route r.

Definition 3 (Bus Stop): A bus stop $stop$ is the end point of a road segment and is also the starting point of the successive road segment. There is a mapping function f for returning a road segment for a given bus stop:

$$f : \text{stop}_j \mapsto seg_i \tag{3}$$

in which $stop_j$ is the starting point of seg_i. Obviously, stop_j is also the end point of seg_{i-1}.

Definition 4 (Trip): A trip $trip$ contains the information about the segments that the bus travels and their corresponding travel times. It is a vector of tuples consisting of road segment and corresponding travel time and time stamp,

$$\text{trip} = [(\text{seg}_1, tt_1, ts_1), (\text{seg}_2, tt_2, ts_2), ..., (\text{seg}_i, tt_i, ts_i), ..., (\text{seg}_n, tt_n, ts_n)] \tag{4}$$

in which tt_i is the travel time on road segment seg_i and ts_i is the time stamp that $trip$ starts to travel on seg_i

Based on the above definitions, we have the following theorem for calculating travel time between two bus stops.

Theorem 1 *(Travel Time between Two Bus Stops): The travel time between two bus stops for a given trip is the sum of corresponding travel times of road segments that the trip travels between the two bus stops:*

$$tts^{jk} = \sum_{i=g(f(stop_j))}^{g(f(stop_k))-1} tt_i \tag{5}$$

in which tts^{jk} *is the travel time from* $stop_j$ *to* $stop_k$ *and* g *is a function returning the sequence of a road segment:*

$$g : seg_i \mapsto i \tag{6}$$

Definition 5 (Travel Time Prediction): The research problem of this study is to build a model Θ that predicts the road segment travel times so that the travel time between two bus stops for a given trip can be calculated by above Eq. 5:

$$\Theta : (\text{trip}^1, ..., \text{trip}^{m-1}, \text{seg}_i, \text{stop}_j, t_j, \text{stop}_k) \mapsto \hat{tt}_i^m \tag{7}$$

in which $\hat{tt}_i^m$ is the predicted travel time for mth trip on road segment seg_i, trip^1, ..., $trip^{m-1}$ are the previous trips that have passed seg_i, $stop_j$ is the last bus stop that the mth trip has passed, t_j is the arrival time at $stop_j$, and the $stop_k$ is the next bus stop that the mth trip will arrive at.

5.2 GPS Data Correction

Due to the well-known issue of GPS accuracy [54], the GPS data is always associated with an error which is a deviation from what the real position of the bus vehicle is. The errors are variable depending on the circumstances, the road network geometry layout and continuity of data transmission in real time. Many other sources could contribute to GPS errors, such as clock error, signal jamming, weather and building blocking. An example of GPS errors is shown in Fig. 3 in which the red dots are the GPS data points sent from the GPS device on a bus while the green line is the actual bus trajectory along the main road. It can be observed that many GPS locations are falling further away from the green line (road centre line) instead of exactly being on it. Consequently, before using the bus GPS data to train the prediction model, we need to correct the GPS data through map matching algorithms by matching every GPS coordinate transmitted by the bus to a correct location on the road centreline.

There are various methods that have been used in the literature for map matching [3, 21, 30, 52]. One native way is the point-to-curve method, which projects GPS points to their closest edges. This method is simplistic and lacks robustness especially

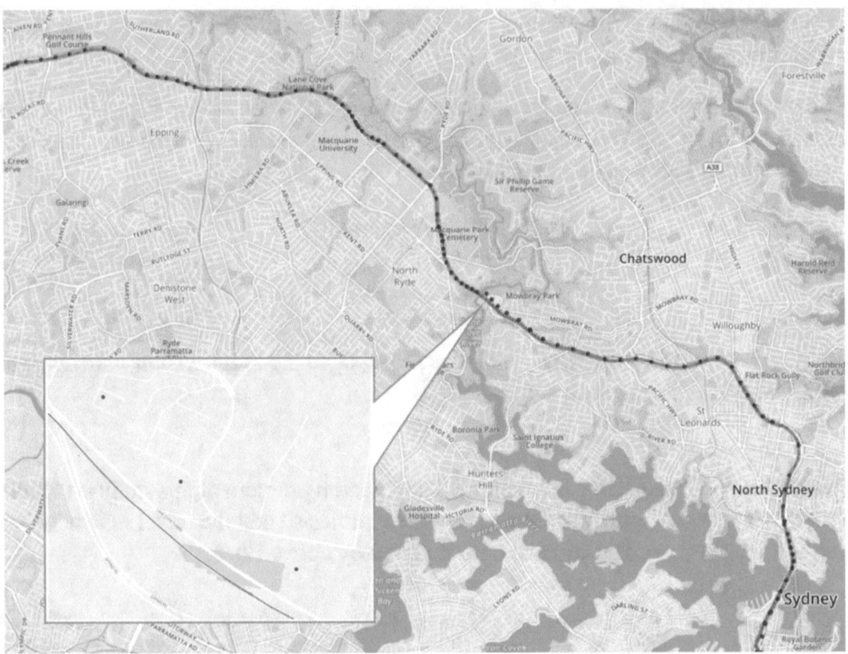

Fig. 3 *An example of GPS errors*: the red dots are the GPS data points sent from the GPS device on a bus while the green line is the actual bus trajectory along the main road. It can be observed that many GPS locations are falling further away from the green line (road centreline) instead of exactly being on it. Best viewed in colour

when the road network has a complicated structure such as in the CBD areas. An improved method is the curve-to-curve method which considers the closeness and similarity between the curve formed by GPS points and the candidate path. However, it still has the same problems under the circumstances of large GPS errors and complicated overlayed networks. Other approaches include using the geometry and topology of the road network [42], Kalman filters [29] and fuzzy rules [39].

To achieve a high accuracy of GPS data correction in real time, our map matching method is based on a hidden Markov model (HMM) [12, 48]. HMMs usually models a system by considering their unobserved states and their observations. In the system, one hidden state can change to any other hidden state by following a state transition probability. Instead of the hidden states, one can observe the values generated from the hidden states with emission probabilities. In this work, we model the road segments on which the bus is as the hidden states and the GPS readings as the observations as shown in Fig. 4. Under this setting, the emission probability is defined in following Eq. 8,

$$P(\mathrm{GPS}^t|\mathrm{seg}_i^t) = \frac{1}{\sqrt{2\pi}\sigma}e^{\frac{gd\mathrm{GPS}^t,\mathrm{GPS}_i^t)^2}{2\sigma^2}} \tag{8}$$

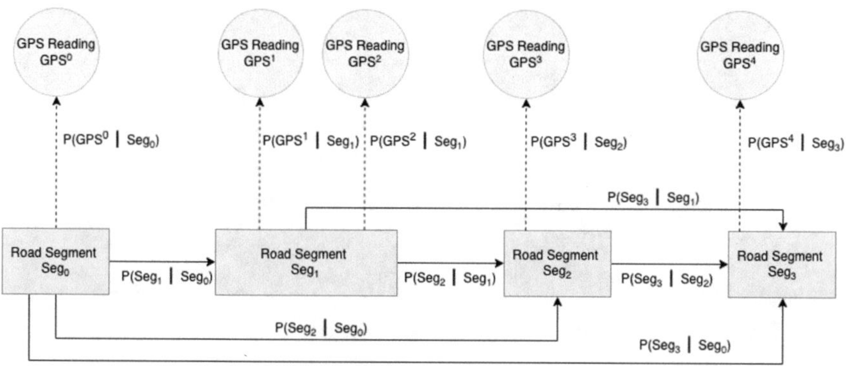

Fig. 4 *Hidden Markov model for map matching*: the blue rectangles are the hidden states of the road segments on which the bus is while the yellow circles are the observations of the GPS readings. Best viewed in colour

in which GPS^t is the bus GPS reading at time t, seg_i^t is the road segment i that the bus is on at time t, GPS_i^t is the projection of GPS^t on seg_i^t, gd is the great circle distance between two geolocations, and σ is the stand deviation of the GPS device error.

Furthermore, the transition probability is defined in following Eq. 9,

$$P(\text{seg}_j^{t+1}|\text{seg}_i^t) = \frac{gd(\text{GPS}^t, \text{GPS}^{t+1})}{rd(\text{GPS}_i^t, \text{GPS}_j^{t+1})} \tag{9}$$

in which rd is the distance between two geolocations along the road segment path.

Given a sequence of GPS readings as the observations, we can utilize the Viterbi algorithm [13] to find out the most likely sequence of road segments as the hidden states.

5.3 LSTM-Based Travel Time Prediction

Our approach to predict the arrival time at next bus stop is composed of two steps including (1) predicting the travel time for each segment that is between current location to the next bus stop (2) and then summing up the travel times for all above segments. One advantage of our approach is that predicting the segment-based travel time can capture the characteristics of each segment at a finer level of granularity than directly predicting the travel time from current location to the next bus stop as a whole. Another advantage of our approach over the method of simply predicting travel time between two bus stops is that it can be used for real-time prediction. Our approach can keep updating the prediction when a bus is travelling by updating the bus' location.

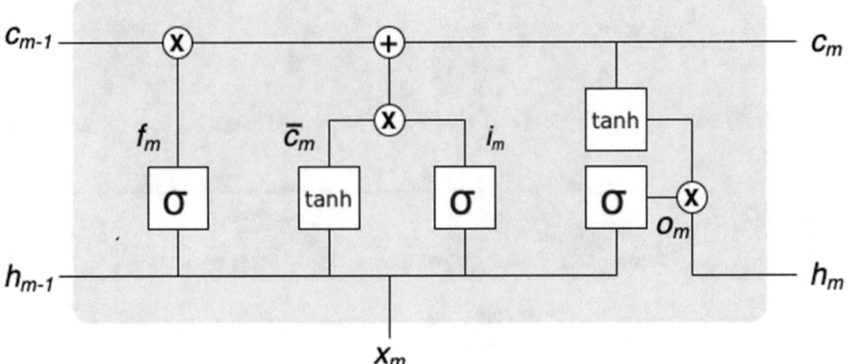

Fig. 5 *Long short-term memory unit*: the structure of a LSTM unit

In order to predict the travel time on a road segment, we build a model based on long short-term memory (LSTM) network [15, 18, 23]. LSTM networks are a type of recurrent neural network (RNN) which are well suitable for time series data. LSTM networks are improved for dealing with the issue of vanishing gradient [22] that the traditional RNNs usually suffer from. When the gradient values become extremely small during the training of RNNs, the weights are prevented from changing their values and the neural networks stop further learning. LSTM networks overcome the vanishing gradient problem by using a mechanism called gates to control the information flow into and out the memory of the network.

Figure 5 shows the LSTM unit that is used in our approach. It consists of a cell which is the memory of the network and three gates including forget gate, input gate and output gate.

The sequence data set Ψ used for training the LSTM network for a road segment is defined as follows:

$$\Psi = \{..., (X_m, tt_{m+1}), ...\} \tag{10}$$

$$X_m = (x_{m-n},\ x_{m-n+1},\ ...,\ x_m) \tag{11}$$

$$x_m = [tt_m, s_m, stop_j, t_j] \tag{12}$$

in which tt_m is the travel time of the mth trip trip^m on the road segment, s_m is the seconds from midnight derived from the time stamp that trip^m starts to travel on the road segment, stop$_j$ is the last bus stop trip^m has passed, t_j is the arrival time at bus stop stop$_j$, and n is the length of a sequence.

After building the sequence data set Ψ, we train the LSTM network by the following equations.

$$f_m = \sigma(W_{xf}x_m + W_{hf}h_{m-1} + b_f) \tag{13}$$

$$i_m = \sigma(W_{xi}x_m + W_{hi}h_{m-1} + b_i) \tag{14}$$

$$\bar{c}_m = \phi(W_{xc}x_m + W_{hc}h_{m-1} + b_c) \tag{15}$$

$$c_m = \bar{c}_m \odot i_m + f_m \odot c_{m-1} \tag{16}$$

$$o_m = \sigma(W_{xo}x_m + W_{ho}h_{m-1} + b_o) \tag{17}$$

$$h_m = o_m \odot \phi(c_m) \tag{18}$$

in which f_m is the forget gate, i_m is the input gate, $\bar{c}_m$ is the cell input, c_m is the cell state, o_m is the output gate, h_m is the output, σ is the sigmoid activation function, ϕ is the tanh activation function, W_* is the weight matrices, and b_* is the bias vectors.

6 Case Study

6.1 Case Study Setting

Our proposed methodology has been applied to an area of Sydney to predict bus travel time. The area for our case study is shown in Fig. 6. We focused on the road segments that are highlighted in blue. There are multiple bus routes which are operating on these road segments. In total, there are sixteen bus stops on the road segments as

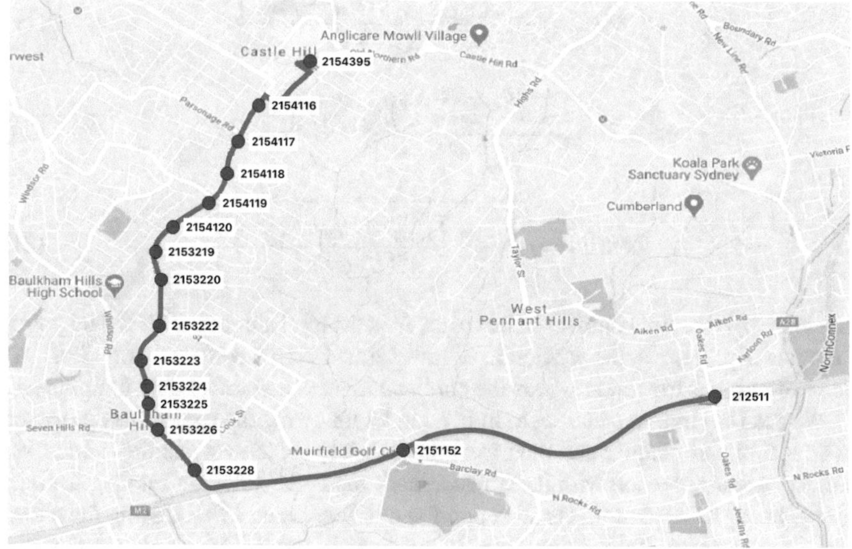

Fig. 6 *Area for the case study*: blue line represents the road segments while the purple dots stand for the bus stops. The numbers beside the bus stops are the bus stop IDs. Best viewed in colour

represented by the purple dots. Fourteen bus stops including the stops from the first to the fourteenth are on a main road, and the remaining two bus stops are on a motorway. One major reason why we choose these road segments is because part of them is on a main road and part of them is on a motorway. We can test our method performance for both types of road.

We collected the GTFS real-time data using the method introduced in Sect. 4.1 of this chapter. The data covers six months of real-time bus GPS location data in the study area. There are more than 2.1 million GPS data points generated from 37,622 bus trips from May 2019 to October 2019. We used the method presented in Subsection 5.2 of this chapter to correct the GPS data by map matching them to the corresponding locations on the road segments.

The six-month data was split into a training data set for training the model and a test data set for evaluating the model's performance. They cover four months and two months of time period, respectively. We evaluated our approach against other three methods including moving average, linear regression and support vector machine.

6.2 *Experimental Results*

Three metrics were used for evaluating the model performance, including mean absolute error (MAE), symmetric mean absolute percentage error (SMAPE) and root mean-squared error (RMSE). They are defined by the following equations, respectively.

$$\text{MAE} = \frac{\sum_{m=1}^{M}\sum_{n=1}^{N-1}|\hat{tts}_{mn} - tts_{mn}|}{M(N-1)} \tag{19}$$

$$\text{SMAPE} = \frac{\sum_{m=1}^{M}\sum_{n=1}^{N-1}\frac{|\hat{tts}_{mn} - tts_{mn}|\times 2}{|\hat{tts}_{mn}|+|tts_{mn}|}}{M(N-1)} \times 100\% \tag{20}$$

$$\text{RMSE} = \sqrt{\frac{\sum_{m=1}^{M}\sum_{n=1}^{N-1}(\hat{tts}_{mn} - tts_{mn})^2}{M(N-1)}} \tag{21}$$

in which M is the total number of bus trips, N is the total number of GPS data points for a bus trip, $\hat{tts}_{mn}$ is the prediction of travel time in minutes for the nth GPS data point of mth bus trip, and tts_{mn} is the corresponding actual travel time in minutes.

We used the training data set to train a model following the approaches proposed in Sect. 5 of this chapter and then used the test data set to evaluate the model. We compared our approach with three benchmark methods including moving average (MA), linear regression (LR) and support vector regression (SVR), using the above evaluation metrics. Table 1 provides the evaluation results, which shows that our approach outperforms the other methods for all evaluation metrics.

Table 1 Comparison of prediction errors for four models

Methods	MAE (min)	SMAPE (%)	RMSE (min)
MA	0.72	19.42	0.94
LR	0.55	18.32	0.86
SVR	0.54	18.77	0.84
Our approach	0.50	17.37	0.72

Table 2 Comparison of prediction errors for four models (weekday versus weekend)

	Methods	MAE (min)	SMAPE (%)	RMSE (min)
Weekday	MA	0.83	19.19	0.97
	LR	0.59	17.91	0.92
	SVR	0.55	17.97	0.89
	Our approach	0.51	17.31	0.74
Weekend	MA	0.59	19.55	0.81
	LR	0.51	18.54	0.72
	SVR	0.48	18.82	0.73
	Our approach	0.46	17.65	0.64

Table 3 Comparison of prediction errors for four models (weekday peak hours versus weekday non-peak hours)

	Methods	MAE (min)	SMAPE (%)	RMSE (min)
Morning peak hours	MA	0.77	19.39	1.02
	LR	0.59	18.27	0.91
	SVR	0.57	18.16	0.87
	Our approach	0.53	16.31	0.78
Non-peak hours	MA	0.69	18.95	0.88
	LR	0.51	17.75	0.79
	SVR	0.52	17.79	0.77
	Our approach	0.46	16.64	0.65
Afternoon peak hours	MA	0.57	19.72	0.97
	LR	0.56	19.47	0.93
	SVR	0.55	19.34	0.84
	Our approach	0.51	19.16	0.73

Table 4 Comparison of prediction errors for four models (motorway versus non-motorway)

	Methods	MAE (min)	SMAPE (%)	RMSE (min)
Motorway	MA	1.01	18.41	1.20
	LR	0.92	17.87	1.14
	SVR	0.93	18.01	1.12
	Our approach	0.89	13.00	1.13
Non-motorway	MA	0.67	20.13	0.89
	LR	0.51	19.19	0.81
	SVR	0.47	19.23	0.77
	Our approach	0.40	18.57	0.56

To further investigate the performance of our approach, we compared it with the three benchmark methods in different scenarios. The first scenario is that we divided the test data set into two data sets for weekday and weekends, respectively, and used them to evaluate the methods. The second scenario is to split the time period from 6AM to 22PM into three parts including morning peak hours (from 6:30AM to 10AM), afternoon peak hours (from 3PM to 7PM) and non-peak hours (the remaining). The third is to evaluate the methods in the scenario that the bus stops are on a motorway. The evaluation results for the above three scenarios are given in Table 2, 3 and 4, respectively, which show that our approach consistently beats other methods.

7 Discussion

Artificial intelligence is regarded as one of the most revolutionary developments in human history. Nowadays, we are witnessing its transformative power. There are so many AI-based cutting-edge solutions solving the most critical challenges faced by the society.

The research work presented in this chapter is one of the examples—AI technologies are used in solving the challenging problem of bus travel time prediction. The proposed AI-based solution can process large amount of vehicle movement data and predict bus travel time in real time, which helps manage the critical issue of traffic congestion. It demonstrates that AI technologies can largely improve the efficiency of our workplace and empower high-performance organizations, governments and communities.

8 Conclusion

In this chapter, we study the research problem of bus travel prediction which is significant to our societies as it helps to improve our daily lives. In order to address this research problem, we propose an approach to predict bus travel time using real-time bus GPS location data. The proposed method involves real-time data collection and processing and adopts the state-of-the-art machine learning technologies.

To verify our approach, a case study was carried out to predict the bus travel time in an area of Sydney. In the case study, three benchmark methods are used to compare with our approach. The evaluation results based on three evaluation metrics show that our proposed approach consistently outperforms the three benchmark methods in a variety of scenarios. In future, we will further improve our approach by applying graph neural networks.

The proposed method in this chapter can support traffic congestion management by providing the information of real-time bus arrival time and delay. This information can help not only transport operators proactively manage traffic congestion and take actions for mitigating the impact of delay, but also commuters better schedule their travel plans accordingly. The research work shows the power of AI technologies to promote productivity in traffic congestion management.

References

1. Agatonovic-Kustrin, S., Beresford, R.: Basic concepts of artificial neural network (ann) modeling and its application in pharmaceutical research. Journal of pharmaceutical and biomedical analysis **22**(5), 717–727 (2000)
2. Bin, Y., Zhongzhen, Y., Baozhen, Y.: Bus arrival time prediction using support vector machines. Journal of Intelligent Transportation Systems **10**(4), 151–158 (2006)
3. Brakatsoulas, S., Pfoser, D., Salas, R., Wenk, C.: On map-matching vehicle tracking data. In: Proceedings of the 31st international conference on Very large data bases, pp. 853–864 (2005)
4. Braz, T., Maciel, M., Mestre, D.G., Andrade, N., Pires, C.E., Queiroz, A.R., Santos, V.B.: Estimating inefficiency in bus trip choices from a user perspective with schedule, positioning, and ticketing data. IEEE Transactions on Intelligent Transportation Systems **19**(11), 3630–3641 (2018)
5. Chen, M., Liu, X., Xia, J., Chien, S.I.: A dynamic bus-arrival time prediction model based on apc data. Computer-Aided Civil and Infrastructure Engineering **19**(5), 364–376 (2004)
6. Chien, S.I.J., Ding, Y., Wei, C.: Dynamic bus arrival time prediction with artificial neural networks. Journal of transportation engineering **128**(5), 429–438 (2002)
7. Chu, L., Oh, J.S., Recker, W.: Adaptive kalman filter based freeway travel time estimation (2005)
8. Coffey, C., Pozdnoukhov, A., Calabrese, F.: Time of arrival predictability horizons for public bus routes (2011). DOI 10.1145/2068984.2068985
9. D'Angelo, M.P., Al-Deek, H.M., Wang, M.C.: Travel-time prediction for freeway corridors. Transportation Research Record **1676**(1), 184–191 (1999)
10. Farber, S., Fu, L.: Dynamic public transit accessibility using travel time cubes: Comparing the effects of infrastructure (dis) investments over time. Computers, Environment and Urban Systems **62**, 30–40 (2017)

11. Farber, S., Morang, M.Z., Widener, M.J.: Temporal variability in transit-based accessibility to supermarkets. Applied Geography **53**, 149–159 (2014)
12. Fine, S., Singer, Y., Tishby, N.: The hierarchical hidden markov model: Analysis and applications. Machine learning **32**(1), 41–62 (1998)
13. Forney, G.D.: The viterbi algorithm. Proceedings of the IEEE **61**(3), 268–278 (1973)
14. Fransen, K., Neutens, T., Farber, S., De Maeyer, P., Deruyter, G., Witlox, F.: Identifying public transport gaps using time-dependent accessibility levels. Journal of Transport Geography **48**, 176–187 (2015)
15. Gers, F.A., Schmidhuber, J., Cummins, F.: Learning to forget: Continual prediction with lstm (1999)
16. Google: Google transit apis. https://developers.google.com/transit
17. Google: Public feeds wiki. https://code.google.com/archive/p/googletransitdatafeed/wikis/PublicFeeds.wiki
18. Greff, K., Srivastava, R.K., Koutník, J., Steunebrink, B.R., Schmidhuber, J.: Lstm: A search space odyssey. IEEE transactions on neural networks and learning systems **28**(10), 2222–2232 (2016)
19. Guthrie, A., Fan, Y., Das, K.V.: Accessibility scenario analysis of a hypothetical future transit network: social equity implications of a general transit feed specification–based sketch planning tool. Transportation research record **2671**(1), 1–9 (2017)
20. Hadas, Y.: Assessing public transport systems connectivity based on google transit data. Journal of Transport Geography **33**, 105–116 (2013)
21. Hashemi, M., Karimi, H.A.: A critical review of real-time map-matching algorithms: Current issues and future directions. Computers, Environment and Urban Systems **48**, 153–165 (2014)
22. Hochreiter, S.: The vanishing gradient problem during learning recurrent neural nets and problem solutions. International Journal of Uncertainty, Fuzziness and Knowledge-Based Systems **6**(02), 107–116 (1998)
23. Huang, Z., Xu, W., Yu, K.: Bidirectional lstm-crf models for sequence tagging. arXiv preprint arXiv:1508.01991 (2015)
24. Jeong, R., Rilett, R.: Bus arrival time prediction using artificial neural network model. In: Proceedings. The 7th International IEEE Conference on Intelligent Transportation Systems (IEEE Cat. No.04TH8749), pp. 988–993 (2004). DOI 10.1109/ITSC.2004.1399041
25. Jeong, R., Rilett, R.: Bus arrival time prediction using artificial neural network model. In: Proceedings. The 7th international IEEE conference on intelligent transportation systems (IEEE Cat. No. 04TH8749), pp. 988–993. IEEE (2004)
26. Jiann-Shiou Yang: Travel time prediction using the gps test vehicle and kalman filtering techniques. In: Proceedings of the 2005, American Control Conference, 2005., pp. 2128–2133 vol. 3 (2005). DOI 10.1109/ACC.2005.1470285
27. Kwon, J., Coifman, B., Bickel, P.: Day-to-day travel-time trends and travel-time prediction from loop-detector data. Transportation Research Record **1717**(1), 120–129 (2000)
28. Leung, H., Haykin, S.: The complex backpropagation algorithm. IEEE Transactions on signal processing **39**(9), 2101–2104 (1991)
29. Li, L., Quddus, M., Zhao, L.: High accuracy tightly-coupled integrity monitoring algorithm for map-matching. Transportation Research Part C: Emerging Technologies **36**, 13–26 (2013)
30. Lou, Y., Zhang, C., Zheng, Y., Xie, X., Wang, W., Huang, Y.: Map-matching for low-sampling-rate gps trajectories. In: Proceedings of the 17th ACM SIGSPATIAL international conference on advances in geographic information systems, pp. 352–361 (2009)
31. Mitchell, T.M., et al.: Machine learning (1997)
32. Nassir, N., Khani, A., Lee, S.G., Noh, H., Hickman, M.: Transit stop-level origin–destination estimation through use of transit schedule and automated data collection system. Transportation research record **2263**(1), 140–150 (2011)
33. Transport for NSW, A.: Transport for nsw's open data portal. https://opendata.transport.nsw.gov.au/
34. Okutani, I., Stephanedes, Y.J.: Dynamic prediction of traffic volume through kalman filtering theory. Transportation Research Part B: Methodological **18**(1), 1–11 (1984)

35. Owen, A., Levinson, D.M.: Modeling the commute mode share of transit using continuous accessibility to jobs. Transportation Research Part A: Policy and Practice **74**, 110–122 (2015)
36. Patnaik, J., Chien, S., Bladikas, A.: Estimation of bus arrival times using apc data. Journal of public transportation **7**(1), 1 (2004)
37. Publications, U.N.: World Urbanization Prospects: The 2018 Revision. UN (2019). https://books.google.com.au/books?id=Kp9AygEACAAJ
38. Ramakrishna, Y., Ramakrishna, P., Lakshmanan, V., Sivanandan, R.: Use of gps probe data and passenger data for prediction of bus transit travel time. In: Transportation Land Use, Planning, and Air Quality, pp. 124–133 (2008)
39. Ren, M., Karimi, H.A.: Movement pattern recognition assisted map matching for pedestrian/wheelchair navigation. The journal of navigation **65**(4), 617–633 (2012)
40. Shalaby, A., Farhan, A.: Bus travel time prediction model for dynamic operations control and passenger information systems. Transportation Research Board **2** (2003)
41. Sinn, M., Yoon, J.W., Calabrese, F., Bouillet, E.: Predicting arrival times of buses using real-time gps measurements. In: 2012 15th International IEEE Conference on Intelligent Transportation Systems, pp. 1227–1232. IEEE (2012)
42. Srinivasan, D., Cheu, R.L., Tan, C.W.: Development of an improved erp system using gps and ai techniques. In: Proceedings of the 2003 IEEE International Conference on Intelligent Transportation Systems, vol. 1, pp. 554–559. IEEE (2003)
43. Stephanedes, Y.J., Kwon, E., Michalopoulos, P.: On-line diversion prediction for dynamic control and vehicle guidance in freeway corridors. 1287 (1990)
44. Sun, D., Luo, H., Fu, L., Liu, W., Liao, X., Zhao, M.: Predicting bus arrival time on the basis of global positioning system data. Transportation Research Record **2034**(1), 62–72 (2007)
45. Sun, F., Dubey, A., Samal, C., Baroud, H., Kulkarni, C.: Short-term transit decision support system using multi-task deep neural networks. In: 2018 IEEE International Conference on Smart Computing (SMARTCOMP), pp. 155–162. IEEE (2018)
46. Sun, F., Pan, Y., White, J., Dubey, A.: Real-time and predictive analytics for smart public transportation decision support system. In: 2016 IEEE International Conference on Smart Computing (SMARTCOMP), pp. 1–8. IEEE (2016)
47. Vanajakshi, L., Subramanian, S.C., Sivanandan, R.: Travel time prediction under heterogeneous traffic conditions using global positioning system data from buses. IET intelligent transport systems **3**(1), 1–9 (2009)
48. Varga, A., Moore, R.: Hidden markov model decomposition of speech and noise. In: International Conference on Acoustics, Speech, and Signal Processing, pp. 845–848. IEEE (1990)
49. Wall, Z.R.: An algorithm for predicting the arrival time of mass transit vehicles using automatic vehicle location data. Ph.D. thesis, University of Washington (1998)
50. Wessel, N., Allen, J., Farber, S.: Constructing a routable retrospective transit timetable from a real-time vehicle location feed and gtfs. Journal of Transport Geography **62**, 92–97 (2017)
51. Wessel, N., Widener, M.J.: Discovering the space–time dimensions of schedule padding and delay from gtfs and real-time transit data. Journal of Geographical Systems **19**(1), 93–107 (2017)
52. White, C.E., Bernstein, D., Kornhauser, A.L.: Some map matching algorithms for personal navigation assistants. Transportation research part c: emerging technologies **8**(1-6), 91–108 (2000)
53. Williams, B., Hoel, L.: Modeling and forecasting vehicular traffic flow as a seasonal arima process: Theoretical basis and empirical results. Journal of Transportation Engineering **129**, 664–672 (2003). DOI 10.1061/(ASCE)0733-947X(2003)129:6(664)
54. Williams, S.D., Bock, Y., Fang, P., Jamason, P., Nikolaidis, R.M., Prawirodirdjo, L., Miller, M., Johnson, D.J.: Error analysis of continuous gps position time series. Journal of Geophysical Research: Solid Earth **109**(B3) (2004)
55. Wu, J., Zhou, L., Cai, C., Dong, F., Shen, J., Sun, G.: Towards a general prediction system for the primary delay in urban railways. In: 2019 IEEE Intelligent Transportation Systems Conference (ITSC), pp. 3482–3487. IEEE (2019)

56. Yu, B., Yang, Z.Z., Wang, J.: Bus travel-time prediction based on bus speed. In: Proceedings of the Institution of Civil Engineers-Transport, vol. 163, pp. 3–7. Thomas Telford Ltd (2010)
57. Zahabi, S.A.H., Ajzachi, A., Patterson, Z.: Transit trip itinerary inference with gtfs and smartphone data. Transportation Research Record **2652**(1), 59–69 (2017)

The Future of Transportation: How to Improve Railway Operation Performance via Advanced AI Techniques

Boyu Li, Ting Guo, Yang Wang, and Fang Chen

1 Introduction

Transportation is a vital part of the development of modern cites [15]. The quality of life and the economy all depends on the performance of the transportation system. A well-performing transportation system can significantly improve the operation level of the cities, thereby reducing unnecessary costs [19]. Furthermore, a transportation system depends not only on a well-designed structure but also on efficient management. However, there is a challenge to maintain the performance of the transpiration systems. First, with population growth, it is hard for the existing transportation network to meet the increased demand, which reduces transportation efficiency. Continuously expanding the transportation system is an effective solution. Whereas it is costly on time and economy, it also makes the system too complicated and influences safety. Second, the data generated by the transportation network continues to increase. These data are valuable but also too complicated to analysis [2, 21]. Properly analyzing these data will bring a lot of effective support to the system. Therefore, it is necessary to establish some approaches to manage the transportation system, which can reduce the cost of expansion and significantly improve the transportation system's efficiency and safety.

With the development of technologies, the urban transportation system has been constructed into advanced information networks, such as by deploying sensors on the transportation networks [1, 10]. The information networks generate colossal amounts of data every day. For this reason, data-driven methods like intelligent transportation systems (ITS) have been proposed to analyze these data and lean knowledge, which makes the transportation system smarter [22]. ITS is an advanced application that

B. Li (✉) · T. Guo · Y. Wang · F. Chen
Data Science Institute, University of Technology Sydney, Sydney, Australia
e-mail: boyu.Li@uts.edu.au

T. Guo
e-mail: ting.guo@uts.edu.au

Y. Wang
e-mail: yang.wang@uts.edu.au

F. Chen
e-mail: fang.chen@uts.edu.au

F. Chen and J. Zhou (eds.), *Humanity Driven AI*,
https://doi.org/10.1007/978-3-030-72188-6_5

mainly focuses on using scientific methods to support transportation management and control [6]. ITS has some critical components, e.g., traffic forecasting, incident management, and road enforcement. All of these components benefit the transportation networks, such as incident management helps protect lives and reduces congestion, and road enforcement aims to reduce dangerous behaviors.

Meanwhile, artificial intelligence (AI) makes great achievements and progress in recent years. Thus, researchers' interest in applying artificial intelligence to transportation management has consistently grown. Machine learning , a branch of artificial intelligence, can learn the hidden pattern from big data and model a system's behavior. Besides, its processing time is reasonable, which benefits from the mighty computational power. Considering that the problems in the transportation field mainly include large and complex data and real-time requirements, these features of machine learning are suitable for solving these problems [4, 5].

Compared with conventional solutions in transportation areas, machine learning methods have shown a more valuable investment return [17]. For instance, vehicle plate recognition is a practical approach to manage the vehicle. Traditional plate recognition methods mostly reply to specific algorithms. These algorithms are designed based on the characteristics and properties of different plates, which are expensive and have low generalization ability [7]. Likewise, machine learning methods like convolution neural networks (CNNs) can recognize license plates more accurately and quickly with training limited labeled license plate images. They cost less and are compatible with different situations [16]. Moreover, machine learning is also powerful in data mining. It can capture the more hidden pattern of data than traditional data analysis methods [13]. Take traffic forecasting as an example, previous studies have applied some statics methods like ARIMA to predict future traffic, but these methods only capture limited data correlations. With the introduction of machine learning, recently studies have transfers traffic networks into graph structure and use graph neural networks to learn both the spatial and temporal hidden relationships, which achieve a more accurate predicted result [9, 11]. Benefits from these features of machine learning, the urban transportation system has become smarter.

Among all kinds of transportation, emerging railway networks defined completely new patterns of accessibility and travel behavior [14, 20]. There is an increasing development worldwide for urban railway network as an effective transportation mode to alleviate traffic congestion in cities [3]. Reliability is one of the critical evaluation criteria in railway service for both passengers and cargo [12]. Many factors are contributing to the measure, such as the delays spanning over spatial and temporal dimensions. Machine learning has the potential to streamline operational performance by increasing the level of effectiveness in decision making and improve overall efficiency. For rail, this seems like an opportunity worth further exploration, as it also calls for a profound culture change [8, 18].

Inspired by machine learning and key challenges in transportation systems, we focus on applying advanced artificial intelligence techniques to solve problems in the transportation field, especially urban railway services. In this chapter, we represent valued solutions about train timetable evaluations and case studies for the Sydney Train systems(as shown in Figs. 1, 2), which is one of the largest transportation parts

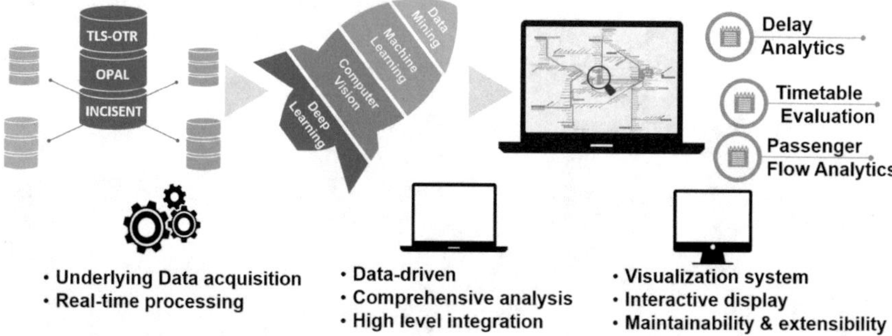

Fig. 1 Data-driven timetable evaluation model development

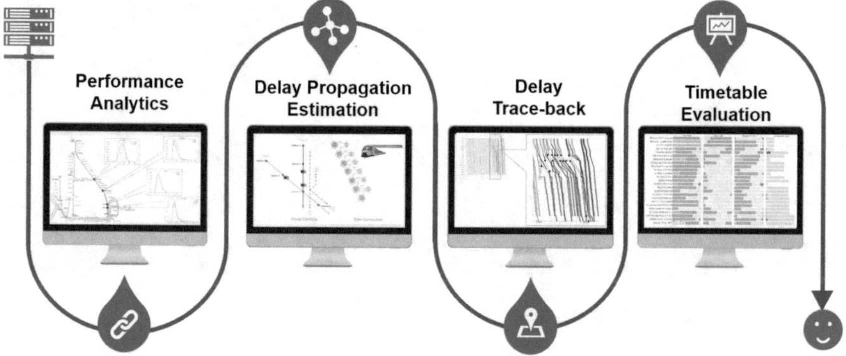

Fig. 2 Smart solutions to railway operation management

of the Great Sydney area. The smart solutions involve a comprehensive analysis of the massive data from whole Sydney Trains, which includes performance analytic, delay propagation estimation, delay trace-back, and timetable evaluation. Based on our solutions, Sydney Trains met their performance metrics and improve both efficiency and effectiveness.

2 Background

As mentioned in Sect. 1, we will focus on AI applications on railway services, especially the real-world applications for Sydney Trains. In this section, we introduce the background of the Sydney Trains and problem definition.

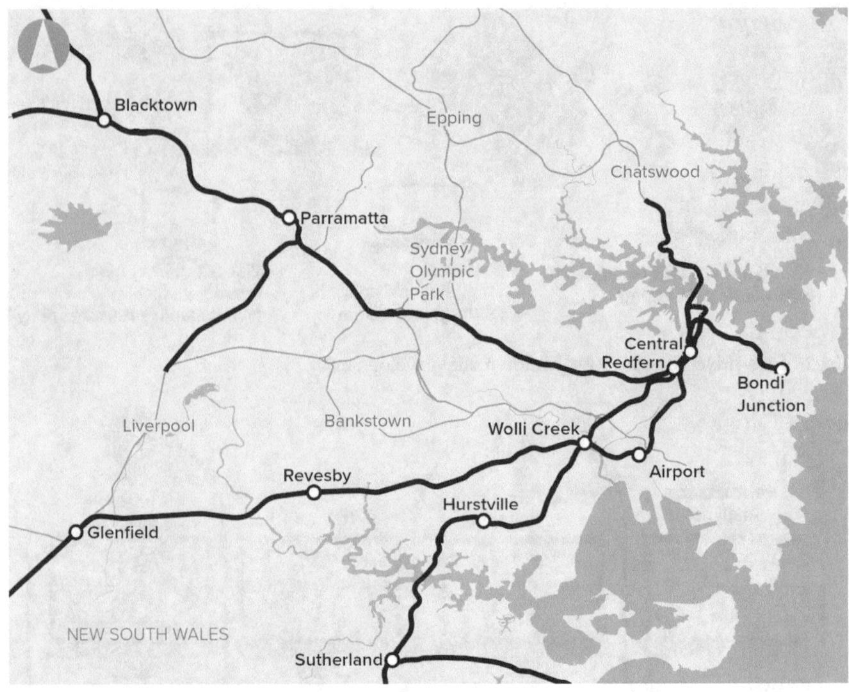

Fig. 3 Geographic Sydney trains map

2.1 *Sydney Urban Rail Transit*

Sydney Trains is the rail service provider across the metropolitan Sydney area with the vision of keeping Sydney moving by delivering safe, customer-focused, reliable, and clean services (as shown in Fig. 3). Here are some information about Sydney Trains:

- The Sydney Train network is a hybrid suburban-commuter railway across the Greater Sydney area, which covers over 1,617km of track and 175 stations (700+ platforms) over nine lines, with annual patronage of over 377.1 million last year.
- The network has 21 h a day operation with metro-like train frequencies of every three minutes or better in the underground core, 5–10 min at most major stations all day, 15 min at most minor stations all day

Overall, Sydney Trains greatly influence the daily life of Sydney residents. It would be highly economically efficient to keep the Sydney Train stable and good performance.

2.2 Problem Definition

On-time running is becoming increasingly important and challenging for Sydney Trains to meet customer expectations since patronage on Sydney's train network has grown steadily over the past few years. On-time running is highly related to capacity utilization, which is a measure of how the timetable utilizes the capacity of a network. A high utilization level might indicate high sensitivity of the railway system to delays and difficulty in recovering from incidents.

Different timetable strategies can result in varying performance and risk levels. Evaluating the robustness of various timetables can help to reduce delays and optimize on-time performance. With sufficient robustness in the timetable, trains can keep their planned slot despite unexpected/inevitable small disturbances. If, however, delays to one rail service are regularly causing a cascading effect across the rail network, it highlights a lack of robustness and the timetable will most likely need adjustment.

Track capacity derived from the fleet, signaling and infrastructure capacity, using train simulation products, is the primary focus in developing Standard Working Timetables. However, this historical simulation approach does not adequately consider the range of "on the day" factors that impact a railway operator's ability to deliver reliability and effectively recover from incidents. These factors include speed restrictions, customer behavior, variability in fleet performance, the impact of weather and infrastructure failures, etc.

There is a wealth of historical train performance, customer and incident data that can be utilized to help create more robust timetables; however, at present, they have not been used. This justifies the initiation of a research to develop a broader "data-driven" approach to timetable evaluation, an exercise that AI techniques have had great success in.

The objective of this research is to develop a timetable robustness evaluation model using analytical/statistical methods and advanced machine learning techniques. The model is able to assess timetables and response plans to ensure that that timetables/response plans are operationally robust and resilient. The model also enables railway services to meet performance metrics and recover from incidents with consideration of a range of impacting factors.

3 AI Solutions for Railway System

Growth demand in railway transport makes adequate capacity management essential. Although current planning rules fail to prevent conflicts and others even cause them. Detailed data-driven performance analysis (operation analysis) can reveal these problems by using historical records. In this section, we will measure the railway performance from three aspects: (1) systematic delay; (2) throughput, and (3) occupancy time.

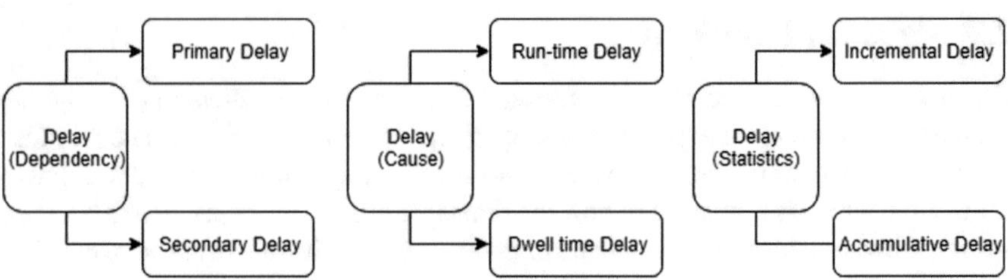

Fig. 4 Delay types under different standards

3.1 Systematic Delay Analysis

Delay is defined as the variation time between actual time and scheduled time. In the railway networks, the delay can be further decomposed into different types according to different definitions as shown in Fig. 4.

During operations, it is unavoidable that trains get delayed. Reasons for delays are manifold: customers blocking doors, train connections, scarce track capacities, weather, technical problems, etc. From a planner's point of view, some causes for the delay just have to be accepted, such as customer behavior, and some have to be dealt with in disruption management, such as power failure due to catastrophic weather conditions. There are, however, also systematic delays, which are inherent to the timetable and can be influenced by careful planning. In this section, we use historical TLS-OTR data to analyze the delay pattern on the station and platform level. TLS-OTR is the train service schedule and historical running dataset. Systematic delay can be divided into two types: systematic runtime delay and systematic dwell time delay. We use delay distribution to show the station/platform-level delay pattern for different delay types, as shown in Fig. 5, 6 and 7.

The delay patterns of systematic run-time/dwell time delay reveals which stations/platforms have best/worst performance. A run-time delay from Stations A to B is defined as (Actual arrival time at B—Actual departure time at A)—(Planned arrival time at B—Planned departure time at A); and the dwell time delay at Station A is defined as (Actual departure time at A—Actual arrival time at A)—(Planned departure time at A—Planned departure time at A). Then, the incremental departure delay at Station B from Station A is the sum of the run-time delay from Station A to B and the dwell time delay at Station B. In Fig. 5 and 6, we show the delay patterns of run time and dwell time of Station A in T9 Northern Line using TLS-OTR data (from 2018/01/01 to 2018/06/30). We can see that the run-time delay patterns have negative values, which means the actual run time is shorter than the planned run time. The overestimation of run time makes the railway network have high robustness to the emergent events caused delays. On the other hand, the delay patterns of the dwell time are positive. It means that the actual dwell time is longer than expected. Part of the reason is the overestimated run time causing that the trains have to wait for departure on scheduled time. This phenomenon is not only observed at Station A but also at other stations. The delay analysis of run time, dwell time, and departure time

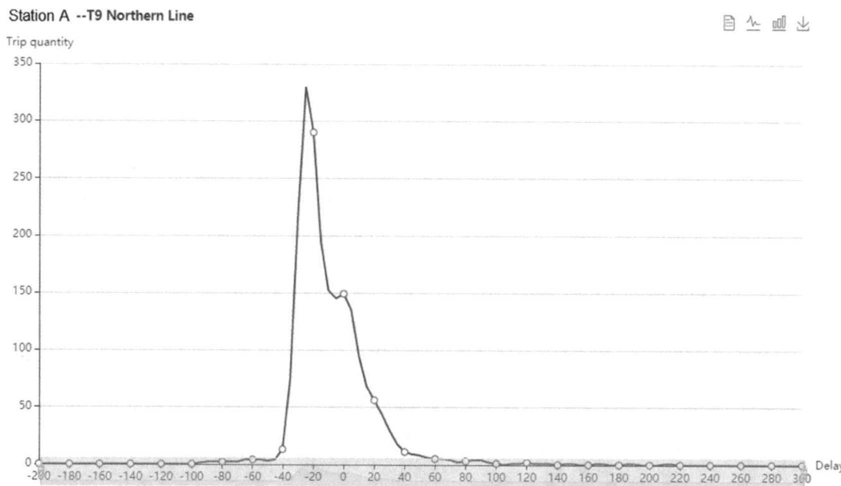

Fig. 5 Upstream run-time delay distribution for Station A in T9 Northern line

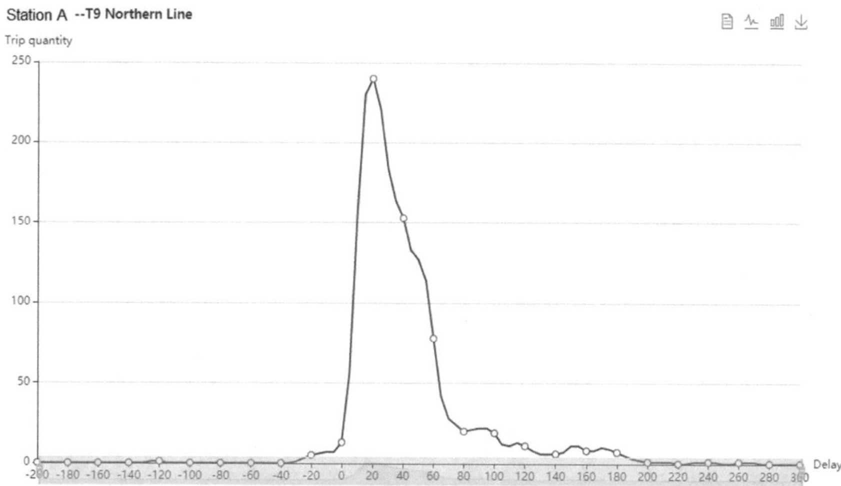

Fig. 6 Upstream dwell delay distribution for Station A in T9 Northern line

on the whole network is integrated into our visualization tool, in which results can be shown for different train lines and time periods (date, peak, and off-peak hours) as shown in Fig. 8. The line-level analysis is also conducted, as shown in Fig. 9.

To provide more intuitive insights from systematic delay, we also find the top delay hotspots based on the operation-oriented impact. The operation-oriented impact takes both systematic delay time and the number of trips into consideration. This is because the impact of a busy station with a 5-min systematic delay should be bigger than the one of an idle station with the same systematic delay. So we developed an operation-

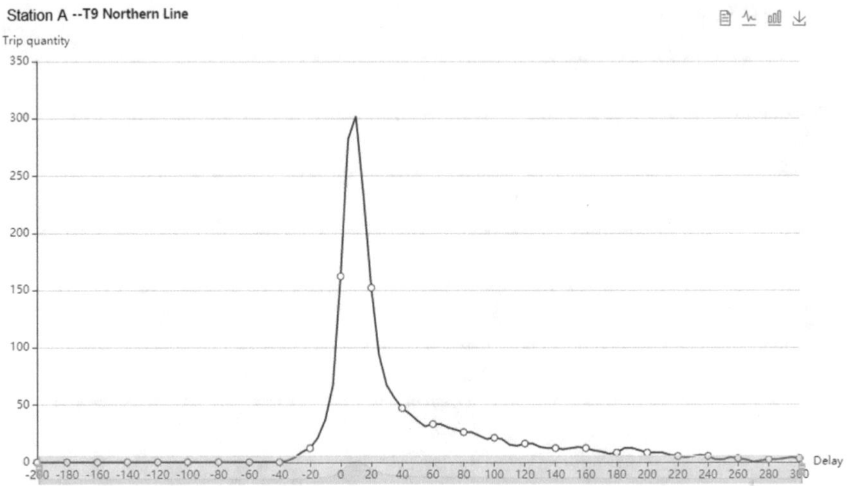

Fig. 7 Upstream departure delay distribution for Station A in T9 Northern line

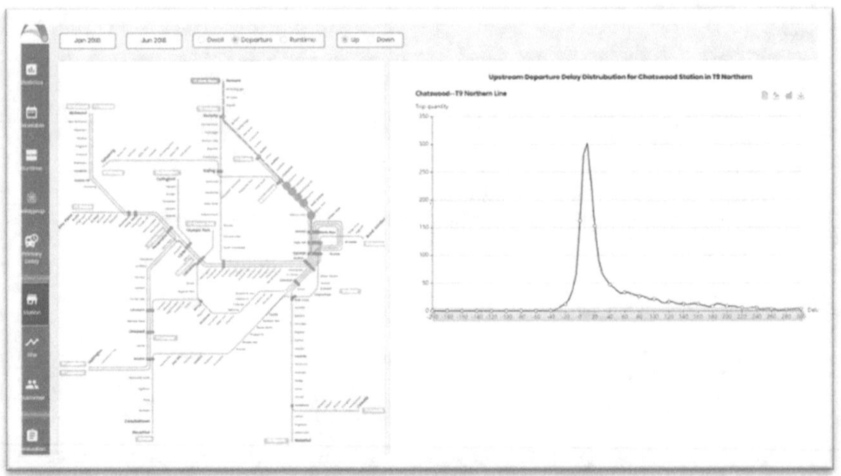

Fig. 8 Screenshot of the visualization tool on station-level systematic delay analysis

oriented method to evaluate the impact of systematic delay on any stations along a given Line L:

$$\text{Impact}\,(S_i) = \text{Systematic\_delay} * \frac{N_c^L\,(S_i)}{N_{\min}^L} \tag{1}$$

Here, $N_c^L(S_i)$ means the number of trips along Line L (per day) stop at Station S_i and N_{min}^L is the number of trips that the station of Line L with a minimum of trains standing on. We can sort the hotspots based on the operation-oriented impact for run-

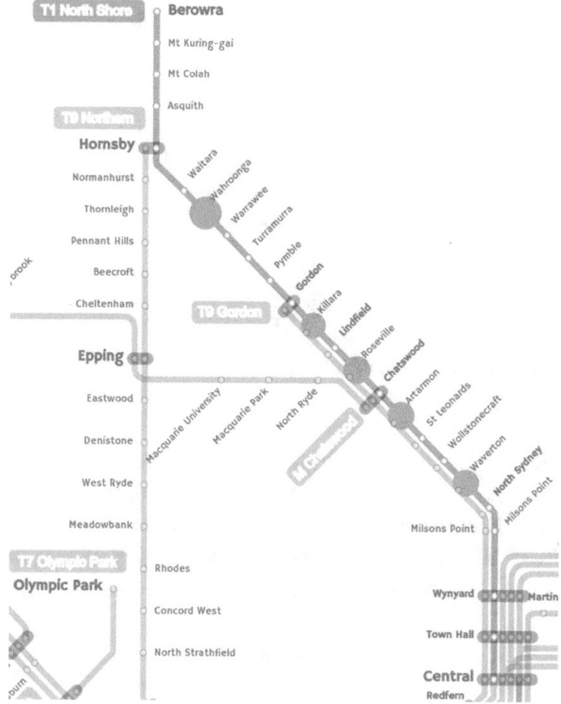

Fig. 9 Top 5 run-time delay hotspots on T1 North Shore Line with the highest operation-oriented impact (Upstream).

time delay, dwell time delay and departure delay, which take both systematic delay time and the number of trips into consideration. Figure 9 shows an example of the top 5 run-time delay hotspots for T1 North Shore Line (upstream), and the systematic delay is calculated by using TLS-OTR data (from 2018/01/01 to 2018/06/30).

Systematic delay analysis on station/line level is the first step of the collection and review of performance data, such as punctuality and process cycle time. It is also a key step in the continuous improvement of transport services.

3.2 *Throughput Estimation*

Route capacity is the maximum number of vehicles, people, or amount of freight that can travel a given route in a given amount of time, usually an hour. It may be limited by the worst bottleneck in the transport system. For the railway system, route capacity is generally the capacity of each train times the number of trains per hour (i.e., throughput). In this way, route capacity is highly dependent on throughput, especially the maximal throughput of a given platform. Traditionally, the throughput of a given platform is calculated only by:

$$\text{Throughput} = \frac{60}{\text{headway}} \tag{2}$$

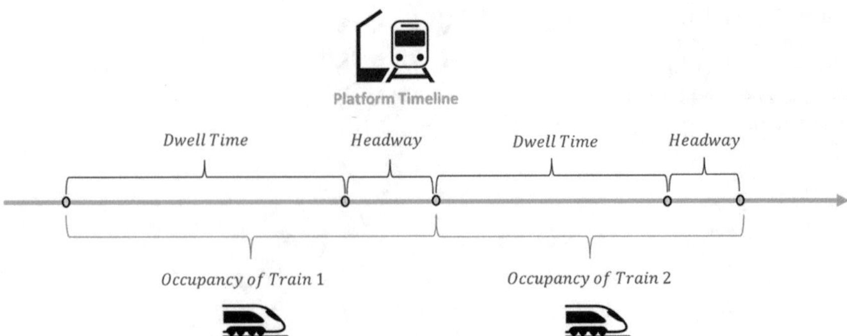

Fig. 10 Throughput definition

Here, Headway (or frequency) is a measurement of the distance or time between vehicles in a transit system. The minimum headway is the shortest such distance or time achievable by a system without a reduction in the speed of vehicles. However, dwell time is another factor that will highly affect the actual throughput and should not be ignored as shown in Fig. 10. So the definition of throughput should be changed to

$$\text{Throughput} = \frac{60}{\text{headway} + \text{dwell time}} \tag{3}$$

The estimation of throughput can be divided into two parts: Minimum headway estimation and dwell time estimation.

3.2.1 Minimum Headway Estimation

Headway is the time taken by the following train to pass past a given point on track after the previous train has passed it, subject to the minimum separation permitted by the signaling system. As the railway system is a complex distributed engineering system with several subsystems, the throughputs of different stations/platforms could be quite different. We proposed a novel data-driven method for headway estimation. Figure 11 illustrates how to idealize the headway. For Case 1, if the expected arrival time of the connecting train (Train 2) is before the actual departure time of the preceding train (Train 1), the incremental run-time delay of Train 2 must be bigger than the sum of expected dependency delay (rest of Train 1's dwell time) and the minimal headway. While for Case 2, as Train 2 does not have a dependence delay (delay caused by Train 1), we cannot estimate the headway through the dependency between the two trains.

Therefore, the relationship among expected dependence delay of Train 2 (denoted by X), the actual incremental run-time delay of Train 2 (denoted by Y), and the headway between Train 1 and Train 2 (denoted by H) is:

$$Y \geq X + H \geq X + \min(H) \tag{4}$$

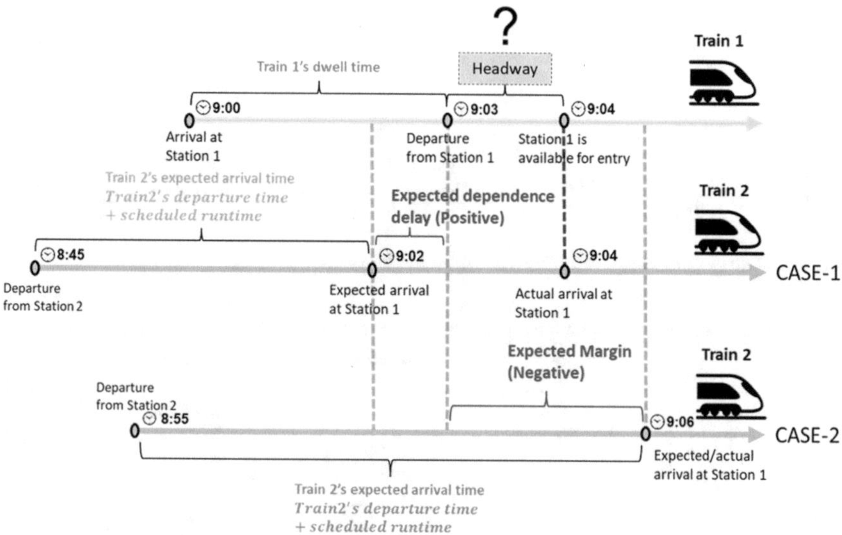

Fig. 11 Illustration of headway estimation

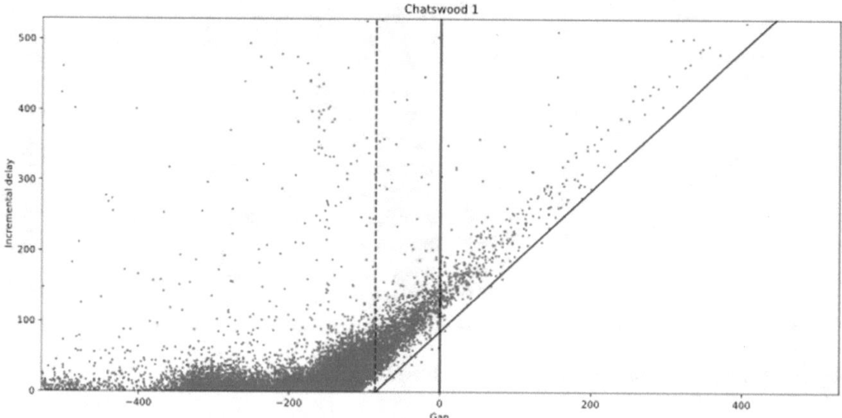

Fig. 12 Minimum headway estimation for Platform 1 of Station A

Here, $\min(H)$ is the minimum headway. As $< X, Y >$ of a given station/platform can be calculated by using historical TLS-OTR data, the $\min(H)$ is the intersection point on the Y-axis of the lower bound of $Y = X + H$ as shown in Fig. 12.

3.2.2 Dwell Time Estimation

Dwell time is another factor that highly influences the occupancy time of a train. The statistical analysis on the whole railway network shows that the distribution fit of the dwell times approximately obeys the lognormal distribution (as shown in Fig. 13).

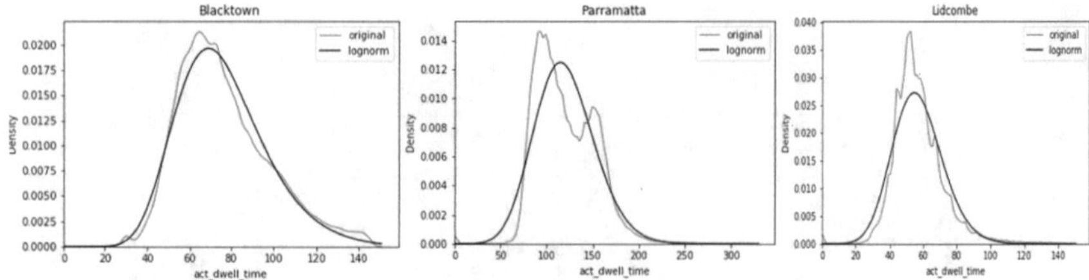

Fig. 13 Distribution fit of dwell times at different platforms

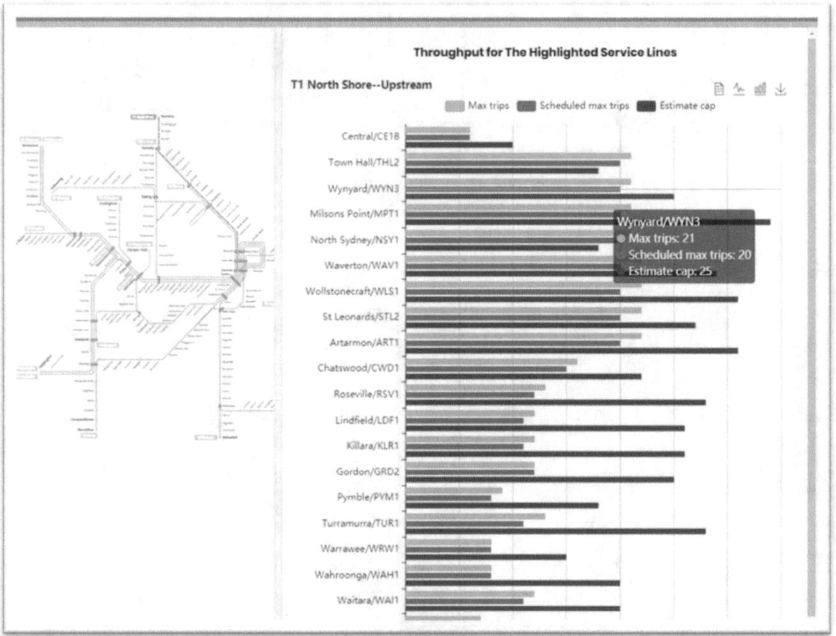

Fig. 14 Throughput estimation for T1 North Shore Line (Upstream).

In order to make the throughput estimation more reliable and robust, we assume the estimated dwell time (denoted by E) of a given platform should cover 85% of all historical dwell time records, which means 85% fitted cumulative distribution: $P\,(dwell\ time\ \leq E) = 85\%$.

Therefore, the estimated throughput (the number of trips per hour) of a given platform can be re-written as follow:

$$\text{Throughput} = \frac{60}{\min(H) + E} \tag{5}$$

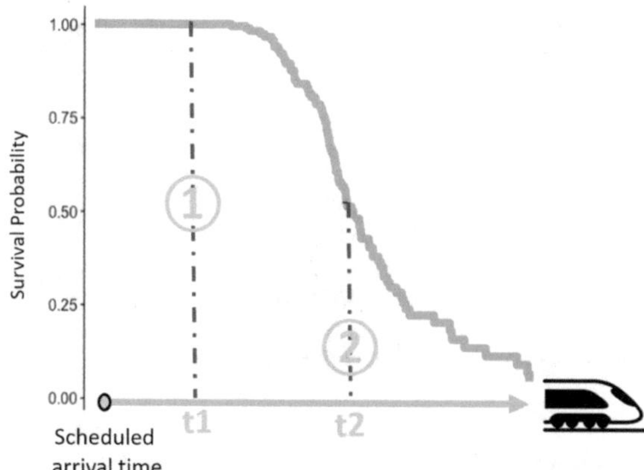

Fig. 15 Survival model for a single trip

here E is 85% fitted cumulative distribution and $\min(H)$ is the minimum headway. Figure 14 shows the throughput estimation for the T1 North Shore Line and the "Estimate cap" is the throughput estimation result.

3.3 Occupancy Time Planning

Occupancy time planning is one of the core parts of railway timetabling and rescheduling. Determining the appropriate value of the occupancy time for different platforms would significantly influence the performance of the railway. In this section, we propose a survival model for occupancy time planning. Survival analysis is a branch of statistics for analyzing the expected duration of time until one or more events happen, such as a death in biological organisms and failure in mechanical systems. We use the survival model here to simulate the probability of train occupancy time at a given platform. As shown in Fig. 15, given the historical dwell time records for a platform, the survival model for a single trip can be defined as:

$$\mathrm{S(t)} = P(T > t) = 1 - F(t) \tag{6}$$

For the case of consecutive trains, the minimum headway has to be considered, so the survival model can be re-written as:

$$\mathrm{S}\left(\mathrm{t}'\right) = \mathrm{S}(\mathrm{t} + \min(H)) = P(T > t) = 1 - F(t) \tag{7}$$

As shown in Fig. 16, if the time interval between consecutive trains is big (Train 1 and Train 2), there is a flexible margin between the two trains. While if the time interval is small, then there is a very high probability of dependence delay (secondary delay) occurred when unexpected incidents happen. Therefore, the incrementalen to the preceding train delays. So the occupancy time planning for any two consecutive trains should take it into consideration. A threshold of occupancy time planning is proposed based on empirical analysis (5% is used in Sydney Trains' case). Given

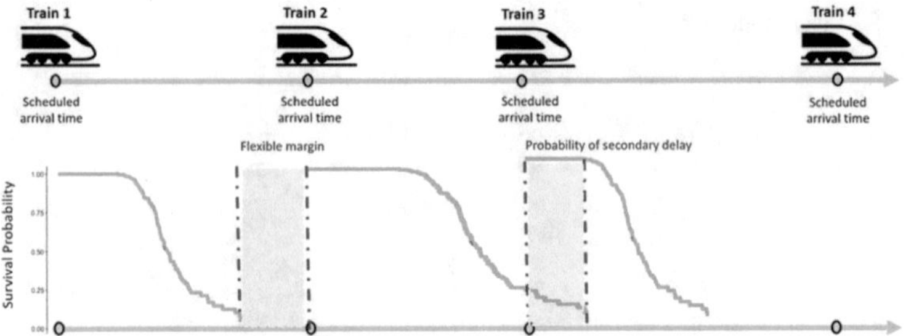

Fig. 16 Survival model for consecutive trains

a time interval value t, the probability of dwell time remaining is $S\left(t'\right)$, where t' = t+min (H): (1) if $S\left(t'\right) \geq 5\%$, it means there is a considerable probability that the preceding train will cause the following train's dependence delay, and (2) if $S\left(t'\right) < 5\%$, the capacity can still be improved as there is still a flexible margin and the time interval between the consecutive trains can be further reduced.

4 Delay Analysis

Reliability is one of the key evaluation criteria in railway service for both passengers and cargo. Many factors are contributing to the measure, such as the delays spanning over spatial and temporal dimensions. One way to increase the reliability is to avoid the systematic delay propagation by better timetable design to reduce the interdependencies between trains caused by route conflicts and train connections. In this section, we will introduce the proposed data-driven models for predicting the propagation of delays on Sydney Trains railway network and tracing back the primary delay by providing the actual running timetable after delays happening.

4.1 Problem Setup and Background

4.1.1 Train Delay

In this section, we will consider both primary delay and secondary delay and divided them based on delay cause and then estimate the distribution of incremental delay on station level by using historical data, and finally give the accumulative delay and influences to the whole railway network. Run time and dwell time delay are considered as variation time with respect to run time and dwell time of a given train, respectively. The incremental run time from Station i to Station j is defined as:

$$R_{ij} = t_j^a - t_i \tag{8}$$

Here, t_j^a is the arrival time at Station j and t_i is the departure time at Station i. Then, the incremental run-time delay from Station i to Station j is computed by Actual $\left(t_j^a\right) - Schedualed(t_i)$. Similarly, the incremental dwell time from Station i

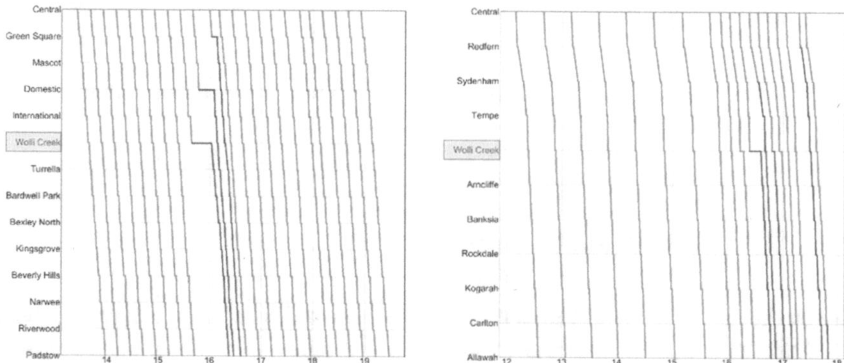

Fig. 17 Delay propagation and impacts

to Station j is:

$$D_j = t_j - t_j^a \tag{9}$$

Therefore, the incremental dwell time delay can be computed by Actual (t_j) − Schedueld (t_j) = Actual $\left(t_j - t_j^a\right)$ − Scheduled$(t_j - t_j^a)$.

4.2 *Delay Propagation*

As discussed in the Introduction section, the delay can have a domino effect and one delayed single trip (primary delay) can cause secondary delays to follow trains and crossing-line trains, and this phenomenon is defined as delay propagation as shown in Fig. 17. Specifically, four typical scenarios have been specified to capture all the delay propagation possibilities as shown in Fig. 4 above.

- Self-propagation: If a train T_1 has a delay at Station 3, the delay will propagate and influence T_1 itself at the following stops.
- Cross-line propagation: If a train T_1 has a delay at Station 3, the delay may propagate and influence trains that are from cross-lines arriving at Station 3 during the time period that T_1 parked at Station 3 unscheduled.
- Backward propagation: If a train T_1 has a delay at Station 3, the delay may propagate and influence the following trains that would arrive at Station 3 during the time period that T_1 parked at Station 3 unscheduled.
- Train-connection propagation: As trains always need to run round trips or connected trips each day, there is always train-connection effects : a train arrives late at the destination will cause a start delay for its next trip.

Cross-line and backward effects of a train's delay are also called route conflict effects. And, all of these different kinds of delay propagation are calculated through a conditional Bayesian model.

5 Case Study

In this section, we introduce different case studies within our proposed models for the performance evaluation.

5.1 Delay Propagation Analysis

We predict the delay propagation by using the proposed conditional Bayesian model for different scenarios introduced in Sect. 4.2 and compare it with the observed values. When a primary delay at the given station is specified, the predicted means and confidence intervals of secondary delays for the impacted following, cross-line, and connected trips are calculated. In Fig. 18, we show the predicted delay propagation pattern (The blue line is the mean, and the blue band is the confidence interval) and the actual running records of the trip (the red line). The dots represent the predicted/actual dwell time at stations, and the stars indicate the predicted/actual run time between two consecutive stations. The model is applied from the beginning of the trip (taking the starting time as the input of the proposed model and predict the dwell/running time for the following stations). It can be seen that when there is no delay, the proposed model can be used for normal running/dwell time prediction (the accumulated delay can be considered as the noise to the scheduled running/dwell time), and the mean of the predicted values are similar to the actual ones. When we specified a delay that happened between Kings Cross and Martin Place (a run-time delay), we just updated the input of the model and re-run it for the following stations. The predicted delay propagation pattern matches the actual one well, and the difference between actual and predicted mean at the trip destination (Central Station) is less than 30 s, which demonstrates the reliability of the proposed model. Similar performance can be found for other delay scenarios. Figures 19 and 20 show the predicted delay propagation on the cross-line trip/ following trip. Figure 19 shows that the cross-line trains would be affected by the primary delay (left figure) occurred at Station Milsons Point and the predicted delays of the cross-line trip (right figure) are close to the actual ones, with difference within 10 s (the difference between actual values and predicted means). Figure 21 shows the start delays (right figure) caused by the train-connection delay (left figure). The delay of the preceding trip propagated to the following trip as the two trips using the same train.

5.2 Primary Delay Tracing Back

In urban railway lines, it is usually observed that once a small delay happens and it widely spreads out to many other trains (as shown in Fig. 22). During the busiest hours in urban railways, a lot of trains are operated densely and once a delay occurs, even if it is small, the delay easily propagates to other trains. The delay that happens first is called a primary delay and the delays caused by the primary delay are called

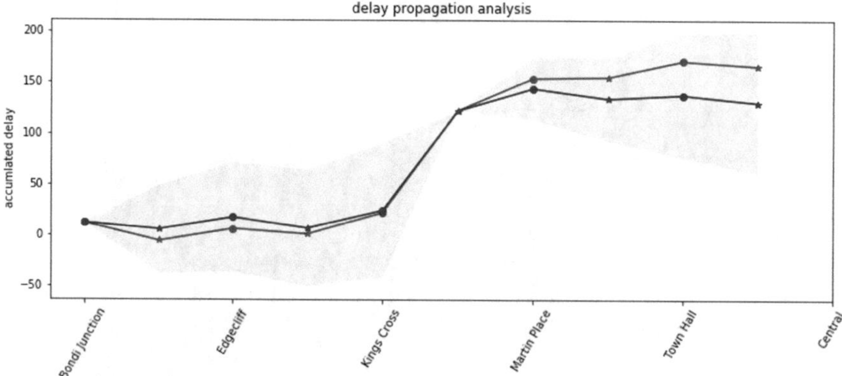

Fig. 18 Delay self-propagation

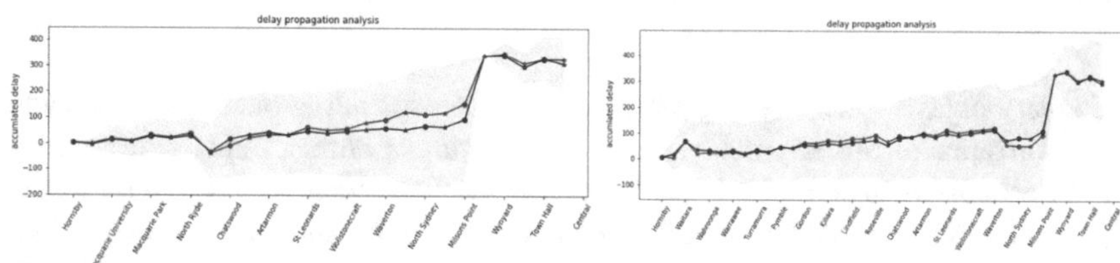

Fig. 19 Delay cross-line propagation

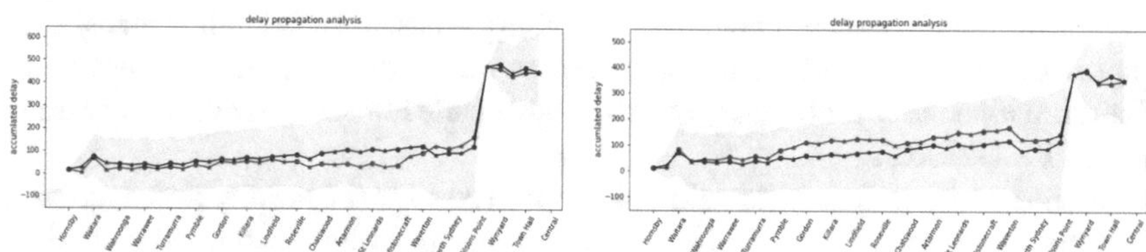

Fig. 20 Delay backward propagation

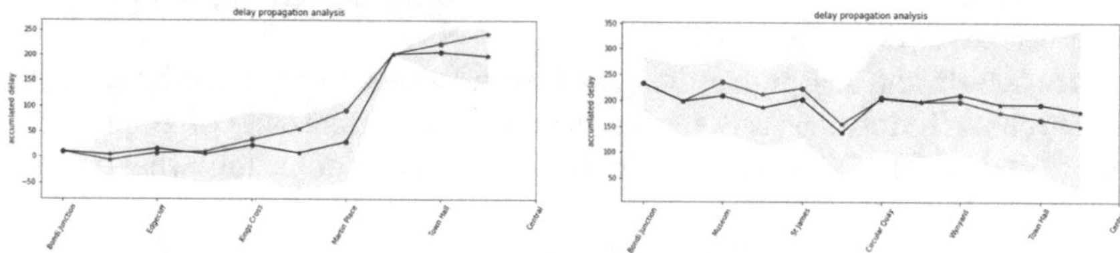

Fig. 21 Delay train-connection propagation

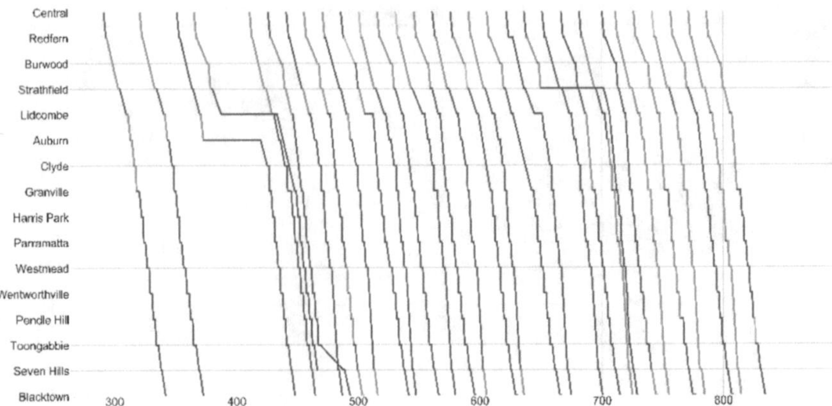

Fig. 22 Delays gradually increase and spread out

secondary delays. One way to prevent delays from spreading out is to try to avoid the occurrence of primary delay. It is very difficult or almost impossible to avoid all the primary delays. But it is considered to be very effective if we could reduce primary delays which very often happen and give a wide influence on many other trains. Therefore, the first and most important thing we have to do is to identify such primary delays. If we can identify such primary delays, we could take effective countermeasures to reduce those primary delays by modifying timetables (to adjust dwell times, to give some supplement to running times, to adjust buffer times, etc.), improving deployment of station staff, and so on. In this section, we focus on an algorithm to identify primary delays which give wide influence to many other trains using TLS-OTR data.

In order to identify a cause of a delay, we need to find causality and trace back the causality toward the origin (as shown in Fig. 23). In this section, we introduce the following ideas to estimate an existence of primary delay: (1) find significant incremental delay on each delayed trip (delayed more than 5mins) and (2) split primary delay and secondary delay based on the delay dependency of consecutive trains (known as dependence delays).

In order to distinguish primary delay and secondary delay of consecutive trains, we need to check the relations between the incremental departure delay of the preceding train (X-axis in Fig. 24) and the incremental arrival delay of the following train (Y-axis in Fig. 24).

A dependence delay is given if a train waits for another one to maintain a connection. Hence, the delay of the preceding train may propagate to the arrival event of the connecting train at a specific station. In order to find such dependencies in the data, we formulate an idealized model of the dependence delay. Ignoring for a moment that the victim may depend on more than one delayer and may also suffer from other sources of delay, we can model an idealized waiting dependency as follows. First, there usually is some buffer time s up to which the preceding train may be delayed

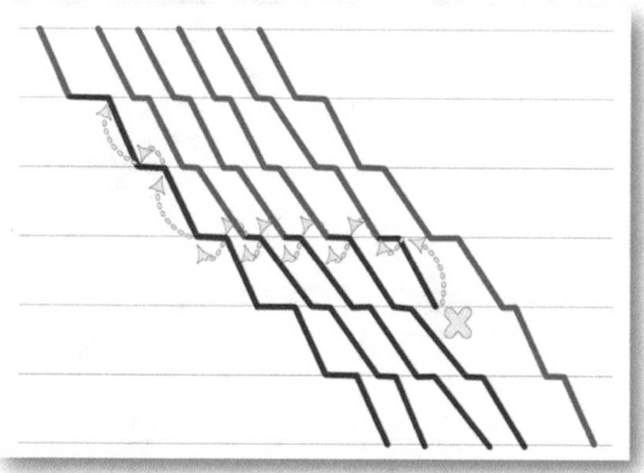

Fig. 23 Tracing back the primary delay

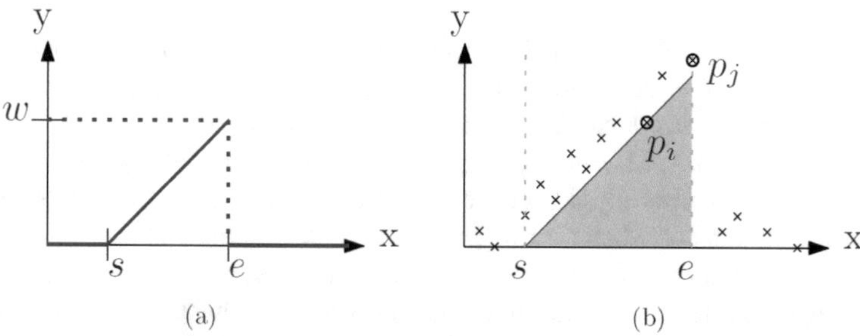

Fig. 24 Dependence delay identification: Waiting dependency of the delay of a connecting train y on the delay of a feeder train *x* within the interval [s, e]

without affecting the following train. If the preceding train is delayed by more than s, the following train will wait to maintain the connection, but only up to a maximal waiting time w, i.e., a maximal delay $e = s + w$ of the preceding train. Denoting by X_d the delay of the preceding train on day d and by train X.

5.3 Timetable Evaluation

Different timetable strategies can result in varying performance and risk levels as shown in Fig. 25. Evaluating the robustness of various timetables can help to reduce delays and optimize on-time performance. With sufficient robustness in the timetable, trains can keep their planned slot despite unexpected small disturbances.

Timetable reliability is typically measured as the percentage of train arrivals actually performed on the day of operation compared to the number of train arrivals planned according to the published schedule. An obvious drawback of the measure is that reliability is measured regardless of the actual arrival time as long as it occurred within the planning horizon. This means that, while significant delays may

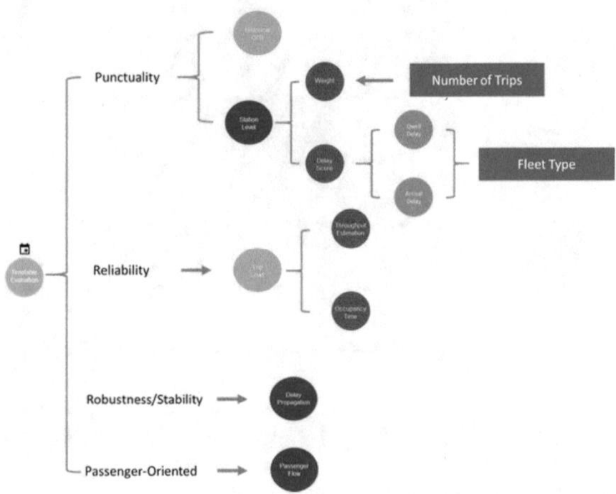

Fig. 25 Time table evaluation criteria

occur, the measured reliability will remain high as long as all the scheduled arrivals take place. Another effective criterion is punctuality, which is mostly measured as the percentage of trains departing from/arriving at stations within a predefined time threshold for the delay. The most used approach to accommodate punctuality issues is to introduce timetable supplements either at the track segments between two stations, at the stations or when turning the trains at the terminal stations. Robustness is in this context the ability of a railway system to resist consecutive delays. Since initial delays are often exogenous, these may be to some extent unavoidable, whereas consecutive delays may occur because of a too-tight schedule. This fact leads to a big issue when considering the robustness of a timetable. The trade-off between having a very tight schedule, which in a non-disturbed environment is able to accommodate the most trains and then having a robust timetable which is able to absorb some of the disturbances is one of the planners' main challenges.

To estimate the robustness of time tables, we would like to build a machine learning model to measure the relationship between the time table performance of a single day and the on-time rate of trains of the corresponding day as shown in Fig. 26. On-time running is becoming increasingly important and challenging for Sydney Trains to meet customer expectations since patronage on Sydney's train network has grown steadily over the past few years. On-time running is highly related to capacity utilization, which is a measure of how the timetable utilizes the capacity of a network. A high utilization level might indicate high sensitivity of the railway system to delays and difficulty in recovering from incidents. Thus, the on-time rate could be an effective criterion to evaluate time tables.

Neural networks are a class of machine learning algorithms used to model complex patterns in datasets using multiple hidden layers and non-linear activation functions. A neural network is defined as a computing system that consists of a number of simple but highly interconnected elements or nodes, called "neurons," which are organized in layers which process information using dynamic state responses to external inputs as shown in Fig. 27. This algorithm is extremely useful in finding patterns that are too

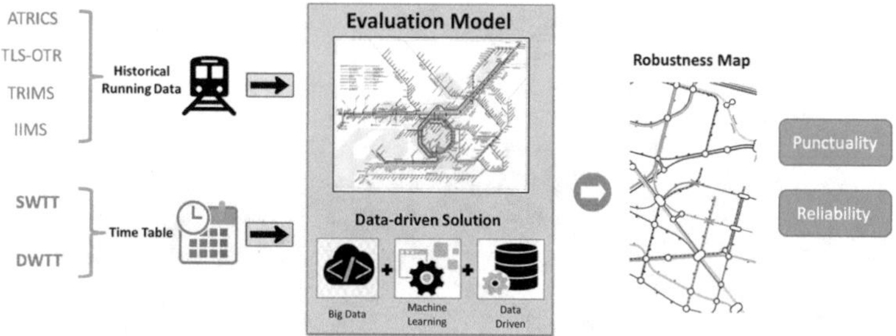

Fig. 26 Model development framework

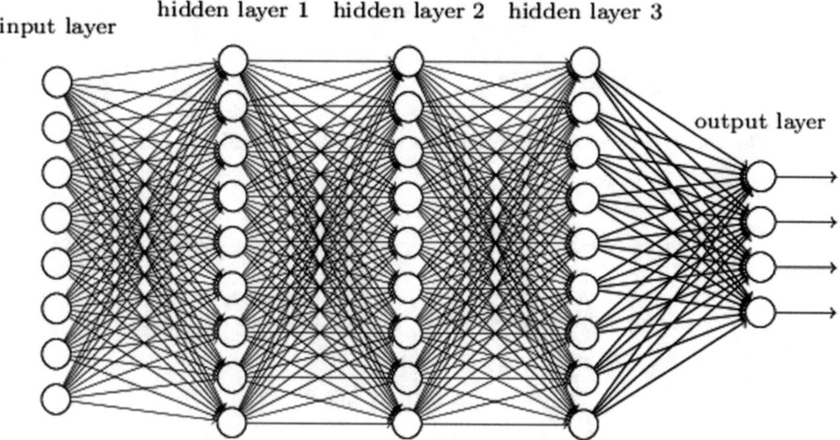

Fig. 27 Neural network model

complex for being manually extracted and taught to recognize the machine. Patterns are introduced to the neural network by the input layer that has one neuron for each component present in the input data and is communicated to one or more hidden layers present in the network. The last hidden layer is linked to the output layer for each possible desired output. We refer to neural network because of its robustness to model nonlinear and implicit relationship between variables.

We would extract features from the time table data as the input for the neural network model and calculate train on-time rate from TLS-OTR data as the model output. We extracted four types of features from data of a single day time table:

- **Fleet type counting**: the number of cargos of each fleet type.
- **Throughput:** the maximum throughput of each platform calculated as described in Sect. 4.2 as shown in Fig. 28.
- **Occupancy time**: the estimated platform free time in the busiest hour. It is calculated by firstly estimating the dwell time distribution for each platform as shown

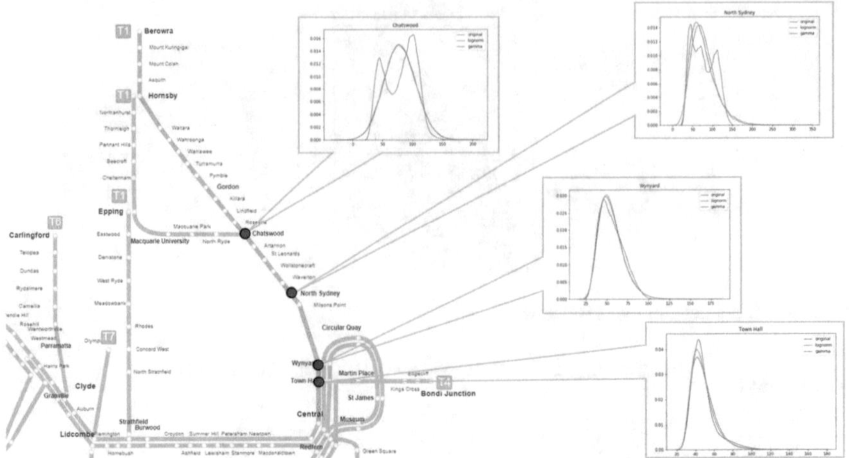

Fig. 28 Throughput estimation—minimal headway estimation—dwell time data-fitting

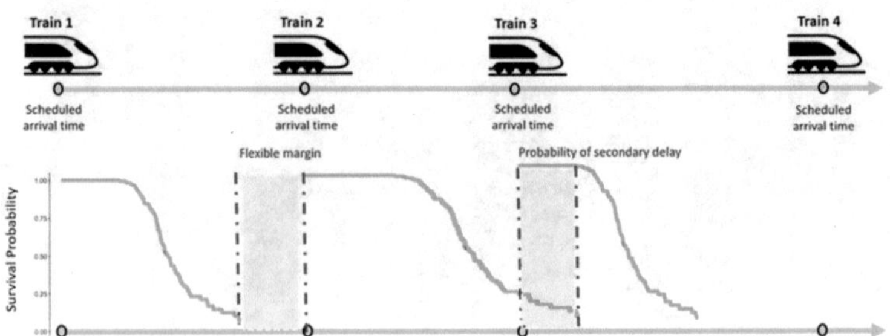

Fig. 29 Occupancy time planning

in Fig. 29. The dwell time for a platform is defined as the 85% quantile value over the distribution. (Details of occupancy time computing can be found in Sect. 3.3):

- **Run-time margin**: the estimated run-time margin between a pair of adjacent stations. It is obtained by grouping TLS-OTR data with actual stop stations, and then for a pair of stations, we obtain the minimum train run time $T_{\min}$ by setting it to be the 15% quantile value of actual run-time values over different trips. (If there is no actual run-time data, the minimum run-time equals to the average of planned run time value and the margin would be 0.) Then, we calculate the average of planned run time T_{mean} over trips. The run-time margin of each station pair is.

$$\text{runtime\_marging} = T_{\text{mean}} - T_{\min} \quad (10)$$

The features were extracted for each platform of the entire traffic network. To improve the model performance, features were pre-selected with the random forest model which gives out an important measurement for each feature. Then, the top N

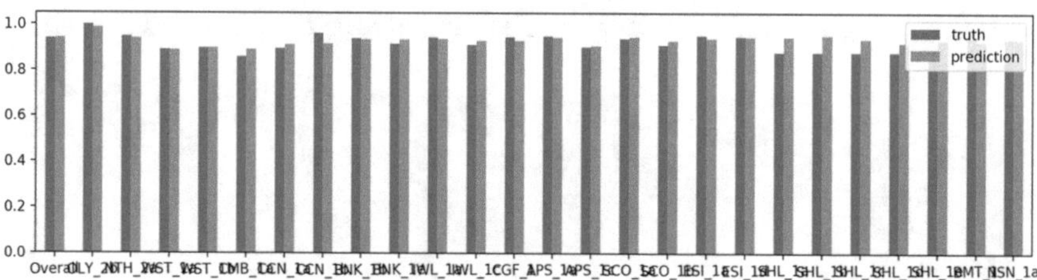

Fig. 30 Network-level and line-level model performance

most important features would be the neural network model training features. The output of the model would be the on-time rate (OTR) calculated from the actual trip arrival status recorded in TLS-OTR datasets. OTR is calculated over three levels:

$$\text{Network-level OTR} = \frac{\text{number of on-time trips}}{\text{total number of trips}} \tag{11}$$

$$\text{Customer line-level OTR} = \frac{\text{number of on time trips of customer line } L_i}{\text{total number of trips of customer line } L_i} \tag{12}$$

$$\text{Station-level OTR} = \frac{\text{number of on-time trips of station } S}{\text{total number of trips of station } S} \tag{13}$$

Model training data were extracted over three-year TLS-OTR data, and about 1000 records were obtained. We would discard records with low OTR (under 85%) as low OTR of a day is highly likely caused by accidents and unable to be predicted by the extracted features. A three-layer neural network model was used to fit the training data at three levels: entire traffic network level, customer line level, and station level. The model reaches less than 2% error rate on the network level and less than 4% on the customer line and station level as shown in Figs. 30, 31, 32.

6 Discussion

Transportation, the industry that deals with the movement of commodities and passengers from one place to another, has gone through several studies, researches, trials, and refinements to reach where it is now. Reliability is one of the critical evaluation criteria in transportation service for both passengers and cargo. Many factors are contributing to the measure, such as the delays spanning over spatial and temporal dimensions. Machine learning has the potential to streamline operational performance by increasing the level of effectiveness in decision making and improve overall efficiency. For rail, this seems like an opportunity worth further exploration, as it also calls for a profound culture change. Different from traditional statistical

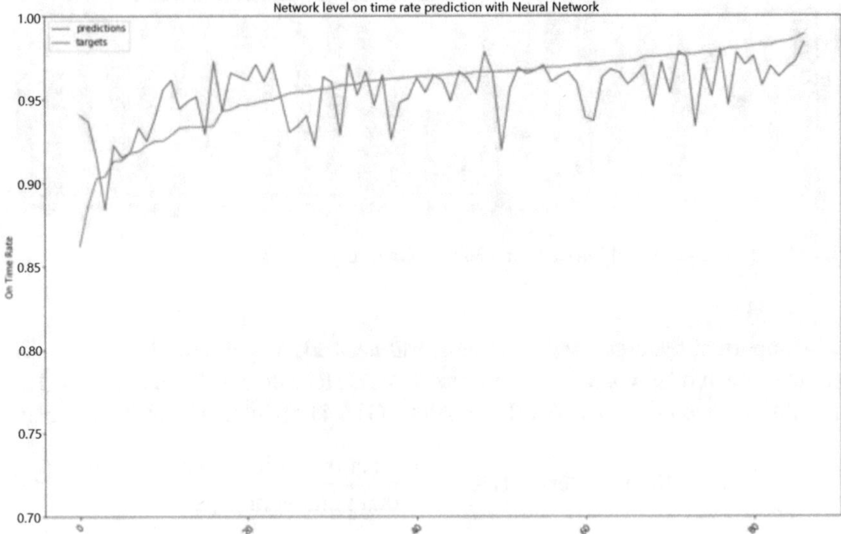

Fig. 31 Network-level model prediction

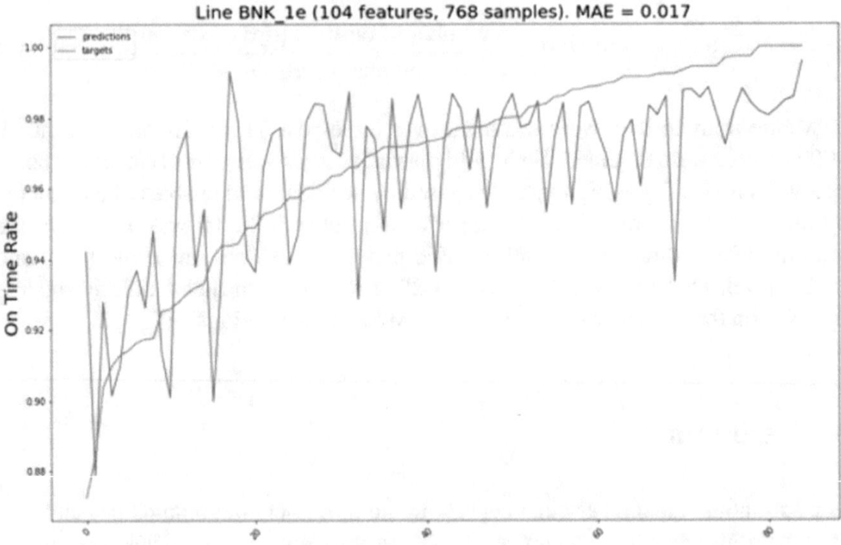

Fig. 32 Line BNK_1e model prediction

methods, AI can be defined as a technology that powers machines with human intelligence. Machines, having AI capabilities, can mimic humans, automate manual tasks, and learn on the go just like humans. Traditionally, most of the applied features need to be identified by domain experts to reduce the complexity of the data and make patterns more visible to learning algorithms to work. While machine learning is powered by massive amount of data. It tries to learn high-level features from data in an incremental manner. This eliminates the need of domain expertise and hard-core feature extraction.

7 Conclusion and Future Work

In this chapter, we propose a smart solution for timetable evaluation, based on a comprehensive analysis of the Sydney Trains historical operation data and with the application of advanced artificial intelligence techniques. Various insights about factor influences have been derived from this research. These insights help understand the importance of different factors and help build an accurate timetable evaluation model based on neural networks. The model considers intrinsic delay patterns caused by the timetable and historical traffic situations together for evaluating the performance of the designed timetable. Many valuable comments were provided on various analyses, e.g., the selection of influential factors for analysis, explanations of the impact of factors, domain expertise on the mechanism of delays, etc. It is also worth noting that the correlation between factors and delay behaviors plays a key role in the analyses. The importance of factors is measured based on correlation. Indeed, correlation does not indicate causation. But common sense and domain experts' knowledge ensured that the considered factors are causal factors.

Train network performance has major effects on transit service reliability and on customer satisfaction. Since patronage on Sydney's train network has grown steadily over the past few years, customer demand and impact become significant factors to evaluate whether the train network is performing well or not. Although the rail industry provides a comprehensive database of passengers records, which provides the station of origin and station of destination of the passenger, data on the characteristics of rail users are not generally available at the level of spatial detail that meets the rail industry's performance evaluation requirements, e.g., the future passenger load on trains. For future work, we propose to develop a performance evaluation model using machine learning techniques from the customer perspective.

References

1. Ashebo, D.B., Tan, C.A., Wang, J., Li, G.: Feasibility of energy harvesting for powering wireless sensors in transportation infrastructure applications. In: Nondestructive Characterization for Composite Materials, Aerospace Engineering, Civil Infrastructure, and Homeland Security 2008, vol. 6934, p. 69340Y. International Society for Optics and Photonics (2008)
2. Bask, A., Spens, K., Stefansson, G., Lumsden, K.: Performance issues of smart transportation management systems. International Journal of productivity and performance management

(2009)
3. Bhattacharjee, S., Goetz, A.R.: Impact of light rail on traffic congestion in denver. Journal of Transport Geography **22**, 262–270 (2012)
4. Bhavsar, P., Safro, I., Bouaynaya, N., Polikar, R., Dera, D.: Machine learning in transportation data analytics. In: Data analytics for intelligent transportation systems, pp. 283–307. Elsevier (2017)
5. Chowdhury, M., Sadek, A., Ma, Y., Kanhere, N., Bhavsar, P.: Applications of artificial intelligence paradigms to decision support in real-time traffic management. Transportation research record **1968**(1), 92–98 (2006)
6. James, W.: Intelligent transport system (2004). US Patent 6,810,817
7. Lotufo, R., Morgan, A., Johnson, A.: Automatic number-plate recognition. In: IEE Colloquium on Image Analysis for Transport Applications, pp. 6–1. IET (1990)
8. Martin, L.J.: Predictive reasoning and machine learning for the enhancement of reliability in railway systems. In: International Conference on Reliability, Safety, and Security of Railway Systems, pp. 178–188. Springer (2016)
9. Moayedi, H.Z., Masnadi-Shirazi, M.: Arima model for network traffic prediction and anomaly detection. In: 2008 international symposium on information technology, vol. 4, pp. 1–6. IEEE (2008)
10. Morgul, E.F., Yang, H., Kurkcu, A., Ozbay, K., Bartin, B., Kamga, C., Salloum, R.: Virtual sensors: Web-based real-time data collection methodology for transportation operation performance analysis. Transportation Research Record **2442**(1), 106–116 (2014)
11. Nagy, A.M., Simon, V.: Survey on traffic prediction in smart cities. Pervasive and Mobile Computing **50**, 148–163 (2018)
12. Perpinya, X.: Reliability and safety in railway. BoD–Books on Demand (2012)
13. Ratner, B.: Statistical and Machine-Learning Data Mining:: Techniques for Better Predictive Modeling and Analysis of Big Data. CRC Press (2017)
14. Ren, X., Wang, F., Wang, C., Du, Z., Chen, Z., Wang, J., Dan, T.: Impact of high-speed rail on intercity travel behavior change. Journal of Transport and Land Use **12**(1), 265–285 (2019)
15. Schnore, L.F.: The use of public transportation in urban areas. Traffic Quarterly **16**(4) (1962)
16. Špaňhel, J., Sochor, J., Juránek, R., Herout, A., Maršík, L., Zemčík, P.: Holistic recognition of low quality license plates by cnn using track annotated data. In: 2017 14th IEEE International Conference on Advanced Video and Signal Based Surveillance (AVSS), pp. 1–6. IEEE (2017)
17. Tizghadam, A., Khazaei, H., Moghaddam, M.H., Hassan, Y.: Machine learning in transportation (2019)
18. Tokody, D., Flammini, F.: The intelligent railway system theory. International Transportation **69**(1), 38–40 (2017)
19. Vasirani, M., Ossowski, S.: A market-inspired approach for intersection management in urban road traffic networks. Journal of Artificial Intelligence Research **43**, 621–659 (2012)
20. Wu, J., Sun, H., Wang, D.Z., Zhong, M., Han, L., Gao, Z.: Bounded-rationality based day-to-day evolution model for travel behavior analysis of urban railway network. Transportation Research Part C: Emerging Technologies **31**, 73–82 (2013)
21. Zeng, W., Fu, C.W., Müller Arisona, S., Erath, A., Qu, H.: Visualizing waypoints-constrained origin-destination patterns for massive transportation data. In: Computer Graphics Forum, vol. 35, pp. 95–107. Wiley Online Library (2016)
22. Zhang, J., Wang, F.Y., Wang, K., Lin, W.H., Xu, X., Chen, C.: Data-driven intelligent transportation systems: A survey. IEEE Transactions on Intelligent Transportation Systems **12**(4), 1624–1639 (2011)

AI for Well-being

Federated Learning for Privacy-Preserving Open Innovation Future on Digital Health

Guodong Long, Tao Shen, Yue Tan, Leah Gerrard, Allison Clarke, and Jing Jiang

1 Introduction

Using AI techniques to enhance or assist healthcare applications has the potential to improve healthcare efficiency, increase healthcare service outcomes, and benefit human well-being. The recent development of data-driven machine learning and deep learning has demonstrated success in many industry sectors, including health care [52, 58]. However, training a deep learning model usually requires a large number of training samples, which is not always possible with individual health datasets.

Personal health information is considered to be highly sensitive data, as it contains not only diagnostic and health care-related information but also identifiable details about individuals. From the consumer perspective, data privacy is also one of the public's critical concerns, and data breaches can result in reduced public trust of their

G. Long (✉) · T. Shen · Y. Tan · L. Gerrard · J. Jiang
Faculty of Engineering and Information Technology, Australian Artificial Intelligence Institute, University of Technology Sydney, Sydney, NSW, Australia
e-mail: Guodong.Long@uts.edu.au

T. Shen
e-mail: Tao.Shen@student.uts.edu.au

Y. Tan
e-mail: Yue.Tan@student.uts.edu.au

L. Gerrard
e-mail: Leah.Gerrard@student.uts.edu.au

J. Jiang
e-mail: Jing.Jiang@uts.edu.au

A. Clarke
Data and Analytics Branch, Health Economics and Research Division, Australian Department of Health, Canberra, NSW, Australia
e-mail: Allison.Clarke@health.gov.au

F. Chen and J. Zhou (eds.), *Humanity Driven AI*,
https://doi.org/10.1007/978-3-030-72188-6_6

data. For these reasons, healthcare data is governed by strict laws and regulations to prevent the risk of re-identification and data breaches.

Key examples of standards that protect certain health information include the Health Insurance Portability and Accountability Act of 1996 (HIPAA) and the General Data Projection Regulation (GDPR) [13]. While these standards are necessary for security and privacy purposes, they can make it challenging to share and link healthcare information. This includes sharing information between medical centres, hospitals, and governments. As a consequence, valuable data are often confined to individual institutions and are unable to be leveraged for analysis, hindering the application of deep learning in the healthcare context. In order to leverage the value of existing health datasets meanwhile maintaining protection of user privacy, a new deep learning technique is desired for sensitive data especially in the health field.

To this end, federated learning (FL) is proposed as a new machine learning paradigm that can learn a global machine learning model without direct access to each contributor's private data, which can include hospital, device, or user data. It aims to build a collaborative training framework where each participant can train a model independently using their data and then collaboratively share this model's information without releasing the data used to train the model. An optimisation framework still guides the overall learning procedure, and the private data does not need to be centrally collected or shared. The shared information includes the model parameters and gradients. This allows machine learning algorithms to learn from a broad range of datasets which exist at different locations, by essentially "de-centralising" the machine learning process. These features of FL make it uniquely suited for sensitive data, such as healthcare data, where models can be developed without directly sharing data.

Intuitively, the setting of FL is highly compatible with a recently popular concept in the industry—open innovation. It is defined as "a distributed innovation process based on purposely managed knowledge flow across organisational boundaries" [8]. While previous approaches to innovation were primarily developed internally by businesses, there is now recognition that an openness to innovation can be valuable, as external involvement brings new knowledge, expertise, and ideas [62]. Some industry sectors (such as open banking) have already taken action to embrace open innovation. However, further work is needed to enable open innovation for the health industry sector [22]. The recent development of digital health indicates that the future of health care is to provide integrated information support across multiple service providers. However, how to collaboratively use health data in a privacy-preserving way is a critical challenge. FL offers a solution to this challenge by training models without direct access to individual participant's data.

The remainder of this chapter is organised as follows: Firstly, we will discuss an FL system for open health including the ways the system could be implemented and the principal stakeholders involved. Then, we will describe the key existing challenges in health care in relation to data security, privacy, and heterogeneity and provide examples of how FL is addressing these issues. Finally, we will discuss the implications of solving these key health challenges and the benefits this will offer the healthcare industry.

2 A Federated Learning System for Open Health

Open health, which describes an open innovation framework in the healthcare industry, is focused on driving innovation and capability in health through collaborative partnerships between healthcare organisations and researchers. In this framework, there is recognition that good ideas can come from both within and outside an organisation to successfully advance processes and outcomes [10]. There are various forms of open innovation, including crowd-sourcing, organisational partnerships, and strategic joint projects [10].

Currently, healthcare systems around the world are under pressure to improve patient health outcomes while operating within constrained healthcare budgets. There are a number of factors that are threatening healthcare system sustainability including ageing populations, increased chronic disease incidence, new medical treatments and technologies, and limited use of data [6]. It is therefore essential to explore avenues, such as FL, that have potential to benefit patient outcomes and the healthcare system.

A lack of data sharing has been identified as one of the barriers to innovation in health care [22]. This is stalling potential progress on patient care delivery, patient outcomes, and health data research [22]. Often the data required for training machine learning and deep learning algorithms are not large enough in individual institutions [49]. Additionally, individual institutions can have data with biases that result in models that do not generalise well and perform poorly when applied to other unseen datasets [49]. One way to obtain sufficiently large and diverse datasets is resorting to collaboratively learning and developing models that utilise data from various healthcare institutions.

Given the importance of data security and privacy in the healthcare sector, FL offers a way of maintaining patient privacy while also facilitating open health. This is because it encourages collaborative relationships for health research that was previously not possible, thereby driving innovation and improvements in health care. Below we expand on this idea by providing an overview of the ways in which FL can be constructed for open health and the key stakeholders that stand to benefit from an FL system (Fig. 1).

2.1 Types of Federated Learning Systems

An FL system can be categorised into two groups: cross-silo and cross-device (as discussed in [44]). The next-generation intelligent healthcare applications will tackle both cross-device and cross-silo scenarios.

The vanilla federated learning [26, 41] proposed by Google aims to solve the large-scale machine learning problem in mobile networks and can be categorised as cross-device. It is designed to learn a model across mobile phones without direct access to user's data. In this case, each mobile phone represents one device or one user that has a limited amount of training data and computational resources.

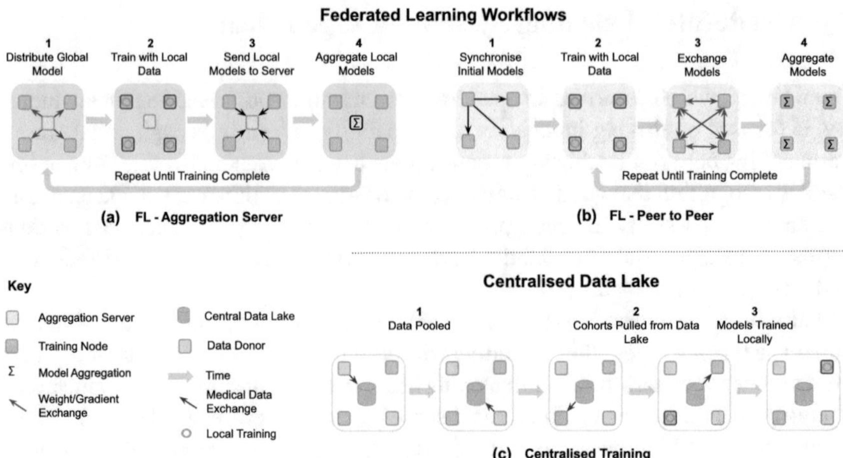

Fig. 1 Workflow comparison between federated learning and traditional machine learning, as found in [45]

The cross-silo FL is designed for knowledge sharing from data across companies, institutions, or organisations. Take an industry sector, e.g. banking or health care, where different banks or hospitals have data only for their own customers. Due to privacy requirements and laws, hospitals cannot link their data to the data of other hospitals. With cross-silo FL, a shared model can be trained without direct access to each hospital's data.

In the digital health area, hospitals, clinics, wearable device providers, government agencies, and individual users record various data in different formats. The survey of federated learning (by Yang et al. [61]) aims to solve the cross-silo data sharing problem across different organisations. Devices usually have very limited computing power and training data, and their communication is often limited and unstable. The cross-silo FL has powerful servers in each participant and has a centralised dataset. However, they require much higher data protection criteria, and there are some existing external factors that can impact data sharing, such as competitions and cybersecurity concerns. This demonstrates that more work is needed to fully enable cross-silo FL.

2.2 Key Stakeholders

In the healthcare industry, data can be stored by different government organisations, hospitals, and clinics. Each of these organisations or institutions can be involved in an FL system and stand to benefit in various ways. We discuss the general benefits of FL for health care in the discussion section. Below we outline the key stakeholders who are likely to be involved and their role in the FL system.

Third-party platforms. A company can provide a platform to enable different health industry participants to join the platform, and this platform is implemented based on FL. Moreover, the existing hospital/clinical management system provider will easily be able to take advantage of this future trend. Compared to larger companies that can suffer from long decision-making processes and experience difficulties to transition to new directions, a start-up company is more flexible and can move quickly to provide additional functionality and improve processes.
Governments. Governments can transition existing governance towards an FL-based framework. In this framework, governments still maintain storage of the data; however, now they can offer other governments and researchers to join in a collaboration so that important research can be undertaken without compromising individual's private information. Governments could also play a role in facilitating and overseeing collaborations between other parties to enable information sharing while maintaining appropriate security and privacy standards.
Medical institutions. The hospitals and clinics may jointly act together to conduct a data-sharing collaboration supported by an FL technique. Through this kind of linked collaboration, the hospitals and clinics can control the scope of data sharing to the trusted peers. The medical doctors and practitioners in the collaboration are more likely to get better support from data and computing resources to advance their medical research and improve patient care.
Wearable service providers. The wearable service provider, such as Apple watch, can easily collect the client's health-related information. Sometimes, the program in the mobile phone can record the user's Internet behaviour combined with the GPS trajectory. These information can also provide a very good indicator to user's health status. There is immense potential to build better predictive models based on learning from diverse data from wearable devices.

3 Security and Privacy Challenge for Federated Learning

In this section, we elaborate on the security and privacy problems in FL systems. FL, intrinsically with a privacy-preserving attribute, plays a significant role in various industry domains that involve sensitive personal data. In an open healthcare scenario for example, each hospital or medical research centre holds sensitive diagnostic data and strictly cannot share this with others, but desire to learn from data across affiliations. Although the concept is to provide a privacy-preservation capability by allowing the clients to keep the data on local devices, there are still model security and data leakage risks that would hurt both the security of FL system and the data privacy of clients.

The risks can be regarded as vulnerabilities or weaknesses from multiple aspects associated with the general FL framework. Thus, we provide a list of common vulnerabilities [43] for comprehensive insights.

- *Client Data Manipulations*: The local device or client is not always verified by the FL system, so a compromised device/client may learn on malicious data intentionally or unintentionally and upload incorrect parameters to the global server.
- *Communication Protocol*: Although the data on a device will not be uploaded, there are still network communications between the client and the centre to (1) download global parameters in the centre server to the local device/client and (2) upload the parameters (or the corresponding gradient updates) from the local device/client to the centre. This poses a risk of "eavesdropping" for further attacks.
- *Weaker Aggregation Algorithm*: An aggregation algorithm, deployed in the central server, is developed to integrate the updates sampled from local devices into the global model. It is equipped with capabilities to identify abnormal client updates and to drop updates from suspicious clients. However, a weak algorithm, such as FedAvg [42], does not provide such a configuration to check and drop abnormal updates, making the system more vulnerable to data manipulations in client devices.

These risks lead to both security and privacy problems, which are detailed in the following.

Security Problem. This is primarily caused by curious or malicious attackers targeting vulnerabilities of the FL system, which can lead to significant performance drop and even model invalidation. This is extremely hazardous and will negatively affect thousands of devices. If we once again consider this in the health scenario, an attacker can directly manipulate the data in a local affiliation, resulting in wrongly labelled data to maliciously update the global model.

Privacy Problem. This problem is even more severe than the security problem when vulnerabilities cause user data leakage, as it weakens the basics of FL that are specifically designed for privacy-preservation across multi-device machine learning. For instance, if the communication data packages between the central server and a local device (i.e. global model and local gradient updates) are intercepted, gradient-based reconstruction attack algorithms can be applied to recover the training data in the local device. In healthcare applications, the leakage data could be patient's personal or healthcare information, which presents a severe ethical problem that deserves our attention (Fig. 2).

Therefore, it is advised that we must correctly identify the vulnerabilities of an FL system and resist unauthorised access to curious or malicious attackers. This will help develop a more secure system by implementing prerequisites for defending loopholes. This is a mandatory step for an FL engineer to check for all possible vulnerabilities and enhance defences for security and privacy.

In the remainder of this section, we detail two kinds of attacks, i.e. backdoor and gradient attacks, and their potential solutions. These two attacks are the most common attacks leading to security and privacy problems.

Fig. 2 Examples of backdoor attack, which are copied from [55]. **a** Airplanes labelled as "truck" in CIFAR10 dataset. **b** Handwritten characters "7" labelled as "1" in MNIST dataset. **c** People in traditional Cretan costumes labelled incorrectly in ImageNet dataset. **d** Positive tweets on director Yorgos Lanthimos (YL) labelled as "negative" on sentiment analysis task. **e** Sentences regarding the city of Athens completed with words of negative connotation on language modelling task

3.1 Backdoor Attack and Solutions

Under most FL settings, it is assumed that there is no central server that verifies the training data of local devices, which exposes FL to adversarial attacks during decentralised model training [4, 5, 21]. The goal of a training-time adversarial attack is to degrade the global model stored in the central centre for a poor or even random performance.

As firstly proposed by Bagdasaryan et al. [3], a new attack paradigm is to insert "backdoors" in the training phase of FL. The goal is to corrupt the global FL model into a targeted mis-prediction on a specific sub-task, e.g. by forcing an image classifier to misclassify green cars as frogs. This can be performed by gradually replacing the global model with a malicious model from the attacker. Usually, a backdoor attack occurs by data poisoning or model poisoning in a compromised malicious or curious client, where the poisoning is more directional in the backdoor attack to force the global model to misclassify on a specific sub-task. Two types of poisoning include black-box and write-box attacks, and we merely focus on black-box attacks, i.e. data poisoning, since its conditions and configurations are readily satisfied. Furthermore, even entire model replacement is possible, with two prerequisites that (1) the FL system (i.e. the global system) is about to converge and (2) the adversary has adequate knowledge about the whole system (e.g. number of users and scale of data).

More recently, edge-case backdoors [55] are presented as strong adversarial attack schemes that are hard to detect and avoid. Specifically, an edge-case backdoor forces the global model to misclassify on seemingly easy examples that are, however, unlikely to be part of the training or test data, i.e. located on the tail of the data distribution. And edge-case backdoor would only attack some unusual inference scenarios and only affect small user groups.

Below, we introduce three ways, from naive to sophisticated, to conduct backdoor attacks via manipulating training data in a local device (indexed by i). First of all, we assume we have a training set $\mathcal{D} = \mathcal{D}_t \cup \mathcal{D}_f$ where $\mathcal{D}_t$ denotes correctly labelled set and $\mathcal{D}_f$ denotes label-manipulated set. And after local gradient updates on $\mathcal{D}$, we obtain new model parameters denoted as $\mathbf{w}_i$ compared to the original parameters $\mathbf{w}$ in the central server.

- *Black-box attack*: As the most straightforward attack approach, the client performs normal weight updates (e.g. SGD) and uploads $\mathbf{w}_i$ to the central server. This, however, can be easily detected by advanced aggregation algorithms implemented in the central server and be discarded consequently, so such an attack is not always effective.
- *Projected gradient descent (PGD) attack*: As the weight updates in the client are derived from applying SGD to the manipulated training set in local client, the updates $\mathbf{w}_i$ would be significant and far from the original parameters $\mathbf{w}$. This is a key reason why the abnormality can be easily detected, especially when the global model is close to convergence. Therefore, a popular adversary strategy is to apply normalisation to $\mathbf{w}_i$ so that $\mathbf{w}_i$ is spatially close to $\mathbf{w}$, i.e. $||\mathbf{w}_i - \mathbf{w}|| < \delta$ where δ is small enough.
- *PGD attack with model replacement*: This attack scheme takes a step further and attempts to replace the global model with a manipulated one to hit the final goal of backdoor. Again, an important prerequisite is that the global model is close to convergence so the updates from other clients are almost the same as $\mathbf{w}$. Hence, extended from PGD attack, the weight updates can be further defined as $\mathbf{w}_i \leftarrow n_S/n_i(\mathbf{w}_i - \mathbf{w}) + \mathbf{w}$, where n_S/n_i is to re-scale for attacking central aggregation. Note that n_S denotes the total example number in the federated learning system and n_i denotes the example number in i-th device. Hence, the aggregation algorithm in the central server will be attacked and perform $\mathbf{w} \leftarrow \mathbf{w} + \sum_j n_j/n_S(\mathbf{w}_j - \mathbf{w}) = \mathbf{w}_i$.

It is interesting to know how to exclude backdoor attacks or data poisoning, and what is the cost of defences. Of course, many defence methods have been proposed to resist a backdoor attack, which are detailed below.

Anomaly Detection. This is the most straightforward idea to resist backdoor attacks and detects abnormal activities and updates from the perspective of the central server. The detection is established by effectively contrasting the updates from thousands of clients with a normal pattern, where the normal pattern can be derived from statistical analysis or expertise. Under the FL framework, backdoor attacks, through either data or model poisoning, will upload abnormal updates (e.g. considerable update step and/or significant deviation from original model), which is well-captured by a sophisticated algorithm and thus removed from aggregation. Shen et al. [51] apply a clustering technique to each client update for a defence against malicious client updates. Blanchard et al. [5] utilise Euclidean distance as the Krum model to measure a deviation between the global model and each client model and then eliminate malicious client updates. Similarly, Li et al. [29] discuss how to detect abnormal updates from clients in a federated learning framework. Furthermore, such defence can also be implemented by auto-encoders or variational auto-encoders, which help to find the malicious client updates [14, 30]. And Fang et al. [14] propose a loss function-based and error rate-based rejection to resist the negative effects of local model poisoning attacks.

However, anomaly detection becomes less effective and even useless when edge-case backdoor attacks appear. Specifically, Wang et al. [55] indicate that edge-case failures can unfortunately be hard-wired through backdoors to federated learning systems. Moreover, directly applying anomaly detection defences has an adverse effect as the clients with diverse enough data would also be removed. This presents a trade-off between fairness and robustness, which is also mentioned in [21] but unexplored in recent works.

Data Sanitisation. As a common technique to defend backdoor and poisoning attacks in FL, data sanitisation [9] is employed in anomaly detection to filter out suspicious training examples. However, stronger data poisoning attacks are likely to break data sanitisation defences [25].

Pruning. Another defence technique against backdoor attacks is "pruning". Rather than directly filtering out the data, this technique evaluates if a unit is supposed to be inactive on clean data but activated in the updates [35]. However, the access to clean holdout data violates the privacy principle of FL and is therefore the biggest concern of this defence technique.

3.2 Gradient Attack and Solutions

Although FL is designed to train a machine learning model without the access to clients' private data, recent research works have revealed that its default setting still suffers from privacy leakage attacks by gradient-based reconstruction [15, 63, 64]. Gradient attack, also known as client privacy leakage attack, is able to accurately reconstruct the private training data in the local client, given only a local gradient update shared from a client to central server. So, in gradient privacy attack, we assume that clients can be compromised in a limited manner. That is, an attacker cannot directly access the private training data $\mathcal{D}$ but only the gradient updates $\nabla \mathbf{w}_i$ calculated by SGD on $\mathcal{D}$. The gradient update data is intercepted by a malicious attacker via a compromised central server or eavesdropping of insecure network communication. This not only violates local data privacy but also the federated learning system by monitoring client confidential data illegally and silently, exposing federated learning into privacy leakage attacks (Fig. 3).

Client Privacy Leakage Attack. This attack technique is to conduct a gradient-based feature reconstruction, where the adversary aims at developing a learning-based reconstruction algorithm that takes the gradient update $\nabla \mathbf{w}_i(t)$ at step t to reconstruct the private data used to calculate the gradient. In the following, we mainly focus on the application scenarios of computer vision in federated learning, where the inputs are images or videos. Therefore, the learning-based reconstruction algorithm will begin from a random attack seed that can be a dummy image with the same resolution as that of the local client. Then, we can perform a forward inference given the dummy image and compute a gradient loss by measuring spatial distance between the current gradient with respect to the model parameters and the actual gradient from the client. Then, we minimise the gradient loss with respect to the dummy-initialised image to approach actual client private data. Thereby, the goal of this reconstruction algorithm is to iteratively modify the dummy image and finally approximate the original data

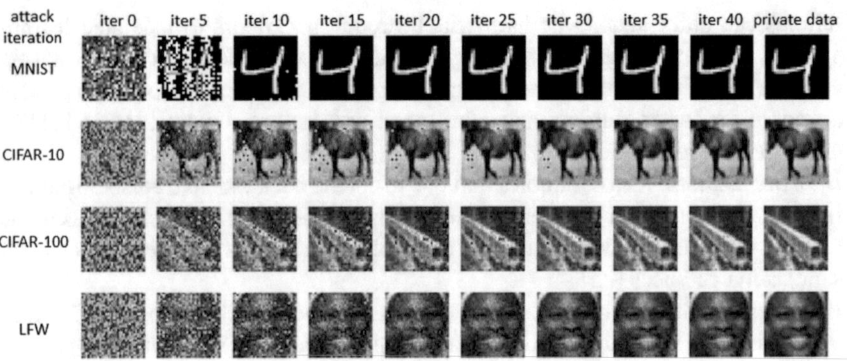

Fig. 3 Examples of gradient attack, which are copied from [56]

in a local device if the gradient loss is converged to be minimal. In summary, this learning-based reconstruction algorithm fixes the parameters of a neural network model and tries to optimise the dummy-initialised image with regard to the gradient loss. Namely, compared to traditional machine learning, this algorithm takes the model $\mathbf{w}$ as its input but takes the image as its learnable parameters.

The open question still remains about how to effectively resist gradient-based client privacy leakage attack. The most effective way, of course, is to prevent the attack from its sources, e.g. encrypting network communication and strengthening server firewalls. When intercepting or eavesdropping is inevitable, differential privacy can be leveraged to eliminate privacy leakage.

Differential Privacy. As a widely applied privacy-preserving technique, differential privacy is proposed to add noise into client privacy data, which thus prevents privacy leakage of personal data [12]. Meanwhile, this comes with an acceptable cost of statistic data quality loss, which is caused by random noise from each client. In this gradient-based attack scenario, differential privacy is implemented by adding noise to the gradient updates from the clients of the federated learning system, which thereby makes it more difficult to reconstruct the client data. However, this privacy-preserving technique introduces randomness into the gradient updates and thus leads to model degeneration. This technique also makes the central server difficult to check the uploaded models from its clients, possibly resulting in conflicts with aforementioned anomaly detection.

Fortunately, there are also other ways to perform defences against gradient-based attacks by increasing attack difficulty, which do not compromise performance degeneration to the same extent. As suggested by Wei et al. [56], according to the principles of client privacy leakage attacks, we can lift the attack difficulty by either adding more parameters for an adversary or increasing estimation complexity. Therefore, this can be reached by (1) increasing batch size of mini-batch SGD in the clients, (2) lifting training image or video resolution in local clients, (3) making more steps of gradient updates before uploading to the central server, and (4) changing activation function in the local model.

4 Data Heterogeneity Challenge for Federated Learning

Heterogeneity widely exists in healthcare and medical data. It is introduced by not only the variety of modalities, dimensionality, and characteristics, but also the data acquisition differences. For example, the medical devices with different brands or local demographics can lead to significantly different source data distributions [45]. FL has addressed this heterogeneous data distribution issue as a critical challenge, and a number of FL algorithms are proposed to tackle heterogeneity in federated networks [61].

4.1 Statistical Heterogeneity

Conventional machine learning is always built upon an independently and identically distributed (IID) assumption of a uniform dataset. However, statistical heterogeneity is an inherent characteristic across the distributed medical data providers, which can be identified as a non-IID problem, as is shown in Fig. 4. Usually, medical data is not uniformly distributed across different institutions and sometimes can introduce a local bias [31, 50]. Recently, some methods have been proposed to handle the statistical heterogeneity in the FL setting. These methods can be applied to most open health scenarios to enhance the robustness of existing distributed machine learning methods and tolerate heterogeneity across data providers. There are two main types of solutions for this, one is to cluster or group the data providers, each cluster/group will have a unique global model, and the other is by personalisation techniques where each medical data provider has both the shared part and the personalised part of model [37].

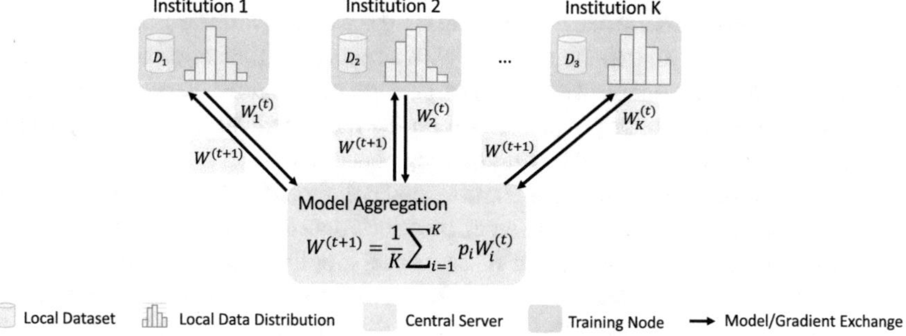

Fig. 4 Statistical heterogeneity problem in federated learning

Clustered FL. According to the input data distribution, models with the same or similar data distribution can be clustered into the same cluster. Weight aggregation can be done inside the cluster. Below are the related methods for clustered federated learning.

In [59], the authors propose a novel multi-centre aggregation mechanism for heterogeneous federated learning which is common in various real-world applications. Multiple global models are learned from the non-IID data by optimising the predefined objective function, namely multi-centre federated loss. In particular, the loss function of the proposed framework is defined as

$$\sum_{i=1}^{n} p_i \cdot \min_k \left\| W_i - W^{(k)} \right\|^2, \tag{1}$$

where p_i is the weight that is typically proportional to the size of the i-th client local dataset, W_i is the parameter of the i-th client's local model, and $W^{(k)}$ is the parameter of the k-th cluster. Any distance metric can be integrated into this framework. This paper takes the simplest L2 distance into consideration and uses K-means as the clustering method.

The distance measurement for clustering methods can be of different forms. Apart from L2 distance, there are more sophisticated distance measurements represented in a hierarchical form, which can be leveraged for specific sets of medical data silos. In [46], geometric properties of the FL loss surface are used for client clustering. Clients within the same cluster have jointly trainable data distributions.

Although clustered FL better utilises the similarity among the users, there are still challenges when performing it in open health. For example, the cluster identities of a hospital or clinic are usually unknown, so it is essential to identify the cluster membership of these data providers first and then optimise each of the cluster models in a distributed setting. To achieve this efficiently, [16] designs a framework known as iterative federated clustering algorithm (IFCA) for clustered FL. IFCA alternately estimates the cluster identities and minimises the loss functions so as to allow the model to converge at an exponential rate with a relaxed initialisation requirement.

Personalised FL. Personalised FL aims to provide personalised services to participating medical institutes or patients based on the their medical images, fragmented data sources, and healthcare data with privacy concerns.

The balance between individual learning and collaboration has been discussed in [11] in a theoretical way. As a result, when the user's data distribution does not deviate too much from the data distribution of other users, collaboration can be beneficial to reduce the local generalisation error. When some users data is too different from the data of others to represent the overall data distribution, independent training is preferable.

Sometimes, it is possible to train one personalised model per client. A theoretic study of personalisation in FL is presented in [40]. The authors propose to use data interpolation as a personalisation technique.

Data interpolation realises personalisation by domain adaptation. Local dataset D_k is regarded as target domain, and global dataset or the cluster dataset $\mathcal{C}$ is regarded as source distribution. The objective function is optimised based on concatenated dataset,

$$\lambda \cdot \mathcal{D}_k + (1 - \lambda) \cdot \mathcal{C}, \tag{2}$$

where λ is a hyperparameter that can be obtained by cross-validation.

Some other popular methods for personalised FL can be categorised as personalisation layers where part of the layers is shared and aggregated across multiple clients. The rule of shared layer selection can vary. For example, in [1], representation layers act as the personalised components, while the decision layers are shared across participants. By contrast, in [32], the representation layers are shared across participants, and decision layers remain local as a personalised component.

4.2 Model Architecture Heterogeneity

Medical data providers tend to use robust statistical models from their local medical data, which is collected in huge amounts by modern healthcare systems [45]. This brings about model heterogeneity to an FL system. Model architecture heterogeneity in Fig. 5, as the main form of model heterogeneity, will hinder the model aggregation procedure in traditional FL algorithms.

To solve this problem and train a robust statistical model from distributed medical data, knowledge distillation, proposed by Hinton et al. [17] in 2015, is widely used to transfer knowledge between models with different architectures. Lin et al. [33] propose ensemble distillation for robust model fusion. It allows for heterogeneous client data and models and clients with different neural architectures to be considered in one FL system. It defines p distinct model prototypes with different architectures. During the aggregation procedure in each communication round, all received client

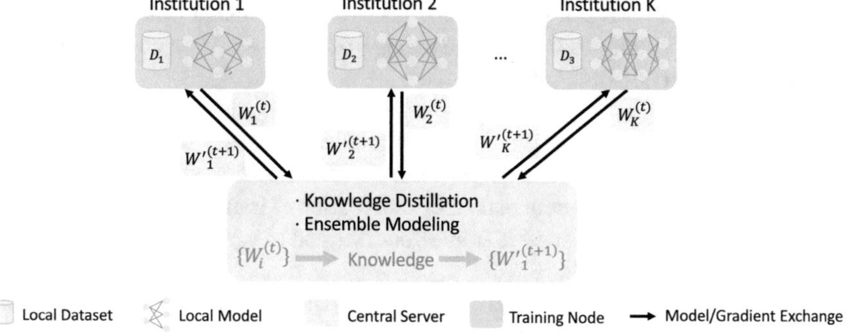

Fig. 5 Model heterogeneity problem in federated learning

models are distilled to p model prototypes without additional computation burden on clients. Then, the fused prototype models are sent to activated clients for the next round.

The authors in [54] also borrow the concept of prototypes and use them to represent classes rather than models. Prototype aggregation is applied in the server to solve the heterogeneous setting in FL.

Sometimes, as a result of various dataset sizes and computation abilities, the model for a specific medical data provider is independently designed. This makes the model unique, and the use of traditional averaging aggregation is no longer possible. To solve this problem, Li and Wang propose federated learning via model distillation (FedMD) which is a universal framework enabling FL to work with uniquely designed local models [28]. Assume there are k clients, and each client owns not only a private dataset $\mathcal{D}_k$ but also a public dataset $\mathcal{D}_0$, $k = 1 \ldots m$. Each client computes the class scores $f_k\left(x_i^0\right)$ on the public dataset and transmits the result to a central server. Instead of model parameter aggregation, the server computes an updated consensus on the average of these class scores. This is realised through knowledge distillation that can transmit learned information in a model-agnostic way.

Although knowledge distillation works well for the model architecture heterogeneity challenge, the communication and computation costs remain a problem. Jeong et al. propose to minimise the communication overhead while enjoying the benefit brought by a massive amount of private data providers [20]. A new distributed training algorithm named federated distillation (FD) has been developed to improve communication efficiency for an on-device machine learning framework. It exchanges the model output rather than the model parameters, which significantly decreases the communication payload from model size to output size.

4.3 *Transfer Learning for Cross-silo Federated Learning*

Existing medical data is not fully exploited by traditional machine learning methods because it sits in data silos and privacy concerns restrict access to this data. As a result of insufficient data, a gap between research and clinical practice exists. FL provides an opportunity to take full advantage of cross-silo data and significantly contribute to open health in future decades.

Transfer learning, as a special case of machine learning, is introduced to solve the heterogeneity problem, expand the scale of medical datasets, and further improve the performance of the final model [36]. For the distributed medical data silos with different kinds of private patient data, the combination of transfer learning and federated learning can lead to a flexible framework adapted to various secure multi-party machine learning tasks [60].

Classical FL methods like FedAvg require that all contributors share the same feature space [41]. However, the scenario with such common entities is rare in reality. In most cases, data contributors share heterogeneous feature spaces and/or model architectures. The authors in [36] address this limitation of existing FL approaches and utilise transfer learning to provide solutions for the entire feature space under a federation. Their work has formalised the federated transfer learning (FTL) problem in a privacy-preserving setting where all parties are honest-but-curious. Next, they propose an end-to-end method to solve the FTL problem. Compared with non-privacy-preserving transfer learning, the proposed method achieves comparable performance in terms of convergence and accuracy. Moreover, novel privacy-preserving techniques, i.e. homomorphic encryption (HE) and secret sharing, can be incorporated with learning models, i.e. neural networks, under the proposed FTL framework without much modifications.

Such privacy-preserving FTL solution is well suited for cross-silo open health scenarios, because it is a well-developed framework that takes all the related aspects into account, including performance, scalability, computation, and communication. FTL is superior to non-federated self-learning approaches and performs as well as non-privacy-preserving approaches.

5 Discussion

In the above sections, we identified key challenges and possible solutions for FL in the healthcare industry. Here, we discuss the implications of solving the healthcare challenges and explore the benefits of a successful open innovation framework with FL.

5.1 Implications of Solving the Security, Privacy, and Heterogeneity Challenges

If the existing security, privacy, and heterogeneity challenges can be solved, there are a number of implications for various industries, including health care. Below we detail three primary implications.

Shared knowledge and expertise. Having a secure way to learn from various local health datasets will increase shared knowledge and expertise among different healthcare institutions. Organisations are likely to be more willing to use their data for collaborative research when they can ensure the privacy of their own patient data and are not required to provide copies of their data. Certainly, it will be essential to identify and engage organisations and institutions that are willing to explore the use of FL for healthcare purposes and to have legal and privacy experts who can verify whether methods comply with existing privacy standards and regulations. Solving the heterogeneity problem will also drive knowledge sharing as it will allow for diverse data to be used to develop more useful global models.

Adoption of deep learning. Deep learning has already demonstrated potential to enhance patient care in the healthcare industry. Previous reviews [2, 52, 58] present numerous applications of deep learning to electronic health records (EHRs), and deep learning has also shown success with image data from medical images and tissue samples [23]. Despite the potential for deep learning to improve patient care, adoption in the healthcare industry is slow. This is often due to models being developed in single healthcare institutions using single datasets, resulting in a lack of robustness across populations [60].

If healthcare information can be shared with the help of an FL system, this will overcome existing limitations. Healthcare institutions that previously did not adopt deep learning due to potential bias issues that can arise from training in single institutions would now have access to models with better generalisability due to training on larger and more representative populations. Furthermore, smaller institutions which were incapable of building predictive algorithms due to small data sizes will now have access to risk prediction models. This will provide these institutions with increased functionality that can be used to help improve clinical care.

Generalised methodologies. The security and privacy challenges, as well as the data heterogeneity problems mentioned above, are not only found in health data. Therefore, designing methods that can address these challenges will facilitate the healthcare sector but will also be relevant to other industries with sensitive data (such as banking or insurance). Methodologies developed could be directly applied to these other relevant industries. Furthermore, general FL research will help advance the field of FL, and in a time where learning joint models from siloed datasets can provide immense potential, particularly in health care, it is paramount that the development of FL algorithms is continued.

5.2 Benefits of an Open Innovation Framework with FL to Healthcare

If a successful open innovation FL system was implemented in the healthcare sector, it stands to benefit in a multitude of ways. These benefits will be received by participants, patients, and the healthcare system.

Participants. In addition to the benefit of knowledge and expertise sharing as indicated in the above section, participants also stand to benefit from FL system through the development of collaborative partnerships. These types of frameworks are the very definition of open innovation, as various external parties will be involved to provide expertise, including clinicians, healthcare professionals, healthcare institution managers, data scientists, and software engineers. We expect that implementation of FL systems will lead to long-term partnerships between medical centres, hospitals, and governments.

Patients. Because FL systems will enhance the adoption of deep learning algorithms, implementation of these algorithms has potential to directly benefit patients and their outcomes in both the cross-device and cross-silo settings.

In the cross-device setting, patients can benefit through shared information from wearable devices. Wearable devices can be used for monitoring health and safety of patients, managing chronic diseases, assisting in the diagnosis and treatment of conditions, and for monitoring rehabilitation [38]. For example, in [53], data from wearable devices was used to create a fall detection system that could produce emergency alerts so that immediate treatment could be provided to patients. Wearables have also been used by patients with chronic obstructive pulmonary disease to help screen for early disease deterioration [57]. They have also found relevance in rehabilitation, helping to understand stroke recovery and modify treatment plans in line with recovery progress [19]. With the help of FL, model information from individual patient devices can be used to help develop more generalised models that offer improvements in identifying falls, disease deterioration, and patient monitoring. This would help optimise care for patients and lead to more personalised treatments, driving improvements in patient outcomes.

In the cross-silo setting, patients can benefit through shared information across healthcare institutions. Much research to date on machine learning and deep learning for healthcare data has utilised the Medical Information Mart for Intensive Care (MIMIC-III), due to it being a freely available database. It has been used for the development of deep learning algorithms to predict mortality, sepsis, future diagnosis, and hospital readmissions [18, 34, 39, 47]. All these outcomes have potential to prevent poor health outcomes for patients and provide optimised care at end-of-life. However, MIMIC-III data is from a single healthcare centre and includes only patients that are admitted to the intensive care unit (ICU) in the hospital. Therefore, many of the predictive models developed on this dataset will not perform equivalently in other health datasets. By using FL, global models can be developed from multiple healthcare institutions that offer improved performance due to training on larger and more diverse health data [60]. These improved predictive models can provide additional information to clinicians about risks and benefits of different treatment options and outcomes [60]. This has potential for more effective treatment earlier, leading to improved patient outcomes.

The promise of FL to improve patient outcomes has already been demonstrated in the healthcare sector, for both risk prediction and identifying similar patients. Brisimi et al. [7] used an FL framework to develop a prediction model for hospitalisations due to heart diseases based on information in EHRs. The decentralised model achieved similar performance to the centralised method, and the authors extracted important features to facilitate interpretability. Sharma et al. [48] compared an FL framework with a centralised approach for predicting in-hospital mortality and also found that the FL approach provided comparable performance to the centralised setting. Lee et al. [27] used a privacy-preserving federated environment to identify similar patients across healthcare institutions without sharing patient-level information. Similarly, Kim et al. [24] performed computational phenotyping without sharing patient-level data. These examples demonstrate the success of FL compared to typically centralised approaches and its potential in the healthcare industry to improve care of patients.

Healthcare system. Given the current pressure for healthcare systems to enhance sustainability, an FL system is an attractive option. With the use of FL, it is possible

to develop more generalisable models that can assist in providing clinical care. More effective and targeted treatment of patients may result in less time spent visiting emergency departments and hospitals, slowed disease progression for chronic disease, and better outcomes sooner [45]. This has potential to reduce healthcare system costs, hence contributing to a more sustainable healthcare system.
Data Structure. The healthcare activity may produce data with various structure, for example, images from medical imaging, texts on clinic reports, tabular data in hospital's database, sequential patient journey in healthcare service system, and time series from wearable devices or ICU. Different data structure needs to tackle with different data processing techniques. Moreover, the data fusion of multi-modal data is also a common solution to build intelligent healthcare application. To model the complex data of real world is a practical challenge. This chapter demonstrates the FL framework using image data. However, the discussed problem and solution can be generally applied to a broad scenario with different data structures.

6 Conclusion

FL holds promising potential to enable shared healthcare information, knowledge, and expertise between institutions, while preserving privacy of individuals. Although there remain challenges for data security, privacy, and heterogeneity, this is an active area of FL research with solutions already being identified. The implications of FL for health are many, including facilitating sharing of healthcare information, increasing adoption of deep learning algorithms that can produce more generalised models, and the development of improved methodologies that are applicable to industries beyond health care. Long-term benefits will result from FL-enabled open innovation of health, which will be felt at the participant, patient, and healthcare system level. We believe that FL will help leverage existing health data assets to directly impact patient care and therefore offers immense opportunity for open innovation in the healthcare sector.

References

1. Manoj Ghuhan Arivazhagan, Vinay Aggarwal, Aaditya Kumar Singh, and Sunav Choudhary. Federated learning with personalization layers. arXiv:1912.00818, 2019.
2. Jose Roberto Ayala Solares, Francesca Elisa Diletta Raimondi, Yajie Zhu, et al. Deep learning for electronic health records: A comparative review of multiple deep neural architectures. *J. Biomed. Inform*, 101:103337, 2020.
3. Eugene Bagdasaryan, Andreas Veit, Yiqing Hua, Deborah Estrin, and Vitaly Shmatikov. How to backdoor federated learning. In *AISTATS*, volume 108, pages 2938–2948, 2020.
4. Gilad Baruch, Moran Baruch, and Yoav Goldberg. A little is enough: Circumventing defenses for distributed learning. In *NeurIPS 2019*, pages 8632–8642, 2019.
5. Peva Blanchard, El Mahdi El Mhamdi, Rachid Guerraoui, and Julien Stainer. Machine learning with adversaries: Byzantine tolerant gradient descent. In *NeurIPS*, 2017.

6. Jeffrey Braithwaite, Yvonne Zurynski, Kristiana Ludlow, Joanna Holt, Hanna Augustsson, and Margie Campbell. Towards sustainable healthcare system performance in the 21st century in high-income countries: A protocol for a systematic review of the grey literature. *BMJ Open*, 9:bmjopen–2018, 01 2019.
7. Theodora S. Brisimi, Ruidi Chen, Theofanie Mela, Alex Olshevsky, Ioannis Ch. Paschalidis, and Wei Shi. Federated learning of predictive models from federated electronic health records. *International Journal of Medical Informatics*, 112:59–67, 2018.
8. Henry Chesbrough, Wim Vanhaverbeke, and Joel West. *New frontiers in open innovation*. OUP Oxford, 2014.
9. Gabriela F. Cretu, Angelos Stavrou, Michael E. Locasto, Salvatore J. Stolfo, and Angelos D. Keromytis. Casting out demons: Sanitizing training data for anomaly sensors. In *IEEE Symposium on S&P*, pages 81–95. IEEE Computer Society, 2008.
10. Patricia Dandonoli. Open innovation as a new paradigm for global collaborations in health. *Globalization and health*, 9:41, 08 2013.
11. Yuyang Deng, Mohammad Mahdi Kamani, and Mehrdad Mahdavi. Adaptive personalized federated learning. *arXiv preprint* arXiv:2003.13461, 2020.
12. Cynthia Dwork. Differential privacy. In *ICALP*, volume 4052. Springer, 2006.
13. Council of the European Union European Parliament. General data protection regulation (gdpr). Technical report, 2016.
14. Minghong Fang, Xiaoyu Cao, Jinyuan Jia, and Neil Zhenqiang Gong. Local model poisoning attacks to byzantine-robust federated learning. In *USENIX Security Symposium*, pages 1605–1622. USENIX Association, 2020.
15. Jonas Geiping, Hartmut Bauermeister, Hannah Dröge, and Michael Moeller. Inverting gradients - how easy is it to break privacy in federated learning? In *NeurIPS*, 2020.
16. Avishek Ghosh, Jichan Chung, Dong Yin, and Kannan Ramchandran. An efficient framework for clustered federated learning. *arXiv preprint* arXiv:2006.04088, 2020.
17. Geoffrey Hinton, Oriol Vinyals, and Jeff Dean. Distilling the knowledge in a neural network. arXiv:1503.02531, 2015.
18. Nianzong Hou, Mingzhe Li, et al. Predicting 30-days mortality for mimic-iii patients with sepsis-3: a machine learning approach using xgboost. *Journal of Translational Medicine*, 18, 12 2020.
19. Chandrasekaran Jayaraman and et al. Variables influencing wearable sensor outcome estimates in individuals with stroke and incomplete spinal cord injury: A pilot investigation validating two research grade sensors. *Journal of NR*, 15, 03 2018.
20. Eunjeong Jeong, Seungeun Oh, Hyesung Kim, Jihong Park, Mehdi Bennis, and Seong-Lyun Kim. Communication-efficient on-device machine learning: Federated distillation and augmentation under non-iid private data. arXiv:1811.11479, 2018.
21. Peter Kairouz, H. Brendan McMahan, et al. Advances and open problems in federated learning. *CoRR*, abs/1912.04977, 2019.
22. Christopher Kelly and Anthony Young. Promoting innovation in healthcare. *Future Healthcare Journal*, 4:121–125, 06 2017.
23. Justin Ker, Lipo Wang, Jai Rao, and Tchoyoson Lim. Deep learning applications in medical image analysis. *IEEE Access*, 6:9375–9389, 2018.
24. Yejin Kim, Jimeng Sun, Hwanjo Yu, and Xiaoqian Jiang. Federated tensor factorization for computational phenotyping. In *SIGKDD*, pages 887–895. ACM, 2017.
25. Pang Wei Koh, Jacob Steinhardt, and Percy Liang. Stronger data poisoning attacks break data sanitization defenses. *CoRR*, abs/1811.00741, 2018.
26. Jakub Konečný, H Brendan McMahan, Felix X Yu, Peter Richtárik, Ananda Theertha Suresh, and Dave Bacon. Federated learning: Strategies for improving communication efficiency. *arXiv preprint* arXiv:1610.05492, 2016.
27. Junghye Lee, Jimeng Sun, Fei Wang, Shuang Wang, Chi-Hyuck Jun, and Xiaoqian Jiang. Privacy-preserving patient similarity learning in a federated environment: Development and analysis. *JMIR Med Inform*, 6(2):e20, 2018.

28. Daliang Li and Junpu Wang. Fedmd: Heterogenous federated learning via model distillation. arXiv:1910.03581, 2019.
29. Suyi Li, Yong Cheng, Yang Liu, Wei Wang, and Tianjian Chen. Abnormal client behavior detection in federated learning. *CoRR*, abs/1910.09933, 2019.
30. Suyi Li, Yong Cheng, Wei Wang, Yang Liu, and Tianjian Chen. Learning to detect malicious clients for robust federated learning. *CoRR*, abs/2002.00211, 2020.
31. Wenqi Li, Fausto Milletarì, et al. Privacy-preserving federated brain tumour segmentation. In *International Workshop on Machine Learning in Medical Imaging*, pages 133–141. Springer, 2019.
32. Paul Pu Liang, Terrance Liu, Liu Ziyin, Ruslan Salakhutdinov, and Louis-Philippe Morency. Think locally, act globally: Federated learning with local and global representations. arXiv:2001.01523, 2020.
33. Tao Lin, Lingjing Kong, Sebastian U Stich, and Martin Jaggi. Ensemble distillation for robust model fusion in federated learning. *NeurIPS*, 33, 2020.
34. Yu-Wei Lin, Yuqian Zhou, Faraz Faghri, Michael Shaw, and Roy Campbell. Analysis and prediction of unplanned intensive care unit readmission using recurrent neural networks with long short-term memory. 08 2018.
35. Boyi Liu, Lujia Wang, and Ming Liu. Lifelong federated reinforcement learning: A learning architecture for navigation in cloud robotic systems. *IEEE Robotics Autom. Lett.*, 4(4):4555–4562, 2019.
36. Yang Liu, Yan Kang, Chaoping Xing, Tianjian Chen, and Qiang Yang. Secure federated transfer learning. *arXiv preprint* arXiv:1812.03337, 2018.
37. Guodong Long, Yue Tan, Jing Jiang, and Chengqi Zhang. Federated learning for open banking. In *Federated Learning*, pages 240–254. Springer, 2020.
38. Lin Lu, Jiayao Zhang, and et al. Wearable health devices in health care: Narrative systematic review. *JMIR Mhealth Uhealth*, 8(11):e18907, 2020.
39. Fenglong Ma, Yaqing Wang, Houping Xiao, Ye Yuan, Radha Chitta, Jing Zhou, and Jing Gao. A general framework for diagnosis prediction via incorporating medical code descriptions. In *BIBM*, pages 1070–1075, 2018.
40. Yishay Mansour, Mehryar Mohri, Jae Ro, and Ananda Theertha Suresh. Three approaches for personalization with applications to federated learning. *arXiv preprint* arXiv:2002.10619, 2020.
41. Brendan McMahan, Eider Moore, Daniel Ramage, Seth Hampson, and Blaise Aguera y Arcas. Communication-efficient learning of deep networks from decentralized data. In *Artificial Intelligence and Statistics*, pages 1273–1282. PMLR, 2017.
42. Brendan McMahan, Eider Moore, Daniel Ramage, Seth Hampson, and Blaise Agüera y Arcas. Communication-efficient learning of deep networks from decentralized data. In *AISTATS*, volume 54, pages 1273–1282, 2017.
43. Viraaji Mothukuri, Reza M. Parizi, Seyedamin Pouriyeh, Yan Huang, Ali Dehghantanha, and Gautam Srivastava. A survey on security and privacy of federated learning. *Future Generation Computer Systems*, 115:619 – 640, 2021.
44. Sashank Reddi, Zachary Charles, Manzil Zaheer, Zachary Garrett, Keith Rush, Jakub Konečný, Sanjiv Kumar, and H Brendan McMahan. Adaptive federated optimization. *arXiv preprint* arXiv:2003.00295, 2020.
45. Nicola Rieke, Jonny Hancox, Wenqi Li, et al. The future of digital health with federated learning. *Nature partner journals: Digital Medicine*, 2020.
46. Felix Sattler, Klaus-Robert Müller, and Wojciech Samek. Clustered federated learning: Model-agnostic distributed multitask optimization under privacy constraints. *IEEE Transactions on Neural Networks and Learning Systems*, 2020.
47. Matthieu Scherpf, Felix Gräßer, Hagen Malberg, and Sebastian Zaunseder. Predicting sepsis with a recurrent neural network using the mimic iii database. *Computers in Biology and Medicine*, 113:103395, 08 2019.
48. Pulkit Sharma, Farah E. Shamout, and David A. Clifton. Preserving patient privacy while training a predictive model of in-hospital mortality. *CoRR*, abs/1912.00354, 2019.

49. Micah Sheller and et al. Federated learning in medicine: facilitating multi-institutional collaborations without sharing patient data. *Scientific Reports*, 10, 07 2020.
50. Micah J Sheller, G Anthony Reina, Brandon Edwards, Jason Martin, and Spyridon Bakas. Multi-institutional deep learning modeling without sharing patient data: A feasibility study on brain tumor segmentation. In *International MICCAI Brainlesion Workshop*, pages 92–104. Springer, 2018.
51. Shiqi Shen, Shruti Tople, and Prateek Saxena. Auror: defending against poisoning attacks in collaborative deep learning systems. In *Proceedings of the 32nd Annual Conference on Computer Security Applications, ACSAC 2016, Los Angeles, CA, USA, December 5–9, 2016*, pages 508–519. ACM, 2016.
52. Benjamin Shickel and et al. Deep EHR: A survey of recent advances on deep learning techniques for electronic health record (EHR) analysis. *CoRR*, abs/1706.03446, 2017.
53. Jung Sungmook, Seungki Hong, Jaemin Kim, Sangkyu Lee, Taeghwan Hyeon, Minbaek Lee, and Dae-Hyeong Kim. Wearable fall detector using integrated sensors and energy devices. *Scientific Reports*, 5:17081, 11 2015.
54. Yue Tan, Guodong Long, Lu Liu, Tianyi Zhou, and Jing Jiang. Fedproto: Federated prototype learning over heterogeneous devices. *arXiv preprint* arXiv:2105.00243, 2021.
55. Hongyi Wang, Kartik Sreenivasan, et al. Attack of the tails: Yes, you really can backdoor federated learning. In *NeurIPS*, 2020.
56. Wenqi Wei, Ling Liu, Margaret Loper, Ka Ho Chow, Mehmet Emre Gursoy, Stacey Truex, and Yanzhao Wu. A framework for evaluating gradient leakage attacks in federated learning. *CoRR*, abs/2004.10397, 2020.
57. Robert Wu, Daniyal Liaqat, Eyal de Lara, Tatiana Son, Frank Rudzicz, Hisham Alshaer, Pegah Abed-Esfahani, and Andrea S Gershon. Feasibility of using a smartwatch to intensively monitor patients with chronic obstructive pulmonary disease: Prospective cohort study. *JMIR Mhealth Uhealth*, 6(6):e10046, Jun 2018.
58. Cao Xiao, Edward Choi, and J. Sun. Opportunities and challenges in developing deep learning models using electronic health records data: A systematic review. *Journal of the American Medical Informatics Association*, 25, 06 2018.
59. Ming Xie, Guodong Long, Tao Shen, Tianyi Zhou, Xianzhi Wang, and Jing Jiang. Multi-center federated learning. *arXiv preprint* arXiv:2005.01026, 2020.
60. Jie Xu and Fei Wang. Federated learning for healthcare informatics. *arXiv preprint* arXiv:1911.06270, 2019.
61. Qiang Yang, Yang Liu, Tianjian Chen, and Yongxin Tong. Federated machine learning: Concept and applications. *TIST*, 10(2):1–19, 2019.
62. Andy Wai Kan Yeung et al. Open innovation in medical and pharmaceutical research: A literature landscape analysis. *Frontiers in Pharmacology*, 11, 01 2021.
63. Bo Zhao, Konda Reddy Mopuri, and Hakan Bilen. idlg: Improved deep leakage from gradients. *CoRR*, abs/2001.02610, 2020.
64. Ligeng Zhu, Zhijian Liu, and Song Han. Deep leakage from gradients. In *NeurIPS*, pages 14747–14756, 2019.

AI-Enhanced 3D Biomedical Data Analytics for Neuronal Structure Reconstruction

Heng Wang, Yang Song, Zihao Tang, Chaoyi Zhang, Jianhui Yu, Dongnan Liu, Donghao Zhang, Siqi Liu, and Weidong Cai

1 Introduction

3D neuron reconstruction, also known as neuron tracing, is a process to digitise the tree-like morphological model of a single neuron from 3D optical microscopic image stacks [24]. It is a critical step in the neuron analysis domain since neuronal structures are fundamental to the definition of neuron identity phenotype, the determination of neuron functionality, the observation of synaptic activities, and further-

H. Wang · Z. Tang · C. Zhang · J. Yu · D. Liu · W. Cai (✉)
School of Computer Science, University of Sydney, Sydney, NSW, Australia
e-mail: tom.cai@sydney.edu.au

H. Wang
e-mail: hwan9147@sydney.edu.au

Z. Tang
e-mail: ztan1463@sydney.edu.au

C. Zhang
e-mail: czha5168@sydney.edu.au

J. Yu
e-mail: jiyu9437@sydney.edu.au

D. Liu
e-mail: dliu5812@sydney.edu.au

Y. Song
School of Computer Science and Engineering, University of New South Wales, Sydney, NSW, Australia
e-mail: yang.song1@unsw.edu.au

D. Zhang
Monash e-Research Centre, Monash University, Melbourne, VIC, Australia
e-mail: donghao.zhang@monash.edu

S. Liu
Digital Services, Digital Technology & Innovation, Paige AI, New York, NY, USA

F. Chen and J. Zhou (eds.), *Humanity Driven AI*,
https://doi.org/10.1007/978-3-030-72188-6_7

more the interactions between neurons among neuron circuits [21]. Investigation of neuronal morphology is fundamental to understanding higher-order cognition functions happening in human brains [17, 33, 39] and thus critical to drug development and treatment for neurological and psychiatric disorders [28]. How to automatically and precisely obtain the neuron structures as point representation consisting of coordinates, radius, and connectivity from the 3D microscopy images thus became essential. The stacks of microscopic images are often generated through confocal or multi-photon laser scanning techniques [58]. Different scanning designs focus on different aspects, such as improving the imaging resolution and enhancing the sampling contrast. Before computational resources came into existence, it is always a time-consuming and labour-intensive task for biologists to obtain the neuron arborisation by pen and paper [42]. With the development of computers, semi-automatic reconstruction algorithms have been invented to help reduce the load. But these algorithms still depend on experts who are experienced in neuron morphology to produce the final precise structure model. As more and more large-scale data are being produced nowadays, the demand for automatic and accurate neuron reconstruction methods without human intervention is becoming urgent.

However, one of the main obstacles in automatic neuron reconstruction is the image quality. Common neuronal data are produced through the scanning of the specimen. Even though laser scanning techniques [51] improve the image resolution, the laser damage to the sample could distort the underlying structures and make the intensity distribution uneven. The multi-photon microscopes have been developed to ensure the sampling rate in depth equal as well and create less damage to the sample. Besides, the Point Spread Function technique is often imposed on produced image stacks to restore the isotropic resolution among different planes [27, 34, 41]. In a nutshell, the main challenges caused by imaging are as follows: (1) inevitable imaging noises or irrelevant structure components; (2) discontinuous intensity among neuronal structures; and (3) low intensity contrast between the objects of interest and the background. As shown in Fig. 1a, the 3D optic image has been polluted by a large area of noise which could be caused by the imaging process or the transportation of neuron data. To correctly distinguish between the noise and the neuronal structures is one critical criterion to evaluate a good reconstruction. Figure 1b presents the verified manual reconstruction ground truth of the noisy image, and different colours indicate different neuronal segments. Figure 1c, d displays an exemplar with disconnected neuronal shape especially around the dendritic area and its corresponding ground truth, respectively. The uneven distribution of intensity value could be caused by different factors, one of which is when the fluorescent markers do not expand around the dendrites evenly. Low-signal contrast could always prevent the automatic reconstruction algorithms from correct tracing, since it is hard to tell the salient features of the neuronal structures such as axons and dendrites out of the background which has the similar intensity distribution in this case. Figure 1e and 1f provides one of such low-signal contrast challenging examples and its ground truth annotation.

Apart from the low quality of neuron data, the intrinsic complexity and variability in the neuron structures also make the precise reconstruction process difficult to achieve. Recently, the successful host of the DIADEM competition [4] and

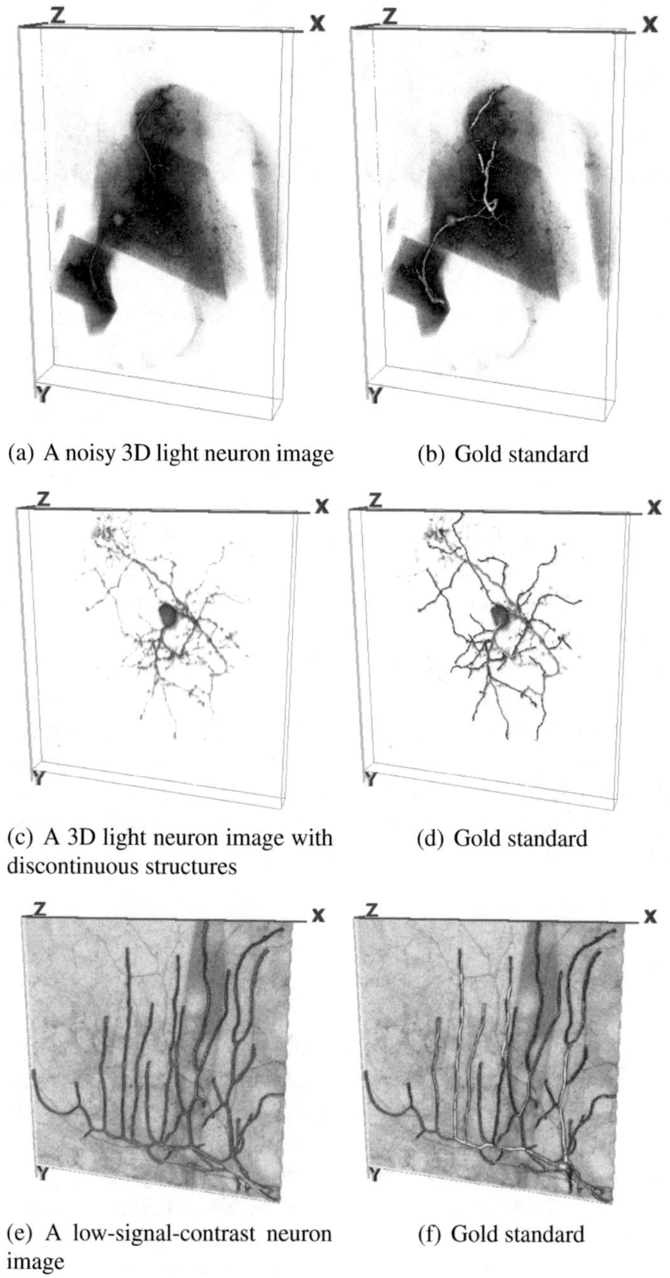

(a) A noisy 3D light neuron image

(b) Gold standard

(c) A 3D light neuron image with discontinuous structures

(d) Gold standard

(e) A low-signal-contrast neuron image

(f) Gold standard

Fig. 1 **a**, **c**, and **e**: Noise-polluted, discontinuous, and low-contrast structures of 3D neuron images. **b**, **d**, and **f**: Manually labelled reconstruction overlapped with the original image for better visualisation

Fig. 2 Overview of the single 3D neuron reconstruction task

the BigNeuron project [35, 37] have encouraged a bunch of 3D semi-automatic or automatic algorithms [3, 6, 22, 24, 30–32, 41, 47, 54, 58, 59, 61] by providing open-source data resources and auxiliary softwares. Even though there have been a number of different algorithms proposed so far, all of them share the same core of design which is to build an automatic pipeline of (1) preprocessing the 3D light image stacks to enhance the quality; (2) tracing the tree-like structures from the preprocessed input; and (3) postprocessing the reconstruction if necessary [22, 24, 47, 61]. Since dense neurons can be separated using particular tissue labelling techniques such as Brainbow [10], the dense neuron reconstruction task can be decomposed to several single neuron reconstruction subtasks. Hence, we focus on single neuron reconstruction algorithms.

In this chapter, we will consider phases (2) and (3) as one phase named tracking. The schematic illustration of the single 3D neuron reconstruction task is shown in Fig. 2. The neuronal structures are first detected and segmented using recent deep learning-based techniques, and then the enhanced 3D image is fed into the later tracking phase to perform the reconstruction intelligently. In the following sections, we will present our latest work on deep learning-based preprocessing techniques and intelligent tracking algorithms with detailed case studies.

2 Efficient Segmentation Model

With the development of deep learning recently, the convolutional neural networks (CNNs [20]) have played a critical part in virtually every single automatic image analysis tasks. CNNs adopt convolutional operations where a set of learnable sliding windows aggregate the semantic information among a sub-region covered by the window from input image. The learning is happening through back-propagation of objective loss every iteration from the training data. The nonlinearity among the hidden layers of CNNs enables the extraction of high-dimensional feature representation of grid-based regular data, including 2D and 3D images. The utilisation of skip connection [12] further boosts the possibility of deeper network with stronger learning ability. The successful employment of CNNs in global image-level recognition tasks such as image classification and local-level dense prediction tasks such as object detection, semantic segmentation, instance segmentation, and panoptic segmentation has inspired a burst of improvement in biomedical image analysis tasks. The invent of U-Net [7] and the subsequent V-Net [29] have made the encoder–decoder-like architecture the de facto standard backbone in medical image segmentation by providing one-stage end-to-end pixel-level prediction. The encoder path of U-Net extracts higher-level semantic information while compressing the input size layer by layer, and the decoder path decodes the segmentation prediction out of the compact semantic embedding while recovering the feature size to the input size. However, the optimisation of CNNs for complex structures like the 3D neuronal arbours often involves a large number of parameters which could prohibitively affect the deployment in real-time practice. In this section, we present two deep learning methods for neuron segmentation tackling the inefficiency challenge in detecting the arborisation of large-scale 3D neuron images. Section 2.1 introduces the data compression method by extracting additional diagonal 2D stacks from original 3D input to save the computational costs in 3D data processing, while Sect. 2.2 presents the later work on compressing the segmentation model rather than the input to keep the information of the source data.

2.1 Input Compression Via Triple-Crossing 2.5D CNN

Since 3D data require more computational resources to aggregate the underlying features, 2.5D CNN [40] has been proposed to use only 2D projection data to learn the representation. Based on 2.5D CNN, we proposed a triple-crossing 2.5D CNN [23] with additional sectional planes being considered to add more information while keeping the efficiency of 2D operations. Since the intensity distributions among different data samples are various, a gradient-based intensity normalisation technique is employed to preprocess the dataset, thus making the later learning more efficient and smooth. Details are presented in Sect. 2.1.1. To highlight the skeleton of the neuronal arbours, we generated the ground truth segmentation based on scale-space distance transform, as will be discussed in Sect. 2.1.2. The schematic illustration of the overall 2D segmentation model architecture will be presented in Sect. 2.1.4.

2.1.1 Gradient-Based Image Preprocessing

It is necessary to make sure the input data for training a neural network follow the similar distribution to help the training converge quickly. However, conventional histogram matching normalisation methods do not perform very well on microscopy images [44] whose intensity distribution always varies among different image. Hence, to suppress the difference of intensity distributions for different input, we use the gradient-based image normalisation technique [44]. The normalisation follows the similar diagram where a reference image is needed to compute the source profile. In our case, we use an average gradient variant of the profile calculation for each intensity value i which is defined as follows:

$$p_i = \sum_{g=0}^{L-1} b_{ig} g / \sum_{g=0}^{L-1} b_{ig} \tag{1}$$

where L refers to the level of intensity which is 256 in our case. b_{ig} refers to the number of occurrence of voxels whose intensity is i, and gradient is g in a bivariate histogram. More details can be found in [44]. This calculated profile will not be affected by the total number of voxels, and it will only be influenced by the gradient distribution. We then use this profile to map the input data to normalise the distribution before feeding them into the network.

2.1.2 Ground Truth Definition

The manually annotated neuronal structures are represented as a set of connected points whose coordinates, radius, and parent point are stored into SWC files. To generate the pixel-level segmentation ground truth from neuronal points information stored in the SWC files, we use a scale-spaced distance transform technique [45] to highlight the centreline. The scale-space distance transform is formulated as follows:

$$D(p, r) = \|p - p_{\min}\|_2^2 + w\,(r - r_{\min}) \tag{2}$$

where $p_{\min}$ and $r_{\min}$ are the coordinate and the radius of the nearest point along the skeleton to the point p. Then to highlight the skeleton and to suppress points far away from the centreline, the final neuronal structure ground truth is defined as follows:

$$d(p, r) = \begin{cases} e^{\alpha \cdot (1 - \frac{D(p,r)}{d_M})} - 1 & \text{if } D(p, r) \leq d_M \\ 0 & \text{otherwise} \end{cases} \tag{3}$$

where d_M is a threshold parameter to control the extent of how the skeleton is highlighted.

Since the manual conversion from the SWC annotation to the regression map $d(p, r)$ is a general estimation to the precise segmentation of the neuronal structures, we use a fixed threshold (0.4) to apply on the predicted segmentation with the aim to filter out most background noise. Then based on this enhanced input, precise tracing of the neuronal structures can be performed using later tracking algorithms.

2.1.3 Triple-Crossing Patches Generation

Patch-based deep 3D segmentation is to use the contextual information of a cube of size S^3 centred at each voxel i to classify the possibility of each voxel belonging to the foreground object. To reduce the cubic computation for each single voxel, 2.5D CNN [40] has been proposed to replace the neighbouring cube with only three orthogonal 2D planes of size S^2 only. Therefore, 3D CNN would be reduced to 2D CNN which saves a great deal of computing resources. In our work, we proposed that the planes along diagonal axes also contain useful contextual information.

In 2.5D CNN, the input data to a learnable model are three planes P^0_{XY}, P^0_{XZ}, and P^0_{YZ} which are perpendicular to axes Z, Y, and X, respectively. In our proposed triple-crossing 2.5D (TC2.5D) work, we add two more diagonal planes for each orthogonal plane. $P_*^{+\frac{\pi}{4}}$ and $P_*^{-\frac{\pi}{4}}$ refer to the diagonal plane $\frac{\pi}{4}$ and $-\frac{\pi}{4}$ to the original orthogonal plane P^0_*, respectively, where $*$ represents XY, XZ, and YZ. Therefore, in our work, the input data contain nine separate planes leading to richer contextual information without too much overhead. To enrich the input data, we also apply data augmentation techniques such as random rotation to these patches.

2.1.4 Triple-Crossing 2.5D Model Architecture

Figure 3 presents the structure of the proposed triple-crossing 2.5D network. The inputs to the network are the nine triple-crossing patches centred at a random voxel after random augmentation. After a sequence of a CNN block, two residual blocks, and a fully connected layer, the probability value of the voxel belonging to the neuronal structure will be predicted. More specifically, the CNN block consists of a convolutional layer with the kernel of the size 3×3 and the number of output channels being 64, a batch normalisation layer [14] to correct the distribution after convolutional operation, and a nonlinear ELU [8] layer to transform the feature maps. In order to enhance the learning capability, we use the residual connection proposed in [12] to alleviate the degradation problem. In our two residual blocks, we introduce a skip connection after two sequences of convolution layers, batch normalisation layer, and ELU nonlinear layer. The number of output channels is doubled after each convolution layer. At the end of both the CNN block and the residual block, we have a 2×2 max pooling layer to enlarge the receptive field and a random 25% Gaussian dropout layer to avoid over-fitting. For fair prediction, the prediction after several observations at a voxel would be averaged.

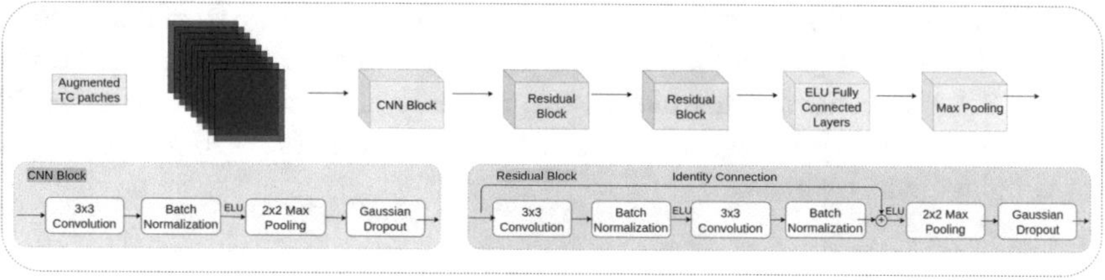

Fig. 3 Overview of the proposed network structure

2.1.5 Discussion

In this work, 3D data are projected into 2D patches from different angles with the aim of using 2D network to tackle 3D problem in a more computation-friendly way. Since the loss of information would affect the aggregation of the neighbourhood information when predicting the probability value of a single voxel, the proposed method includes six additional diagonal angles to reserve more information. Experiments show that the proposed method outperforms the previous 2.5D CNN. Nevertheless, there is still information loss when 3D data are transformed into 2D patches. It is still less accurate compared to the full-size 3D method. In next section, a 3D approach to enhance the efficiency of 3D neuron segmentation model is introduced.

2.2 *Model Compression Via Teacher-Student Network*

To address the downside of information loss when discarding most details in depth of neuron image stacks as mentioned in Sect. 2.1.5, we proposed to maintain the input source as 3D data while reducing the computational cost from the aspect of model complexity. As large models might have more powerful learning ability, the redundant time they take to do the inference hinders the deployment in practical. Also, the likelihood for large model to be over-fitting to the training set is much higher due to their complex structures, but the learned knowledge is key to avoid under-fitting problems in small-size networks. Inspired by recently proposed transfer learning techniques [13, 19], we proposed a teacher-student-based model [56] to compress the inference model through knowledge distillation. In this proposed method, a complex model is employed to sufficiently learn different scales of features from the training set, and then a small-capacity model is trained from the same set but with the guidance of the complex network. More details about the network architectures are included in Sect. 2.2.1. Since the relationship between these two networks simulates the real-world teacher-student interaction, the complex model is referred to as the teacher model while the small model is considered accordingly the student model. We elaborate more about how the teacher network guides the student one in Sect. 2.2.2. The proposed method was evaluated on the Janelia sequences from the BigNeuron project [35, 37], and the results of the experiments presented in Sect. 2.2.3 demonstrate that our method not only outperforms the baseline 3D U-Net [7] in accuracy in segmenting the neuron structures but also requires much less computational overhead.

2.2.1 Teacher-Student Network Architecture

The schematic diagram of the proposed teacher–student framework is shown in Fig. 4. Both the complex teacher and the lightweight student model are variants of the prevalent 3D U-Net [7]. Since the complex model is expected to capture finer details

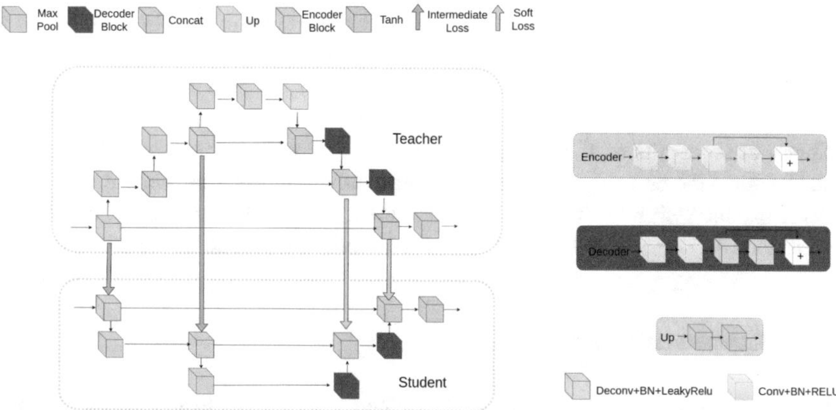

Fig. 4 Architecture of our proposed teacher–student network

of the neuron structures, the designed teacher network consists of four encoders with a set of convolutional operations, one up block at the smallest resolution layer, and two decoders. All the convolutional kernels have the window size $3 \times 3 \times 3$. As for upsampling path, the deconvolutional kernel size is $2 \times 2 \times 2$. The channel number of output feature maps for the first encoder in the teacher network is 16 and gets doubled for subsequent encoders. The number of feature maps after the up block and the two decoders is 64, 32, and 16, respectively. At the end of the teacher network, we use the Tanh nonlinear function so that we can calculate the $L1$ loss between the prediction and the scale-space distance transformed [45] ground truth. The architecture of the student network is the same as the teacher except its size is half that of the teacher one. Both the teacher and student model include residual connection [12] to improve the gradient flow.

2.2.2 Knowledge Distillation

The passing of extracted information from the teacher model is achieved through two additional losses, namely the intermediate and the soft loss as highlighted in Fig. 4 as four wide arrows, apart from the regular training of the student model via the ground truth which we refer as the hard loss. Formally, the learning objective of the student network is formulated as below:

$$L = \zeta L_{\text{hard}} + \beta L_{\text{soft}} + \gamma L_{\text{intermediate}} \tag{4}$$

where L_{hard} is the $L1$ loss between the prediction of the student model and the ground truth segmentation; L_{soft} denotes the $L1$ loss between the prediction from the trained teacher network and that from the training student network; $L_{\text{intermediate}}$ represents the average $L1$ loss between the intermediate feature maps from the two networks. The three hyperparameters ζ, β, and γ are set empirically to be 0.8, 0.1, and 0.1, respectively, to balance these three losses. In this end-to-end teacher-student framework, the student is trained towards the teacher but also has its own learning towards the ground truth. Hence, the student network is capable of distilling the primary components of the teacher model with almost half the size of the teacher one. To boost the converge to the optimal point when training the student model, we further use the weights of the first as well as the third encoder and the second as well as the third decoders of the trained teacher network to initialise the student network.

2.2.3 Experimental Results

The Janelia dataset used in this study contains 42 3D neuron images of adult Drosophila nervous system. These image stacks were captured by optical microscopes with combinatorial multicolour stochastic labelling method, namely the Brainbow labelling technique [25]. Thirty-eight out of 42 images were taken as training data and the rest four images as testing data with the average size of $197 \times 199 \times 165$ and $262 \times 159 \times 181$, respectively. The learnable parameters of the student network (603,281) are approximately $\frac{1}{5}$ of that of the teacher network (2,868,529). We use random flipping and random rotation to enlarge the training set. During each training iteration, a patch of the size $160 \times 160 \times 8$ is randomly extracted from the training image. During the inference, each trained model is applied as a sliding window to the input image, and the generated outputs will be stitched together to produce the final segmentation results.

We compared the performance among the 3D U-Net regression baseline (UR), the teacher regression network (TR), the naive student regression network (SR) with only half the size of TR but without the guidance from TR, and our proposed distilled student regression network instructed by trained TR (DSRI). We use precision-recall curve to evaluate the results since the proportion between the foreground and background class is imbalanced. The precision and recall are defined as follows:

$$\text{Precision} = \frac{\text{TP}}{\text{TP} + \text{FP}}, \quad \text{Recall} = \frac{\text{TP}}{\text{TP} + \text{FN}} \tag{5}$$

where TP, FP, and FN denote the number of true positive, false positive, and false negative voxels, respectively. As shown in Fig. 5, there is large improvement after using the skip connection in TR compared to the baseline UR. The reason why the small-capacity SR outperforms TR is probably the model with larger architecture tends to be over-fitting. But it is noticeable that after distilling knowledge from TR, the small-size student network was further enhanced. It is expected since the complex TR contains fine features which are rarely detected in SR.

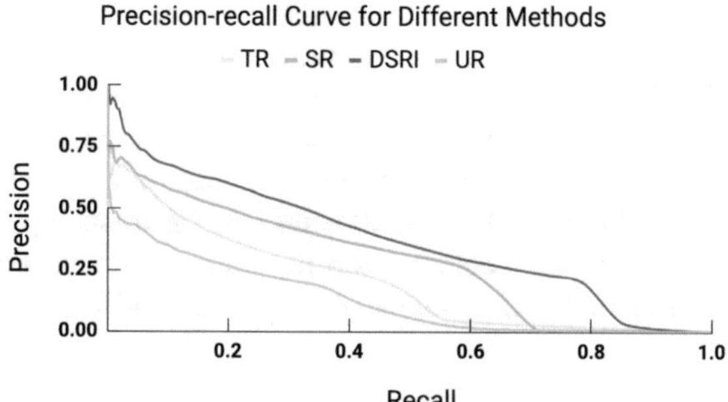

Fig. 5 Precision-recall curves of the Janelia dataset using different methods. TR, SR, DSRI, and UR represent the teacher network, student network, student network guided by the teacher one, and the baseline 3D U-Net, respectively

3 Accuracy-Enhanced Segmentation Model

Apart from efficiency, the other equivalently important aspect of neuron segmentation performance resides in the accuracy. Our later works were designed to tackle with this precise segmentation problem. The challenges of accurate segmentation reside in two aspects. On the one hand, neuron morphology is complex, varying from blob-shape soma centre to fibre-like branches. It is challenging to segment such multiscale neuronal structures. Recently, we proposed an end-to-end 3D multiscale kernel fusion network (MKF-Net) [55] and a graph-based U-Net [53] to tackle this challenge. In Sect. 3.1, we mainly introduce our MKF-Net since it is the inspiration of our later work [53]. We designed a 3D segmentation network with multiple scale convolutional operations with the aim of extracting features of different scales. The fusion of multiscale features is demonstrated to improve the accurate neuron segmentation after experiments on the Janelia dataset as firstly introduced in Sect. 2.2.3. We also applied the segmented images to the later tracing phase and experiments show that the preprocessing segmentation enhances the ability of later tracing algorithm. On the other hand, the common shortcoming of applying machine learning-related approaches on biomedical images analysis task is the lack of sufficient training data. However, the learning ability of models is correlated with the training data. If the model observes more different data, the better it would generalise to unseen data. It is not exceptional for neuron image analysis. Therefore, we proposed a method to alleviate such data shortage in training set by synthesising real-like neuron images using Generative Adversarial Neural Networks (GANs). More details will be elaborated in Sect. 3.2.

3.1 Towards Multiscale Feature Representation

In this work [55], we proposed a multiscale kernel fusion network (MKF-Net) to use spatial fusion convolutional blocks to aggregate neuronal features of various scales into the hidden representation, in order to enhance the segmentation of different structures. We will introduce this novel block in Sect. 3.1.2. The overall network follows the basic structure of the 3D version of the prevalent U-Net [7]. More details will be discussed in Sect. 3.1.1. Evaluated on the Janelia dataset from the BigNeuron project [35, 37], our proposed method outperforms the baseline U-Net. And the integration of our proposed segmentation approach into the tracing algorithm further improves the overall neuron reconstruction performance, compared to other state-of-the-art reconstruction algorithms without deep learning-based segmentation preprocessing. Quantitative results are provided in details in Sect. 3.1.3.

3.1.1 Multiscale Kernel Fusion Network

Our 3D segmentation network follows the general architecture of the U-Net [7] with a contraction path and an expansion path to achieve the end-to-end segmentation performance. Figure 6 displays the schematic diagram of the proposed network.

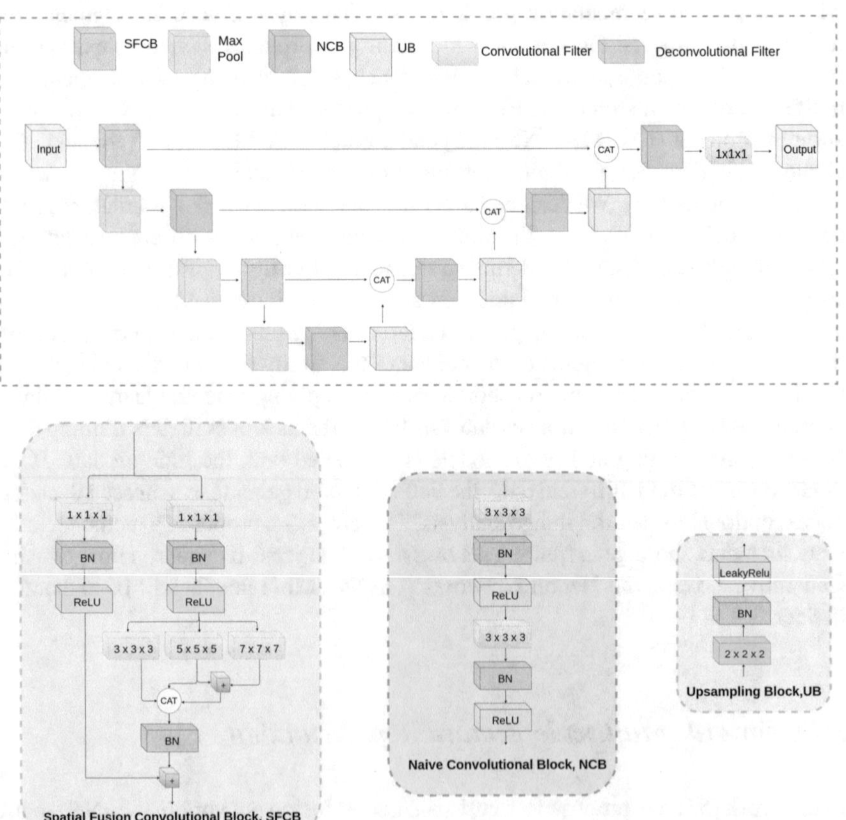

Fig. 6 Architecture of our proposed multiscale kernel fusion network

Different from U-Net, we replace the first and third convolutional blocks in U-Net, named as Naive Convolutional Block (NCB), with our proposed Spatial Fusion Convolutional Blocks (SFCBs). Inside an SFCB, a parallel of filters with different receptive fields are integrated together to extract feature maps of different scales. More details will be elaborated later in Sect. 3.1.2. The output feature maps of each layer along the contraction path contain 16, 32, 64, and 128 channels. Along the expansion path, the number of output channels after each Upsampling Block (UB) is 64, 32, and 16, respectively, from lower to higher layer. The same design goes for each NCB along the expansion path. The detailed architectures of NCB and UB are presented in the bottom part of Fig. 6. NCB is two repetitions of a sequence of convolution with kernel size $3 \times 3 \times 3$, 3D batch normalisation [14], and ReLU activation layer, while UB is just a sequence of deconvolution with the kernel size of $2 \times 2 \times 2$, 3D batch normalisation, and LeakyReLU to avoid gradient vanishing.

3.1.2 Spatial Fusion Convolutional Operation

As shown in the bottom left of Fig. 6, the input feature maps will be examined by three different convolutional kernels whose size is $3 \times 3 \times 3$, $5 \times 5 \times 5$, and $7 \times 7 \times 7$, respectively. The output from two larger kernels will be aggregated first since they contain more contextual information. Then the aggregated features are concatenated with the output from the small kernel and medium kernel together. The fusion among feature maps with different receptive field is beneficial to the detection of different scale of features. At the end of the proposed SFCB, a residual connection with the input is introduced. Since the output channel is expected to be doubled compared to the input, we employ the $1 \times 1 \times 1$ unit convolution to change the feature dimension.

3.1.3 Experimental Results

The experiments were conducted on the same Janelia dataset as introduced in Sect. 2.2.3. We split the dataset into training, validation, and testing set which contains 35, 3, and 4 3D neuron images, respectively, where the average size is $196 \times 197 \times 176$, $206 \times 219 \times 41$, and $262 \times 159 \times 181$, respectively. We use data augmentation techniques such as random flipping and random angle rotation along different axes to enlarge the training set. All the models were trained using the Adam [18] optimiser with a learning rate of 1×10^{-3} and a weight decay of 5×10^{-4}. The training loss is cross-entropy loss. The batch size is 8, and each input data is randomly extracted patch of the size $128 \times 128 \times 128$. During the inference, we apply the trained model as a sliding window to the input image and stitch the outputs together.

Table 1 presents the quantitative comparison between the proposed MKF-Net and the baseline U-Net on the task of segmenting neuron images. The ground truth is generated through the space-scale distance transform [45]. Our proposed method outperforms the baseline in all three metrics. It is because the deployed spatial fusion

Table 1 Quantitative segmentation comparison between the baseline 3D U-Net and our proposed 3D MKF-Net on four testing Janelia fly images

Segmentation method	Metric	Fly1	Fly2	Fly3	Fly4	Overall results
3D U-Net	Precision	0.58	0.32	0.26	0.35	0.38 ± 0.14
	Recall	0.74	0.90	0.51	0.25	0.60 ± 0.28
	$F1$	0.65	0.47	0.34	0.29	0.44 ± 0.16
3D MKF-Net	Precision	0.56	0.37	0.25	0.35	$\mathbf{0.38 \pm 0.13}$
	Recall	0.79	0.84	0.54	0.33	$\mathbf{0.63 \pm 0.24}$
	$F1$	0.66	0.52	0.35	0.34	$\mathbf{0.47 \pm 0.15}$

Table 2 Quantitative comparison of reconstructed points with SWC ground truth between our proposed method, Ensemble [52], TreMap [63], APP2 [58], Snake [57], Neutube [9], MOST [30], and SmartTracing [6]. The number of the successful reconstructions is shown beside the method name

Reconstruction method	Precision	Recall	$F1$
Ensemble (4/4)	0.1 ± 0.04	$\mathbf{0.99 \pm 0.03}$	0.684 ± 0.07
TreMap (4/4)	0.80 ± 0.16	0.38 ± 0.19	0.48 ± 0.14
APP2 (4/4)	0.87 ± 0.09	0.33 ± 0.28	0.42 ± 0.31
Snake (4/4)	$\mathbf{0.9 \pm 0.05}$	0.57 ± 0.22	0.68 ± 0.17
Neutube (4/4)	0.88 ± 0.10	0.52 ± 0.18	0.63 ± 0.15
MOST (4/4)	0.33 ± 0.28	0.26 ± 0.21	0.2 ± 0.13
SmartTracing (3/4)	0.75 ± 0.06	0.97 ± 0.02	0.84 ± 0.05
MKF-Net + MEIT [54] (4/4)	0.79 ± 0.24	0.95 ± 0.05	$\mathbf{0.85 \pm 0.16}$

block is able to aggregate features of various scales, thus making the hidden representation more stable to predict the segmentation output. We also combine the MKF-Net with our tracing algorithm. As shown in Table 2, our proposed framework with MKF-Net and MEIT which we will discuss in Sect. 4.3 achieves the highest $F1$-score among all state-of-the-art tracing algorithms without deep learning-based preprocessing, demonstrating the effectiveness of the proposed MKF-Net in improving the input quality. Our framework is also capable of reconstructing all the testing images while SmartTracing [6] fails one image.

3.2 Data Augmentation Through Skeleton-to-Neuron Translation

In addition to improving the model complexity, our later work [48] focuses on the variability of training data. Inspired by recent development in applying generative adversarial networks (GANs) to synthesise unavailable training data from available data [16, 60], we proposed an image-to-image synthesis network to transform the manual annotation of neuron morphology into its 3D microscopy source image. Given that there are some neuronal structures whose original optical inputs are missing in NeuroMorpho.Org [2], our proposed method could generate the neuron images for these skeletons, and the synthesised 3D neuron images could be in return beneficial to enlarge the training set for training segmentation models. We will discuss the proposed translation framework in Sect. 3.2.1. Then in Sect. 3.2.2, the learning objective of the proposed network will be elaborated in detail.

3.2.1 GAN-Based Translation Framework

The GAN-based skeleton-to-neuron translation framework is illustrated in Fig. 7. The neuron skeleton is generated from manual annotation through scale-space distance transform [23, 45, 55, 56]. For each training neuron skeleton, there is a corresponding 3D optical neuron image, which is named as real neuron image. The neuron skeleton will be fed into a generator to generate a microscopy-realistic neuron image, which is named as fake neuron image. Like 3D U-Net [7], the proposed generator possesses an encoder-decoder architecture with bypass between mirror encoder and decoder. Unlike 3D U-Net, we discard the usage of max pooling to reduce the resolution along the contraction path. Instead, we use convolutional kernels with the stride of 2 to allow more contextual information. Furthermore, inspired recent work on multiscale feature learning [46, 55], we propose a multi-resolution filtering sub-module to aggregate information of different scales. The detailed structure of the proposed sub-module is displayed in the rightmost part of Fig. 7. It consists of four different paths with scales $1 \times 1 \times 1$, $3 \times 3 \times 3$, and $5 \times 5 \times 5$ where $5 \times 5 \times 5$ is represented as two

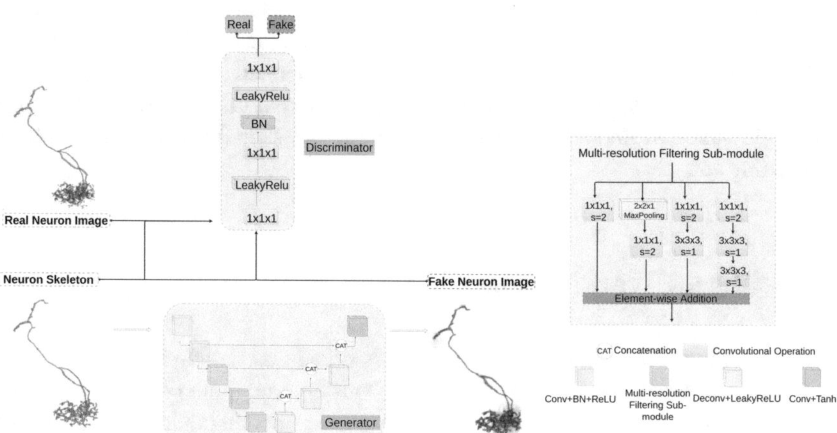

Fig. 7 Architecture of our proposed translation framework

stacks of filters of the size $3 \times 3 \times 3$. The generator aims to synthesise as much realistic as possible fake neuron images. In the design of GANs, a discriminator is there to distinguish between the real data from the fake data. In our framework, we use $1 \times 1 \times 1$ pixel GAN [26] as our discriminator. It contains a sequence of convolutional layer, leaky ReLU, convolutional layer, 3D batch normalisation (BN), leaky ReLU, and final convolutional layer to output a single value as real or fake. The input to the discriminator is a pair of neuron skeleton and a neuron image.

3.2.2 3D Skeleton-to-Neuron Synthesis

The generator and the discriminator introduced in Sect. 3.2.1 are trained iteratively with the adversarial learning objective as below [15]:

$$G^* = \arg\min_G \max_D L_{cGAN}(G, D) + \lambda L_{l1}(G) \tag{6}$$

where G, D, L_{cGAN}, and L_{l1} refer to the generator, the discriminator, the conditional GAN loss, and the $L1$ loss, respectively. The $L1$ loss controls the low-frequency synthesis while the conditional GAN loss improves the contextual-level high-frequency generation by calculating the GAN loss conditioned on the input skeleton image. This adversarial learning encourages the generator to generate towards more real-like fake microscopy images from the skeleton input.

3.2.3 Discussion

This work improves the learning ability of segmentation model through enlarging the training set. It uses a conditional generative adversarial design to generate microscopy-realistic neuron images from a skeleton annotation. To our knowledge, it is the first time when image-to-image translation technique has been used on neuron segmentation task. However, the variability of the generated fake neuron images has not been investigated. How to generate multiple different fake neuron images from one single skeleton annotation could be a challenging task in future to further enlarge the training set.

4 Intelligent Tracking Algorithms

In this section, we focus on algorithms working on neuron tracing instead of neuron segmentation elaborated in Sects. 2 and 3. Neuron tracing, also known as neuron tracking, is the successive step after the neuron image segmentation. While neuron image segmentation methods target at enhancing the neuron image quality, neuron tracing aims to extract the various neuron morphologies out of the 3D input as a tree graph where each point has a coordinate and an estimated radius. Since manual annotation requires expert knowledge and is time and labour expensive, automatic neuron tracing algorithms have been developed rapidly these years. In the following subsections, we will introduce three intelligent tracking algorithms. Specifically, Rivulet1 [22, 61] was first proposed to tackle the main challenge in automatic 3D neuron tracing, which is with the low image quality and the complex neuronal structures. We will explain the main idea of this approach in Sect. 4.1. Later on, Rivulet2 [24] was designed to deal with the disadvantages in Rivulet1 and is capable of better performance. More details will be elaborated in Sect. 4.2. Lastly, MEIT [54] came up as to solve the large computational overhead in large-scale neuron image tracking. We will discuss more in Sect. 4.3.

4.1 *Rivulet1*

To alleviate the effect of broken branches and gaps during the tracing, we proposed to highlight the centreline skeleton of neuronal arborisation in Rivulet1 [22, 61] by applying the greyscale weighted distance transform (GWDT) method used in APP2 [58] on the segmented neuron images. After GWDT, voxels near the centrelines are assigned higher intensity while voxels near the boundary are darker. To obtain smooth neuronal curves, a variant of fast-marching (FM) algorithm [43], namely multi-stencils fast-marching (MSFM) [11], is applied on the distance transform results to get estimation of the geodesic distance with sub-voxel precision. More details will be discussed in Sect. 4.1.1. After MSFM, a time-crossing map will be generated. The voxels with larger map value are voxels further away from the centreline. Hence, a gradient-based iterative back-tracking algorithm is employed to track the neuronal branch from the furthest point on the time-crossing map. We will elaborate more on this back-tracking algorithm in Sect. 4.1.2. After a potential branch is produced, a confidence score is calculated to determine whether it is a real neuronal structure or a tracing error. The criteria about how to discard and merge a traced branch will be discussed in Sect. 4.1.3. In the end, if the traced branches take up over a specific ratio of the overall segmented foreground, the tracing will stop.

4.1.1 Multi-stencils Fast Marching

In our proposed tracing method, a time-crossing map is required to do further back-tracking. The fast-marching (FM) algorithm [43] is commonly used in neuron reconstruction [3, 50, 58] to compute such time-travelling map. It is able to progressively detect the neuron regions from a starting point, which is usually the soma centre point. It starts the marching process by solving the Eikonal equation [1, 49] formulated as below:

$$|\nabla T|F = 1, \quad T(\Gamma_0) = 0 \tag{7}$$

where the initial level set Γ_0 is set to have the zero travel time since it is the starting point. In our proposed method, the speed map F is defined based on the GWDT distance map $F = \frac{\text{GWDT}(B)}{\text{GWDT}_{\max}}^4$ where B is the segmented binary neuron image and $GWDT_{\max}$ is the maximum distance transform value. Instead of following the solution by the FM method, we use the multi-stencils fast-marching (MSFM) algorithm [11] to obtain a more accurate estimation to Eq. (7) in 3D space. The time-crossing map T is therefore computed along a set of different stencils within each grid point's neighbourhood. Let U_1, U_2, U_3 define the directional derivatives for three unit vectors v_1, v_2, v_3, respectively, and α, β, γ be the three rotating angles between the stencils and the unit vectors. The three different neighbourhoods covered by the rotating stencils are denoted as T_1, T_2, T_3 among the time-crossing map. Then, the relationship between the directional derivatives U and the speed map F is as follows:

$$U^T \left(RR^T\right)^{-1} U = \tfrac{1}{F^2(x)},\qquad RR^T = \begin{pmatrix} 1 & \cos\alpha & \cos\gamma \\ \cos\alpha & 1 & \cos\beta \\ \cos\gamma & \cos\beta & 1 \end{pmatrix} \tag{8}$$

where $RR^T = \left(RR^T\right)^{-1} = 1$ when the rotating angles are all $\frac{\pi}{2}$.

If $T(x)$ is larger than its neighbourhood, it can be approximated as follows:

$$\sum_{t=1}^{3} g_t(h)\left(a_t T^2(x) + b_t T(x) + c_t\right) = \frac{1}{F^2(x)} \tag{9}$$

where the three coefficients a_t, b_t, c_t are defined as follows:

$$\left[\, a_t \; b_t \; c_t \,\right] = \left[\, 1 \; -2T_t \; T_t^2 \,\right], t = 1, 2, 3 \tag{10}$$

Otherwise, $T(x)$ is defined as follows:

$$\min\left(T_t + \frac{\|x - x_t\|}{F(x)}\right), t = 1, 2, 3 \tag{11}$$

The point with the minimum time-crossing map value resides near the soma centre of the neuron image. It can be detected using soma detection algorithms [62] or specified manually.

4.1.2 Gradient-Based Iterative Back-Tracking

Based on the time-crossing map T, for each tracing iteration i, the tracking of neuronal structures starts from the furthest point p^i_f which has the largest T value among all the untraced points. All the points along the tracked path from p^i_f back to the source point p_s will be marked as traced once this path is verified as neuronal branch. The tracking continues from the furthest point based on its gradient. Specifically, from a current point p_i, the gradient of it would be calculated, and then the next point p_{i+1} to trace is computed through the classical 4-th Runge–Kutta (RK4) algorithm which is formulated as follows:

$$\begin{cases} p_{i+1} = p_i + \frac{h}{6}\left(k_1 + 2k_2 + 2k_3 + k_4\right) \\ k_1 = f\left(p_i\right) \\ k_2 = f\left(p_i + \frac{h}{2}k_1\right) \\ k_3 = f\left(p_i + \frac{h}{2}k_2\right) \\ k_4 = f\left(p_i + hk_3\right) \end{cases} \tag{12}$$

where $f(\cdot)$ is the normalised 3D interpolation of the gradient $\nabla T\ (p_i)$ at point p_i. The step size h is set to 1 empirically. The back-tracking design in our proposed algorithm is not firstly seen [50]. The difference between our proposed one and the previous one is that ours only computes the time-crossing map once. That is, each point will be only visited once which saves a large amount of computational resources. The tracing stops when (1) it reaches the soma area; (2) it steps on background for a certain number of iterations; (3) it steps outside the image boundary; (4) it keeps trapped in the same point for a certain number of iterations; (5) the time-crossing map value for the current point is less than or equal to zero (i.e. the tracing steps on traced branch). For a verified branch, we compute the radius r for each point along the branch using the sphere growing method [36] from the greyscale input image. Then we set the T value for all the area covered by the sphere of the size $\frac{4}{3}\pi r^3$ as -1 corresponding to the fifth rule mentioned before.

4.1.3 Branch Removal and Merging

To decide whether a branch should be kept or not, we use a simple confidence score $C = \sum_{i=0}^{l} B_i/l$ where B_i is 1 when the traced point is on the foreground image otherwise 0, inspired by SmartTracing [6]. If the traced branch starts from a noisy point, its confidence score would probably tend to be very small. Therefore, we check if the confidence score for a newly visited branch is lower than a specific value, i.e. 50%, then we can discard the path traced so far. We also dump a branch if the total number of points along it is less than eight. When we are making decision about whether to add a new branch into the neuron trunk or not, we check the Euclidean distance D between the endpoints p_n of the new branch and the closest point $p_{\min}$ on the trunk. The point is merged if $D(p_n, p_{\min}) < R \times (r_n + 3)$ or $D(p_n, p_{\min}) < R \times (r_{\min} + 3)$. R is a wiring threshold which depends on the image quality. The tracing stops when the traced region covers a specific coverage ratio of the overall foreground image. The ratio is set as 98% empirically. The coverage ratio parameter ensures that our proposed algorithm will not under-trace the neuronal structures.

4.1.4 Discussion

Compared to previous methods [36, 50, 58], our proposed tracing algorithm only requires the fast-marching computation once. Also, the proposed confidence score controls the filtering of false branches from the noise points. In conclusion, our proposed algorithm achieves better performance with less computational complexity. However, the dependency on some manually specified parameters hinders the generalisation ability to images of various quality. In next Sect. 4.2, we introduce the improved version of Rivulet1, named as Rivulet2 to see how Rivulet2 gets rid of these parameters to further enhance the performance of the tracing algorithm.

4.2 Rivulet2

In Rivulet1, a simple confidence score is used to determine whether the traced branch belongs to neuronal structures or not. One of the disadvantages of this score is that it cannot stop the tracing early if the branch is a fake structure. Another shortcoming of this post confidence score is it cannot distinguish noisy part and the real fibre part if the branch steps on neuronal fibres after several steps on noisy points. To deal with these disadvantages, our later work Rivulet2 [24] proposed an online confidence score to compute the liability of a traced branch in real time. We will discuss more details in Sect. 4.2.1. In addition, we propose a new way to merge branches to avoid the dependency on the wiring threshold used in Rivulet1. More details will be elaborated in Sect. 4.2.2.

4.2.1 Robust Stopping Criteria

Instead of checking the confidence score when the tracing of one branch finishes, in Rivulet2, an online confidence score is computed during each tracing step and the tracing could stop early at any time once the online confidence score is smaller than a fixed value, which is 0.2 in our case. Different to the confidence score defined in Sect. 4.1.3, the updated online confidence score is formulated as follows:

$$C = \sum_{i=0}^{l} B_i / l + 1 \tag{13}$$

where l represents the total number of points which have been visited. The $+1$ term here is to make sure the score starts from 0.5. If the branch is traced from a noise point, the online confidence score would decrease rapidly, once the score tends to be lower than 0.2, the tracing could stop, and the branch would be discarded. Apart from this naive situation, a more challenging case is when the tracing starts from some noises but soon it steps on real neuronal fibres. In this case, the confidence score will decrease for a small time interval and increase soon when they touch the neuronal structure. And it is expected to discard those noises while keeping the later real neuronal structures. To tackle this corner case, we use two exponential moving average (EMA) measures with the window size of 4 and 10, respectively. The EMA is commonly used in the financial analysis to detect such corner case. EMA at time t is calculated based on its previous values which is defined as follows:

$$E_t^W = E_{t-1}^W + \frac{2 \times \left(P(c(t), B(x)) - E_{t-1}^W\right)}{W+1} \tag{14}$$

where W is the window size. If the lowest value of the online confidence score appears between the two crossing points of the short-term EMA E_t^4 and the long-term EMA E_t^{10}, then we discard all the points traced towards the point with the smallest confidence score and keep all the points after.

Together the 0.2 threshold bottom boundary with the EMA measures, the new online confidence score is able to skip noises from gaps. Apart from that, there might be gaps between two irrelevant neuron structures. For example, Brainbow [10] images could contain several single neurons. Therefore, to avoid tracing of unrelated neuronal structures, we propose to use a continuous gap check $G(t)$ during the tracing. The tracing stops when $G(t) > 8 \times R(c(t))$ where $c(t)$ is the traced branch at step t and $R(c(t))$ is the average estimated radius of all the points along $c(t)$.

4.2.2 Branch Merging and Postprocessing Pruning

In Rivulet1 [22, 61], one of the stopping criteria is when the tracing steps on previously traced region. Then as introduced in Sect. 4.1.3, a wiring threshold is used to check whether to conduct the merging process or not. To get rid of this ill-posed parameter, in Rivulet2 [24], the tracing continues even though it touches visited area. But when it starts stepping on traced region, it will look for the closest point $p_{\min}$ satisfying either $\| p_i - p_{\min} \| < R_{p_i}$ or $\| p_i - p_{\min} \| < R_{p_{\min}}$. Once it finds such a point, the branch will be merged.

Once all the candidate branches have been traced, the largest connected graph will be kept while other small structures will be dumped, since those separate small structures are mostly background noises or irrelevant structures which does not belong to the same neuron cell. If dendrites spines are not required during the reconstruction, curvilinear structures of length shorter than 4 could also be discarded.

4.2.3 Discussion

Rivulet2 optimises the confidence score and the wiring threshold to improve the overall performance with less dependency on human intervention compared to Rivulet1. The online confidence score could prevent the redundant time wasted on tracing noisy branches, and the intelligent branch cut of noisy part avoids both under-fitting when discarding the whole structure and over-fitting when including the noisy points. The merging process does not depend on the wiring threshold which is error prone to noises. Instead, the tracing will continue until it finds a real closest point. Therefore, Rivulet2 achieves a more accurate tracing of the overall neuron structures compared to previous methods. However, for both Rivulet1 and Rivulet2, the computation of the time-crossing map is conducted on the whole input image. It is not efficient especially when the input 3D neuron image is of large-scale size. To alleviate such memory and computational burden, we proposed a block-wise tracing framework MEIT [54] which is the last case study in this chapter.

4.3 MEIT

To deal with the tracing efficiency challenge, our later work MEIT [54], which stands for Memory (and Time) Efficient Image Tracing, applies a computation-friendly block-wise tracing paradigm into the Rivulet2 algorithm. Instead of tracing the whole image at once, inspired by UltraTracer [38, 64], we start from an initial small block and expand towards the outside of this block to complete the tracing. The difference between UltraTracer and our method is that we use fast marching to compute the exact four endpoints closest to the four boundary faces. The main computational costs in computing the fast-marching time-crossing map for a whole image then would be reduced to a small block each iteration. In Sect. 4.3.1, we define how the initial block is generated. We then discuss the main block-wise tracing paradigm in Sect. 4.3.2. Such block-wise tracing design helps save both memory and computational time while achieving competitive tracing accuracy performance. Detailed experiment results are included in Sect. 4.3.3.

4.3.1 Initial Block Definition

We decide to start from the soma centre area which is expected to contain the maximum distance transform value among the entire image. Because whether the detection of the soma centre is accurate would not affect too much about our later tracing as long as we start from the similar area. To save the computational cost when computing the distance transform map for the whole image with the size of $W \times H \times D$ where W, H, and D denote the width, height, and depth, respectively, we firstly downsample the image I by $\frac{1}{4}$ into I'. We then perform the 3D distance transform technique on the binary shrank image B' after segmentation to obtain the point with the maximum value. A block of size $\text{crop}_x \times \text{crop}_y \times D$ centred at this point is generated as the initial block bk_0, and this point is the source point $\text{SP}(\text{bk}_0)$ from which the first iteration of tracing is conducted. Empirically, we set the width crop_x and the height crop_y of the block bk_0 as both 100.

4.3.2 Block-Wise Large-Scale Neuron Tracing Paradigm

Rather than performing the fast-marching algorithm on the whole binary image B like Rivulet2, we proposed to compute the time-crossing map block by block from the initial block. Once we have the initial block, we perform tracing using Rivulet2 or any other tracing algorithms inside this small region with the source point SP(bk_0) as the initial zero level-set. As shown in the top part of Fig. 8, there are two endpoints touching the boundary faces of the initial block bk_0 which we highlight them in yellow square. The tracing continues based on such endpoints. Based on their time-crossing map values, the endpoints are pushed into a source point queue Q with the rule of large first in and small first out. For boundary faces without endpoints generated, we check whether the adjacent block of the same size as bk_0 contains enough foreground points (tracing ability threshold α). If the foreground ratio exceeds α, then the point closest to this boundary face within bk_0 is pushed into Q with the time-crossing map manually set as the maximum time-crossing map value among the queue Q plus 1. Then, the tracing continues by popping the endpoint with the smallest time-crossing map value out. Such point is assigned as the source point of the adjacent block for the fast-marching algorithm to start in order to maintain the connectivity. As illustrated in Fig. 8, the endpoint on the left face of bk_0 has smaller time-crossing map value, therefore, the next block to trace is the one left to bk_0. The same process is repeated for this new block bk_1. However, the new endpoints generated during this iteration would be assigned the time-crossing map value as

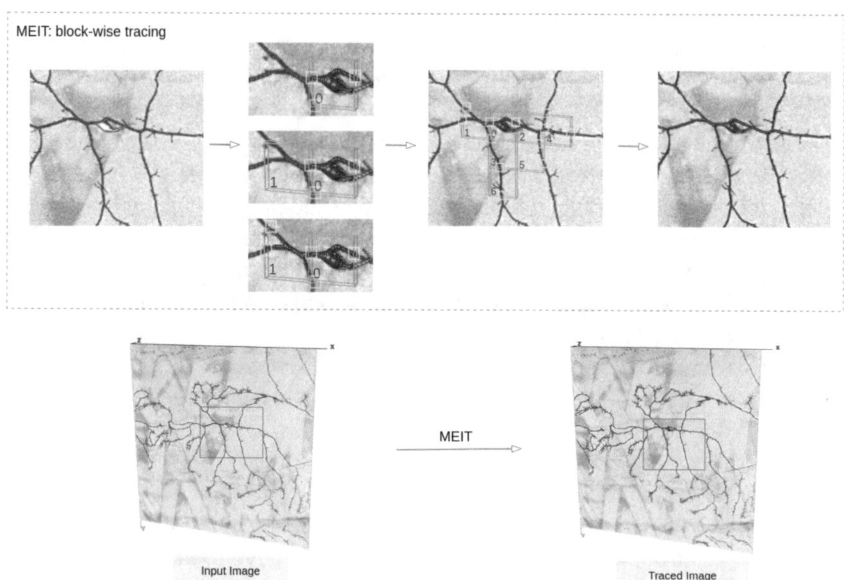

Fig. 8 Illustration of how MEIT works to trace a neuron image of size 2048 × 2048 × 21 efficiently

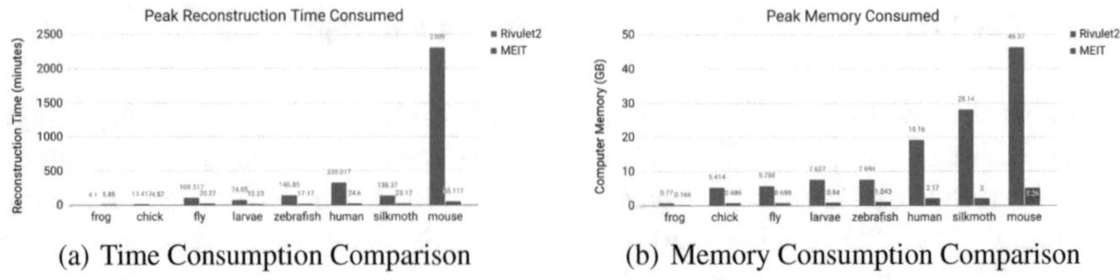

(a) Time Consumption Comparison (b) Memory Consumption Comparison

Fig. 9 Time and memory consumption comparison between our proposed method MEIT and the state-of-the-art Rivulet2

$T_{\text{global}}(\text{end point}) = T_{\text{global}}(\text{bk}_1) + T_{\text{local}}(\text{end point}) - T_{\text{local}}(\text{SP}(\text{bk}_1))$. That is, when we push endpoints into Q, we only record its global time-crossing map value, and it is estimated based on the accumulation of previous tracing time-crossing map values. Following this tracing pattern, the whole neuron image would be traced adaptively. The tracing stops when 0.98 of the whole foreground part has been traced.

4.3.3 Experimental Results

The evaluation was conducted on the 156 3D neuron images from the BigNeuron project [35, 37] with eight different species including fruitfly larvae (12), fly (79), zebrafish (13), silkmoth (7), frog (1), mouse (29), chick (8), and human (7). Each neuron image is accompanied with an expert-labelled annotation. The total number of voxels varies from 632,520 to 629,145,600.

We compared the reconstruction time and memory usage when using the proposed MEIT algorithm and the state-of-the-art Rivulet2 method. The results are presented in Fig. 9. Note that MEIT is a framework where the inner tracing algorithm can be replaced by any other solid tracing method. Figure 9a displays the time consumption comparison. For all the species except the frog, our proposed method outperforms the Rivulet2 by a large margin. Since MEIT traces the image block by block while Rivulet2 computes the time-crossing map for the whole image, MEIT is more efficient when the image is larger. Figure 9b presents the consumed memory comparison. Since MEIT only loads a small block of the entire image each iteration, the memory required is way less than that used in Rivulet2.

We also compared the reconstruction accuracy between these two methods to prove that our proposed method achieves the competitive reconstruction accuracy as the state-of-the-art Rivulet2. The quantitative results are presented in Table. 3. It can be observed that MEIT outperforms Rivulet2 regarding the $F1$-score in the fruitfly larvae, the fly, the zebrafish, the silkmoth, and the frog subsets. The reason is that MEIT utilises a block-wise tracing pattern which captures more local information when tracing. The higher recall of MEIT is because MEIT avoids the accumulation of errors introduced by fast marching through efficient block traceability determination. However, the less attention on the entire image area in MEIT results in less precision in some cases compared to Rivulet2.

Table 3 Quantitative comparison between Rivulet2 and MEIT. The number beside the dataset name is the number of 3D images in each dataset. The number of the successful reconstructions is shown beside the method name

	Precision	Recall	$F1$
Rivulet2 (12/12)	**0.617 ± 0.147**	0.902 ± 0.105	0.722 ± 0.117
MEIT (12/12)	0.599 ± 0.127	**0.983 ± 0.026**	**0.736 ± 0.100**
fly 79			
Rivulet2 (79/79)	**0.925 ± 0.105**	0.908 ± 0.076	0.912 ± 0.084
MEIT (79/79)	0.911 ± 0.102	**0.987 ± 0.023**	**0.944 ± 0.065**
zebrafish 13			
Rivulet2 (13/13)	0.587 ± 0.176	0.911 ± 0.052	0.698 ± 0.147
MEIT (13/13)	**0.588 ± 0.137**	**0.983 ± 0.009**	**0.725 ± 0.118**
silkmoth 7			
Rivulet2 (7/7)	**0.877 ± 0.078**	0.916 ± 0.119	0.890 ± 0.080
MEIT (7/7)	0.876 ± 0.039	**0.989 ± 0.013**	**0.929 ± 0.023**
frog 1			
Rivulet2 (1/1)	0.670 ± 0.000	0.970 ± 0.000	0.790 ± 0.000
MEIT (1/1)	**0.810±0.000**	**1.000 ± 0.000**	**0.890 ± 0.000**
mouse 29			
Rivulet2 (28/29)	**0.607 ± 0.169**	0.889 ± 0.066	**0.706 ± 0.141**
MEIT (29/29)	0.480 ± 0.186	**0.981 ± 0.020**	0.624 ± 0.166
chick 8			
Rivulet2 (8/8)	**0.414 ± 0.204**	0.781 ± 0.124	**0.525 ± 0.208**
MEIT (8/8)	0.333 ± 0.172	**0.935 ± 0.048**	0.470 ± 0.194
human 7			
Rivulet2 (7/7)	**0.824 ± 0.108**	0.891 ± 0.094	**0.851 ± 0.079**
MEIT (7/7)	0.707 ± 0.193	**0.966 ± 0.032**	0.804 ± 0.133

5 Discussion and Future Work

On the one hand, the combination of automatic segmentation and intelligent tracking saves human experts from tedious and time-consuming labour tasks and enables the fast and accurate collection of digital neuron structures thus speeding up the analysis of neuron-related problems. However, for now, segmentation and tracking are two separate stages for neuron reconstruction. How to group these two stages as an end-to-end pipeline could be a prospective direction in the future. On the other hand, the proposed deep learning-based segmentation methods improve the neuron image quality by a great deal compared to that with only binary thresholding. Also, the thresholding value is hard to unify for different neuron images, and it always relies on expert decision to choose a liable one. However, deep learning-based methods rely on training data to learn the features, and it is possible that some features would never appear in training set, and in this situation, deep learning-based approaches would not perform well for a neuron image with unseen features. With the recently rising deep active learning [5], coupling powerful learning ability of deep networks with human experts occasional guidance could be one interesting direction as human–AI interaction and mutual progress. Apart from that, the explainability of the decision made by AI-based models could hinder the practical deployment in industry. How to make deep models more interpretable and explainable could also be one future direction of deep learning-based methods.

6 Conclusion

In this chapter, we have presented a general review of our recent works on AI-enhanced 3D biomedical data analytics for neuronal structure reconstruction, with focus on neuron segmentation and neuron tracking for 3D optical microscopy images. For neuron segmentation, we presented four different methods which can be divided into two categories. One group is to deal with the segmentation efficiency when using deep learning-based model by compressing the input 3D data or compressing the deployment model. Compressing the 3D data into 2D projection can enable the usage of 2D model which saves lots of computational costs. However, the reduction of input data could result in loss of information. Hence, we design the later model compression method to keep the input information. The other group is to improve the segmentation accuracy by designing multiscale feature aggregation mechanism or enlarging the dataset using GAN-based adversarial learning techniques. Using different scales of feature to predict the final segmentation can improve the capturing ability of both local and global information and thus improving the final segmentation result, while enlarging the dataset solves the problem from the other side. The latter one provides more training data to the model so that the model can learn features of variability and thus improving the generalisation ability to unseen data. For neuron tracing, we described three different intelligent automatic approaches. The first approach employs multi-stencil fast marching to track iteratively from the furthest points. Based on this approach, the second method designs a better stopping criteria to get rid of simple parameters which could hinder the deployment to different data sets. The last approach is more like a general framework where the first two methods can be used locally. It utilises a block-wise tracing paradigm to save the computational time and memory for large-scale neuron image tracing. To the end, the performance of artificial intelligence-based methods depends on the model complexity and data complexity. The rapid development of artificial intelligence boosts the proposal of different kinds of model architectures targeting at different aspects of neuron reconstruction tasks. Various ways to produce and utilise the neuron image data also contribute to the robustness of proposed models. With more and more automatic and solid 3D neuron reconstruction methods coming into existence, scientists thus can focus more on the analysis of neuron morphology rather than spending lots of time on tedious reconstruction task, which can further enhance the research on brain science by a great deal.

References

1. Adalsteinsson, D., Sethian, J.A.: A fast level set method for propagating interfaces. J. Comput. Phys. **118**(2), 269–277 (1995)
2. Ascoli, G.A., Donohue, D.E., Halavi, M.: Neuromorpho. org: a central resource for neuronal morphologies. J. Neurosci. **27**(35), 9247–9251 (2007)
3. Basu, S., Racoceanu, D.: Reconstructing neuronal morphology from microscopy stacks using fast marching. In: Proc. ICIP., pp. 3597–3601. IEEE (2014)
4. Brown, K.M., Barrionuevo, G., Canty, A.J., De Paola, V., Hirsch, J.A., Jefferis, G.S., Lu, J., Snippe, M., Sugihara, I., Ascoli, G.A.: The DIADEM data sets: representative light microscopy images of neuronal morphology to advance automation of digital reconstructions. Neuroinformatics **9**(2–3), 143–157 (2011)
5. Budd, S., Robinson, E.C., Kainz, B.: A survey on active learning and human-in-the-loop deep learning for medical image analysis. arXiv preprint arXiv:1910.02923 (2019)
6. Chen, H., Xiao, H., Liu, T., Peng, H.: SmartTracing: self-learning-based neuron reconstruction. Brain informatics **2**(3), 135–144 (2015)
7. Çiçek, Ö., Abdulkadir, A., Lienkamp, S.S., Brox, T., Ronneberger, O.: 3D U-Net: learning dense volumetric segmentation from sparse annotation. In: Proc. MICCAI., pp. 424–432. Springer (2016)
8. Clevert, D.A., Unterthiner, T., Hochreiter, S.: Fast and accurate deep network learning by exponential linear units (elus). arXiv preprint arXiv:1511.07289 (2015)
9. Feng, L., Zhao, T., Kim, J.: neutube 1.0: a new design for efficient neuron reconstruction software based on the SWC format. eNeuro **2**(1) (2015)
10. Hampel, S., Chung, P., McKellar, C.E., Hall, D., Looger, L.L., Simpson, J.H.: Drosophila brainbow: a recombinase-based fluorescence labeling technique to subdivide neural expression patterns. Nature methods **8**(3), 253–259 (2011)
11. Hassouna, M.S., Farag, A.A.: Multistencils fast marching methods: A highly accurate solution to the eikonal equation on cartesian domains. IEEE Trans. Pattern Anal. Mach. Intell. **29**(9), 1563–1574 (2007)
12. He, K., Zhang, X., Ren, S., Sun, J.: Deep residual learning for image recognition. In: Proc. CVPR., pp. 770–778 (2016)
13. Hinton, G., Vinyals, O., Dean, J.: Distilling the knowledge in a neural network. arXiv preprint arXiv:1503.02531 (2015)
14. Ioffe, S., Szegedy, C.: Batch normalization: Accelerating deep network training by reducing internal covariate shift. arXiv preprint arXiv:1502.03167 (2015)
15. Isola, P., Zhu, J.Y., Zhou, T., Efros, A.A.: Image-to-image translation with conditional adversarial networks. In: Proc. CVPR., pp. 1125–1134 (2017)
16. Jin, D., Xu, Z., Tang, Y., Harrison, A.P., Mollura, D.J.: CT-realistic lung nodule simulation from 3D conditional generative adversarial networks for robust lung segmentation. In: Proc. MICCAI., pp. 732–740. Springer (2018)
17. Kandel, E.R., Schwartz, J.H., Jessell, T.M., Siegelbaum, S., Hudspeth, A.J., Mack, S.: Principles of neural science, vol. 4. McGraw-hill New York (2000)
18. Kingma, D.P., Ba, J.: Adam: A method for stochastic optimization. arXiv preprint arXiv:1412.6980 (2014)
19. Kong, B., Sun, S., Wang, X., Song, Q., Zhang, S.: Invasive cancer detection utilizing compressed convolutional neural network and transfer learning. In: Proc. MICCAI., pp. 156–164. Springer (2018)
20. Krizhevsky, A., Sutskever, I., Hinton, G.E.: Imagenet classification with deep convolutional neural networks. Advances in neural information processing systems **25**, 1097–1105 (2012)
21. Li, R., Zeng, T., Peng, H., Ji, S.: Deep learning segmentation of optical microscopy images improves 3-D neuron reconstruction. IEEE Trans. Med. Imag. **36**(7), 1533–1541 (2017)
22. Liu, S., Zhang, D., Liu, S., Feng, D., Peng, H., Cai, W.: Rivulet: 3D neuron morphology tracing with iterative back-tracking. Neuroinformatics **14**(4), 387–401 (2016)

23. Liu, S., Zhang, D., Song, Y., Peng, H., Cai, W.: Triple-crossing 2.5 D convolutional neural network for detecting neuronal arbours in 3D microscopic images. In: Proc. MLMI. Workshop, pp. 185–193. Springer (2017)
24. Liu, S., Zhang, D., Song, Y., Peng, H., Cai, W.: Automated 3-D neuron tracing with precise branch erasing and confidence controlled back tracking. IEEE Trans. Med. Imag. **37**(11), 2441–2452 (2018)
25. Livet, J., Weissman, T.A., Kang, H., Draft, R.W., Lu, J., Bennis, R.A., Sanes, J.R., Lichtman, J.W.: Transgenic strategies for combinatorial expression of fluorescent proteins in the nervous system. Nature **450**(7166), 56–62 (2007)
26. Makhzani, A., Frey, B.J.: Pixelgan autoencoders. In: Proc. NeurIPS., pp. 1975–1985 (2017)
27. McNally, J.G., Karpova, T., Cooper, J., Conchello, J.A.: Three-dimensional imaging by deconvolution microscopy. Methods **19**(3), 373–385 (1999)
28. Meijering, E.: Neuron tracing in perspective. Cytometry Part A **77**(7), 693–704 (2010)
29. Milletari, F., Navab, N., Ahmadi, S.: V-Net: Fully convolutional neural networks for volumetric medical image segmentation. In: Proc. 3DV., pp. 565–571. IEEE (2016)
30. Ming, X., Li, A., Wu, J., Yan, C., Ding, W., Gong, H., Zeng, S., Liu, Q.: Rapid reconstruction of 3D neuronal morphology from light microscopy images with augmented rayburst sampling. PloS one **8**(12), e84,557 (2013)
31. Mukherjee, A., Stepanyants, A.: Automated reconstruction of neural trees using front re-initialization. In: SPIE Med. Imag., vol. 8314, p. 83141I. International Society for Optics and Photonics (2012)
32. Mukherjee, S., Condron, B., Acton, S.T.: Tubularity flow field—a technique for automatic neuron segmentation. IEEE Trans. Image Process. **24**(1), 374–389 (2014)
33. Nicholls, J.G., Martin, A.R., Wallace, B.G., Fuchs, P.A.: From neuron to brain, vol. 271. Sinauer Associates Sunderland, MA (2001)
34. Pawley, J.: Handbook of biological confocal microscopy, vol. 236. Springer Science & Business Media (2006)
35. Peng, H., Hawrylycz, M., Roskams, J., Hill, S., Spruston, N., Meijering, E., Ascoli, G.A.: Bigneuron: large-scale 3D neuron reconstruction from optical microscopy images. Neuron **87**(2), 252–256 (2015)
36. Peng, H., Long, F., Myers, G.: Automatic 3D neuron tracing using all-path pruning. Bioinformatics **27**(13), i239–i247 (2011)
37. Peng, H., Meijering, E., Ascoli, G.A.: From diadem to bigneuron (2015)
38. Peng, H., Zhou, Z., Meijering, E., Zhao, T., Ascoli, G.A., Hawrylycz, M.: Automatic tracing of ultra-volumes of neuronal images. Nature methods **14**(4), 332–333 (2017)
39. Purves, D., Cabeza, R., Huettel, S.A., LaBar, K.S., Platt, M.L., Woldorff, M.G., Brannon, E.M.: Cognitive neuroscience. Sunderland: Sinauer Associates, Inc (2008)
40. Roth, H.R., Lu, L., Liu, J., Yao, J., Seff, A., Cherry, K., Kim, L., Summers, R.M.: Improving computer-aided detection using convolutional neural networks and random view aggregation. IEEE Trans. Med. Imag. **35**(5), 1170–1181 (2015)
41. Santamaría-Pang, A., Hernandez-Herrera, P., Papadakis, M., Saggau, P., Kakadiaris, I.A.: Automatic morphological reconstruction of neurons from multiphoton and confocal microscopy images using 3D tubular models. Neuroinformatics **13**(3), 297–320 (2015)
42. Senft, S.L.: A brief history of neuronal reconstruction. Neuroinformatics **9**(2-3), 119–128 (2011)
43. Sethian, J.A.: Level set methods and fast marching methods: evolving interfaces in computational geometry, fluid mechanics, computer vision, and materials science, vol. 3. Cambridge university press (1999)
44. Sintorn, I.M., Bischof, L., Jackway, P., Haggarty, S., Buckley, M.: Gradient based intensity normalization. J. Microsc. **240**(3), 249–258 (2010)
45. Sironi, A., Türetken, E., Lepetit, V., Fua, P.: Multiscale centerline detection. IEEE Trans. Pattern Anal. Mach. Intell. **38**(7), 1327–1341 (2015)
46. Szegedy, C., Vanhoucke, V., Ioffe, S., Shlens, J., Wojna, Z.: Rethinking the inception architecture for computer vision. In: Proc. CVPR., pp. 2818–2826 (2016)

47. Tang, Z., Zhang, D., Liu, S., Song, Y., Peng, H., Cai, W.: Automatic 3D single neuron reconstruction with exhaustive tracing. In: Proc. ICCV. Workshop, pp. 126–133 (2017)
48. Tang, Z., Zhang, D., Song, Y., Wang, H., Liu, D., Zhang, C., Liu, S., Peng, H., Cai, W.: 3D conditional adversarial learning for synthesizing microscopic neuron image using skeleton-to-neuron translation. In: Proc. ISBI., pp. 1775–1779. IEEE (2020)
49. Tsitsiklis, J.N.: Efficient algorithms for globally optimal trajectories. IEEE Trans. Autom. Control. **40**(9), 1528–1538 (1995)
50. Van Uitert, R., Bitter, I.: Subvoxel precise skeletons of volumetric data based on fast marching methods. Medical physics **34**(2), 627–638 (2007)
51. Wallén, P., Carlsson, K., Liljeborg, A., Grillner, S.: Three-dimensional reconstruction of neurons in the lamprey spinal cord in whole-mount, using a confocal laser scanning microscope. J. Neurosci. Methods **24**(2), 91–100 (1988)
52. Wang, C.W., Lee, Y.C., Pradana, H., Zhou, Z., Peng, H.: Ensemble neuron tracer for 3D neuron reconstruction. Neuroinformatics **15**(2), 185–198 (2017)
53. Wang, H., Song, Y., Zhang, C., Yu, J., Liu, S., Peng, H., Cai, W.: Single neuron segmentation using graph-based global reasoning with auxiliary skeleton loss from 3D optical microscope images. ISBI (2021)
54. Wang, H., Zhang, D., Song, Y., Liu, S., Gao, R., Peng, H., Cai, W.: Memory and time efficient 3D neuron morphology tracing in large-scale images. In: Proc. DICTA., pp. 1–8. IEEE (2018)
55. Wang, H., Zhang, D., Song, Y., Liu, S., Huang, H., Chen, M., Peng, H., Cai, W.: Multiscale kernels for enhanced U-shaped network to improve 3D neuron tracing. In: Proc. CVPR. Workshop, pp. 1105–1113 (2019)
56. Wang, H., Zhang, D., Song, Y., Liu, S., Wang, Y., Feng, D., Peng, H., Cai, W.: Segmenting neuronal structure in 3D optical microscope images via knowledge distillation with teacher-student network. In: Proc. ISBI., pp. 228–231. IEEE (2019)
57. Wang, Y., Narayanaswamy, A., Tsai, C.L., Roysam, B.: A broadly applicable 3-D neuron tracing method based on open-curve snake. Neuroinformatics **9**(2-3), 193–217 (2011)
58. Xiao, H., Peng, H.: App2: automatic tracing of 3D neuron morphology based on hierarchical pruning of a gray-weighted image distance-tree. Bioinformatics **29**(11), 1448–1454 (2013)
59. Yang, J., Gonzalez-Bellido, P.T., Peng, H.: A distance-field based automatic neuron tracing method. BMC bioinformatics **14**(1), 1–11 (2013)
60. Yang, J., Liu, S., Grbic, S., Setio, A.A.A., Xu, Z., Gibson, E., Chabin, G., Georgescu, B., Laine, A.F., Comaniciu, D.: Class-aware adversarial lung nodule synthesis in CT images. In: Proc. ISBI., pp. 1348–1352. IEEE (2019)
61. Zhang, D., Liu, S., Liu, S., Feng, D., Peng, H., Cai, W.: Reconstruction of 3D neuron morphology using rivulet back-tracking. In: Proc. ISBI., pp. 598–601. IEEE (2016)
62. Zhang, D., Liu, S., Song, Y., Feng, D., Peng, H., Cai, W.: Automated 3D soma segmentation with morphological surface evolution for neuron reconstruction. Neuroinformatics **16**(2), 153–166 (2018)
63. Zhou, Z., Liu, X., Long, B., Peng, H.: TReMAP: automatic 3D neuron reconstruction based on tracing, reverse mapping and assembling of 2D projections. Neuroinformatics **14**(1), 41–50 (2016)
64. Zhou, Z., Sorensen, S.A., Peng, H.: Neuron crawler: An automatic tracing algorithm for very large neuron images. In: Proc. ISBI., pp. 870–874. IEEE (2015)

Artificial Intelligence for Fighting the COVID-19 Pandemic

Rohit Salgotra, Iman Rahimi, and Amir H. Gandomi

1 Introduction

With more than 25 million confirmed cases and around one million deaths, the severe acute respiratory syndrome coronavirus 2 (SARS-Cov-2) or simply coronavirus disease 2019 (COVID-19) has emerged as a global pandemic and has affected more than 90% countries of the world. What started in December 2019 as a potential threat has taken almost all nations by storm. The rapid contagion of SARS-CoV-2, causing the COVID-19 disease, which is around ten times deadlier than the common cold or the seasonal flu, challenges healthcare systems across the world [16]. The population is not immune to the novel coronavirus strains, and effective therapies are not available, which benefits the enormous pace of the spreading. The World Health Organization (WHO) then declared that a global coronavirus has been identified and isolated. The movement of people across the various provinces in China and to other countries of the world were put under serious scanner, and every person reaching from China was investigated at the respective airports [40]. The authorities tried to contain the virus by imposing strict restrictions on travelling and mass gathering by closing airports, state roadways, public transport, local transport and all other services such as public gathering, gaming events, mass events and any other activity where chances of social contacts or public interactions were higher [41]. The Chinese administration started collecting the travel histories and required information of people travelling to and from various provinces across the country, by calculating the infectious disease vulnerability index (IDVI) according to the user data records International Air Transport Association (IATA) [25]. It was further noted that IDVI has a range of [0, 1], and if the value of IDVI is higher, the risk of transmission and vulnerability is the higher. The data thus collected was used as the primary source of information for analysing the effect of virus outside China.

R. Salgotra (✉)
Department of Electronics and Communication Engineering, Thapar Institute of Engineering and Technology, Patiala, India

I. Rahimi · A. H. Gandomi
Faculty of Engineering and Information Technology, University of Technology Sydney, Sydney, NSW 2007, Australia
e-mail: gandomi@uts.edu.au

F. Chen and J. Zhou (eds.), *Humanity Driven AI*,
https://doi.org/10.1007/978-3-030-72188-6_8

Despite rigorous efforts, the first case outside China was reported in Thailand on 13 January 2020 [38], and by 19 January 2020 numerous cases were reported in Bangkok, Hong Kong, Japan and Taipei, all having an IDVI greater than 0.65 [39]. The virus started escalating towards the Third World countries, and on 31 January 2020, WHO declared an emergency condition. By 11 March 2020, the virus was declared as a global pandemic with a daily increase in the total number of cases by 25–30% in the total number of confirmed cases [29]. As of March 2021, the United States of America (USA) is the most affected country of the world with around 10 million confirmed cases (CC) and a total death count (DC) of more than 500,000 people. The second most affected is India with a total of more than 7 million CC (200,000 DC) and followed by Brazil with more than 4 million CC (100,000 DC) [29]. Thus. it can be said that the virus which started from a single human being is currently multiplying as a community level transmission agent. Though numerous efforts have been put into place by the respective governments, the virus is still escalating at a rapid pace.

The pandemic became a game-changer for the health and economic lifestyle of the world's population. Despite rigorous efforts, the exponential spreading burdens the whole medical care system. During this crisis, predominantly developing countries struggle to stabilize their economy and healthcare system [21]. When nations faced the first contagion wave (around April 2020), most organizations which require face-to-face contact (e.g. hotels, cinemas, restaurants, universities and others) faced heavy restrictions. As a result, this measure caused a significant rise in unemployment. The pandemic forced governments of all countries to deal with such a health economic dilemma (HED) [12]. The pandemic is a frightening example that trade-offs between health and economy are sometimes inevitable and regulators have to come up with appropriate actions to deal with it [12].

The potential effect of COVID-19 has prompted various studies, and numerous articles have been published to analyse the possible impact of the virus and derive potential vaccine and provide solutions to the policy-makers for the global pandemic [5]. Figure 1 shows distribution of documents by subject area. As it is clear from Fig. 1, medicine has the most contribution in the area (53%) followed by biochemistry (7%), social science (6%) and immunology (5%) while, for example, mathematics, computer science and agricultural sciences possess the least contribution (1%). Initial studies showed that the virus has a very devastating effect on people of elder age, with heart-related aliments, respiratory disorders and other ailments [8, 28]. These studies further predicted that the virus has an incubation period of around 5.1 days, and the minimum quarantine time is around 14–21 days [7]. Some other studies showed that the transmission rate ranges from [0.001 2.3] [24], whereas the reproduction number lies in the range of [2.3 3.9] [44]. Apart from these studies, it has also been projected that the transmission of the virus is limited on a global scale with only few hundreds of people getting affected per one million peoples [30, 31]. Some of the recent studies on COVID-19 include Weibull distributed modelling [1], logarithmic distribution [43], exponentially growing patterns [11] and others [20]. While most of the studies predicted that the virus is growing at an exponential rate, some studies predicted that the growth curve is logarithmic which stagnates towards later stages

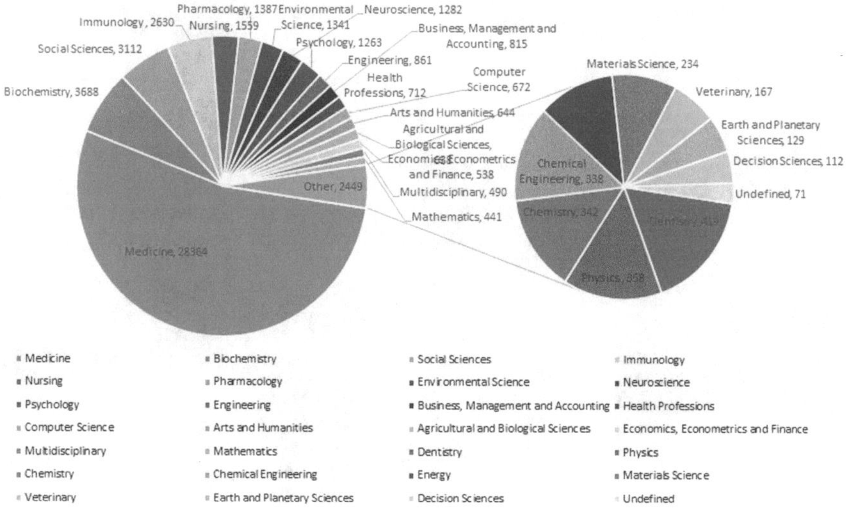

Fig. 1 Distribution of documents by subject areas

[11, 43]. These studies have provided some basic insight into the initial background of AI and its application to find the exact pattern of COVID-19 and what possible impact it will create in the near future.

In present work, the role of AI-based techniques and their possible impact in the battle against COVID-19 pandemic are presented.

2 Can AI Solve Real-World Problems?

During unprecedented and chaotic times, the science and technology have provided significant contribution for the implementation of government propaganda and policies. This can be understood from the fact that numerous AI-based models and approaches are being used to solve real-world problems. Figure 2 presents different classes of AI. Although there are several fields in AI, only few studies have been used for dealing with the pandemic. Implementing AI into our lives has been studied for years now, and things are getting more real. In the field of data science, useful information is turned into valuable resources, and hence, new creative business models and strategies are designed. AI-based natural language processing has been used for communications with intelligent systems using languages such as English and is required to instruct intelligent systems such as robots for deriving new decisions from certain clinical experts and other major tasks. AI models based on machine learning and deep learning are used to develop computer-based programs to learn and adapt as per the user requirements. Apart from that, deep learning which is a sub-field of machine learning helps in modelling high-level abstractions in the available data by

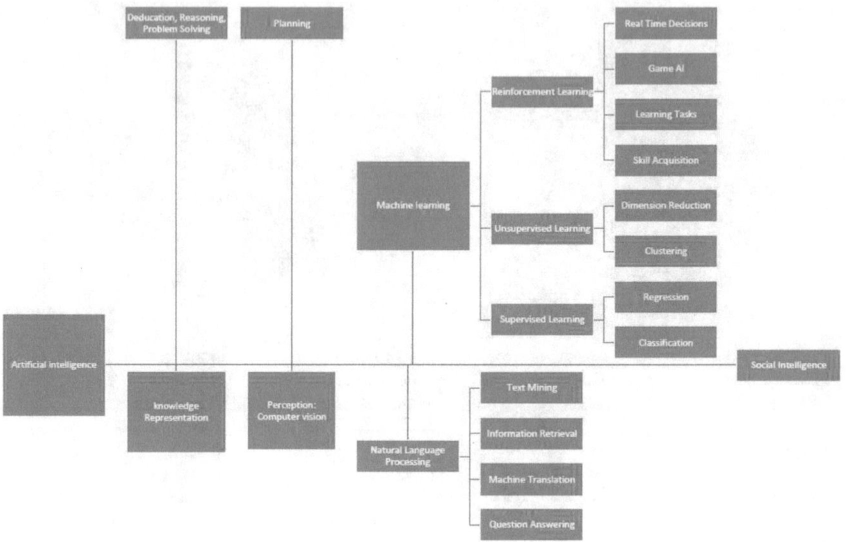

Fig. 2 Different classes of artificial intelligence

using deep graphical models with multiple neural network layers that are composed of multiple linear and nonlinear transformations. Apart from that automatic extraction of data, its analysis and understanding of the useful information from images or simply computer vision are also an important branch of AI which aims at providing better capabilities to machines. A deeper understanding of these concepts is beyond the scope of this chapter.

Also when compared to the current pandemic scenario or an emergency condition, the traditional machines learning classifiers require special attention so that decisions can be made consistently without wasting time for training and analysis. This is because the real-world data available in the literature will not be available for months or even years for proper analysis and experimentation. This implies that instead of using a traditional or conventional set of data, AI-driven tools can be used to analyse the impact of such emergency conditions by using interactive learning or self-learning over time. The main aim is to learn iteratively over time to adapt and formulate new data without forgetting its existing limited knowledge. While significant changes can be brought over time using anomaly detection techniques, these techniques help to identify rare items, events or observations that may be different from the normal data for that particular condition.

In health care, several important healthcare facilities such as hospital beds, ventilators, medical masks, capacity and others are very limited and doctors are forced to provide judgement without proper inspection. As a result of that, AI-based systems can be used to make such decisions, and various AI-inspired decision support systems can be actively used to provide clinical support to the patients [17]. Various diseases such as epilepsy [22], heart rhythms [3], nerve and muscle disease [18] have been successfully interpreted by using machine learning classifiers. Deep learning-based algorithms have also been used to predict cancer [26], various viruses [4] and other biomedical studies [33]. Apart from that, transfer learning-based models can be used for analysing existing literature and provide predictions for other current state of the art.

3 AI and COVID-19

The primary purpose of AI-based techniques is that they do not require complete data sets for training, testing and validation of models. Instead, these can be implemented from the initial data collection scenario, in conjugation with the experts from the domain research where active learning is required. To achieve higher accuracy level during decision-making, rather than relying on single type of data, several different types of data are employed. Apart from testing, training and validation for prediction analysis, AI-based models can be used for detecting viruses with high sensitivity and speed. Neural network-based classifiers can be used for screening and monitoring of patients overtime. In this section, a detailed study on the role of AI in tackling the problem of COVID-19 is highlighted with respect to the existing literature. Figure 3a presents network, and Fig. 3b presents density visualization found by VOSviewer software [35]. From Fig. 3, it can be seen that forecasting and deep learning are the most interested areas of artificial intelligence applied to COVID-19. Figure 3 has been provided based on clustering algorithm that 1000 items are distributed in the different clusters (Table 1 shows the top items with the most occurrences in each cluster).

Various efforts have been made to develop novel diagnostic approaches using deep learning, neural networks and machine learning algorithms. Transfer learning-based SARS-CoV-2 assay design for screening of patients has been designed using CRISPR-based virus detection system [23]. In an enhanced version, neural network-based classifiers were developed for screening on large scale. This type of system is based on the respiratory patterns of the patients [37]. Deep learning-based enhancements have also been proposed for automatic detection and monitoring of COVID-affected patients by analysing systematic thoracic CT-scanned images [15]. It has already been known that the hallmark of COVID-19 is patchy shadows and opaque ground glasses distributed bilaterally within the respiratory system. So deep learning-based methods were used to extract the radiological graphical features for diagnosing the coronavirus [36]. Similarly, chest images classification using multi-objective differential evolution-based convolution neural networks has also been done [34]. These studies not only pave way for increased accuracy and speed but can also help in reducing the total number of healthcare workers required to complete the same task. Apart from that, contactless healthcare system will minimize or reduce the chances of disease transmission to the healthcare workers.

A second aspect where AI has played a significant role in combating the COVID-19 pandemic is the prediction and forecasting of expected rise in the number of

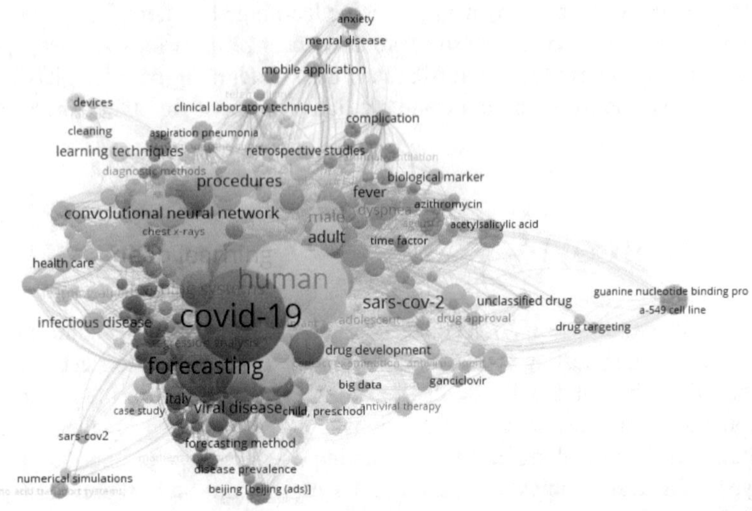

(a) Network visualization

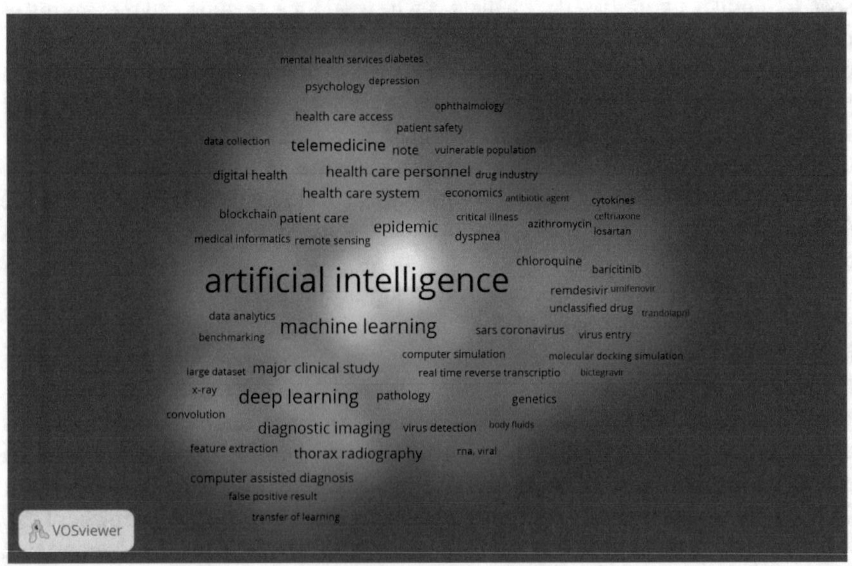

(b) Density visualization

Fig. 3 Visualization found by VOSviewer software

Table 1 Top keywords in each cluster

Clusters	1	2	3
Item 1	Accuracy	Automation	Artificial ventilation
Item 2	ARIMA	Chest CT	Consensus
Clusters	4	5	6
Item 1	Body temperature	China	Analysis
Item 2	2019 novel coronavirus	Coronavirus	Biotechnology
Clusters	7	8	9
Item 1	Anorexia	Case series	Anxiety
Item 2	Case series	Chest X-ray image	Artificial intelligence
Clusters	10	11	12
Item 1	Drug targeting	Big data	AI applications
Item 2	Gen ontology	Clinical feature	Computer scientist
Clusters	13	14	15
Item 1	Climate	Metabolism	Deep learning
Item 2	Environment	Molecular dynamics	Medical Imaging
Clusters	16	17	18
Item 1	Climate	Metabolism	Chest CT
Item 2	Environment	Molecular dynamics	Image recognition

cases in any particular region. Initial studies included adaptive neuro fuzzy inference system using flower pollination algorithm and salp swarm algorithm for forecasting total new cases in mainland China [2]. Deep learning-based long short-term memory (LSTM) networks were used to predict ending point of outbreak without using loosing temporal components [9] . Wide range of mathematical and statistical models such as autoregressive moving average (ARIMA), moving average and others have also been used to model the transmission dynamics of COVID-19 pandemic [10]. Genetic programming-based models have also been proposed to analyse and forecast the impact of virus in different countries of the world [30, 31]. Also, along with epidemiological data, environmental factors have also been studied to analyse and forecast the possible effect of temperature, humidity and other factors on the increase in COVID-19 cases [24]. Apart from that, various other algorithms such as krill herd [13] and naked mole rat [5] can be used for analysis and prediction of COVID-19 case. These studies have helped to predict and forecast the possible effect of COVID-19 in coming days and helped the authorities to come up with certain solutions such as imposing lockdown, strict travel restrictions, limiting mass events and others. Also transfer learning-based techniques can be used to analyse the possible impact of COVID-19. As an example, the possible impact of COVID-19 in China, Italy, USA, Brazil and India can be used and extended to analyse and predict the effect in other countries. It means a model trained in Italy or China or India can be used to automatically detect coronavirus in Singapore or Australia. In other words, for a respiratory syndrome such as COVID-19, cross-population training and testing-based AI models must be designed so that automated detection can be processed. In parallel, the COVID data sets generated by AI-based models can be used for decision-based training without the formal requirement of whole data. In the next section, a detailed study of AI-based techniques with respect to COVID-19 is presented.

Instead of diagnostic, monitoring and forecasting studies, there is a need of effective therapeutic strategy to treat COVID-19-affected patients at a rapid pace. As clinical trials for various drugs are under way, there is an urgent need to analyse previous potential drug candidates against the deadly virus. A machine learning-based positioning and purposing strategy has been designed to prioritize existing drugs against COVID-19 for clinical trials [14]. Also, novel drug like compounds have been discovered by using deep learning-based drug discovery pipelines [42]. Google platform DeepMind has also come up with the protein structure associated with the COVID-19, which if done by traditional experimental formulations may take months to compile [33]. A reverse vaccination tool using integrated technology and machine learning has also been proposed in [27] to tackle the ongoing scenario. Molecular transformer drug target interaction-based deep learning model has been used to identify commercially available antiviral drugs to potentially reduce or disrupt the effect of viral component such as proteinase, polymerase and helicase from the SARS-CoV-2 viral component [6]. Thus, tremendous efforts are being carried out to produce a potential vaccine for COVID-19 as the earliest possible, and AI is playing a very significant role to subsequently transform minimal available information into useful resources for easy access and implementation. Figure 4 shows the citation network based on authors. The minimum number of documents and citation of an author has been set 1 resulted in 422 authors selected. Selda- Enriquez G., Sola Ortigosa J., Ruiz- Villaverde R., Roncero Riesco M. are among top cited authors in the field. AI also plays significant role in helping humanity on a whole by providing a general framework for health, economy and policy-making in order to deal with the pandemic. This can be better understood from the fact that AI is considered as the major non-pharmaceutical interventions and the most effective tool to contain pandemic. This can help the whole population to reach herd immunity. These containment measures have a prominent effect on reducing the spreading speed of the virus, although it is necessary to find an optimal strategy to implement them [32]. Generally, there are two tactics: a restrictive one, using a protective approach to handle the population by imposing lockdowns and self-isolation (e.g. Japan or South Korea), and a relaxed approach, for not taking any precautions at all to reach herd immunity faster (e.g. Sweden or the UK in the early phase of the pandemic). A protective strategy prevents healthcare systems from collapsing while putting large pressure on the economy. Contrary, the second approach helps to provide a stable economy. However, the number of case fatalities would rise dramatically. Thus, the top priority is to not overstrain the capacity of the healthcare system and simultaneously keeping the economy going. This shows a need for a trade-off strategy between the containment of the pandemic and economic health [19]. Overall in this scenario

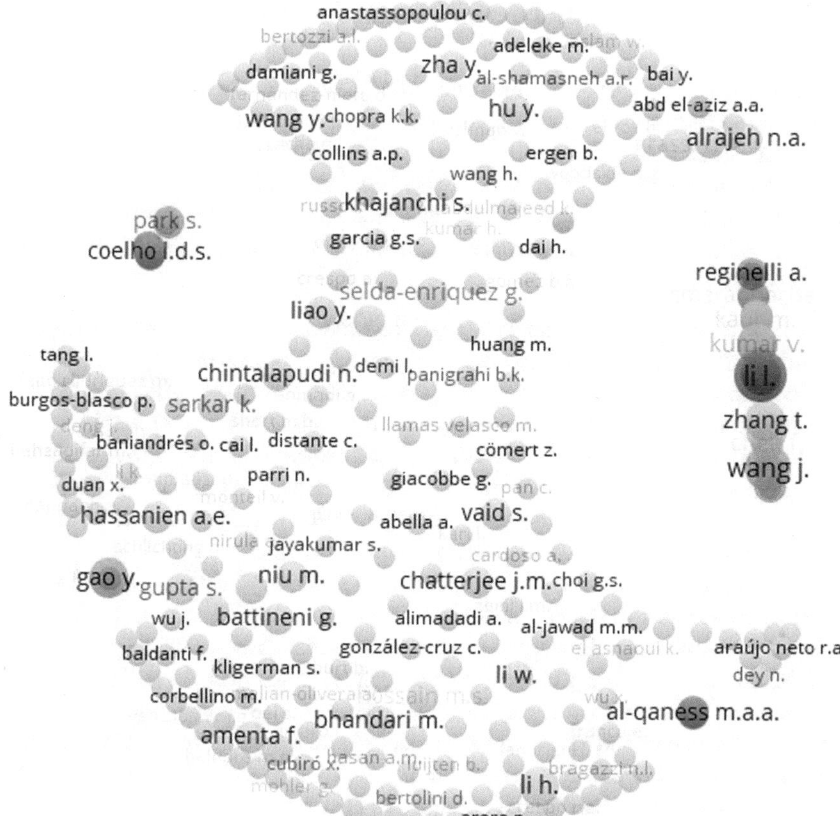

Fig. 4 Citation network

also, AI can be used to find optimal trade-off between both health and economic constraints [21].

Apart from the above discussed advantages of AI in handling the COVID-19 pandemic, there are some points that need to be dealt with, and in most of the cases, human needs to be in the loop to make final decisions. This can be better understood from the health economic dilemma problem which is highlighted by the fact that whatever the scenario is, policy-makers and involved persons work in collaboration to deal with the pandemic. For example, the AI-based models can provide numerous possible solutions to deal with the health and economic aspect of pandemic. Based on these solutions, the policy-makers can decide how to deal with the whole scenario in an organized manner.

4 Insightful Implications and Future Direction

Healthcare organizations are in urgent need of decision-making or more precisely multi-criteria decision-making to handle the coronavirus and get proper suggestions to limit its spread. AI plays a very significant and vital role in an efficient way to mimic human like intelligence. It may also provide possible understanding of the basic protein structure of COVID-19 and hence suggesting the development of a potential vaccine. Overall, important conclusions and some insightful implications can be drawn as follows:

- For forecasting prediction analysis, various models can be integrated including ARIMA models, Weibull function, evolutionary approaches and others. These models have already been used for analysis of various diseases, and integration of these into one another can make the system more convenient and reliable.
- Predicting protein structure of COVID-19 and their interaction with host human proteins and the cellular environment is another important aspect which can be dealt by using AI-based techniques. This may help to analyse the basic structure of the virus, and hence, potential vaccine can be derived.
- Incorporating indicators such as population density, age distribution, individual and community movements, healthcare facilities available can be included in regression or computational models to enhance prediction accuracy.
- AI-based real-time forecasting, wireless sensors, camera for surveillance, visual tracking of symptoms from the affected persons and using apps such as Arogya Setu, worldometer and others to keep a check on the number of infected cases.
- Analysis of social media data sets from platforms such as Twitter, Facebook and others for real-time collection of epidemiological data.
- Contactless treatment using AI-based robots, for drug delivery, treating patients at remote locations without the involvement and direct contact of medical staff.
- Risk assessment with different age grouped person can be analysed and predicted. This will help to find which section of the population is most vulnerable and needs to be given more intensive care.

Overall, there are numerous factors where AI plays a significant role in keeping a check on the spread of the virus, providing primary care to patients and searching a potential vaccine for curing the disease. The research is still on, and as compared to traditional testing mechanisms, AI has contributed significantly towards its advancements. Research data from diseases such as pneumonia and others has been used as basic preliminaries to formulate new hypothesis for COVID-19 pandemic and analyse its effect. Apart from that, models have been made to make a possible vaccine using deep learning epidemiological data. Thus, we can say that, with the advent of AI, even diseases such as COVID-19 can be brought under scanner, and possible solutions can be obtained.

5 Conclusion

In this study, we analyse the overall significance of AI-based techniques in order to fight with the COVID-19 pandemic. Typically, AI-based tools can assist mankind in various forms from detection of various infections to treating infected patients and from forecasting of the total number infections to keeping track of the various advances for proper policy-making. Detailed discussed study shows that AI can track the COVID-19 crisis under various constraints such as medical, climatic conditions and others. AI can also be used to facilitate research by analysing already available literature. Apart from that, it can serve as the basis for providing proper treatment to patients, prevention, vaccine development, policy-making and other tasks for humans to make the final decision.

References

1. Akhmetzhanov, A.R., Mizumoto, K., Jung, S.m., Linton, N.M., Omori, R., Nishiura, H.: Epidemiological characteristics of novel coronavirus infection: A statistical analysis of publicly available case data. medRxiv (2020)
2. Al-Qaness, M.A., Ewees, A.A., Fan, H., Abd El Aziz, M.: Optimization method for forecasting confirmed cases of covid-19 in china. Journal of Clinical Medicine **9**(3), 674 (2020)
3. Alfaras, M., Soriano, M.C., Ortín, S.: A fast machine learning model for ecg-based heartbeat classification and arrhythmia detection. Frontiers in Physics **7**, 103 (2019)
4. Andriasyan, V., Yakimovich, A., Georgi, F., Petkidis, A., Witte, R., Puntener, D., Greber, U.F.: Deep learning of virus infections reveals mechanics of lytic cells. bioRxiv p. 798074 (2019)
5. Backer, J.A., Klinkenberg, D., Wallinga, J.: Incubation period of 2019 novel coronavirus (2019-ncov) infections among travellers from wuhan, china, 20–28 january 2020. Eurosurveillance **25**(5), 2000,062 (2020)
6. Beck, B.R., Shin, B., Choi, Y., Park, S., Kang, K.: Predicting commercially available antiviral drugs that may act on the novel coronavirus (sars-cov-2) through a drug-target interaction deep learning model. Computational and structural biotechnology journal (2020)
7. Boldog, P., Tekeli, T., Vizi, Z., Dénes, A., Bartha, F.A., Röst, G.: Risk assessment of novel coronavirus covid-19 outbreaks outside china. Journal of clinical medicine **9**(2), 571 (2020)
8. Chang, S.L., Harding, N., Zachreson, C., Cliff, O.M., Prokopenko, M.: Modelling transmission and control of the covid-19 pandemic in australia. arXiv preprint arXiv:2003.10218 (2020)
9. Chimmula, V.K.R., Zhang, L.: Time series forecasting of covid-19 transmission in canada using lstm networks. Chaos, Solitons & Fractals p. 109864 (2020)
10. Dehesh, T., Mardani-Fard, H., Dehesh, P.: Forecasting of covid-19 confirmed cases in different countries with arima models. medRxiv (2020)
11. Eubank, S., Guclu, H., Kumar, V.A., Marathe, M.V., Srinivasan, A., Toroczkai, Z., Wang, N.: Modelling disease outbreaks in realistic urban social networks. Nature **429**(6988), 180–184 (2004)
12. Fernandes, N.: Economic effects of coronavirus outbreak (covid-19) on the world economy. Available at SSRN 3557504 (2020)
13. Gandomi, A.H., Alavi, A.H.: Krill herd: a new bio-inspired optimization algorithm. Communications in nonlinear science and numerical simulation **17**(12), 4831–4845 (2012)
14. Ge, Y., Tian, T., Huang, S., Wan, F., Li, J., Li, S., Yang, H., Hong, L., Wu, N., Yuan, E., et al.: A data-driven drug repositioning framework discovered a potential therapeutic agent targeting covid-19. bioRxiv (2020)

15. Gozes, O., Frid-Adar, M., Greenspan, H., Browning, P.D., Zhang, H., Ji, W., Bernheim, A., Siegel, E.: Rapid aid development cycle for the coronavirus (covid-19) pandemic: Initial results for automated detection & patient monitoring using deep learning ct image analysis. arXiv preprint arXiv:2003.05037 (2020)
16. Huang, C., Wang, Y., Li, X., Ren, L., Zhao, J., Hu, Y., Zhang, L., Fan, G., Xu, J., Gu, X., et al.: Clinical features of patients infected with 2019 novel coronavirus in wuhan, china. The lancet **395**(10223), 497–506 (2020)
17. Jiang, F., Jiang, Y., Zhi, H., Dong, Y., Li, H., Ma, S., Wang, Y., Dong, Q., Shen, H., Wang, Y.: Artificial intelligence in healthcare: past, present and future. Stroke and vascular neurology **2**(4), 230–243 (2017)
18. Karthick, P., Ghosh, D.M., Ramakrishnan, S.: Surface electromyography based muscle fatigue detection using high-resolution time-frequency methods and machine learning algorithms. Computer methods and programs in biomedicine **154**, 45–56 (2018)
19. Khadilkar, H., Ganu, T., Seetharam, D.P.: Optimising lockdown policies for epidemic control using reinforcement learning. Transactions of the Indian National Academy of Engineering **5**(2), 129–132 (2020)
20. Liu, T., Hu, J., Kang, M., Lin, L., Zhong, H., Xiao, J., He, G., Song, T., Huang, Q., Rong, Z., et al.: Transmission dynamics of 2019 novel coronavirus (2019-ncov) (2020)
21. Mandal, M., Jana, S., Nandi, S.K., Khatua, A., Adak, S., Kar, T.: A model based study on the dynamics of covid-19: Prediction and control. Chaos, Solitons & Fractals **136**, 109,889 (2020)
22. Memarian, N., Kim, S., Dewar, S., Engel Jr, J., Staba, R.J.: Multimodal data and machine learning for surgery outcome prediction in complicated cases of mesial temporal lobe epilepsy. Computers in biology and medicine **64**, 67–78 (2015)
23. Metsky, H.C., Freije, C.A., Kosoko-Thoroddsen, T.S.F., Sabeti, P.C., Myhrvold, C.: Crispr-based surveillance for covid-19 using genomically-comprehensive machine learning design. BioRxiv (2020)
24. Mohsen, M., Salgotra, R., Holloway, D., Gandomi, A.H.: Covid-19 time series forecast using transmission rate and meteorological parameters as features. IEEE Computational Intelligence Magazine (2020)
25. Moore, M., Gelfeld, B., Adeyemi Okunogbe, C.P.: Identifying future disease hot spots: infectious disease vulnerability index. Rand health quarterly **6**(3) (2017)
26. Munir, K., Elahi, H., Ayub, A., Frezza, F., Rizzi, A.: Cancer diagnosis using deep learning: a bibliographic review. Cancers **11**(9), 1235 (2019)
27. Ong, E., Wong, M.U., Huffman, A., He, Y.: Covid-19 coronavirus vaccine design using reverse vaccinology and machine learning. BioRxiv (2020)
28. Read, J.M., Bridgen, J.R., Cummings, D.A., Ho, A., Jewell, C.P.: Novel coronavirus 2019-ncov: early estimation of epidemiological parameters and epidemic predictions. MedRxiv (2020)
29. Riou, J., Althaus, C.L.: Pattern of early human-to-human transmission of wuhan 2019 novel coronavirus (2019-ncov), december 2019 to january 2020. Eurosurveillance **25**(4), 2000,058 (2020)
30. Salgotra, R., Gandomi, M., Gandomi, A.H.: Evolutionary modelling of the covid-19 pandemic in fifteen most affected countries. Chaos, Solitons & Fractals p. 110118 (2020)
31. Salgotra, R., Gandomi, M., Gandomi, A.H.: Time series analysis and forecast of the covid-19 pandemic in india using genetic programming. Chaos, Solitons & Fractals p. 109945 (2020)
32. Salgotra, R., Seidelmann, T., Fischer, D., Mostaghim, S., Moshaiov, A.: Optimal control policies to address the pandemic health-economy dilemma. arXiv preprint arXiv:2102.12279 (2021)
33. Senior, A.W., Evans, R., Jumper, J., Kirkpatrick, J., Sifre, L., Green, T., Qin, C., Žídek, A., Nelson, A.W., Bridgland, A., et al.: Improved protein structure prediction using potentials from deep learning. Nature **577**(7792), 706–710 (2020)
34. Singh, D., Kumar, V., Kaur, M.: Classification of covid-19 patients from chest ct images using multi-objective differential evolution–based convolutional neural networks. European Journal of Clinical Microbiology & Infectious Diseases pp. 1–11 (2020)
35. Van Eck, N.J., Waltman, L.: Software survey: Vosviewer, a computer program for bibliometric mapping. scientometrics **84**(2), 523–538 (2010)

36. Wang, S., Kang, B., Ma, J., Zeng, X., Xiao, M., Guo, J., Cai, M., Yang, J., Li, Y., Meng, X., et al.: A deep learning algorithm using ct images to screen for corona virus disease (covid-19). MedRxiv (2020)
37. Wang, Y., Hu, M., Li, Q., Zhang, X.P., Zhai, G., Yao, N.: Abnormal respiratory patterns classifier may contribute to large-scale screening of people infected with covid-19 in an accurate and unobtrusive manner. arXiv preprint arXiv:2002.05534 (2020)
38. WHO: Novel coronavirus—thailand (ex-china); world health organization: Geneva, switzerland, 2020. Available online: https://www.who.int/csr/don/14-january-2020-novel-coronavirus-thailand-ex-china/
39. WHO: Situation report; world health organization: Geneva, switzerland, 2020. Available online: https://www.who.int/emergencies/diseases/novel-coronavirus-2019/situation-reports/
40. WHO: Statement regarding cluster of pneumonia cases in wuhan, china; world health organization: Geneva, switzerland, 2020. Available online: https://www.who.int/china/news/detail/09-01-2020-who-statementregarding-cluster-of-pneumonia-cases-in-wuhan-china
41. WHO: irector-general's opening remarks at the media briefing on covid-19 – 11 march 2020 (2020)
42. Zhavoronkov, A., Zagribelnyy, B., Zhebrak, A., Aladinskiy, V., Terentiev, V., Vanhaelen, Q., Bezrukov, D.S., Polykovskiy, D., Shayakhmetov, R., Filimonov, A., et al.: Potential non-covalent sars-cov-2 3c-like protease inhibitors designed using generative deep learning approaches and reviewed by human medicinal chemist in virtual reality (2020)
43. Zheng, Q., Meredith, H., Grantz, K., Bi, Q., Jones, F., Lauer, S., Team, J.I., et al.: Real-time estimation of the novel coronavirus incubation time. 2020
44. Zhou, T., Liu, Q., Yang, Z., Liao, J., Yang, K., Bai, W., Lu, X., Zhang, W.: Preliminary prediction of the basic reproduction number of the wuhan novel coronavirus 2019-ncov. Journal of Evidence-Based Medicine **13**(1), 3–7 (2020)

AI for Sustainability

Sewer Corrosion Prediction for Sewer Network Sustainability

Jianjia Zhang, Bin Li, Xuhui Fan, Yang Wang, and Fang Chen

1 Introduction

Sewer corrosion is a key issue in wastewater systems worldwide, particularly in warm climate countries such as Australia. As seen in Fig. 1, sewer corrosion results in concrete loss, sewer pipe cracks and ultimately structural collapse [8]. It gradually deteriorates sewer network, which is one of the most critical infrastructure assets for modern urban societies [7], and as a result of this, the value of public assets is being significantly diminished. The mitigation and renewal of corroded sewer pipes are highly costly. The cost of sewer corrosion in Australia is estimated to be hundreds of millions of AUD per year [20] (http://www.score.org.au)—This has not included those indirect costs, e.g. lost time and productivity caused by corrosion-related outages, delays, failures and litigation [10]. Moreover, the cost is expected to increase in future as the ageing sewer pipes continue to corrode. Besides economical costs, sewer corrosion may also lead to other issues, e.g. odour complaints and traffic blockage.

Considering the serious negative effect of sewer corrosion, measures should be taken to mitigate the corrosion process, e.g. dosing chemicals [3, 6, 7] or using protective coatings and liners [2, 14, 16, 19]. A preliminary requirement of these

J. Zhang (✉)
School of Biomedical Engineering, Sun Yat-sen University, Guangzhou, China
e-mail: zhangjj225@mail.sysu.edu.cn

B. Li
Fudan University, Shanghai, China
e-mail: Libin@fudan.edu.cn

X. Fan
The University of New South Wales, Sydney, Australia
e-mail: Xuhui.Fan@unsw.edu.au

Y. Wang · F. Chen
Data Science Institute, University of Technology Sydney, Sydney, Australia
e-mail: yang.wang@uts.edu.au

F. Chen
e-mail: fang.chen@uts.edu.au

F. Chen and J. Zhou (eds.), *Humanity Driven AI*,
https://doi.org/10.1007/978-3-030-72188-6_9

(a) Corroded handlers (b) Corroded roof (c) Concrete loss (d) Structural collapse

Fig. 1 Examples of sewer corrosion effects on the sewer network

preventive operations is to know the corrosion status of the sewer network. However, inspecting the corrosion status of all pipes is infeasible in practice. Firstly, there are a large number of sewer pipes (e.g. several thousands in Sydney) in a modern city. Vast human and material resources are required to inspect all these pipes, making it unaffordable for water utilities. Secondly, many pipes are not easily accessible because of their sizes, locations or hazardous conditions. Therefore, a water utility expects to inspect a small portion of the sewer pipes which are at high corrosion risk.

In this case, predicting sewer corrosion on the entire sewer network is a critical task for water utilities around the globe in order to improve efficiency and save costs in chemical dosing and sewer pipe rehabilitation. The water utility requires a corrosion prediction model built on influential factors that cause sewer corrosion, such as hydrogen sulphide (H_2S) and temperature. However, reliable prediction of sewer corrosion has often been hampered by insufficient observations of influential factors (e.g. H_2S and temperature) and inspections of corrosion status as ground truth for accurate modelling. As aforementioned, increasing the number of monitoring and inspection sites may be infeasible due to cost and accessibility. Therefore, modelling of sewer corrosion on the entire sewer network with a limited number of monitoring sites is non-trivial. Current study of corrosion rate prediction for concrete sewers is mainly conducted in very few testbeds deployed in the sewer system, with an array of coupons installed along with a variety of sensors for measuring different influential factors. However, the physical model [20] is calibrated in a certain testbed, and it may not be versatile in any sewer system of any city due to very different environments and lack of measurements of the required factors.

This chapter attempts to leverage a Bayesian nonparametric method to predict the sewer corrosion risk on the entire sewer network with a limited number of observations. Specifically, this is achieved in two steps: (1) Gaussian process [13] is used to estimate the distributions of the two influential factors, H_2S and temperature, on the entire sewer network; (2) based on the estimation results of influential factors, a second-level Gaussian process is used to further predict the corrosion risk levels on the entire sewer network. Thanks to the Bayesian nonparametric method, the corrosion prediction model based on Gaussian process is able to integrate the physical model developed by domain experts, the sparse H_2S and temperature monitored records and the sewer geometry to predict corrosion risk levels on the entire sewer network. Because of incorporating physical model as prior knowledge, the hypothesis space of the model parameters can be regularized, and the issue of insufficient observations can be mitigated.

The proposed method has the following desirable properties: (1) the proposed method is able to integrate expert domain knowledge (physical model) into the prediction model to alleviate the issue of insufficient data. The adopted data analytics technique is a Bayesian nonparametric method which provides a way to regularize the prediction with domain knowledge; (2) the proposed method is flexible. The prediction model in this work can readily incorporate more factors related to sewer corrosion. Therefore, the model can be easily improved by employing additional data collected in the future. In addition, the proposed model could well handle large-scale sewer networks, making it widely applicable; (3) the proposed model built on Gaussian process not only predicts the sewer corrosion level quantitatively, but also estimates the uncertainty of the prediction. This uncertainty is an important measure in decision-makings and cost-effective sewer operations. For example, it can be used to prioritize high corrosion areas, recommend chemical dosing locations and suggest deployment of sensors.

A case study is conducted on real data set from a water utility in Australia. The empirical study demonstrates that the proposed method could achieve promising sewer corrosion prediction results. The results admit several promising further applications for water utilities, including prioritizing high corrosion areas and recommending chemical dosing profiles.

2 Case Study

This work is to collaborate with an Australian water utility to make use of data analytics techniques for sewer corrosion prediction. The water utility manages around 24,000 km of sewers, of which approximately 900 km is large concrete trunks up to 2 m in diameter. Sewer corrosion is a serious concern for the water utility, who spends about 40 million AUD per year on the rehabilitation of corroded sewer pipes. Therefore, predicting sewer corrosion is a critical task for the utility to improve efficiency and save costs in sewer pipe rehabilitation and chemical dosing. This motivates a collaborative project between the utility and Data61, aiming to assess the feasibility of predicting corrosion in sewer network using data analytics. The data provided by the water utility includes

- **Sewer network geometry data**: including the length and GPS coordinates of the sewer pipes in the sewer system;
- **H_2S Observation data**: including GPS coordinates of 17 observation sites the sewer system, as shown in Fig. 2 (left), and the H_2S records of these sites from January 2011 to December 2015 with a sampling frequency of 15 min;
- **Temperature observation data**: including GPS coordinates of 13 observation sites, as shown in Fig. 2 (right), and the temperature records of these sites from January 2011 to December 2015 with a frequency of 15 min;

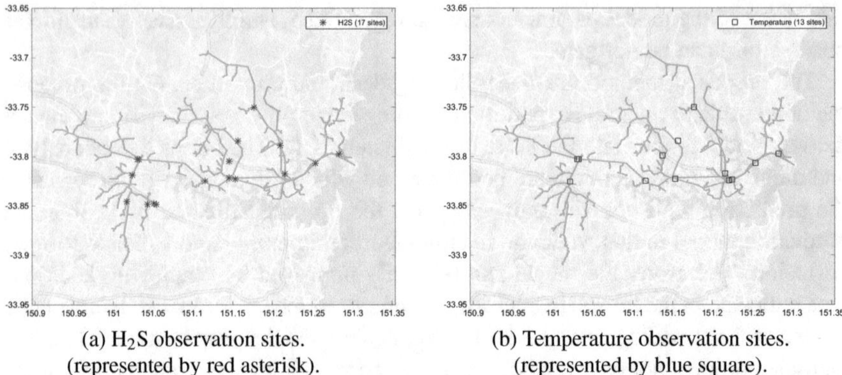

(a) H_2S observation sites. (represented by red asterisk).

(b) Temperature observation sites. (represented by blue square).

Fig. 2 H_2S (Left) and temperature (Right) observation sites on the sewer network

- **Traverse reports**: including two batches of traverse reports conducted during 2007–2010 and 2011–2016, respectively. In each period, a set of sewer pipes are inspected, and their corrosion risk levels (1–5) were recorded. The corrosion risk levels in the reports are shown in Fig. 3a, b.

With the data provided above, sewer corrosion prediction aims to construct a mapping from two influential factors, H_2S and temperature, as input to the corrosion risk level as output. The challenge lies in the data sparsity, that is, the data sampling points on the sewer network are very sparse. Thus, developing a robust sewer corrosion prediction model requires techniques suitable for this particular problem. This study is an attempt to construct a prediction model for sewer corrosion on the entire sewer network.

3 Preliminaries

3.1 Related Work on Sewer Corrosion

In the last decades, extensive research has been conducted on understanding and managing sewer corrosion [4, 5, 7, 11, 22]. It has been verified that the production and emission of hydrogen sulphide (H_2S) are a major cause of corrosion in sewer systems [1, 15]. Sulphate-reducing bacteria residing in the sewer system could turn sulphate in the wastewater into sulphide when anaerobic conditions prevail in a sewer system. During this process, H_2S emits into the sewer atmosphere [8]. In a later stage, H_2S present in the sewer system will be consumed by bacteria, and sulphuric acid will be generated in biological oxidation of H_2S [12, 18]. The sulphuric acid generated in this stage causes internal cracking and pitting in the sewer pipe, which exposes more pipe surface for acid attack [8]. Step by step, mass corrosion of sewer pipe happens.

Also, it has been found that the conversion rate of sulphuric acid in the sewer system from H_2S is proportional to the concentration of H_2S in the sewage [12].

Besides H_2S, temperature is also a marked factor affecting the rate of sewer corrosion since sulphuric acid generation is a biological phenomenon. Specifically, temperature plays an important role in the emission of H_2S from liquid to gas phase [21] and can affect various abiotic and biotic reaction rates important for corrosion [9]. It has been found in [9, 12] that the generation rate of sulphide increases with the rise of temperature.

The findings above motivate this work to first conduct estimation of H_2S and temperature on the entire sewer network; and based on the estimation results, prediction of corrosion risk level on the entire sewer network is further carried out. This is because (1) both H_2S and temperature are well-verified influential factors to sewer corrosion in the literature, and (2) in comparison with inspecting corrosion status of the sewer network, H_2S concentration and temperature can be more conveniently monitored and collected by using electronic sensors and telecommunication techniques.

3.2 Brief Introduction to Gaussian Process

Gaussian process (GP) is a generic supervised learning method designed to solve regression and probabilistic classification problems. The general idea behind GP for regression is illustrated in Fig. 3c. As seen, the unknown value of a certain type of measurement (in the following, we take H_2S for example) at site U can be estimated as a weighted combination of values collected at the observation sites A, B and C.

$$V(U) = w_{A\to U}V(A) + w_{B\to U}V(B) + w_{C\to U}V(C) \tag{1}$$

where $V(U)$ denotes the predicted H_2S at any unknown point U (the green dot in Fig. 3c) on the sewer network while $V(A)$, $V(B)$ and $V(C)$ denote those points with observed H_2S (the three red dots in Fig. 3c). The weights $w_{A\to U}$, $w_{B\to U}$ and $w_{C\to U}$ are learned automatically through the GP. By repeating this prediction for any unobserved point on the network, the estimation of H_2S on the entire network can be obtained, as shown by the red line in Fig. 3c.

GP has several advantages: (1) GP enables integration of prior knowledge, such as the physical model developed by domain experts of sewer corrosion. This prior knowledge could regularize the hypothesis space of the prediction model; (2) the prediction of GP is a Gaussian distribution, such that one can compute empirical confidence interval using the variance of the Gaussian distribution and make decisions based on these confidence intervals. The confidence interval is illustrated in Fig. 3c. As seen, the farther the prediction point away from the observation points (red dots), the more uncertain the prediction result is; (3) GP is flexible and versatile. Different regression objectives can be achieved by simply specifying different kernels (will be

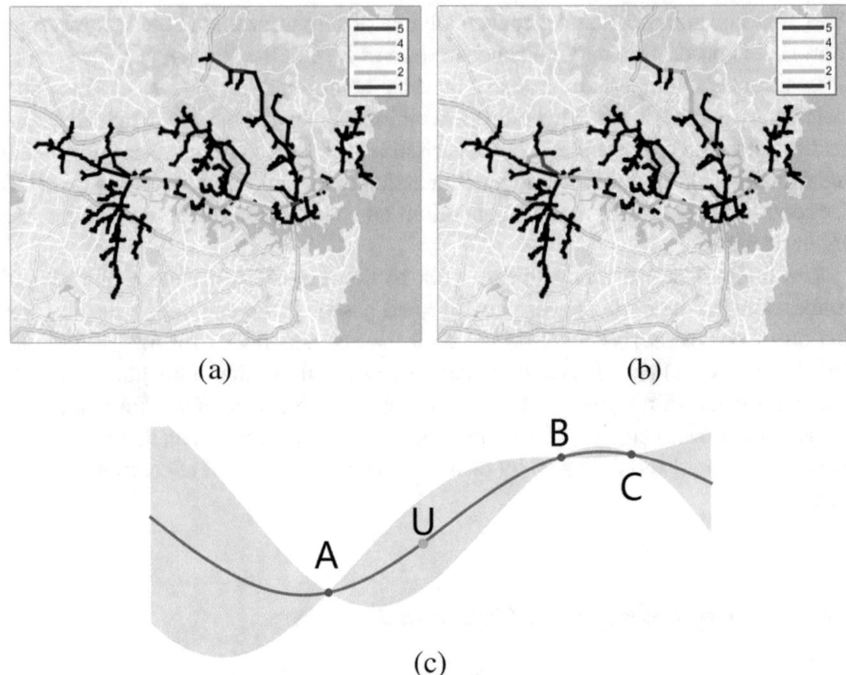

Fig. 3 **a** and **b** Two batches of traverse reports in (2007–2010) and (2011–2016). Five different colours denote five levels of corrosion risk 1–5 (1 for lowest risk and 5 for highest risk) while black lines denote those pipes without a traverse report. **c** Illustration of the prediction and the associated prediction uncertainty of a Gaussian process on a segment of sewer. The red curve denotes the mean value of the prediction, and the bandwidth denotes the uncertainty. The farther the prediction point away from the observation points (red dots), the more uncertain the prediction result is

introduced in the following section). This enables both influential factor estimation and corrosion prediction on the entire sewer network in a similar framework.

A GP is a generalization of the Gaussian distribution in the infinite dimensional space. Similar to a Gaussian distribution, a GP is also fully specified by a mean function and a covariance function (also known as a kernel function). Therefore, the key to use GP is just to specify these two functions for our goals. The design of two functions for influential factor estimation and corrosion prediction will be introduced in the following section.

4 Methodology

The aim of this work is to develop a prediction model based on a Bayesian nonparametric method. A typical Bayesian model is in the form of "Prediction (posterior distribution) = Domain Knowledge (prior distribution) × Data Fitness (likelihood)", where "Domain Knowledge" provides a hypothesis space to the model such that the model is not only driven by the data (in terms of "Data Fitness") when data is sufficient, but also does not deviate too far from the domain expert's hypothesis when data is insufficient.

Through Bayesian modelling, we can thus (1) integrate domain experts' knowledge, for example, using the existing physical model as prior knowledge and (2) conduct prediction as a posterior distribution, whose variance can be viewed as the uncertainty of the prediction. In the following, we first introduce the Gaussian process-based prediction model and then elaborate how it is adapted to H_2S, temperature and corrosion prediction on the entire sewer network.

4.1 Gaussian Process-Based Prediction Model

The prediction problem introduced above is essentially a regression problem on a network. To address this problem, we adopt a Bayesian nonparametric method—Gaussian process (GP) [13] to achieve this goal due to its outstanding performance and desirable properties aforementioned. In order to make this chapter self-contained, this section briefly introduces GP. GP assumes that all the training (observed) and test (unobserved) data can be represented as a joint multivariate Gaussian distribution:

$$\begin{bmatrix} \boldsymbol{y}_O \\ \boldsymbol{y}_U \end{bmatrix} \sim \mathcal{N}\left(\begin{bmatrix} \boldsymbol{\mu}_O \\ \boldsymbol{\mu}_U \end{bmatrix}, \begin{bmatrix} \boldsymbol{K}_{OO} & \boldsymbol{K}_{OU} \\ \boldsymbol{K}_{OU}^\top & \boldsymbol{K}_{UU} \end{bmatrix}\right) \tag{2}$$

where $\boldsymbol{\mu}_O$ and $\boldsymbol{\mu}_U$ denote the means of training and test points, respectively; $\boldsymbol{K}_{OO}$ denotes the covariance matrix of the training set, $\boldsymbol{K}_{OU}$ denotes the covariance matrix between the training set and the test set, and $\boldsymbol{K}_{UU}$ denotes the covariance matrix of the test set.

Given the values of the training set $\boldsymbol{y}_O$, the conditional distribution of the test value $\boldsymbol{y}_U$ can be expressed as follows:

$$\boldsymbol{y}_U | \boldsymbol{y}_O \sim \mathcal{N}\left(\boldsymbol{\mu}_U + \boldsymbol{K}_{OU}^\top \boldsymbol{K}_{OO}^{-1} (\boldsymbol{y}_O - \boldsymbol{\mu}_O), \boldsymbol{K}_{UU} - \boldsymbol{K}_{OU}^\top \boldsymbol{K}_{OO}^{-1} \boldsymbol{K}_{OU}\right) \tag{3}$$

The optimal estimation of $\boldsymbol{y}_U$ is the mean of the above Gaussian distribution:

$$\hat{\boldsymbol{y}}_U = \boldsymbol{\mu}_U + \boldsymbol{K}_{OU}^\top \boldsymbol{K}_{OO}^{-1} (\boldsymbol{y}_O - \boldsymbol{\mu}_O) \tag{4}$$

and the uncertainty of the estimation is reflected in its variance:

$$var(\boldsymbol{y}_U) = \boldsymbol{K}_{UU} - \boldsymbol{K}_{OU}^\top \boldsymbol{K}_{OO}^{-1} \boldsymbol{K}_{OU} \tag{5}$$

As discussed above, a GP is fully specified by its mean function to obtain $\boldsymbol{\mu}_O$ and $\boldsymbol{\mu}_U$ and covariance function $k(\cdot, \cdot)$ to calculate $\boldsymbol{K}_{OO}$, $\boldsymbol{K}_{OU}$ and $\boldsymbol{K}_{UU}$. Please refer to [13] for more details about GP.

In our case study, $\boldsymbol{\mu}_O$ and $\boldsymbol{\mu}_U$ can be the observed and unobserved values of a factor (e.g. H_2S and temperature) or the corrosion risk level, respectively; $\boldsymbol{K}_{OO}, \boldsymbol{K}_{OU}$ and $\boldsymbol{K}_{UU}$ are the covariance matrices between these observed and unobserved sites. The specification of these functions will be introduced in the following.

4.2 Factor Estimation

This section introduces how mean and covariance functions of the GP-based prediction model are specified to estimate H_2S concentration and temperature on the entire sewer network.

4.2.1 Mean Function

The mean function for estimating H_2S is the output of the absorbing state random walks (ASRW)[1] [17]. ASRW is a widely used algorithm for interpolation and extrapolation on a network (e.g. electricity network). The input of an ASRW algorithm is the network structure represented as a directed graph and the values of some observed points on the network; the output of the ASRW is the interpolation and extrapolation results on the entire network. Since the interpolation and extrapolation are based on smoothing, the results can be naturally viewed as a coarse estimation of the mean values of H_2S (assigned with the results of ASRW), with the assumption that the real distribution of H_2S will not be far away from the mean function.

ASRW is adopted as the mean function of the prediction model for the following reasons: (1) ASRW has no specific assumption on the underlying graph structure, and it can be easily applied to sewer networks, which usually have complicated graph structures; (2) the interpolation and extrapolation results of ASRW are smooth on the network, and this coincides with the status of gas phase H_2S, which is smoothly distributed in sewer networks due to diffusion; (3) ASRW is very efficient to compute which makes it applicable to large sewer networks.

4.2.2 Covariance Function

The commonly used exponential kernel function is employed as the covariance function of the GP-based prediction model. Due to the constraints of the network structure, H_2S can only diffuse along the sewer networks. Instead of the traditional Euclidean distance used in the exponential kernel, this work argues that geodesic distance should be used in the kernel function to incorporate the underlying network structure. Therefore, we need to first compute the shortest geodesic distance, denoted as

[1] The introduction to ASRW is out of the scope of this chapter. Interested readers are referred to [17] for details.

d_{ij}, between any two points i and j on the network as the distance between these two points. Then, the exponential kernel can be defined in terms of the shortest geodesic distance as follows:

$$\boldsymbol{K}_{i,j} = \exp\left(\frac{-d_{ij}^2}{\sigma^2}\right) \tag{6}$$

where $\boldsymbol{K}_{i,j}$ denotes the i-th row and j-th column of the kernel matrix and σ is the bandwidth of the exponential kernel. With this kernel function, the covariance matrices $\boldsymbol{K}_{OO}$, $\boldsymbol{K}_{OU}$ and $\boldsymbol{K}_{UU}$ in Eq. (2) can be computed using training–training, training–test and test–test data sets, respectively. Then the mean and variance of the H_2S concentration on the entire sewer network can be estimated by applying Eqs. (4) and (5), respectively. In this way, the spatial H_2S estimation is achieved. By repeating this process for the unknown points at any time point, the estimation of H_2S is finally obtained.

Similar to the H_2S estimation introduced above, the estimation of temperature on the entire sewer network can be obtained in the same manner with the observed temperature.

4.3 Corrosion Prediction

This section introduces how mean and covariance functions of the GP-based prediction model are specified to predict sewer corrosion rate on the entire sewer network.

4.3.1 Mean Function

The mean function, i.e. $\boldsymbol{\mu}_O$ and $\boldsymbol{\mu}_U$ in Eq. (2), is set as the physical model derived from [20]:

$$R_m = A \cdot H^{0.5} \cdot \frac{0.1602\eta - 0.1355}{1 - 0.977\eta} \cdot \mathrm{e}^{\frac{-45,000}{RT}} \tag{7}$$

where A is a constant calibrated empirically using the training data (coupons on the testbed), H denotes the H_2S concentration, η denotes the fractional relative humidity of the sewer atmosphere, which is set as the average humidity of several coupon sites in the sewer network, R denotes the universal gas constant, T denotes the absolute temperature, and the result R_m denotes the corrosion rate.

As aforementioned, Eq. (7) was developed by the domain experts of sewer corrosion research [20] based on the coupons. Therefore, this mean function represents a hypothesis space of the corrosion rate based on domain knowledge such that the prediction of the proposed prediction model will not deviate domain experts' hypothesis too far. In other words, the mean function is used as prior knowledge to regularize the hypothesis space of the proposed prediction model.

4.3.2 Covariance Function

Considering the fact that the sewer corrosion rate is closely related to the sewer network geometry, H_2S concentration and temperature [1, 9, 12, 15], the kernel function of the GP-based prediction model for sewer corrosion is set as a linear combination of three kernels corresponding to these three factors, respectively:

$$\boldsymbol{K} = \alpha_1 \boldsymbol{K}^G + \alpha_2 \boldsymbol{K}^H + \alpha_3 \boldsymbol{K}^T \quad (8)$$

where $\boldsymbol{K}^G$ is the exponential kernel with pairwise geodesic distance defined in Eq. (6), $\boldsymbol{K}^H$ is an exponential kernel with pairwise difference of H_2S concentration between two points as the distance, $\boldsymbol{K}^T$ is another exponential kernel with pairwise difference of temperature between two points as the distance, and α_is are the linear combination coefficients for the three kernel matrices.

With the mean and kernel functions defined above, the corrosion rate prediction can be performed by applying Eqs. (4) and (5) on the entire sewer network at each time point, by assigning $\boldsymbol{\mu}_L$ with the observed corrosion rate calculated based on the two batches of traverse reports.

5 Case Study

In this section, a case study is conducted to evaluate the proposed corrosion prediction model using the data provided by the water utility introduced in Sect. 2.

5.1 Evaluation

In order to predict the sewer corrosion, we first estimate H_2S and temperature distributions on the entire network over five years (2011–2015) using the method introduced in Sect. 4. The training data used in this estimation procedure is the H_2S and temperature records as described in Sect. 2. The hyper-parameters, including σ in Eq. (6), A in Eq. (7) and α_i in Eq. (8), are all tuned automatically by maximizing the log marginal likelihood [13].

The estimation of monthly average H_2S and temperature along with the sewer geometry data are then used as the input to predict corrosion rate as in Sect. 4.3. The ground-truth corrosion rates are derived from the two batches of traverse reports. Specifically, there are 17 sewer pipes having corrosion risk level records in both periods of traverse reports. This enables calculating the ground-truth average corrosion rates, denoted as R_g, of these 17 pipes using the following equation: $R_g = \frac{C(t_2)-C(t_1)}{t_2-t_1}$, where $C(t)$ denotes the corrosion risk level record at time t in the traverse reports.

The case study adopts the commonly used leave-one-out (LOO) evaluation method. Specifically, the 17 sewer pipes with known corrosion rates are used in the evaluation. At each time, one of these 17 pipes is reserved for evaluation, and the remaining 16 sewer pipes are used for training the GP-based prediction model. The trained model is then used to predict the corrosion rate of the reserved pipe. The evaluation is conducted in turn on each of the 17 sewer pipes, and the final prediction accuracy is averaged over the 17 prediction results.

As the input of the GP-based corrosion prediction model is corrosion rate, the direct output of the model is also the corrosion rate, denoted as R_p. In order to obtain the corrosion risk level at a certain time, the following equation can be used: $\tilde{C}(t) = C(t_0) + R_p \cdot (t - t_0)$, where $C(t_0)$ denotes the known corrosion risk level at time t_0 while $\tilde{C}(t)$ denotes the predicted corrosion risk level at time t. Figure 4 plots the predicted corrosion risk levels (in green) for the 17 sewer pipes in comparison with the ground truths (in blue). One can see that the majority of predictions have less than 10% difference comparing to the corresponding ground truths. In average, the prediction error is less than 10% (0.49/5 = 9.8%). The absorbing state random walks (ASRW) are also applied for a comparison with the proposed method. As seen in Fig. 4, ASRW (in yellow) has larger prediction errors than the proposed method for most pipes. Statistically, ASRW has an prediction error of 17.6% (0.88/5 = 17.6%).

The proposed GP-based prediction model is able to perform corrosion prediction at any time on the entire sewer network as long as there are some observed H_2S and temperature records. The prediction results from January 2011 to December 2015 are illustrated in Fig. 5 for example. As seen, the corrosion risk levels are gradually increased from January 2011 to December 2015. It can also be found that the pipes in the same area often share similar corrosion risk levels while the pipes in different areas could vary much. This is probably because the corrosion rate of the pipes in the same area is similar since the two influential factors, H_2S and temperature, are likely

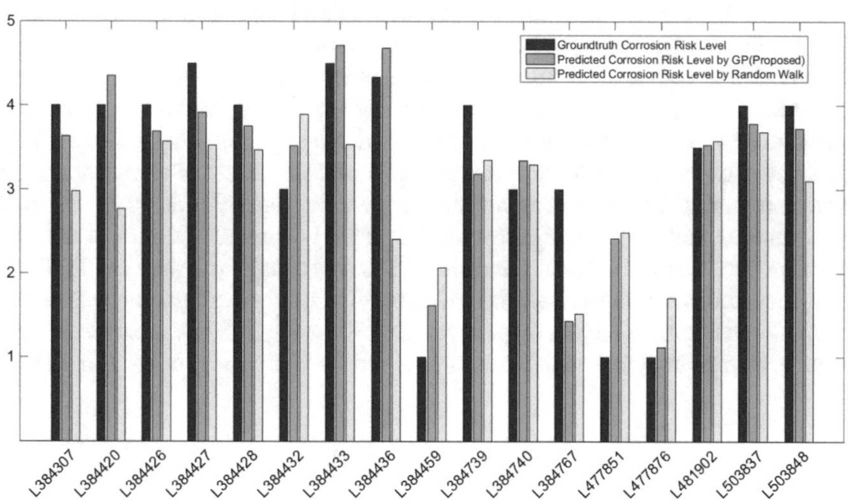

Fig. 4 Evaluation of sewer corrosion prediction

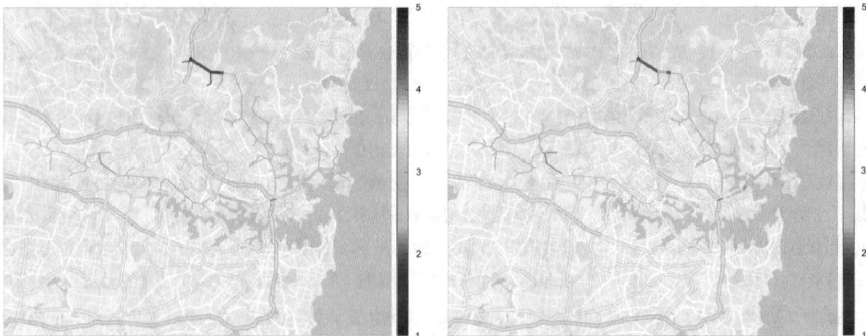

Fig. 5 Example sewer corrosion risk maps in January 2011 (left) and December 2015 (right). The corrosion risk levels on the maps are the prediction results of the proposed corrosion prediction model

to be similar; while these two factors could be significantly different in different areas. For example, the organic or chemical components in the wastewater released in industrial areas could accelerate the generation of H_2S and in turn lead to higher corrosion rates in comparison with residential areas.

5.2 Discussion

The above evaluation results have well demonstrated the high prediction accuracy of the proposed corrosion prediction model. Nevertheless, the model still has space to be improved in the following aspects: (1) the temporal patterns of H_2S or temperature; (2) installing more H_2S and temperature sensors and collecting more H_2S and temperature records and (3) collecting several other factors, e.g. humidity or pH.

Besides improving the model, more applications can be built on the corrosion prediction results. For example, smart chemical dosing is an on-going project tacking advantages of the H_2S and corrosion prediction results. A set of chemical dosing unites are installed to dose certain chemicals, e.g. ferrous chloride, to reduce H_2S concentration and sewer pipe corrosion. However, how much chemical should be dosed at each site to maximally reduce H_2S is a challenging issue. The H_2S and corrosion prediction play an important role in optimizing the dosing strategy. Another example application is odour complaint control. Knowing H_2S on the entire network could enable taking preventative measures to reduce H_2S-caused odour complaints.

6 Conclusion

Data analytics and machine learning techniques are commonly used in many applications and shown great success especially in situations where it is highly complex to analytically model. As a data-driven machine learning technique, Gaussian process (GP) has been successfully used in many applications. Therefore, utilizing Gaussian process to model highly complex aspects of sewer environments is a reasonable approach.

H_2S content in sewers varies with time as well as throughout the network, meaning it has spatiotemporal variations. GPs are proven to capture such trends reasonably well. However, as it is a data-driven approach, the quality of the models is going to be dependent on the quality of the data. Limited and less informative data can weaken the accuracy of the model predictions. On the other hand, analytical models and heuristics may be incorporated in the GP framework to somewhat address the issue of sparseness of data. The GP model proposed by this chapter tries to capture the H_2S distribution reasonably well given the limited number of spatial data points and their locations. In the current Sydney water sewer systems, the number of measurements and their locations might not have been chosen by optimal sampling strategies. Therefore, GP predictions can have reasonably large errors and associated higher uncertainties at some locations. However, the model seems to capture the trends reasonably well.

The corrosion process is highly complex, and accurate modelling of a large network is non-trivial. Currently, the predictions of the model proposed by this chapter are less than 10% difference to the ground truth. The GPs have a reasonably good chance of evolving over time due to availability of more informative data. Both the H_2S predictions and corrosion prediction outputs can be used for developing dosing strategies.

Inputs to the corrosion prediction models are, H_2S, temperature, relative humidity and geometrical distances while its output is the deterioration rate of a pipe. Currently, the H_2S is sampled from a separate GP prediction model or direct observations.

In sum, this chapter proposed a corrosion prediction model based on a Bayesian nonparametric method, named Gaussian process, on the entire sewer network with confidence. The proposed corrosion prediction model was evaluated on a real data set of a water utility in Australia. The evaluation results have demonstrated the high prediction accuracy of the proposed model, with average corrosion risk level prediction error 9.8%, which has been well received by the domain expert in the water utility.

References

1. Boon, A., Lister, A.: Formation of sulphide in rising main sewers and its prevention by injection of oxygen. Prog. Wat. Tech **7**(2), 289–300 (1975)
2. De Muynck, W., De Belie, N., Verstraete, W.: Effectiveness of admixtures, surface treatments and antimicrobial compounds against biogenic sulfuric acid corrosion of concrete. Cement and Concrete Composites **31**(3), 163–170 (2009)

3. Ganigue, R., Gutierrez, O., Rootsey, R., Yuan, Z.: Chemical dosing for sulfide control in australia: an industry survey. Water research **45**(19), 6564–6574 (2011)
4. Hernandez, M., Marchand, E.A., Roberts, D., Peccia, J.: In situ assessment of active thiobacillus species in corroding concrete sewers using fluorescent rna probes. International biodeterioration & biodegradation **49**(4), 271–276 (2002)
5. ISMAIL, N., NONAKA, T., NODA, S., MORI, T.: Effect of carbonation on microbial corrosion of concretes. Doboku Gakkai Ronbunshu **1993**(474), 133–138 (1993)
6. Jiang, G., Keating, A., Corrie, S., O'halloran, K., Nguyen, L., Yuan, Z.: Dosing free nitrous acid for sulfide control in sewers: results of field trials in australia. Water research **47**(13), 4331–4339 (2013)
7. Jiang, G., Sun, J., Sharma, K.R., Yuan, Z.: Corrosion and odor management in sewer systems. Current opinion in biotechnology **33**, 192–197 (2015)
8. Jiang, G., Wightman, E., Donose, B.C., Yuan, Z., Bond, P.L., Keller, J.: The role of iron in sulfide induced corrosion of sewer concrete. Water research **49**, 166–174 (2014)
9. Joseph, A.P., Keller, J., Bustamante, H., Bond, P.L.: Surface neutralization and h 2 s oxidation at early stages of sewer corrosion: influence of temperature, relative humidity and h 2 s concentration. Water research **46**(13), 4235–4245 (2012)
10. Koch, G.H., Brongers, M.P., Thompson, N.G., Virmani, Y.P., Payer, J.H.: Corrosion cost and preventive strategies in the united states. Tech. rep. (2002)
11. Okabe, S., Odagiri, M., Ito, T., Satoh, H.: Succession of sulfur-oxidizing bacteria in the microbial community on corroding concrete in sewer systems. Applied and environmental microbiology **73**(3), 971–980 (2007)
12. Pomeroy, R., Bowlus, F.D.: Progress report on sulfide control research. Sewage Works Journal **18**(4), 597–640 (1946)
13. Rasmussen, C.E.: Gaussian processes in machine learning. In: Advanced lectures on machine learning, pp. 63–71. Springer (2004)
14. Redner, J.A., Hsi, R.P., Esfandi, E.J., Sydney, R., Jones, R., Won, D., Andraska, J.: Evaluation of protective coatings for concrete. Califiornia: County Sanitation Districes of Los Angeles County (1998)
15. Sharma, K., de Haas, D.W., Corrie, S., O'Halloran, K., Keller, J., Yuan, Z.: Predicting hydrogen sulfide formation in sewers: a new model. Water **35**(2), 132–137 (2008)
16. Shook, W.E., Bell, L.W.: Corrosion control in concrete pipe and manholes. Technical Presentation, Water Environmental Federation, Florida (1998)
17. Snell, P., Doyle, P.: Random walks and electric networks. Free Software Foundation (2000)
18. Van Nguyen, L., Kodagoda, S., Ranasinghe, R., Dissanayake, G., Bustamante, H., Vitanage, D., Nguyen, T.: Spatial prediction of hydrogen sulfide in sewers with a modified gaussian process combined mutual information. In: Control Automation Robotics & Vision (ICARCV), 2014 13th International Conference on, pp. 1130–1135. IEEE (2014)
19. Vipulanandan, C., Liu, J.: Performance of polyurethane-coated concrete in sewer environment. Cement and Concrete Research **35**(9), 1754–1763 (2005)
20. Wells, T., Melchers, R.: Concrete sewer pipe corrosion – findings from an australian field study (2016)
21. Yongsiri, C., Vollertsen, J., Hvitved-Jacobsen, T.: Effect of temperature on air-water transfer of hydrogen sulfide. Journal of Environmental Engineering **130**(1), 104–109 (2004)
22. Zhang, L., De Schryver, P., De Gusseme, B., De Muynck, W., Boon, N., Verstraete, W.: Chemical and biological technologies for hydrogen sulfide emission control in sewer systems: a review. Water research **42**(1), 1–12 (2008)

AI Applied to Air Pollution and Environmental Health: A Case Study on Hypothesis Generation

Colin Bellinger, Mohomed Shazan Mohomed Jabbar, Osnat Wine, Charlene Nielsen, Jesus Serrano-Lomelin, Alvaro Osornio-Vargas, and Osmar R. Zaïane

1 Introduction

Exposure to pollution in the environment is a major contributor to disease globally and has economic impacts on the order of billions of dollars each year [45]. Related to this, the field of environmental health aims to monitor and understand factors in the environment that affect human health and disease. This chapter examines the challenges related to understanding airborne chemical dispersion and human exposure along with the resulting adverse health outcomes and discusses how AI contributes to these tasks.

One of the first challenges in environmental health is understanding which airborne chemicals are present and at what levels. Physical pollution models are a standard method to estimate these quantities. Physical models are developed from domain expertise, along with data on the emission sources and chemicals of interest.

C. Bellinger (✉)
Digital Technologies, National Research Council of Canada, Ottawa, Canada
e-mail: colin.bellinger@nrc-cnrc.gc.ca

M. S. M. Jabbar · O. R. Zaïane
Alberta Machine Intelligence Institute, Edmonton, Canada
e-mail: mohomedj@ualberta.ca

O. R. Zaïane
e-mail: zaiane@ualberta.ca

O. Wine · A. Osornio-Vargas
Department of Pediatrics, University of Alberta, Edmonton, Canada
e-mail: osnat@ualberta.ca

A. Osornio-Vargas
e-mail: osornio@ualberta.ca

C. Nielsen
School of Public Health, University of Alberta, Edmonton, Canada
e-mail: ccn@ualberta.ca

J. Serrano-Lomelin
Department of Obstetrics and Gynecology, University of Alberta, Edmonton, Canada
e-mail: jaserran@ualberta.ca

F. Chen and J. Zhou (eds.), *Humanity Driven AI*,
https://doi.org/10.1007/978-3-030-72188-6_10

These are combined with atmospheric and meteorological factors that determine the transportation and evolution of the pollutants in the environment. Models of this nature are limited by the complexity in their design and prediction errors resulting from abstraction. Alternatively, geo-statistical approaches rely on multi-variate linear models that require large-scale spatial monitoring and geographic information systems (GIS) data to model and predict pollutant concentrations. The GIS parameters needed for model development and application are often available on a limited spatial scale, and models cannot generalise across cities [82]. In cases where the necessary data does exist, it is often held by separate institutions and corporations with distinct legal, moral and financial obligations. As a result, the datasets are often small, and the replications of studies are difficult. Nonetheless, there is a growing awareness in the environmental health community about the need for high-quality, accessible data [83]. This shift has opened the door for new and more power data-driven AI methods to play a role.

In addition to air pollution modelling and prediction, there is great need to advance the understanding of the health consequence of exposure to airborne pollutants. The chemicals in the atmosphere co-occur and exist as mixtures that interact with each other. Once inhaled, they persist in the body for varying lengths of time, which, amongst other things, depends on the chemical makeup. Recent evidence suggests that mixtures of chemicals can have a toxicological behaviour that differs from the toxicity of the individual chemicals [20, 77] and may produce greater adverse health outcomes [64, 71]. As a result, there is a growing movement in the environmental health community, including regulators, epidemiologists and health practitioners, to encourage the development of new paradigms of analysis to explore the impact of exposure to mixtures of airborne chemicals on health outcomes [24, 41, 57, 68]. The authors in [13, 57, 75] noted that the traditional tools of analysis are often insufficient to assess the impacts of mixtures of pollutants. There is a strong need for methods that can address the unique challenges presented by high-dimensional (multi-chemical) environmental health data [56]. In addition, there is a need for creative methods to fill the persistent data gaps related to movement and exposure, along with methods that can be applied in rural areas where data is even more sporadic.

Artificial intelligence (AI) is the computational process in which algorithms learning from data or experience, and are applied to analyse large datasets, discover patterns, extract actionable knowledge and predict outcomes of future or unknown events [5, 30]. Methods used in this process come from a combination of computational disciplines including statistics, mathematics, machine learning and database systems. Prior to the application of the AI algorithms, processing steps are often applied to format and clean the data. In addition, a post-processing stage is typically employed to visualise the results of the analysis in an intuitive and easy-to-communicate manner.

AI provides a wide array of scalable and reliable methods that have performed well in complex domains with similar challenges to those in environmental health. When paired with accurate data and domain expertise, AI algorithms have demonstrated a strong potential to support the advancement of knowledge and understanding in applications such as in science, engineering and medicine [35, 53, 69]. Moreover, new frontiers for the application of AI, which often inspire novel algorithms, analyses and evaluation methods, are being explored everyday. This has inspired collaborations between AI and environmental health researchers aimed at the adapting AI methods to analyse modern, big datasets in air pollution epidemiology [10, 61, 79, 82]. Researchers are now utilising the unique abilities of AI to incorporate new data sources, such as satellite and street view images, and social media posts into the analysis [67, 82]. The flexibility of AI has also been used to develop a better understanding of the impact of exposure to airborne chemical mixtures. A recent survey on machine learning applied environmental health found that 52% of the identified studies employed machine learning methods to analysing chemical mixtures [61].

The remaining of this chapter is laid out as follows. Section 2 presents four areas of environmental health related to air pollution in which AI has great potential. Specifically, air quality prediction and forecasting, health outcome analysis, source apportionment, and decision support. A case study of the use of AI to support the advancement of a particular application of environmental health is provided in Sect. 3. In particular, result from the Data Mining & Neonatal Outcomes (DoMiNO) project[1] is presented to illustrate how geo-spacial data mining and data visualisation can be combined with GIS and traditional epidemiological analysis to generate hypotheses about which mixtures of airborne chemicals negatively impact birth outcomes. Finally, Sect. 5 discusses implication, future work and challenges related to the use AI in environmental health related to air pollution and Sect. 6 summarises the finds of this chapter.

2 AI in Environmental Health

This section highlights four areas of environmental health related to air pollution in which AI has great potential. These include air quality prediction and forecasting, health outcome analysis, source apportionment and decision support.

2.1 Air Quality Prediction and Forecasting

A significant portion of the research on AI applied to environmental health deals with the challenge of forecasting and predicting airborne pollution levels. This includes predicting the current air quality or pollution levels, forecasting the future values, given some local or regional input variables, and forecasting the geo-spatial distribution of air quality or pollutants. Predictions of this nature serve to support public policy, planning and health research by simplifying and improving the accuracy of pollution estimates and contributing to the understanding of the impact of a potential future events, such as new highways and factories.

[1] Data MIning and Neonatal Outcomes: https://sites.google.com/a/ualberta.ca/domino/.

Some examples of the application of AI in air pollution prediction include [17, 46, 66, 86]. The authors in [66] compared traditional methods, such as generalised additive models, to the AI methods such as random forest (RF) and support vector machine (SVM) for predicting $PM_{2.5}$ during wildfire events. In [46], the authors evaluated the effectiveness of RF, SVM and artificial neural network (ANN) for estimating the daily distributions of $PM_{2.5}$. An ANN was employed in [17] to predict the indoor air quality based on data recorded at outdoor air monitors, and the authors in [49] employed boosted regression trees to improve the accuracy of common low-cost air pollution sensors.

$PM_{2.5}$ studies are typically limited to ground-based measurements. As a result, they often utilise land-use models to estimate the spatial distributions and exposure. Satellite-based data is expanding the spatial scope of the accessible data and enabling the incorporation of temporal analyses. Aerosol optical dept (AOD) data, collected as a part of NASA's earth observation program, has been used in combination with meteorological, atmospheric and land-use data to develop spatial-temporal $PM_{2.5}$ models [14]. In this work, RF models were trained to predict daily PM concentrations at a resolution of 1×1 km throughout the metropolitan area of Cincinnati, USA.

Whilst the majority of the previous work utilised traditional AI techniques from supervised and unsupervised learning, the power of deep learning is increasingly being recognised and exploited in state-of-the-art public health research [82]. Unlike physical and statistical models, classical methods from machine learning and deep learning methods have the potential to scale up to global coverage by exploiting the increasing supply of ground-based and satellite-based imagery, along with other remote sensing data. This is facilitated by deep learning's unique ability to efficiently generalise from large datasets composed of multiple data formats, such as image, text and sensor. Recently, researchers have utilised deep learning for haze prediction [52, 54] and for $PM_{2.5}$ and PM_{10} classification and exposure prediction [16, 22, 23]

The authors in [51] proposed the deep learning-based long short-term memory (LSTM) method to predict air pollutant concentrations at fixed locations based on historical air pollutant concentration data, meteorological data and other time series data. Their results suggest that the method can more effectively capture spatio-temporal correlations and incorporates auxiliary data to improve predictive performance. In addition to predicting outcomes, the proficiency of deep learning from image data provides the potential to identify prevalent co-occurring exposure "networks" through image recognition and unsupervised learning [62].

2.2 *Health Outcome Analysis and Characterisation*

A major challenge in environmental health is understanding the relationship between exposure to airborne chemicals and health outcomes. This challenge is exacerbated by the complexity of co-occurring airborne chemicals, the persistence of chemicals in the body for varying lengths of time and other risk factors.

In order to shed more light on the complex relationship between exposure and health outcomes, researchers are increasingly looking to existing and novel AI methods for help. The availability of pollutant release data, transfer registries and chemical biomonitoring data has opened the door to the application of AI to analyse large datasets of chemical exposures. The authors in [7], for example, used frequent itemset mining to efficiently and comprehensively evaluate relationships between chemicals and health biomarkers for diseases in the NHANES biomonitoring survey. In [39, 70], the authors developed a new co-location pattern mining algorithm AGT-Fisher (Aggregated Grid Transactionization) to discover spatial associations between mixtures of chemicals and adverse birth outcomes. In [77], an association rule mining-based methodology is used to discover patterns with relevant odds ratios whilst limiting redundancy and control for statistical significance. The author proposed a combined approach that first used AI to identify a subset of interesting associations between air pollutant exposure profiles and children's cognitive skills, and secondly, the approach utilised traditional statistical methods adjusted for confounders in order to estimate the magnitude. The two-stage approach is particularly effective for generating meaningful hypotheses within high-dimensional exposure data.

Unsupervised clustering algorithms are another effective method to help understand the relationship between airborne chemicals and health outcomes. The authors in [63] utilised self-organising maps (SOM) to identify pollutant profiles within the ambient air and associate them with health outcomes. This work improved the understanding of long-term spatial distributions of multiple pollutants and demographic characteristics of populations residing within areas with distinct air quality. Alternatively, K-means and hierarchical clustering were employed to group days with similar chemical profiles at a single site in Boston, USA [6]. The clusters described unique physical and chemical characteristics and are utilised to investigate physical and chemical conditions posing higher health risks. Bayesian clustering techniques are particularly interesting in the context of environmental health as they attempt to account for uncertainty in the data. The authors in [58] utilise Bayesian clustering to characterise the spatial distribution of multiple pollutants and populations at risk in Atlanta, USA.

2.3 Source Apportionment

Many countries regulate and require the reporting of chemicals emitted to the environment. Once released into the atmosphere, however, complex physical and chemical processes determine their fate. In addition, many chemical emissions, such as those from motor vehicles and aeroplanes, are not directly tracked. As a result, it is difficult to accurately associate local air quality measurements with the factors causing them. Source apportionment aims to trace a given decrease in air quality or increase in a given pollutant back to its emission source. Amongst other benefits, the ability to do so accurately can enable regulators to monitor emitters and is helpful for updating laws and taking steps towards mitigating the impact on humans and the broader environment.

Existing studies largely focus on outdoor and urban air pollution and apportioning particular airborne pollutants to potential sources, such as industrial sites, regions and major intersections. Clustering and data analysis methods have been applied to identify correlations and the importance of particular meteorological parameters, traffic, fuel fired equipment and industries to air pollution [18, 19, 73, 76, 80]. The authors in [87] utilised sequential pattern mining technique to investigate spatial-temporal patterns of $PM_{2.5}$.

2.4 Decision Support

As previously stated, accurate predictive models have the potential to support science and drive decision-making related to regulations and urban planning. Given its ability to incorporate multi-modal data, deep learning may serve as an efficient means of predicting past and future exposures based on known or anticipated changes in land use, traffic and the built environment. In addition, it may serve to identify areas to be prioritised for detailed monitoring and/or surveillance [82].

Existing work focused on discovering associations between chemical mixtures and health outcomes combined with source apportionment can serve to guide public policymakers to increase regulations on chemicals association with adverse health outcomes, work with neighbouring regions to reduce the impacts of upwind emissions and change industrial zoning to reduce the risk of the co-occurrence of chemicals that would form harmful mixtures. In addition, predictive models can be used to determine staffing and other public health needs. In [25], the authors use data from PM monitors to predict hospital admission for cardiovascular and respiratory diseases. Multiple data sources, including Twitter and Google searches, are utilised in [65] to predict asthma-related emergency department visits and can guide staffing levels.

3 Case Study: DoMiNO

This case study presents our interdisciplinary research with Data Mining & Neonatal Outcomes (DoMiNO) project.[2] This work serves to bridge the knowledge gap between exposure to airborne chemical mixtures during pregnancy and the occurrence adverse birth outcomes (ABOs). To achieve this, we utilise state-of-the-art methodologies from data mining and knowledge discovery. The developed spatial co-location pattern mining algorithm AGT-Fisher involves transforming the geo-

[2] Data MIning and Neonatal Outcomes: https://sites.google.com/a/ualberta.ca/domino/.

spatial pollution and birth outcome data into transactions for pattern mining with the Kingfisher algorithm. The Kingfisher algorithm discovers dependency rules of the form $A \rightarrow B$, where A is a set of airborne chemicals, and B is a birth outcome [38, 39, 50, 70].

In data-intensive applications, the data mining process often discovers a larger volume of patterns. The number of discovered patters is often greater than can be analysed and understood by the knowledge users. This poses a significant barrier to the effective utilisation of the mining results. In our work, for example, data mining with the AGT-Fisher algorithm [39] produced over 1700 statistically significant co-location patterns on our data with antecedents up to the size of three chemicals. Metrics of interestingness applied to sort the discovered patterns can only partially address this issue.

In order to facilitate the efficient use of the discovered patterns, we created the visualisation tool, Visualisation of Association Rules (VizAR). This tool advances upon the previous work by developing an interactive Web-based software platform for post-pattern mining, exploration and visualisation. Similar to the work of Ltifi et al. in [55], our goal is to support human intelligence with machine intelligence. Our work, however, focuses on geo-spatial environmental health data and the identification of valuable knowledge in mined co-location patterns.

VizAR serves as the final step in the data mining process, as illustrated in Fig. 1. The essential features of VizAR are (a) interactive exploration and (b) visualisations at multiple levels of geo-spatial abstraction. It operates on the mined patterns,end thereby alleviating the end-user from making complex technical decision regarding algorithms and metrics. It enables users to interactively search, sort, filter, explore and visualise the patterns and their geographic distribution at multiple levels of abstraction.

From a domain perspective, VizAR facilitates knowledge translation by enabling the users to connect the discovered pattern with its roots in the mined data. The results of this can both inspire new research questions and hypotheses and drive new public policy directions. In our results, we present two use-cases for the VizAR software that illustrate its ability to identify interesting and epidemiological significant patterns.

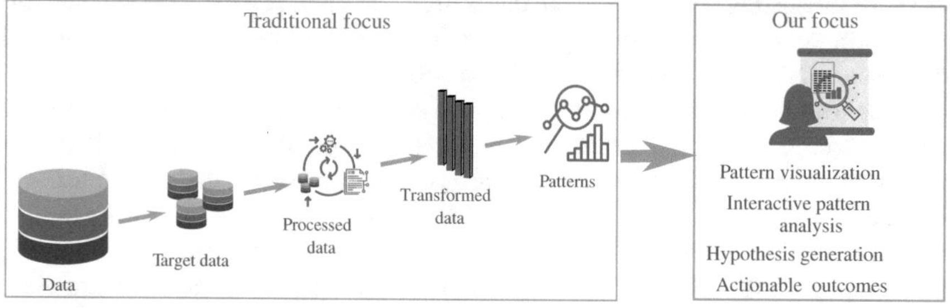

Fig. 1 This work focuses on the final step of the data science process. Specifically, the translation of patterns to actionable user knowledge. This image was inspired by one first appearing in [26]

We evaluate the meaningfulness of a subset of these patterns using the odds ratio, which is a standard approach in epidemiology.

Our evaluation demonstrates that the framework enables users to identify patterns that are pertinent to their work and chemical combinations for which the exposed group is at a greater risk than the unexposed according to the odds ratio. More generally, our user-base finds that pattern discovery via AGT-Fisher and presenting in VizAR enables them to identify new associations that have the potential to initiate research that could lead to healthier births in the future.

3.1 Related Work

In this work, we are interested in association rules, $A \rightarrow B$, where A is a set of airborne chemicals (i.e. antecedents), and B is an adverse birth outcome (i.e. consequent); in the geo-spatial context, these are referred to as co-location patterns. A co-location pattern is a set of spatial features whose instances are often located together in spatial proximity. Due to the significance in multiple fields of study, co-location pattern mining has gained significant importance recently [48]. We address the challenge of co-location pattern mining by transforming the geo-spatial data to a tabular format via aggregated grid transactionization. Transactionization enables the patterns to be discovered with standard association mining algorithms [4, 33].

Measures of interestingness play an essential role in the data mining process. These measures are intended for selecting and ranking patterns according to their potential interest to the user [40]. In addition, they are helpful for saving time and space costs associated with the data mining process [29]. Most of the existing association mining techniques rely on frequency-based prevalence or statistical significance to measure interestingness [4, 33, 85]. These include metrics such as support, confidence, lift and the p-value [29]. Because of the exploratory and interdisciplinary nature of data science, it is often challenging to select a metric that will accurately rank the patterns according to the users subjective preferences. Thus, to avoid pruning rules that may be of interest to the users, a low selection threshold is often used. The result of this is a large number of potentially noisy patterns which are deemed strong or interesting according to the data mining process. A personalised and interactive process is essential to support users in identifying the so-called nuggets of knowledge that are embedded in the discovered patterns.

Visualisation effectively communicates complex ideas and experimental results across disciplines. A significant number of general purpose data visualisation systems have been proposed [12, 34, 81]. These are generic approaches that enable users to load data, cluster it and visualise it in low-dimensional projections. These are limited by their generality, the need to understand algorithms and computer programming and are not designed for searching, exploring and visualising the geographic distribution of mined patterns. Pattern mining researchers have developed some visualisation tools, however, few of these have been proposed for co-location patterns [21], and there is no work in the literature on visualising spatial contrast nor common sets discovered in data mining.

In general, the AI research into pattern visualisation only offers a static perspective on the discoveries; specifically, the user does not have the opportunity to interactively produce the visualisations that are relevant to them in various levels of abstractions. Recent application of data science has noted the importance of interactive and exploratory tools for knowledge discovery and decision support in genetic data and temporal medical data [55, 72].

3.2 Methodology

In this section, we present the datasets, software and evaluation process used in our work.

3.2.1 Data and Preprocessing

The adverse birth outcomes datasets used in this research were acquired from the Alberta Perinatal Health Program (APHP)[3] and the Canadian Neonatal Network (CNN).[4] In each dataset, there are three main adverse birth outcomes: (1) Preterm birth (PTB)—a birth that takes place more than three weeks before the baby is due; (2) Low birth weight at term (LBW)—a birth in which the weight of the baby is less than 2500 g and the gestational age is on or above 37 weeks and (3) Small for gestational age (SGA)—birth in which the baby's weight is in the lower 10th percentile for the gestational age according to Kramer's Canada-wide statistics [42].

The APHP database is a rich dataset including mother's geolocated reported residence by postal code for all live births during the period of 2006–2012 for the province of Alberta, Canada. Specifically, the dataset contains the birth outcome (non-ABO, PTB, SGA, LBW) mother's residence location of 333,247 births. The distribution of the adverse birth outcomes in this dataset is as follows: (1) PTB 22,733 cases; (2) LBW 5,485 cases and (3) SGA 29,679 cases. The CNN data is collected from 19 Census Metropolitan Areas (CMAs) in all provinces across Canada through Neonatal Intensive Care Units (NICUs). This contains mothers admitted to NICUs during the time period of 2006–2010. In particular, the CNN dataset has the geolocated reported residences of 32,836 mothers along with their birth outcomes. The distribution of the adverse birth outcomes in this dataset is as follows: (1) PTB 17261 cases; (2) LBW 1476 cases and (3) SGA 5465 cases.

The industrial air pollutant emissions data were accessed via the National Pollutant Release Inventory (NPRI) of Canada for the time period of 2006–2012. The emissions dataset includes estimates of yearly releases of 136 industrial chemicals.

The NPRI map in Fig. 2 shows the distribution of the 6279 industrial facilities for the province of Alberta. The subsequent maps help demonstrate the distribution

[3] Alberta Perinatal Health Program. http://aphp.dapasoft.com/Lists/HTMLPages/index.aspx.

[4] http://www.canadianneonatalnetwork.org/portal/.

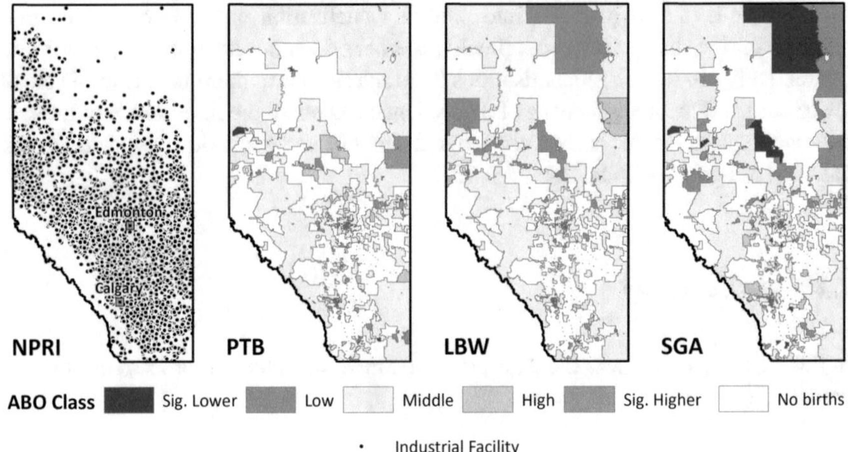

Fig. 2 From left to right, this figure shows the distribution of NPRI sites and the rates of PTB, LBW and SGA for in Alberta during the study period

of births by ABO. To protect individual privacy, the actual locations of residences cannot be shown; therefore, the categories are based on smoothed Bayesian rates that indicate areas of relatively lower (purple) and higher (orange) than the average (yellow) provincial rates of PTB, LBW and SGA. The maps were made available in the Web Mercator projection for knowledge users to access in the visualisation tool.

3.2.2 Transactionization

The above adverse birth outcomes and chemical emission datasets were integrated and tabulated via the transactionization process [39, 50]. To determine the overlapping regions of chemicals and births, we utilised historic weather data from Environment Canada and the Alberta Agriculture weather stations to simulate the atmospheric transportation of airborne chemicals from their point sources. We generated the dispersion region of an air pollutant from an emission point (facility) as a circular buffer where the centre was the emission point, and the radius was defined based on the amount of chemical released. To better reflect the dispersion area, we transform the circular region into an elliptical buffer region based on the average wind speed and direction. The lengths of the major axis and minor axis (a and b, respectively) were computed as follows: $a = r + \gamma|\nu|$; $b = r^2/a$, where r was the radius of the initial circle, and it was equal to the natural logarithm of the amount of chemical released at a given location [r = ln(amounts)]; ν was the wind speed, and γ was the stretching coefficient (=0.3). Detailed information about this process has been published by [39].

As a surrogate of the maternal mobility range during pregnancy, a 5 km radius circles centred on the postal code location of the maternal residence are defined.

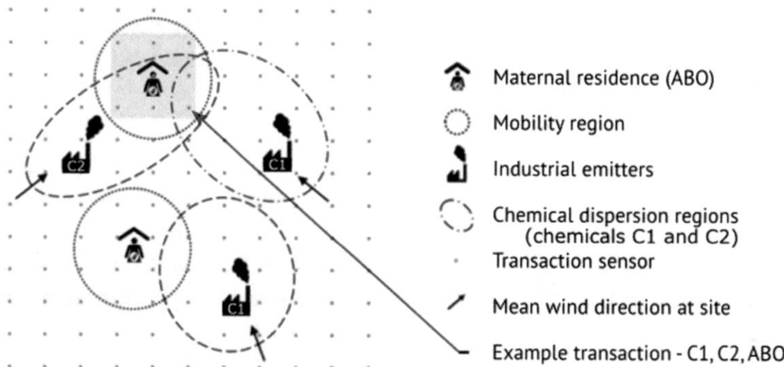

Fig. 3 This figure is recreated from [70]. It presents the process of transactionization. The geospatial region includes the maternal residences and mobility buffers, along with the chemical emission sources and downwind dispersion areas. Transactions record the birth outcomes and chemical occurrences for each grid point on the map according to the overlapping mobility and dispersion regions

This is overlaid with the region of interest (map) with a set of uniformly distributed grid points (1-km grid). This is illustrated in Fig. 3. Each grid point recorded the occurrence or absence of each event (ABO or non-ABO) and each industrial chemical at its location. Thus, an example transaction for a grid point is {SGA = True, LBW = False, ... , benzene = True, chlorine = False, PM = True, ...}. Each grid point is added to the transaction database for co-location pattern mining. As an example, the grid point highlighted in the figure records the co-occurrence of chemical C1, C2 and the ABO. Furthermore, through a transaction aggregation process, this algorithm also captures more complex scenarios where the mother was exposed to multiple chemicals, each with non-overlapping buffer regions.

3.2.3 Data Mining with AGT-Fisher

After the transaction dataset of birth outcomes is created, pattern mining with the Kingfisher dependency rule search technique is applied. Our previous work [39] demonstrated that the Kingfisher algorithm [33] finds non-redundant statistically significant co-location patterns between chemical mixtures and ABO. Kingfisher judges the statistical significance of the association between chemical mixtures and ABO using Fisher's exact test.

The Kingfisher algorithm enumerates trees to search and prune the co-location patterns, thereby discovering likely patterns in a computationally efficient manner. The AGT-Fisher algorithm discovered a set of co-location patterns of the form chemical set → ABO or chemical set → non-ABO, where the pattern satisfied a p-value threshold. A p-value cut-off of 0.05 is used in this work. As previously stated, a common challenge in data mining is that the list of discovered associations remains large (i.e., hundreds). Moreover, it is highly likely that only a small subset of these patterns is of interest to knowledge users. As a result, a subsequent interactive and exploratory processes is needed to enable end-users to understand and isolate the most valuable knowledge in the discovered associations.

3.2.4 VizAR

VizAR is a formalisation for personalised rule identification that enables users to interact with, explore and visualise the discovered co-location patterns at three levels of abstraction:

1. Overview level
2. Pattern level
3. Instance level.

System Architecture: The architecture of VizAR is presented in Fig. 4. VizAR communicates with a central database that stores the previously mined patterns. By mining and storing the patterns in advance, we achieve three desirable outcomes: (a) the technical complexity of data mining is removed from the end-user, (b) the user experience is separated from the time complexity of the data mining, and (c) patient data is securely kept offline. In addition to the patterns, the pattern database includes the anonymised transactions on which the patterns were mined, the corresponding measures of interestingness and meta-data that enables geo-spatial visualisation and exploration of the discovered patterns. VizAR interacts with cloud services to access various kinds of resources such as maps and customised context on adverse birth outcome rates and socio-economic status.

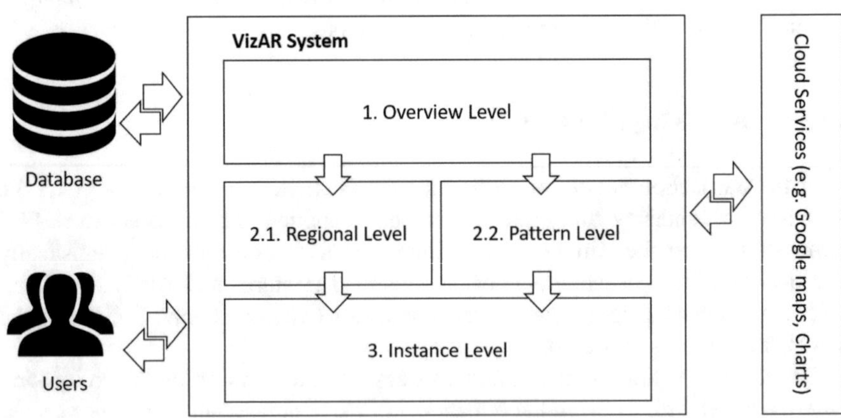

Fig. 4 System architecture of the VizAR framework

VizAR Data Views: The overview level has two components. Users can visualise the geo-spatial distribution of all of the co-location patterns and/or search, sort and filter for a subset of co-location patterns.

The geo-spatial distribution is depicted in the form of an interactive bubble chart in Fig. 5. It enables policymakers and other users to identify common or contrasting trends in sub-regions (CMAs). The CMAs are listed on the y-axis with spacing approximately scaled to the distance between their physical locations. The x-axis specifies the unique identifier of each discovered co-location pattern.

The occurrence of a pattern at a CMA is represented by a circle. In cases where an individual pattern (rule x) is discovered at multiple CMAs, circles are drawn at the intersection of the rule ID on the x-axis and the CMA on the y-axis. For each CMA, the size of the circle indicates the *support* in the dataset for that rule at that CMA. The colour indicates the statistical significance of the pattern at the CMA in terms of Fisher's exact test ($\log(p_F)$) [39].

EX1 in Fig. 5 illustrates an example of contrasting regions (cities in this case) that can be discovered with this view. In this example, Toronto and Moncton are identified as contrasting regions because Toronto has significantly more co-location patterns associated with it than Moncton does. In a similar manner, users can easily identify regions that have association rules in common, such as Toronto and Montreal. We refer to these as geo-spatially common regions, which occur when regions have similar sets of rules. Policymakers can, for example, use this view to identify CMAs with similar issues and initiate working groups to develop focused research on specific chemicals and mixtures in order to support future development of solutions.

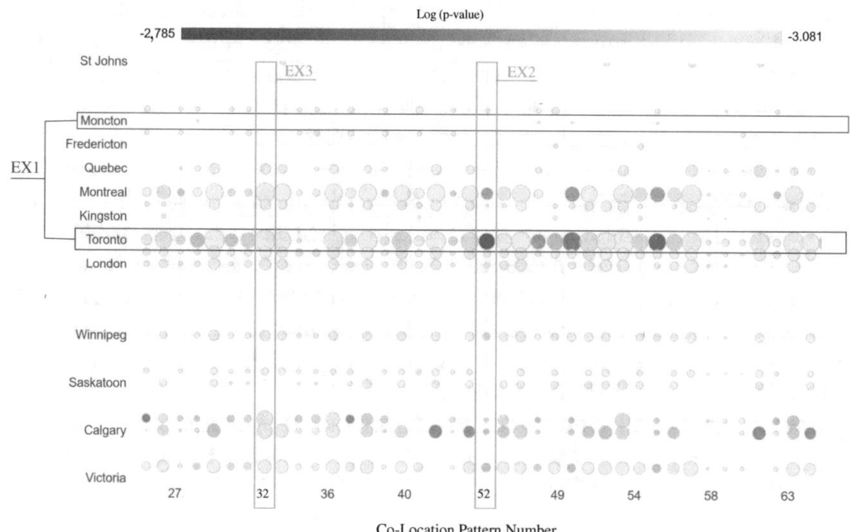

Fig. 5 Regional level visualisation: Bubble sizes represent the support of a rule in a particular spatial region, and the color code represents the $\log(p_F)$ range

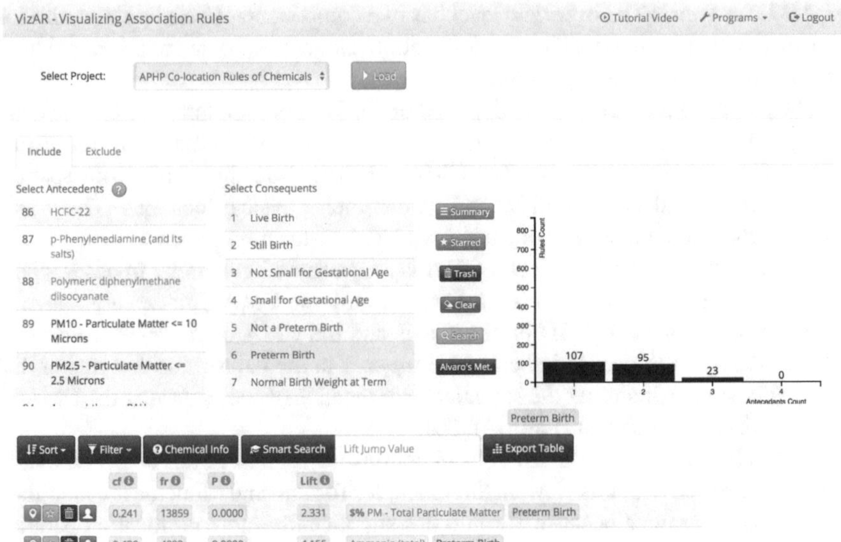

Fig. 6 Search, sort and filter view. This enables the user to find patterns involving chemicals and birth outcomes related to their research

EX2 and EX3 in Fig. 5 demonstrate that users can discover common or contrasting patterns. For instance, EX3 depicts a pattern which is uniformly statistically significant in multiple sub-regions (i.e. common set), whereas EX2 has divergent degrees of significance in different CMAs. Specifically, pattern 52 (i.e. EX2) has strong support and significance in Toronto and weak support elsewhere; thus, it is a contrasting pattern. This can lead policymakers to address the question, why is it prominent in Toronto and nowhere else? Alternatively, pattern 32 is a geo-spatially common pattern with significance and support similar across many CMAs.

The tabular frame in the overview level enables users to find and analyse the occurrence of patterns involving subsets of chemicals and/or adverse birth outcomes. It is shown in Fig. 6. Users can use this feature to reduce the scope of the bubble chart prior to analysis or drill down into the distribution of a specific pattern. In addition, summary statistics describing the number of patterns meeting a search requirement are produced. This includes the bar chart showing the number of patterns of each size that were found. Here, the pattern size refers to the number of chemicals involved. This is depicted on the right-hand side of the view.

Pattern Level Visualisation: Users can drill down to the pattern level view, depicted in Fig. 7, by selecting a pattern of interest at the overview level. This view presents a map of the entire geo-spatial region of interest annotated with the existence of the selected pattern. This gives a perspective on distribution of the pattern of interest across the CMAs in Canada. Once again, the occurrence of the pattern is depicted as a circle, where the support and significance are represented by size and colour. The example in this figure presents another way of identifying geo-spatially common and

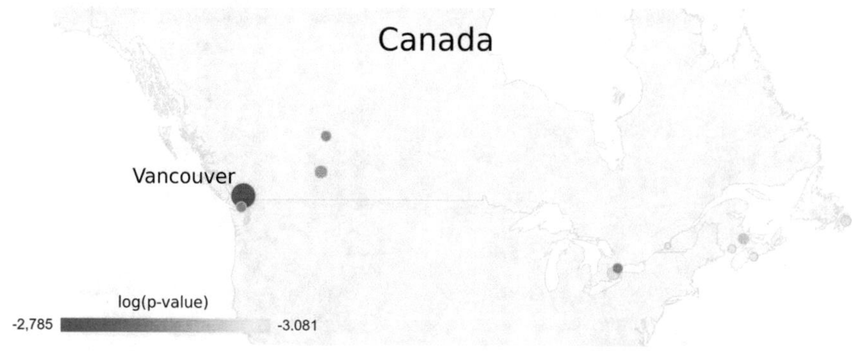

Fig. 7 Visualising a pattern's prevalence/significance in different CMA regions. Size of the bubbles represents the support for the pattern in a particular region, and colour code represents the $\log(p_F)$ (i.e. log of the Fisher's p-value) range

contrasting pattern. In this case, the pattern has much greater support and significance in Vancouver than the other CMAs (i.e. a contrasting pattern/set).

In addition to the map-based analysis, strategies for pattern level analysis based on wind rose plots are provided. A wind rose is typically used to visualise the relative frequency of wind speed at a specific location. It is used here to emphasise the disagreements in the support or significance of a particular pattern across the CMAs.

A spatial-temporal perspective on the patterns is also possible and very useful. This can be achieved using the wind rose plot. Figure 8, for example, demonstrates the visualisation of a pattern across spatial regions in different months. With this visualisation, users can, for instance, discover temporal changes and population shifts leading to a change in the distribution of the pattern.

Instance Level Visualisation: The lowest level of abstraction is formulated as the instance level view. It focuses on exploring a specific pattern in a specific CMA. This view presents the individual occurrences of the pattern on an interactive map. Figure 9 depicts the distribution of the occurrence of the pattern ($PM_{2.5}$, Methyl ethyl keyton, Xylene) $\rightarrow$ PTB in the Edmonton, Canada CMA. Users can zoom in and out on the map in order to gain perspectives on the distribution of the pattern down to the neighbourhood level. In addition, the view allows users to overlay other pertinent information, such as location of the emitting facilities, the interpolated dispersion regions of the chemicals, along birth outcome rates and socio-economic information broken down by denomination area. These help users to better understand the population under study.

4 Results

In order to demonstrate the efficacy of our framework, we present a summary of patterns identified through VizAR by our user-base. In addition, we describe two

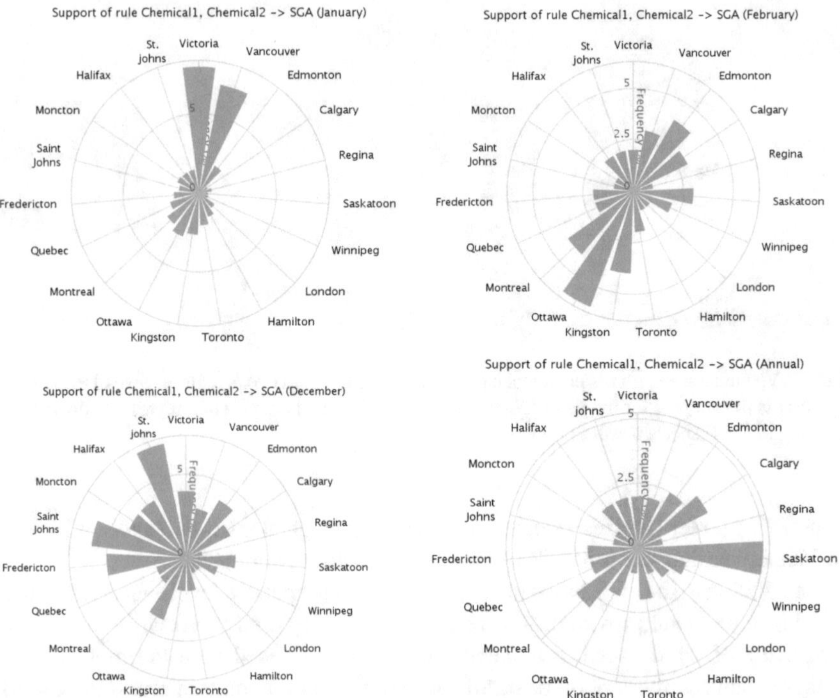

Fig. 8 Demonstration of spatial-temporal analysis by geography and birth month with wind rose plots. This shows a mock-up of the support distribution of contrast sets for January (top left), February (top right), December (bottom left) and annual average (bottom right)

exploration strategies employed by our users and conduct a thorough epidemiological assessment of one of the identified patterns. This is done by calculating the odds ratios of exposure and the outcome [70].

4.1 Identified Patterns of Interest

The user-base includes researchers in environmental health, epidemiology, neonatology, paediatrics and public health. Users were trained to use VizAR and given an opportunity to use it to explore the co-location patterns discovered by our AGT-Fisher algorithm on the datasets. A summary of the chemical mixtures of interest identified by the users via VizAR is provided in Table 1.

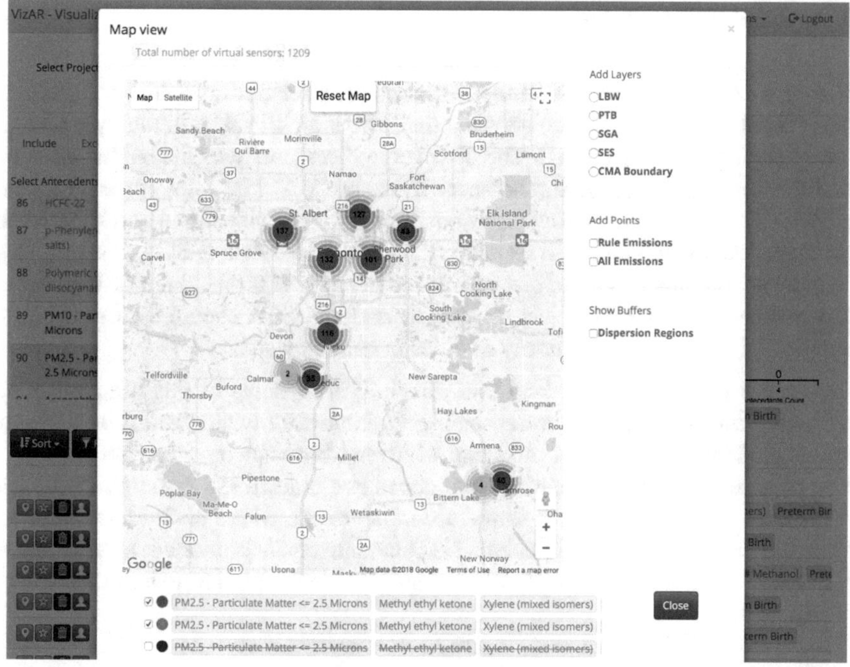

Fig. 9 Instances level visualising of the co-location pattern ($PM_{2.5}$, Methyl ethyl keytone, Xylene) → PTB in the Edmonton CMA. Green colour bubbles represent the places where only the antecedents exist (i.e. air pollutants), whereas the red bubbles represent the places where both the ABO and air pollutants coexist

Table 1 This table presents some chemical mixtures discovered to be associated ABOs via VizAR

Cmemicals	Outcome
Lead + Toluene	ABO
Lead + Xylene	ABO
Lead + Nitrogen dioxide + Particulate matter	ABO
Mercury + Phenanthrene	PTB
Metals + Polycyclic aromatic hydrocarbon	ABO
Toluene + Xylene + Methanol + Carbon monoxide	ABO
Ethylbenzene + Methyl isobutyl ketone	ABO
$PM_{2.5}$ + Methyl ethyl ketone + Xylene	PTB

The mixtures are either associated with general adverse birth outcomes (ABO), or a specific outcome, such as PTB

4.2 Discovery Techniques

Use-case 1 (geo-spatial exploration): This use-case is focused on identifying patterns of the form (chemical mixture) → ABO that have high lift values at multiple CMAs (geo-spatial common patterns). The discovery process analyses the bubble chart to find the rule with greatest significance for each CMA. The rules for each CMA are tabulated, and the most frequently occurring pattern is identified as a significant common pattern. In this case, it identifies that the pattern Lead → SGA to is the most significant common pattern of size one. It has the highest lift in 13 out of 19 CMAs. This indicates that the association between lead and SGA should be a significant question of interest in the majority of cities in our study area.

Use-case 2 (tabular search, sort and filter): The objective of this use-case is to efficiently find subsets of airborne chemical mixtures for which the exposed group has a significantly greater risk of having an adverse birth outcome than not having it. This requires searching and sorting to produce two ordered set P and N. P is a set of patterns $X \rightarrow A = a$ that is sorted according to lift, where the birth outcome is always $A = a$, and X is a set of chemicals. Alternatively, N is a sorted set of negative patterns $Y \rightarrow A = \overline{a}$. A score of the exposure risk is calculated from these sets using the lift ratio:

$$LR(X, A = a) = \text{lift}(X, A = a)/\text{lift}(X, A = \overline{a}) \quad (1)$$

The lift ratio utilises the intuition that all of the mothers in the CMA are exposed to the chemicals X. Thus, the larger the lift ratio, the more significant the association between the exposure and the ABO. The lift ratio is calculated for each pattern in P_i, $\{P_i : X_i \rightarrow A = a\} \in P$ that has a corresponding pattern N_j, $\{N_j : Y_j \rightarrow A = \overline{a}\} \in N$, such that the chemical mixtures are equivalent, $X_i = Y_j$.

Five patterns were discovered using this method, and the pattern ($PM_{2.5}$, Methyl ethyl ketone, Xylene) → PTB was selected to evaluate using odds ratio, which is a standard metric for risk assessment in epidemiology. The odds ratio is defined as the ratio between odds of adverse birth outcome among exposed versus unexposed groups. Thus, an odds ratio greater than 1 indicates a positive relationship between the exposure and the adverse birth outcomes. This pattern has an odds ratio of 1.14, which means that the exposed group is at greater risk than the unexposed group.

Figure 10 gives a relative perspective on the significance of this pattern. It shows the odds ratios, with 95% confidence intervals[5] for smoking and PTB, low socio-economic status (SES) and PTB, our discovered chemical mixture and PTB, along with the combination of all three (smoking, low SES status, rule 1) and PTB. The odds ratios for smoking and SES were calculated using maternal data form the APHP and Census data. In addition to showing that this chemical mixture poses a similar risk as other known factors, it demonstrates that the combination of the chemicals, smoking

[5] Adjusting for maternal confounders including smoking, substance use, past-preterm, mothers' age, socio-economic status, etc.

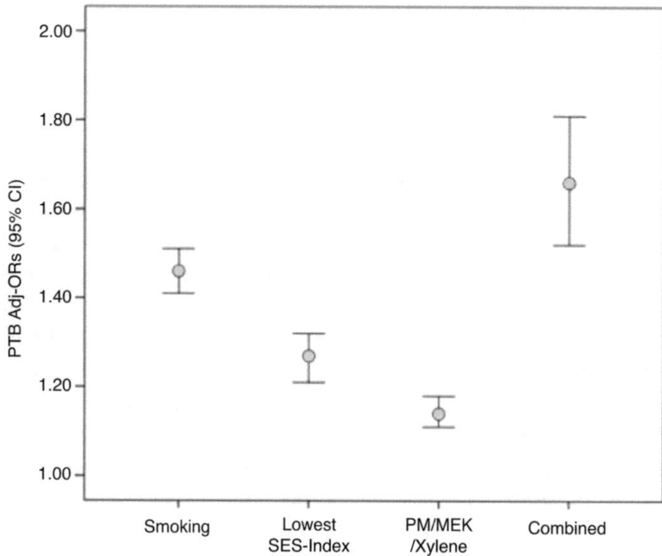

Fig. 10 Comparison of odds ratio (adjusted for relevant maternal confounders and socio-economic status) for an association discovered for preterm birth with other risk factors

and low SES status poses an even greater risk than the individual components. This finding has, in fact, inspired future work and a grant proposal.

5 Discussion

There is a growing body of literature and practical examples that demonstrate the great potential for AI to support the advancement of environmental health. Nonetheless, numerous challenges exist, such as access to a sufficient amount of high-quality data, how optimally pair AI with existing methods in environmental health, appropriate AI algorithm evaluation and parameter tuning methods and techniques to report results in manner that is understandable and reproducible by an interdisciplinary audience. These and related topics are discussed in the subsections below.

5.1 Pattern Filtering and Hypothesis Generation

As demonstrated by the DoMiNO case study, data mining is particularly powerful in contexts involving mixtures of airborne chemicals. The number of patterns discovered by data mining methods, however, can be large and intractable for human analysis. As a result, pattern filtering and visualisations approaches are needed to reduce the volume of discovered patterns. In the DoMiNO project, the lift ratio is utilised to filter the output of the AGT-Fisher algorithm, and hypothesis generation is performed via the interactive visualisation provide by VizAR. The authors in [77] developed two post-pruning criteria to filter the output of the basic Apriori algorithm.

The exploratory nature of data science implies that users are often looking for new insights without a-priori knowledge of the form that the patterns might take. When filtering is applied, it is important to recognise that it risks removing associations between rare, but critical, mixtures and outcomes [62]. Researchers must be careful to achieve the satisfactory balance between reducing the number of patterns and maintaining good sensitivity. The combination of filtering and interactive visualisation can facilitate a better in this respect. Viewing data mining results with GIS tools has also been demonstrated to be a effective way to discover meaningful patterns [63]. Nonetheless, additional research on best practices for pattern filtering and hypothesis generation in the context of environment health is needed.

Because the AI algorithms generally find associations rather than causation, they are better suited to serve as the first step in the hypothesis generation process. The authors in [75] demonstrate AI coupled with traditional methods to narrow the search space. The benefit of such a combined system is that the AI can be applied to high-dimensional, continuous exposure variables, and traditional epidemiological methods control for confounding, assess effect size, investigate various contrasting exposures and identify chemical mixtures of interest.

5.2 Data

Exposome [83] and other ambitious projects are expanding the size and scope of what is traditionally studied in environmental health. To support the characterisation of the breadth of exposures that humans encounter from birth to death necessitates the design and evaluation of novel AI methods for exceptionally high-dimensional spatial-temporal datasets. Advancements, such as those seen in natural language processing with LSTM and transformer networks, are needed in order to discover critical links between events with significant temporal separation.

Regardless of the above-mentioned efforts, the authors in [62] note that the publicly available data remains a significantly limited. Challenges with respect to data access include the cost and complexity of pollution monitoring and dispersion modelling, along with inconsistent collection and privacy concerns related to health records. Whilst the number of potential exposure combinations is immense, the pollution monitoring and health outcome data remain sparse. As a result, the authors claim that the current data may not allow for reproducible findings. New research focused on the application of AI to small, high-dimensional and sparse environmental health data is needed.

Moreover, the quality of the available data is an issue that requires attention. The accuracy of the available data can be compromised on many fronts. This includes due to human error and the accuracy of sensors or the dispersion models used. In addition, the imperfect output of AI algorithms is used as the input to subsequent AI models. This can add a degree of uncertainty to the data that most AI methods cannot account for [74]. AI algorithms that are robust to noise and provide well-calibrated confidence scores will be a great use.

5.3 Robustness and Validity

Unlike traditional statistics, the focus in much of AI is on designing and developing accurate predictive models and discovering frequent, but unknown, patterns. It is critical that collaborators in interdisciplinary application, such as environmental health, understand the implicit assumptions and objectives being optimised by the AI algorithms used (e.g. finding associations versus causal relationships). In many cases, terminology may be used or understood differently between fields. For collaborations to be successful, issues of this nature should be identified in advance and clarified in subsequent publications.

As discussed in [84], interdisciplinary collaborations between AI and environmental health researchers can serve as a gateway to new results and discoveries. These collaborations require that the participants commit time to relationship building, continuous learning and engagement in order to mitigate conflicts and misunderstandings. DoMiNO utilised an iterative process of learning and familiarisation to establish a common ground with regards to data mining methodologies and terminologies. This was found to increase the likelihood of success by providing collaborators from across disciplines with the skill set necessary to proactively participate in the design and undertaking of the data mining process.

In order to promote robust and appropriate use of AI in environmental health, it is advised that practitioners explicitly state the goal of the study in advance, explain why AI is needed and what the assumptions and risks are. Simulation studies and analyses of the AI on artificial datasets that replicate key properties of the target domain are an excellent means of building trust in and understanding of the proposed method. The authors in [44] used a simulated study to assess boosted regression trees' ability to detect relationships between chemical mixtures and metabolic syndrome. This serves to simplify the identification of the limitation of the method, evaluate its robustness to training sets size, noise and correlated exposures.

Results of the AI algorithms and the hypotheses generated from them ought to be considered in the context of the representativeness of the data used. Much like science and society in general, it has been shown that the results of AI algorithms suffer from bias [11, 15]. Recent work has also discussed racism in algorithms deployed in health care [60]. Whilst the representativeness of the data is a major point of consideration in environmental health, it is often overlooked in AI where the academic focus has typically been on theoretical considerations of algorithmic learning. It is only now becoming a critical point of consideration in academic and industrial AI [88]. In the context of AI applied to environmental health, spatial variability in exposure profiles, demographics and contextual characteristics of the subjects in the data must be considered.

5.4 Transparency and Trust

Transparency and trust play an important role when it comes to health and medical applications. The most powerful AI algorithms tend to be complex and are less transparent. This is particularly the case for modern end-to-end deep learning system. Hence, achieving transparency and maintaining trust whilst building a successful AI system is a challenging task, especially in an interdisciplinary setting. In part, the DoMiNO project accomplished this through dialog and mutual learning, but also by facilitating a human-machine interactive process where end-users actively become part of the knowledge discovery process with VizAR. Rather than passively consuming patterns/knowledge provided by the algorithm, the users interactively explored them to understand their foundation and meaningfulness.

5.5 Deep Learning

Artificial neural networks date back to the 1960s. As a result of significant improvements in computing power and dataset size, along with refinements in the learning algorithms, the modern incarnation of artificial neural networks (deep learning) can achieve human-level performance in a wide variety of applications including health [30, 36].

In environmental health, deep learning algorithms designed for object recognition tasks, such as convolutional neural networks (CNNs), have a great potential [43]. Supported by the growing availability of ground- and satellite-based imagery, CNNs provide the potential to simplify and improve large-scale pollution modelling and air quality prediction [82]. A large portion of environmental health data, including that from air pollution senors and medical records, is sequential. Like image recognition, deep learning has made significant breakthroughs in modelling and predicting sequential data, such as natural language [32, 78]. With the growing availability of sequential environmental health data, deep learning architectures, such as LSTMs and transformers, have a great potential to improve the predictive performance beyond the current standard.

Missing data is a common problem in both statistics and AI. In general, it may be handled by removing records with missing values or filling the missing values with estimates and data imputation [5]. However, domain-specific approaches may be devised that produce better results. Missing values, for example, occur in AOD data due to cloud cover and other atmospheric conditions. In [14], the authors addressed this by training two deep learning models, one with and one without AOD data. In other settings, however, training two models may not provide satisfactory performance in all conditions. Deep generative networks, such as generative adversarial networks (GAN) [31], can serve as more powerful data imputation and augmentation methods [37, 47].

Other important challenges in environmental health relate to limited, sparse and class imbalanced data. This includes the lack of pollution data from rural areas and in marginalised and low-income communities. As a result, there is a dearth of knowledge about health issues that are specific to these communities. It is critical that the growing potential of AI in environmental health is utilised to benefit these communities that have traditional been under-served. In addition to new algorithms and data sources, this will require working with communities to better understand their environmental health wants and needs.

Learning from limited data is a challenge that transcends many deep learning applications. It is a quickly developing field of study that has generated a great amount of interest [1–3]. Some exemplary methods with potential in environmental health include data augmentation, transfer learning, domain adaption, few-shot learning and meta-learning. Data augmentation methods serve to correct for class imbalance and artificially inflate the number of samples from underrepresented populations [8, 9, 59]. Few-shot learning and meta-learning aim to utilise knowledge from earlier phases of training to quickly learning new predictive capabilities [27, 28]. In the context of environmental health, this offers the potential for the model to quickly adapt to new health outcomes and new prediction settings. Transfer learning and domain adaption, on the other hand, are techniques that enable models pre-trained one dataset to be quickly refit to new, but typically related, dataset. This can enable better generalisation in the transferred domain and faster learning [30]. A possible application is to develop models for cities with limited data by pre-training on data from cities with a large, representative network of air quality sensors.

6 Summary

Exposure to pollution in the environment is a major contributor to disease globally. There remains, however, a dearth of knowledge about the levels, distribution and types of airborne pollutants in the environment, along with how exposure to complex mixtures of airborne chemicals impacts health outcomes. Research in environmental health aims to monitor and understand factors in the environment that affect human health and disease. Recent collaborations between AI researchers and environmental health have demonstrated a great potential to help advance the science of air pollution epidemiology, urban planning and public policy.

In this chapter, we discussed AI in the context of environmental health related to air pollution. We outlined the importance of the field of study, the challenges that it currently faces and the opportunity for AI to contribute to the advancement of the field. In addition, we presented a case study on the DoMiNO project, which utilised

AI algorithms in combination with pattern visualisation via VizAR and traditional epidemiological analysis to generate hypotheses about which mixtures of airborne chemicals have the greatest impact on birth outcomes. Our results highlight both the great potential for AI in this field along with some interesting challenges for AI researchers to address in future work with environmental health researchers.

References

1. The 2nd learning from limited labeled data (lld) workshop. https://lld-workshop.github.io/. Accessed: 2021-03-29
2. From shallow to deep: Overcoming limited and adverse data. https://s2d-olad.github.io. Accessed: 2021-03-29
3. Workshop on meta-learning (metalearn 2020). https://meta-learn.github.io/2020/. Accessed: 2021-03-29
4. Agarwal, R., Srikant, R., et al.: Fast algorithms for mining association rules. In: Proc. of the 20th VLDB Conference, pp. 487–499 (1994)
5. Aggarwal, C.C.: Data mining: the textbook. Springer (2015)
6. Austin, E., Coull, B., Thomas, D., Koutrakis, P.: A framework for identifying distinct multi-pollutant profiles in air pollution data. Environment international **45**, 112–121 (2012)
7. Bell, S.M., Edwards, S.W.: Identification and prioritization of relationships between environmental stressors and adverse human health impacts. Environmental health perspectives **123**(11), 1193–1199 (2015)
8. Bellinger, C., Corizzo, R., Japkowicz, N.: Remix: Calibrated resampling for class imbalance in deep learning. arXiv preprint arXiv:2012.02312 (2020)
9. Bellinger, C., Drummond, C., Japkowicz, N.: Manifold-based synthetic oversampling with manifold conformance estimation. Machine Learning **107**(3), 605–637 (2018)
10. Bellinger, C., Jabbar, M.S.M., Zaïane, O., Osornio-Vargas, A.: A systematic review of data mining and machine learning for air pollution epidemiology. BMC public health **17**(1), 1–19 (2017)
11. Bolukbasi, T., Chang, K.W., Zou, J., Saligrama, V., Kalai, A.: Man is to computer programmer as woman is to homemaker? debiasing word embeddings. In: Proceedings of the 30th International Conference on Neural Information Processing Systems, pp. 4356–4364 (2016)
12. Bostock, M., Heer, J.: Protovis: A graphical toolkit for visualization. IEEE transactions on visualization and computer graphics **15**(6) (2009)
13. Braun, J.M., Gennings, C., Hauser, R., Webster, T.F.: What can epidemiological studies tell us about the impact of chemical mixtures on human health? Environmental health perspectives **124**(1), A6–A9 (2016)
14. Brokamp, C., Jandarov, R., Hossain, M., Ryan, P.: Predicting daily urban fine particulate matter concentrations using a random forest model. Environmental science & technology **52**(7), 4173–4179 (2018)
15. Buolamwini, J., Gebru, T.: Gender shades: Intersectional accuracy disparities in commercial gender classification. In: Conference on fairness, accountability and transparency, pp. 77–91. PMLR (2018)
16. Chakma, A., Vizena, B., Cao, T., Lin, J., Zhang, J.: Image-based air quality analysis using deep convolutional neural network. In: 2017 IEEE International Conference on Image Processing (ICIP), pp. 3949–3952. IEEE (2017)
17. Challoner, A., Pilla, F., Gill, L.: Prediction of indoor air exposure from outdoor air quality using an artificial neural network model for inner city commercial buildings. International journal of environmental research and public health **12**(12), 15,233–15,253 (2015)

18. Chen, H.W., Tsai, C.T., She, C.W., Lin, Y.C., Chiang, C.F.: Exploring the background features of acidic and basic air pollutants around an industrial complex using data mining approach. Chemosphere **81**(10), 1358–1367 (2010)
19. Chen, M., Wang, P., Chen, Q., Wu, J., Chen, X.: A clustering algorithm for sample data based on environmental pollution characteristics. Atmospheric Environment **107**, 194–203 (2015)
20. Coker, E., Liverani, S., Ghosh, J.K., Jerrett, M., Beckerman, B., Li, A., Ritz, B., Molitor, J.: Multi-pollutant exposure profiles associated with term low birth weight in los angeles county. Environment international **91**, 1–13 (2016)
21. Desmier, E., Flouvat, F., Gay, D., Selmaoui-Folcher, N.: A clustering-based visualization of colocation patterns. In: Proceedings of the 15th Symposium on international database engineering & applications, pp. 70–78. ACM (2011)
22. Di, Q., Amini, H., Shi, L., Kloog, I., Silvern, R., Kelly, J., Sabath, M.B., Choirat, C., Koutrakis, P., Lyapustin, A., et al.: An ensemble-based model of pm2. 5 concentration across the contiguous united states with high spatiotemporal resolution. Environment international **130**, 104,909 (2019)
23. Di, Q., Kloog, I., Koutrakis, P., Lyapustin, A., Wang, Y., Schwartz, J.: Assessing pm2. 5 exposures with high spatiotemporal resolution across the continental united states. Environmental science & technology **50**(9), 4712–4721 (2016)
24. Dominici, F., Peng, R.D., Barr, C.D., Bell, M.L.: Protecting human health from air pollution: shifting from a single-pollutant to a multi-pollutant approach. Epidemiology (Cambridge, Mass.) **21**(2), 187 (2010)
25. Dominici, F., Peng, R.D., Bell, M.L., Pham, L., McDermott, A., Zeger, S.L., Samet, J.M.: Fine particulate air pollution and hospital admission for cardiovascular and respiratory diseases. Jama **295**(10), 1127–1134 (2006)
26. Fayyad, U.M., Piatetsky-Shapiro, G., Smyth, P., Uthurusamy, R.: Advances in knowledge discovery and data mining, vol. 21. AAAI press Menlo Park (1996)
27. Fei-Fei, L., Fergus, R., Perona, P.: One-shot learning of object categories. IEEE transactions on pattern analysis and machine intelligence **28**(4), 594–611 (2006)
28. Finn, C., Abbeel, P., Levine, S.: Model-agnostic meta-learning for fast adaptation of deep networks. In: International Conference on Machine Learning, pp. 1126–1135. PMLR (2017)
29. Geng, L., Hamilton, H.J.: Interestingness measures for data mining: A survey. ACM Computing Surveys (CSUR) **38**(3), 9 (2006)
30. Goodfellow, I., Bengio, Y., Courville, A., Bengio, Y.: Deep learning, vol. 1. MIT press Cambridge (2016)
31. Goodfellow, I.J., Pouget-Abadie, J., Mirza, M., Xu, B., Warde-Farley, D., Ozair, S., Courville, A., Bengio, Y.: Generative adversarial networks. In: Proceedings of the International Conference on Neural Information Processing Systems (NIPS 2014), pp. 2672–2680 (2014)
32. Graves, A., Mohamed, A.r., Hinton, G.: Speech recognition with deep recurrent neural networks. In: 2013 IEEE international conference on acoustics, speech and signal processing, pp. 6645–6649. Ieee (2013)
33. Hämäläinen, W.: Kingfisher: an efficient algorithm for searching for both positive and negative dependency rules with statistical significance measures. Knowledge and information systems **32**(2), 383–414 (2012)
34. Heer, J., Card, S.K., Landay, J.A.: Prefuse: a toolkit for interactive information visualization. In: Proceedings of the SIGCHI conference on Human factors in computing systems, pp. 421–430. ACM (2005)
35. Hermann, J., Schätzle, Z., Noé, F.: Deep-neural-network solution of the electronic schrödinger equation. Nature Chemistry **12**(10), 891–897 (2020)
36. Hinton, G.: Deep learning—a technology with the potential to transform health care. Jama **320**(11), 1101–1102 (2018)
37. Hu, X., Belle, J.H., Meng, X., Wildani, A., Waller, L.A., Strickland, M.J., Liu, Y.: Estimating pm2. 5 concentrations in the conterminous united states using the random forest approach. Environmental science & technology **51**(12), 6936–6944 (2017)

38. Jabbar, M., Zaïane, O., Osornio-Vargas, A.: Discovering spatial contrast and common sets with statistically significant co-location patterns. In: Proceedings of the Symposium on Applied Computing, pp. 796–803. ACM (2017)
39. Jabbar, M.S.M., Bellinger, C., Zaïane, O.R., Osornio-Vargas, A.: Discovering co-location patterns with aggregated spatial transactions and dependency rules. International Journal of Data Science and Analytics **5**(2), 137–154 (2018)
40. Jalali-Heravi, M., Zaïane, O.R.: A study on interestingness measures for associative classifiers. In: Proceedings of the 2010 ACM Symposium on Applied Computing, pp. 1039–1046. ACM (2010)
41. Johns, D.O., Stanek, L.W., Walker, K., Benromdhane, S., Hubbell, B., Ross, M., Devlin, R.B., Costa, D.L., Greenbaum, D.S.: Practical advancement of multipollutant scientific and risk assessment approaches for ambient air pollution. Environmental health perspectives **120**(9), 1238–1242 (2012)
42. Kramer, M.S., Platt, R.W., Wen, S.W., Joseph, K., Allen, A., Abrahamowicz, M., Blondel, B., Bréart, G., of the Canadian Perinatal Surveillance System, F.H.S.G., et al.: A new and improved population-based canadian reference for birth weight for gestational age. Pediatrics **108**(2), e35–e35 (2001)
43. Krizhevsky, A., Sutskever, I., Hinton, G.E.: Imagenet classification with deep convolutional neural networks. Advances in neural information processing systems **25**, 1097–1105 (2012)
44. Lampa, E., Lind, L., Lind, P.M., Bornefalk-Hermansson, A.: The identification of complex interactions in epidemiology and toxicology: a simulation study of boosted regression trees. Environmental Health **13**(1), 1–17 (2014)
45. Landrigan, P.J., Fuller, R., Acosta, N.J., Adeyi, O., Arnold, R., Baldé, A.B., Bertollini, R., Bose-O'Reilly, S., Boufford, J.I., Breysse, P.N., et al.: The lancet commission on pollution and health. The lancet **391**(10119), 462–512 (2018)
46. Lary, D.J., Faruque, F.S., Malakar, N., Moore, A., Roscoe, B., Adams, Z.L., Eggelston, Y.: Estimating the global abundance of ground level presence of particulate matter (pm2. 5). Geospatial health pp. S611–S630 (2014)
47. Lee, H., Liu, Y., Coull, B., Schwartz, J., Koutrakis, P.: A novel calibration approach of modis aod data to predict pm 2.5 concentrations. Atmospheric Chemistry and Physics **11**(15), 7991–8002 (2011)
48. Lee, J.G., Kang, M.: Geospatial big data: challenges and opportunities. Big Data Research **2**(2), 74–81 (2015)
49. Lewis, A.C., Lee, J.D., Edwards, P.M., Shaw, M.D., Evans, M.J., Moller, S.J., Smith, K.R., Buckley, J.W., Ellis, M., Gillot, S.R., et al.: Evaluating the performance of low cost chemical sensors for air pollution research. Faraday discussions **189**, 85–103 (2016)
50. Li, J., Zaïane, O.R., Osornio-Vargas, A.: Discovering statistically significant co-location rules in datasets with extended spatial objects. In: International Conference on Data Warehousing and Knowledge Discovery, pp. 124–135. Springer (2014)
51. Li, X., Peng, L., Yao, X., Cui, S., Hu, Y., You, C., Chi, T.: Long short-term memory neural network for air pollutant concentration predictions: Method development and evaluation. Environmental pollution **231**, 997–1004 (2017)
52. Li, Y., Huang, J., Luo, J.: Using user generated online photos to estimate and monitor air pollution in major cities. In: Proceedings of the 7th International Conference on Internet Multimedia Computing and Service, pp. 1–5 (2015)
53. Litjens, G., Kooi, T., Bejnordi, B.E., Setio, A.A.A., Ciompi, F., Ghafoorian, M., Van Der Laak, J.A., Van Ginneken, B., Sánchez, C.I.: A survey on deep learning in medical image analysis. Medical image analysis **42**, 60–88 (2017)
54. Liu, C., Tsow, F., Zou, Y., Tao, N.: Particle pollution estimation based on image analysis. PloS one **11**(2), e0145,955 (2016)
55. Ltifi, H., Ben Mohamed, E., ben Ayed, M.: Interactive visual knowledge discovery from data-based temporal decision support system. Information Visualization **15**(1), 31–50 (2016)
56. Manrai, A.K., Cui, Y., Bushel, P.R., Hall, M., Karakitsios, S., Mattingly, C.J., Ritchie, M., Schmitt, C., Sarigiannis, D.A., Thomas, D.C., et al.: Informatics and data analytics to support

exposome-based discovery for public health. Annual review of public health **38**, 279–294 (2017)
57. Mauderly, J.L., Burnett, R.T., Castillejos, M., Özkaynak, H., Samet, J.M., Stieb, D.M., Vedal, S., Wyzga, R.E.: Is the air pollution health research community prepared to support a multipollutant air quality management framework? Inhalation toxicology **22**(sup1), 1–19 (2010)
58. Molitor, J., Coker, E., Jerrett, M., Ritz, B., Li, A.: Part 3. modeling of multipollutant profiles and spatially varying health effects with applications to indicators of adverse birth outcomes. Research report (Health Effects Institute) (183 Pt 3), 3–47 (2016)
59. Mullick, S.S., Datta, S., Das, S.: Generative adversarial minority oversampling. In: Proceedings of the IEEE International Conference on Computer Vision, pp. 1695–1704 (2019)
60. Obermeyer, Z., Powers, B., Vogeli, C., Mullainathan, S.: Dissecting racial bias in an algorithm used to manage the health of populations. Science **366**(6464), 447–453 (2019)
61. Oskar, S., Stingone, J.A.: Machine learning within studies of early-life environmental exposures and child health: Review of the current literature and discussion of next steps. Current Environmental Health Reports pp. 1–15 (2020)
62. Patel, C.J., Manrai, A.K.: Development of exposome correlation globes to map out environment-wide associations. In: Pacific Symposium on Biocomputing Co-Chairs, pp. 231–242. World Scientific (2014)
63. Pearce, J.L., Waller, L.A., Sarnat, S.E., Chang, H.H., Klein, M., Mulholland, J.A., Tolbert, P.E.: Characterizing the spatial distribution of multiple pollutants and populations at risk in atlanta, georgia. Spatial and spatio-temporal epidemiology **18**, 13–23 (2016)
64. Rajapakse, N., Silva, E., Kortenkamp, A.: Combining xenoestrogens at levels below individual no-observed-effect concentrations dramatically enhances steroid hormone action. Environmental health perspectives **110**(9), 917–921 (2002)
65. Ram, S., Zhang, W., Williams, M., Pengetnze, Y.: Predicting asthma-related emergency department visits using big data. IEEE journal of biomedical and health informatics **19**(4), 1216–1223 (2015)
66. Reid, C.E., Jerrett, M., Petersen, M.L., Pfister, G.G., Morefield, P.E., Tager, I.B., Raffuse, S.M., Balmes, J.R.: Spatiotemporal prediction of fine particulate matter during the 2008 northern california wildfires using machine learning. Environmental science & technology **49**(6), 3887–3896 (2015)
67. Represa, N.S., Fernández-Sarría, A., Porta, A., Palomar-Vázquez, J.: Data mining paradigm in the study of air quality. Environmental Processes **7**(1), 1–21 (2020)
68. SCHER (Scientific Committee on Health and Environmental Risks): Toxicity and assessment of chemical mixtures (2012). https://doi.org/10.2772/21444. https://ec.europa.eu/health/sites/health/files/scientific_committees/environmental_risks/docs/scher_o_155.pdf
69. Senior, A.W., Evans, R., Jumper, J., Kirkpatrick, J., Sifre, L., Green, T., Qin, C., Žídek, A., Nelson, A.W., Bridgland, A., et al.: Improved protein structure prediction using potentials from deep learning. Nature **577**(7792), 706–710 (2020)
70. Serrano-Lomelin, J., Nielsen, C.C., Jabbar, M.S.M., Wine, O., Bellinger, C., Villeneuve, P.J., Stieb, D., Aelicks, N., Aziz, K., Buka, I., et al.: Interdisciplinary-driven hypotheses on spatial associations of mixtures of industrial air pollutants with adverse birth outcomes. Environment international **131**, 104,972 (2019)
71. Silva, E., Rajapakse, N., Kortenkamp, A.: Something from "nothing"- eight weak estrogenic chemicals combined at concentrations below noecs produce significant mixture effects. Environmental science & technology **36**(8), 1751–1756 (2002)
72. Simon, S., Mittelstädt, S., Kwon, B.C., Stoffel, A., Landstorfer, R., Neuhaus, K., Mühlig, A., Scherer, S., Keim, D.A.: Visexpress: Visual exploration of differential gene expression data. Information Visualization **16**(1), 48–73 (2017)
73. Singh, K.P., Gupta, S., Rai, P.: Identifying pollution sources and predicting urban air quality using ensemble learning methods. Atmospheric Environment **80**, 426–437 (2013)
74. Stingone, J.A., Pandey, O.P., Claudio, L., Pandey, G.: Using machine learning to identify air pollution exposure profiles associated with early cognitive skills among us children. Environmental Pollution **230**, 730–740 (2017)

75. Sun, Z., Tao, Y., Li, S., Ferguson, K.K., Meeker, J.D., Park, S.K., Batterman, S.A., Mukherjee, B.: Statistical strategies for constructing health risk models with multiple pollutants and their interactions: possible choices and comparisons. Environmental Health **12**(1), 1–19 (2013)
76. Thurston, G.D., Spengler, J.D.: A quantitative assessment of source contributions to inhalable particulate matter pollution in metropolitan boston. Atmospheric Environment (1967) **19**(1), 9–25 (1985)
77. Toti, G., Vilalta, R., Lindner, P., Lefer, B., Macias, C., Price, D.: Analysis of correlation between pediatric asthma exacerbation and exposure to pollutant mixtures with association rule mining. Artificial intelligence in medicine **74**, 44–52 (2016)
78. Vaswani, A., Shazeer, N., Parmar, N., Uszkoreit, J., Jones, L., Gomez, A.N., Kaiser, L., Polosukhin, I.: Attention is all you need. arXiv preprint arXiv:1706.03762 (2017)
79. VoPham, T., Hart, J.E., Laden, F., Chiang, Y.Y.: Emerging trends in geospatial artificial intelligence (geoai): potential applications for environmental epidemiology. Environmental Health **17**(1), 1–6 (2018)
80. Wang, H., Zhao, L.: A joint prevention and control mechanism for air pollution in the beijing-tianjin-hebei region in china based on long-term and massive data mining of pollutant concentration. Atmospheric Environment **174**, 25–42 (2018)
81. Ward, M.O.: Xmdvtool: Integrating multiple methods for visualizing multivariate data. In: Proceedings of the Conference on Visualization'94, pp. 326–333. IEEE Computer Society Press (1994)
82. Weichenthal, S., Hatzopoulou, M., Brauer, M.: A picture tells a thousand... exposures: opportunities and challenges of deep learning image analyses in exposure science and environmental epidemiology. Environment international **122**, 3–10 (2019)
83. Wild, C.P.: The exposome: from concept to utility. International journal of epidemiology **41**(1), 24–32 (2012)
84. Wine, O., Zaiane, O.R., Osornio Vargas, A.R.: A collaborative research exploration of pollutant mixtures and adverse birth outcomes by using innovative spatial data mining methods: The domino project. Challenges **10**(1), 25 (2019)
85. Xiong, H., Shekhar, S., Huang, Y., Kumar, V., Ma, X., Yoc, J.S.: A framework for discovering co-location patterns in data sets with extended spatial objects. In: Proceedings of the 2004 SIAM International Conference on Data Mining, pp. 78–89. SIAM (2004)
86. Xu, Y., Yang, W., Wang, J.: Air quality early-warning system for cities in china. Atmospheric Environment **148**, 239–257 (2017)
87. Zhang, L., Yang, G., Li, X.: Mining sequential patterns of pm2. 5 pollution between 338 cities in china. Journal of environmental management **262**, 110,341 (2020)
88. Zou, J., Schiebinger, L.: Ai can be sexist and racist—it's time to make it fair (2018)

SharkSpotter: Shark Detection with Drones for Human Safety and Environmental Protection

Nabin Sharma, Muhammed Saqib, Paul Scully-Power, and Michael Blumenstein

1 Introduction

Marine animals (sharks, dolphins, rays, etc.) are key to the biodiversity and integrity of the marine ecosystem. Marine animals exhibit complex behaviour. Thus, extensive use of the ocean for recreational activities is causing the animals, in particular sharks, attacking humans more frequently than ever before. According to the statistics published by Australian shark statistics for 2015 [1], it recorded 33 unprovoked cases, including two fatal cases and 16 cases with injuries. The statistics show that risk is associated with the ocean when recreational activities are carried out without supervision. However, manual supervision of the beach by a human may miss some of these critical and life-threatening situations. Moreover, manpower for shark detection and deterrence is costly, inaccurate and inadequate. There is a call for effective management of the marine environment using aerial surveillance. However, helicopter and fixed-wing aircraft aerial surveillance are not designed for long flights, and their flights typically last for 5–10 min with tens of thousands per flight. Another concern is their lower accuracy [2, 3], such as 17.1% and 12.5% for analogue sharks observed from helicopters and fixed-wing aircraft, respectively. The accuracy for a human observer to analyse the aerial images is approximately 38% (drone pilot) and 50% (post-flight video analysis) [4], which is not adequate for effective beach safety management and shark detection.

N. Sharma (✉) · M. Saqib · M. Blumenstein
School of Computer Science, Australian Artificial Intelligence Institute,
University of Technology Sydney, Sydney, NSW 2007, Australia
e-mail: Nabin.Sharma@uts.edu.au

M. Blumenstein
e-mail: Michael.Blumenstein@uts.edu.au

P. Scully-Power
Ripper Corporation Pty Ltd, 18 Manning Road, South Brisbane, QLD 4101, Australia
e-mail: psp@rippercorp.com

F. Chen and J. Zhou (eds.), *Humanity Driven AI*,
https://doi.org/10.1007/978-3-030-72188-6_11

Traditionally manned aircraft with experienced crew has been used for aerial surveys and monitoring of beaches. Although the aircraft provides a very good view of the ocean from the sky, the process is manual, time consuming and expensive and requires the constant attention of human observers [2]. This process is susceptible to human error. Hence, automating the whole process is a way forward for such monitoring as it requires high precision and prompt action in case of any emergency. The recent advancement in drone technology has made possible the availability of cheaper drones for videography and entertainment. These drones are equipped with high-resolution cameras capable of capturing images and videos with excellent quality in real-time. Moreover, combined with the advancement in an intelligent system using computer vision and deep learning, the UAVs are an excellent choice for the identification of sharks or other potential threats from the live video stream.

The increase in shark attacks can be attributed to the frequent interaction of humans with the marine ecosystem [5]. Several shark control programmes [6–9] have been widely adopted around the world to decrease the risk by removing/restricting the sharks from areas used for recreation purposes. However, these programmes, in general, do not discriminate sharks from other marine life, which results in interference with the marine ecosystem and can be harmful [10, 11]. Hence, there is a need to explore alternate solutions that facilitate the coexistence of marine life and humans without compromising the safety of humans and marine animals.

Thus, providing safety and security around beaches is essential. Furthermore, safety for both human beings and marine life (e.g. sharks, dolphins, etc.) in general is critical while people continue to use the beaches heavily for recreation and sport. Hence, an efficient, automated and real-time monitoring approach on the beaches for detecting sharks and overall beach surveillance is necessary to avoid unexpected accidents and human/marine life loss. The drone surveillance equipped with advanced computer vision techniques provides an excellent solution for the awareness of surroundings and has obvious advantages in drone search and rescue. This chapter will discuss the application of drones for detecting sharks, deployment as a system, the challenges associated with their operation and their effectiveness in a maritime environment.

2 Critical Challenges in Automatic Shark Detection

Ocean is already a challenging environment, and exploring a potential technology solution for detecting sharks automatically and performing beach surveillance pose additional challenges and open research problems. Quite a few techniques were proposed and used a part of the shark mitigation strategies, which includes shark net, aerial patrols using helicopters, electronic shark deterrents, etc., to mention a few significant ones. Although the shark deterrents [12] are effective, it still has a hidden risk involved as there are various shark species available and some may not respond to the pre-defined frequencies. Moreover, the devices are invasive in the context that they are wearable, and the discharge frequencies can be harmful to both human and sharks or marine life in general. Hence, a technology solution which is non-invasive to the marine ecosystem is desired.

Drones or UAVs equipped with a camera have received a lot of attention due to their low cost, availability and potential usefulness in a wide range of applications, including aerial photography, surveillance, delivery of parcels, agriculture, etc. Intuitive understanding of the streaming visual data becomes vital in such applications for the practical usage of drones. Therefore, the use of computer vision algorithms plays a major role in the successful deployment of drones. Despite the great advancement in general computer vision algorithms for object detection, tracking and segmentation, these algorithms are not optimal for drone-based applications and need customization based on specific requirements.

This section will discuss some of the major challenges in the development and deployment of an automatic shark detection system for visual analysis of marine animals using drone/aerial imagery. The challenges have been categorized into unavailability of datasets, environmental challenges and software & hardware challenges and are discussed below.

2.1 Unavailability of Dataset

The first challenge was the lack of a publicly available dataset for marine animal detection using aerial images. The dataset was collected using drones from different beaches under a variety of conditions over a year. Development of SharkSpotter required a large amount of footage with sharks in different environmental conditions and locations. This was a time-consuming task as it is highly unlikely to spot sharks during every drone flight. Machine learning algorithms and deep learning models, in particular, require a huge amount of data for training and testing. Appropriate videos were selected from large sequences of captured data for data preparation. Annotation of videos, in particular, was a very time-consumming task. A trained human was required to manually draw bounding boxes around the different objects of interest present in video frames, and the information was stored in a particular format required by the deep learning algorithms. The collection, pre-processing and annotations were laborious and challenging before the project's actual start. Moreover, the dataset collection involved approval from government agencies to capture images and videos for research and development. The aim was to cover as many scenarios as possible in the data collection phase. However, classes were added regularly for new marine objects, which enables the machine learning model to detect a variety of objects. Major challenges related to data collection include the following:

- Optimal speed of UAV/drone, altitude, camera resolution for data capture and actual deployment.
- Unconstrained lighting conditions while capturing real-time videos of beaches using the UAV/drone.

2.2 Environmental Challenges

The ocean is a completely unconstrained environment that poses myriads of challenges to the deployment of an automatic shark detection system using a deep learning model. The change in weather conditions such as rain and the low-light condition causes illumination that affects the object detector's performance. Similarly, high tides of water cause the object of interest to be hidden from the object detector causing occlusion. Moreover, power and Internet connectivity are also major bottlenecks when flying drones on remote beaches for rescue and surveillance. Salty water and sandy environment near the beaches are also of major concern as this might damage the computer hardware.

Noisy backgrounds in data due to ocean waves, muddy water, human activities, surf boards, boats, sun glare, etc., make it more complex to design an efficient shark detection system using drones and are the major environment challenges.

2.3 Software and Hardware Challenges

The aim of the SharkSpotter project or an automatic shark detection system is to provide real-time alert for shark detection and other marine species with a significantly high accuracy. Moreover, the challenge is to optimize the deep learning model that can be deployed with limited resources and hardware. The deeper the architecture of the model, the more accurate the model in general. However, the real-time performance considerably decreases with deeper models. Therefore, a trade-off has to be made between the type of model, accuracy and real-time performance keeping in view the capacity of the hardware. On the software side, a wide range of deep learning-based object detection algorithms are available and choosing the appropriate one for the task considering the real-time performance requirement. Ease of deployment of the deep learning model on small form factor hardware is also a challenge given the high performance and real-time processing requirements. Harsh environment near the beach requires a rugged hardware which can withstand high operating temperature while delivering expected performance.

Developing the software (machine/deep learning model, intuitive interface, etc.) involved the following major challenges:

- Tracking and identifying/distinguishing sharks from other large fish/marine life.
- Distinguishing sharks from other objects, namely surfer, swimmers, drone shadows, etc., in noisy background/environment.
- Detecting potentially unusual activities indicating shark attacks.
- Noisy backgrounds due to ocean waves, human activities, surf boards and other objects.
- Real-time alarms for surf life-saving clubs/teams in case of a shark detection/attack.

Major hardware challenges include the following:

- Choice of hardware for deploying the machine/deep learning model without compromising with real-time performance and high accuracy.
- Finding a rugged small form factor hardware for deployment with software optimization.
- Estimating the extreme operating conditions (e.g. harsh environment) to determine the hardware failure situations.

Figure 1 highlights some of the challenges involved in processing the aerial video of the ocean. Among the above-mentioned challenges, some of them required human intervention to potentially find a solution, whereas for others artificial intelligence (AI) can potentially assist in developing an efficient/effective solution. More specifically, tracking and identifying sharks from other marine animals, distinguishing sharks from other objects, unusual activity detection, real-time alerts in case of shark attack are some of the critical challenges which can be solved using AI with high performance. Another important factor for the potential AI solution is to ensure that it does not interfere with the marine ecosystem.

3 Related Approaches Towards an AI Solution

In this section, the recent works on automated marine animal detection are discussed.

Not much work has been reported in the literature to address the problem of automatic marine animal detection [13–15], in general, and shark [16–20] detection in particular. Among the recent work, Mejias et al. [21] presented two algorithms to detect marine species automatically. They focus on detecting dugongs from aerial images, in order to automate the aerial surveys. Two algorithms were proposed; morphological operations and combined colour analysis for blob detection were used in the first algorithm. The second algorithm used a shape profiling method on saturation channel from HSV colour space. The reported result showed very low precision rate and high false positives.

Maire et al. [13] also presented an algorithm for detecting dugongs from aerial imagery. Their approach consisted of two stages. Regions-of-interest are determined in the first stage using colour and morphological filter. In the second stage, shape analysis is performed on the candidate blobs identified from the first stage. A template matching technique is used for finalizing detection results. The system performed better when the sea surface was calm, but the performance degraded as the sea surface became rough.

Shrivakshan [16] presented an analysis of Sobel and Gabor filters for classifying different shark types. The analysis shows that Gabor filters performed better than Sobel filter. Use of multi-spectral imaging for automatic detection of marine animals was studied by Lopez et al. [14]. To the best of our knowledge, the first study on automatic shark detection using deep learning [22–25] was reported by Sharma et al. [17]. Three different CNNs (ZF [26], VGG16 [27] and VGGM [28]) architectures

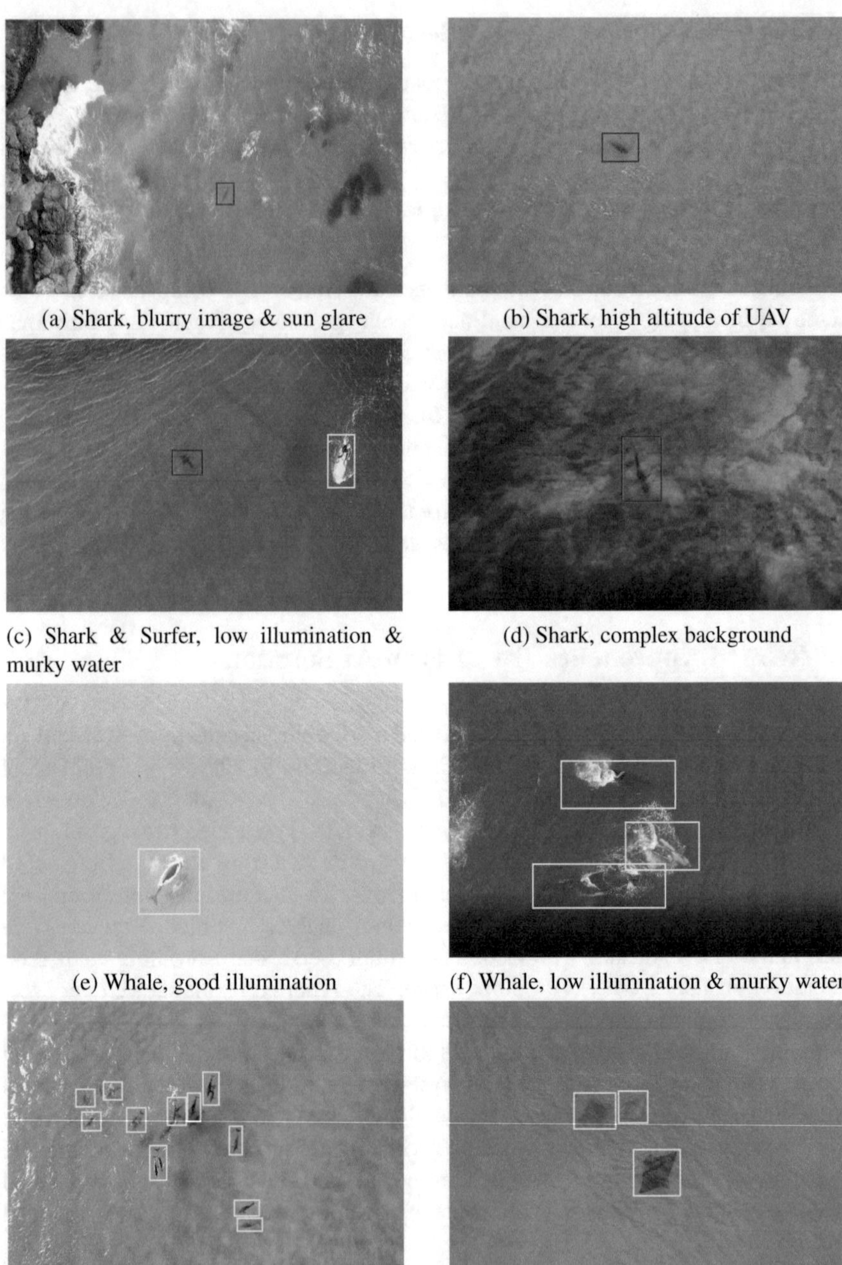

(a) Shark, blurry image & sun glare

(b) Shark, high altitude of UAV

(c) Shark & Surfer, low illumination & murky water

(d) Shark, complex background

(e) Whale, good illumination

(f) Whale, low illumination & murky water

(g) Dolphins, sun glare

(h) Rays, murky water

Fig. 1 Sample aerial images of shark, whale, dolphin, ray and surfer

were used in the study, and a comparative analysis of the performance was presented. Five different objects, namely shark, surfer, large fish, whale and boats, were considered for the experiments. Mean average precision(mAP) of 90.1% was reported using VGG16 architecture.

Recently, Gorkin et al. [18] proposed the Sharkeye system/platform, a personal shark alert system used by the beach goers. The authors used a deep learning-based method. The CNN architecture used by the authors was based on the You Only Look Once (YOLO) methodology. Shark, surfer and ray were considered for the experiments, and an accuracy of 68.7% was achieved during the trials.

To summarize, although global shark attacks in the recent years were quite high, not many works have been reported towards the automation of the detection process, as compared to the severity of the consequences. Most of the works found in the literature used traditional machine learning approach and were quite slow with unacceptable precision. Real-time performance and high precision are an essential requirement for an acceptable solution, which were missing in the discussed approaches. Few of the recent works [17, 18] used deep learning methodologies or CNNs, but extensive experiments are still needed for the development of a commercial grade system.

3.1 The SharkSpotter© AI Solution

SharkSpotter© is the world's first non-destructive and non-invasive technology that uses a deep learning algorithm to detect sharks and other potential threats using real-time aerial video imagery. Operating via cameras attached to drones that fly over the surf, SharkSpotter improves the safety of Australia's beaches by identifying sharks, providing early warnings and protecting sensitive marine ecosystems. It provides 90% accuracy, compared to current shark detection methods that have an accuracy rate of >30%. It is also a highly cost-effective approach to beach safety, costing substantially less than current methods. Deployment of SharkSpotter has gained beachgoers' confidence and reinvigorated beach tourism in areas that have struggled due to a high incidence of shark attacks.

Use of deep learning architecture resulted in an AI-driven algorithm with a high confidence score. Data was prepared by manually annotating drone footage, and the algorithm is trained to detect, identify and classify sharks and other marine objects. Deployment of SharkSpotter across Australian beaches occurred after successful trials and fine-tuning, including improving the user friendliness of the graphical user interface. Field trials and milestone reports were used to assess performance, users were trained, and user manuals were created to ensure SharkSpotter's seamless deployment. SharkSpotter received significant media attention and won several awards in recognition of its important contribution to shark detection and mitigation strategies.

SharkSpotter's capabilities far exceed those of aerial spotters, which make little sense of the dynamic, cluttered ocean environment where sharks and other marine

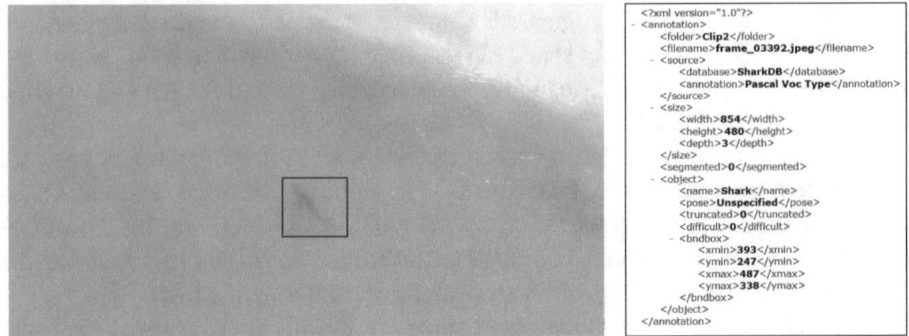

Fig. 2 Sample image of a shark (marked in red) annotation

objects are seen only as moving shadows. SharkSpotter has revolutionized shark detection by using deep learning to distinguish between these shadows—essentially 'seeing' sharks under the water. SharkSpotter's cameras relay these images to lifesavers at a control centre on the beach and provide a visual indication and audible alert when a shark is spotted. The image relay occurs in real-time, with a latency of just one second, quickly alerting lifesavers and beachgoers to the danger of nearby sharks. SharkSpotter relies on lifesavers to make decisions based on the data they are given. They can sound an alarm broadcast by the drones to alert swimmers and surfers to a shark's presence and direct them to leave the water. The deployable lifesaving flotation pod and electronic shark repellent attached to the drone can also be dropped to swimmers and surfers when sharks are nearby.

Over two years, the team used video and image processing, pattern recognition and machine learning techniques to develop SharkSpotter's object detection, identification and classification capabilities. They overcame challenges associated with using the technology in complex environments such as optimal altitude range, potential camera resolution, illumination conditions, the infrequency of shark sightings and the difficulties of distinguishing sharks from other large fish/marine species and surfers, swimmers, boats and other large objects.

The UTS team collected real-time data from Westpac Little Ripper drones flown over Australian beaches and manually annotated the resulting videos by identifying sharks and other marine objects. An example of annotation along with its corresponding video frame/image is shown in Fig. 2. Pascal VOC [29] format was used for creating the corresponding XML files for annotation. Sixteen different objects/categories were considered in the development of SharkSpotter, namely *shark, surfer, swimmer, whale, dolphin, eagle ray, turtle, person, drone, kayak boat, paddle boat, single paddle boat, tent (on beaches), boat(generic category), large fish (generic category) and unknown(generic category)*. The generic boat category represents different types of boats as enough samples were not available to form separate categories/classes. Additionally, the large fish and unknown categories were used to represent large marine animals which are not having clear shape (e.g shadows) in the video/image due to low resolution, glitter, etc., but could be of potential interest or can pose threats

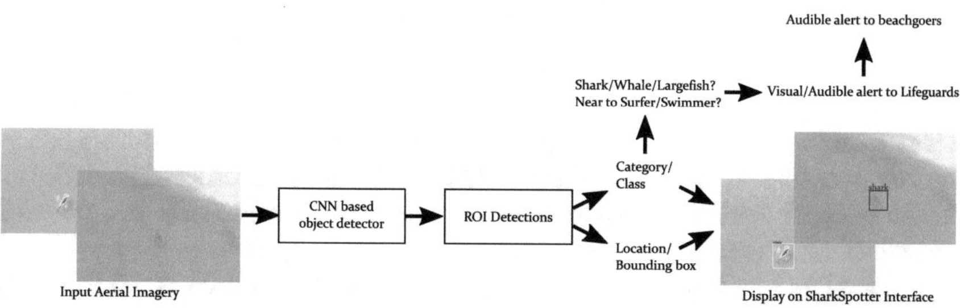

Fig. 3 SharkSpotter© framework version-1

to the beach users. The generic categories were defined to reduce the confusion with sharks and enhance the performance of the system. It also enables the system to detect a broad range of objects in the dynamic ocean environment, which can be verified by the lifeguards/operators.

The team then used cutting-edge deep learning and the transfer learning technique [30] to fine-tune the system, accelerating the algorithm training process and achieving better performance and accuracy. Various convolutional neural network (CNN) architectures were evaluated, and their performance formed the basis of the development of the custom model for SharkSpotter. A high-level framework of the SharkSpotter solution version-1 is shown in Fig. 3. The final algorithm had a high confidence score and efficiently and effectively identified sharks and other marine objects in real-time using image processing techniques, state-of-the-art sensors and AI software. It was then applied to detect, identify and classify sharks via a camera on board a Westpac Little Ripper Lifesaver drone. A simple and intuitive graphical user interface was designed and developed that would relay images from the camera to lifesavers at the control centre on the beach. The aim was to provide a better end user experience, whereby lifesavers could quickly and easily recognize and respond to the presence of nearby sharks after SharkSpotter provided a visual indication and audible alert.

The dataset used for developing the SharkSpotter version-1 solution comprises more than 13K aerial video frames/images. The dataset consists of videos from UAV trials conducted on popular Australian beaches. The dataset was divided in three subsets: for training, validation and testing, with random sampling. The train set consists of 70% of the total dataset, whereas validation and test set consist of 15% each of the total samples, respectively. Based on the initial experiments [17], a custom CNN network architecture was designed and trained. The model was trained with $2 \times$ Nvidia Quadro P6000 GPU, 24 GB, on a Ubuntu server (Core i7 processor, 64 GB RAM). In the training phase, the snapshot of trained models was saved at an interval of $10k$ iterations. Detections with overlap greater than the 50% intersection over union (IOU) threshold with the corresponding ground-truth bounding box are considered as true positive and all other detections as false positive as shown in Eq. 1 [29].

$$\mathrm{IOU} = \frac{\mathrm{area}\left(\mathrm{BBox}_{\mathrm{pred}} \cap \mathrm{BBox}_{\mathrm{gt}}\right)}{\mathrm{area}\left(\mathrm{BBox}_{\mathrm{pred}} \cup \mathrm{BBox}_{\mathrm{gt}}\right)} \tag{1}$$

where $\mathrm{BBox}_{\mathrm{pred}}$ and $\mathrm{BBox}_{\mathrm{gt}}$ are the predicted bounding box and ground-truth bounding box, respectively. Average precision (AP) is calculated from the area under the precision–recall (PR) curve [29] to evaluate the detection performance. Mean average precision (mAP) is the average of AP over all classes/categories.

The mAP of SharkSpotter was ≈ 0.81 with an average precision of >0.90 for the shark category. The performance of large fish category detection was also comparable with an average precision of >0.88. High precision for large fish class justifies its formation to represent a generic class of marine animals which are large in size and could be of potential danger to the beach users. Additionally, large fish category helped in minimizing the confusion with shark and whale categories. Sample detection results are shown in Fig. 4. The resultant images show the robustness of SharkSpotter in detecting shark under different environmental conditions along with other objects such as whales, eagle rays, dolphin, boats, surfer and swimmer.

4 Implications of the SharkSpotter Solution

SharkSpotter was developed with an intention to create a technology solution for shark mitigation, which is more efficient than the existing techniques, cost effective, eco-friendly and easy to use, and can assist the lifeguards in better decision-making in a highly dynamic ocean environment with limited visibility. The SharkSpotter solution achieved majority of the targets with high accuracy and real-time performance.

SharkSpotter's economic impacts are also significant, reducing typical costs associated with patrolling Australian beaches, which exceed \$25 M per annum [31]. The cost of deploying the Westpac Little Ripper Lifesaver drone is substantially less than aerial detection by helicopters. A study was conducted by the Ripper Group over a five-month period (January–May 2018) across 11 beaches in Northern NSW, monitoring high beach-going activity. Using helicopter patrol for 600 hours, spending 5–10 minutes per beach per day, the cost was approximately \$360 K. For around the same cost (\$363 K), Westpac Little Ripper Lifesaver drones could patrol 11 beaches consistently for 5775 hours across the five months and could reliably monitor those beaches via SharkSpotter for an entire day. Secondly, SharkSpotter has had important economic outcomes for the tourism industry. SharkSpotter and Westpac Little Ripper Lifesavers have regained the confidence of tourists and locals in struggling beach locations. For instance, in Ballina, northern NSW, SharkSpotter has shifted the public's view of the town as the 'shark capital of Australia'. This dubious title contributed to a decline in tourism and significant losses for hotels, restaurants and other infrastructure. A 2018 survey by the Ripper Group found that more than 95% of people felt safer due to Little Ripper drones patrolling the beaches they visited.

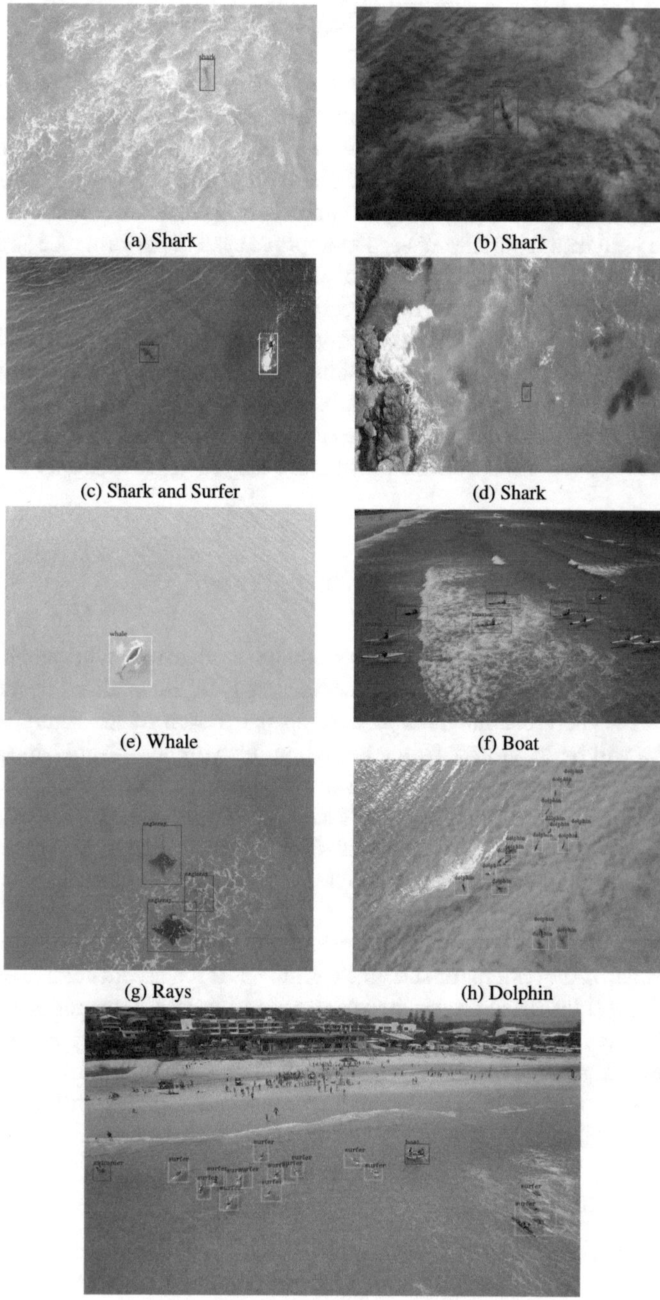

(a) Shark (b) Shark

(c) Shark and Surfer (d) Shark

(e) Whale (f) Boat

(g) Rays (h) Dolphin

(i) Surfers, Swimmer and Boat

Fig. 4 Sample detection results obtained using SharkSpotter model

In December 2017, 17 Westpac Little Ripper Lifesavers trialled SharkSpotter at 15 different Australian beaches to assess performance with respect to various parameters including camera resolution, height above sea level, speed and flight duration, all of which affected the performance of both the drone and the algorithm. Weekly and fortnightly meetings were arranged between UTS and the Ripper Group to monitor progress and maintain the collaboration. The UTS team closely participated in field trials conducted by The Ripper Group to understand operational conditions and challenges, and field trial reports were used to improve system performance and increase user friendliness. Milestone reports were also produced and discussed periodically to mitigate the risks associated with the research.

SharkSpotter also has significant environmental impacts. The increased sense of security has changed beachgoers' emotional relationships with sharks, leading to a reduction in reactionary shark culls in areas of high shark activity. Further, the technology can reduce damage to marine ecosystems by replacing shark nets, which are destructive to the marine environment and costly at approx. $50m per annum.

5 Future of Beach Safety and Surveillance

Australian beaches are well patrolled by volunteer lifesavers who monitor swimmers who swim 'between the flags'. However, many of the fatalities occur 'beyond the flags'. It is therefore intended to develop the 'beach of the future' where an entire beach will be 'patrolled' by the latest high-tech drones—Mini Ripper surveillance drones, Little Ripper fast-reaction rescue drones, tethered drones for continuous surveillance, and Ripper Ranger Coastwatch drones covering several beaches, together with Ocean Guardian electronic shark-repellent buoys. It is also intended to expand the suite of 'Spotter' technologies to include RipSpotter and PeopleSpotter and DistressSpotter to detect people in distress. And further work will address multi-spectral and hyper-spectral to get penetration in water below the surface, coupled with polarization filters for sun glitter removal. It is also intended to expand the suite of 'deployables' from drones for search and rescue (SAR) operations, including flotation devices, emergency packages, defibrillators, medical supplies, etc., which may require parachutes for deployment. And finally, our infrared sensor capabilities for bushfires and night detection will be enhanced, together with algorithms to quantify damages to structures in disaster areas.

6 Summary

Shark attacks have been a very emotive issue in Australia and across the globe. Although numerous shark management programmes are implemented and running globally, the risk of shark attacks is still high and is a serious threat to beach recreation. The existing solutions are invasive to the marine ecosystem, costly and not very effective in terms of performance/accuracy. Although non-lethal shark deterrents are commercially available, they are not extensively tested on all species of sharks and other marine animals, which can still pose potential risk to ocean users. Hence, a technology solution, SharkSpotter, is presented in this chapter. To the best of our knowledge, SharkSpotter is the world's first AI solution for detecting sharks. A deep learning-based approach has been used to develop the AI solution. Trained and tested using a large dataset comprising 16 different categories of objects are commonly found in a beach environment. SharkSpotter solution has been trialled and deployed across several Australian beaches with high user acceptance. It is cost-effective, highly accurate and an eco-friendly alternative to the existing shark mitigation techniques. Moreover, it works in real-time and is able to detect sharks with $\sim$90% accuracy. SharkSpotter paired with drone/UAV can provide both better visibility (aerial view) and an efficient decision-making companion to the lifeguards and assist them to make the beach recreation much safer. Further reseach is in progress to build a multiple sensors (multi-spectral, thermal)-based AI solution, in order overcome the existing issues and making the beaches smarter and safer.

Acknowledgements The authors would like to thank the Ripper Group (Now Ripper Corporation) for providing the data samples for the experiments. The Ripper Group operated the Westpac Little Ripper Lifesaver UAV/drones at beaches in NSW and QLD in conjunction with Surf Life Saving Australia. This research was funded by the Ripper Group under a research contract with the University of Technology Sydney (UTS).

References

1. https://taronga.org.au/conservation/conservation-science-research/australian-shark-attack-file/2015
2. Robbins WD, Peddemors VM, Kennelly SJ, Ives MC (2014) Experimental Evaluation of Shark Detection Rates by Aerial Observers. PLOS ONE 9(2): e83456. 1 https://doi.org/10.1371/journal.pone.0083456
3. Robbins, W.D., Peddemors, V.M. and Kennelly, S.J., (2012) Assessment of shark sighting rates by aerial beach patrols. Fisheries Final Report Series No. 132. Cronulla, NSW, Australia. 38pp. ISSN 1837–2112.
4. Butcher Paul A., Piddocke Toby P., Colefax Andrew P., Hoade Brent, Peddemors Victor M., Borg Lauren, Cullis Brian R., "Beach safety: can drones provide a platform for sighting sharks?", Wildlife Research, 2019, 46, 701–712.
5. West J (2011) Changing patterns of shark attacks in Australian waters. Marine and Freshwater Research 62: 744–754.
6. Wetherbee BM, Lowe C., C G. (1994) A Review of Shark Control in Hawaii with Recommendations for Future Research. Pacific Science 4: 95–115.
7. House D (2014) Western Australian Shark Hazard Mitigation Drum Line Program 2014–17: Public Environmental Review. Western Australia: The Department of the Premier and Cabinet. 85 p.
8. Reid D, Robbins W, Peddemors V (2011) Decadal trends in shark catches and effort from the New South Wales, Australia, Shark Meshing Program 1950–2010. Marine and Freshwater Research 62: 676–693.

9. Dudley SFJ (1997) A comparison of the shark control programs of New South Wales and Queensland (Australia) and KwaZulu-Natal (South Africa). Ocean and Coastal Management 34: 1–27.
10. Cliff G (1995) Sharks caught in the protective gill nets off Kwazulu-Natal, South Africa. 8. The great hammerhead shark Sphyrna mokarran (Ruppell). South African Journal of Marine Science 15: 105–114.
11. Cliff G, Dudley S, Jury M (1996) Catches of white sharks in KwaZulu-Natal, South Africa and environmental influences. Great white sharks: The biology of Carcharodon carcharias: 351–362.
12. Kempster RM, Egeberg CA, Hart NS, Ryan L, Chapuis L, et al. (2016) How Close is too Close? The Effect of a Non-Lethal Electric Shark Deterrent on White Shark Behaviour. PLOS ONE 11(7): e0157717. https://doi.org/10.1371/journal.pone.0157717
13. F. Maire, L. Mejias, A. Hodgson, and G. Duclos. Detection of Dugongs from Unmanned Aerial Vehicles. IEEE/RSJ International Conference on Intelligent Robots and Systems, 2013.
14. J. Lopez, J. Schoonmaker and S. Saggese, "Automated detection of marine animals using multispectral imaging," 2014 Oceans - St. John's, St. John's, NL, 2014, pp. 1–6.
15. M. Saqib, SD Khan, N Sharma, P Scully-Power, P Butcher, A Colefax and M Blumenstein, "Real-Time Drone Surveillance and Population Estimation of Marine Animals from Aerial Imagery," 2018 International Conference on Image and Vision Computing New Zealand (IVCNZ), Auckland, New Zealand, 2018, pp. 1–6.
16. G. T. Shrivakshan, "An analysis of SOBEL and GABOR image filters for identifying fish," 2013 International Conference on Pattern Recognition, Informatics and Mobile Engineering, 2013, pp. 115–119.
17. Sharma N., Scully-Power P., Blumenstein M. (2018) Shark Detection from Aerial Imagery Using Region-Based CNN, a Study. In: Mitrovic T., Xue B., Li X. (eds): Advances in Artificial Intelligence. AI 2018, pp 224–236. Lecture Notes in Computer Science, vol. 11320. Springer.
18. Gorkin, Robert and Adams, Kye and Berryman, Matthew J and Aubin, Sam and Li, Wanqing and Davis, Andrew R and Barthelemy, Johan, "Sharkeye: Real-Time Autonomous Personal Shark Alerting via Aerial Surveillance", Drones, vol. 4, no. 2, article no. 18, 2020
19. Suthep Gururatsakul, Danny Gibbins, David Kearney, A Simple Deformable Model for Shark Recognition, Canadian Conference on Computer and Robot Vison, pp. 234–240, 2011.
20. Gururatsakul, D. Gibbins, D. Kearney and I. Lee, Shark detection using optical image data from a mobile aerial platform, 25th International Conference of Image and Vision Computing New Zealand (IVCNZ), 2010, pp. 1–8, 2010.
21. L. Mejias, G. Duclos, A. Hodgson, and F. Maire. Automated Marine Mammal Detection From Aerial Imagery. To Appear in MTS/IEEE OCEANS, San Diego, USA, 2013.
22. R. Girshick: Fast R-CNN. In Proceedings of the IEEE International Conference on Computer Vision, pp. 1440–1448, 2015
23. R. Girshick, J. Donahue, T. Darrell, and J. Malik: Rich feature hierarchies for accurate object detection and semantic segmentation. In Proceedings of the IEEE conference on computer vision and pattern recognition, pp. 580–587, 2014
24. S. Ren, K. He, R. Girshick, and J. Sun: Faster r-cnn: Towards real-time object detection with region proposal networks. In Advances in neural information processing systems, pp. 91–99, 2015
25. Y. Jia, E. Shelhamer, J. Donahue, S. Karayev, J. Long, R. Girshick, S. Guadarrama, and T. Darrell: Caffe: Convolutional architecture for fast feature embedding. In Proceedings of the 22nd ACM international conference on Multimedia, pp. 675–678. ACM, 2014
26. M. D. Zeiler and R. Fergus: Visualizing and understanding convolutional networks. In European conference on computer vision, pp. 818–833. Springer, 2014
27. K. Simonyan and A. Zisserman: Very deep convolutional networks for large-scale image recognition. International Conference on Learning Representations (ICLR), 2014
28. K. Chatfield, K. Simonyan, A. Vedaldi, A. Zisserman: Return of the Devil in the Details: Delving Deep into Convolutional Nets. British Machine Vision Conference (BMVC), 2014
29. Everingham, Mark and Eslami, SM Ali and Van Gool, Luc and Williams, Christopher KI and Winn, John and Zisserman, Andrew: The pascal visual object classes challenge: A retrospective. International Journal of Computer Vision, pp. 98–136. 2015

30. J. Deng, W. Dong, R. Socher, L.-J. Li, K. Li, and L. Fei-Fei: Imagenet A large-scale hierarchical image database. In Computer Vision and Pattern Recognition, 2009. IEEE Conference on, pp. 248–255. IEEE, 2009
31. https://sls.com.au/surf-life-saving-australia-asks-beachgoers-to-be-a-life-saver-too/

AI + Human Partnership

Learner Engagement Examination Via Computer Usage Behaviors

Kun Yu, Jie Xu, Yuming Ou, Ling Luo, and Fang Chen

1 Introduction

The rapid development of technologies has been revolutionizing various aspects of education, including teaching and learning. Traditional learning involves a teacher and students gathering in the same space, where the teacher and the books are the primary sources of knowledge. With the aid of computers, learning has been gradually shifting from using static materials, such as books, to interactive media in computer-aided learning (CAL) and online learning that can provide personalized content and feedback.

During the course of CAL, learners naturally develop their own interaction style with computers which involves the movements and clicks of mouse, usage of keyboards and the way they look at the screen. Such interaction styles can be translated into quantifiable patterns to characterize learners' behavior during learning. These patterns allow teachers to understand learners' engagement, which is crucial to the learning outcome [1].

K. Yu (✉) · J. Xu · Y. Ou · F. Chen
Data Science Institute, University of Technology Sydney, Sydney, NSW, Australia
e-mail: kun.yu@uts.edu.au

J. Xu
e-mail: jie.xu@uts.edu.au

Y. Ou
e-mail: yuming.ou@uts.edu.au

F. Chen
e-mail: fang.chen@uts.edu.au

L. Luo
School of Computing and Information Systems, University of Melbourne,
Melbourne, VIC, Australia
e-mail: ling.luo@unimelb.edu.au

F. Chen and J. Zhou (eds.), *Humanity Driven AI*,
https://doi.org/10.1007/978-3-030-72188-6_12

Online learning provides and facilitates unlimited participation and open access to learners. Massive Open Online Course (MOOC) is a good example of online learning. Most MOOC courses allow for self-paced learning, featured with the convenience and feasibility for people that are not able to attend the course at fixed times, which are generally required by the traditional teaching and learning in classroom. However, criticism has never ceased for online learning, and a recent investigation suggests that around 90 percent registrations of self-paced online courses have not been finished. Furthermore, subjective engagement has become a challenge for online courses, as the lack of classroom environment decreases the opportunities of communication between teachers and learners, which negatively impacts the attention of the learners.

Researchers have compared traditional classroom learning with online learning. In the research of Carlsson et al. [2], studying at school significantly raises scores of students in terms of knowledge usage. Based on a comparative study, Norton and Hathaway [3] have found the role of a student as a group member had a significant impact on teacher–learners' perception of the learning environment. The group was sometimes seen as a powerful source of support, insight, and collaboration. Lavy's examination outcome [4] also aligns with this finding to some extent, which echoed that more hours spending in schools help to increase the test scores. These findings could be attributed to the decreased motivation of students for learning when they are absent from school or limited methods that could be used to encourage their engagements. The school lockdowns during the pandemic period could be used as a test for the education technology available for remote online learning. Unfortunately, few systems arrived at this point are fully prepared, in many aspects including learning material development, student engagement awareness, and student assessment.

In this chapter, we investigate learner engagement modeling under the modern learning environment. In particular, we study how to model learning engagement by using computer usage behaviors. This chapter is organized as follows: Related work is reviewed in Sect. 2, followed by the method in Sect. 3. Section 4 presents the experiment results, which is discussed in Sect. 5. Section 6 draws the conclusions.

2 Related Work

The advance of technologies has significantly reshaped learning. As engagement is a vital part of learning, we first review in Sect. 2.1 how technologies have impacted engagement measurement in learning. Since learning materials have evolved in tandem with technologies, we then study in Sect. 2.2 how learning materials should develop to meet the needs of students, assisted by current technologies. Lastly, we discussed how technologies can help to assess the learning in Sect. 2.3.

2.1 Engagement

Engagement has been widely recognized as the holy grail of learning by researchers and practitioners. Researchers have put enormous effort in conceptualizing student engagement, or academic engagement, as a complex multi-dimensional construct that captures a diverse range of states, such as behavioral, cognitive, and emotional states [5]. Unfortunately, practical advances have lagged behind theoretical progress. Traditional measures of engagement often take a uni-modal approach to source either sensor-free student interaction data or uni-modal behavioral data [6]. Examples of them include questionnaires, teacher ratings, video coding, etc. [7].

The advance of technology has enabled researchers to adopt a multimodal approach. This approach employs advanced computational techniques for recording the measurement of multiple aspects of engagement. It is emerging as a vial complement to the uni-modal approach. One such example is the AutoTutor [8], a multimodal affect detector that aggregated conversational cues, gross body language, and facial features. Features from those sensory channels were combined to discriminate among boredom, engagement/flow, confusion, frustration, delight, and neutral. Experiment results indicated that combination of channels yielded super-additive effects for some affective states. Similarly, the Student Engagement Analytics Technology (SEAT) [9] used student appearance and interaction logs as two modalities to detect engagement in real time. SEAT was able to support various usage scenarios including providing engagement states to (1) students for improving self-awareness; (2) integrating this information in educational platforms; and (3) providing input to teachers for implementing personalized interventions. Related to SEAT, [10] combined the information from the learning context and the students' appearance to examine the affective states with an 8-s window. However, to achieve real-time tracking of students' engagement, more refined examination is required, as a few different tasks can be conducted within an 8-s time frame. In consequence, the specific behaviors of learners with higher temporal resolution, e.g., mouse usage, gazing, etc., could be potential solutions for student engagement tracking. The keyboard and mouse usage have been identified as feasible indicators of human emotional states [11–13], . However, to our knowledge, very few has been done to understand their relationship with subjective emotions or learning outcome.

2.2 Learning Material Development

In addition to traditional course materials, such as filmed lectures, readings, and problem sets, many MOOCs provide interactive courses with user forums or social media discussions to support community interactions among students, professors, and teaching assistants (TAs), as well as immediate feedback to quick quizzes and assignments.

However, different learning materials and teaching formats should be developed to meet the needs of students with different learning styles, so that learners can select appropriate activities based on their preference. In the work of Ally, different learning styles have been mentioned with their special needs [14]. Concrete experience learners work well with specific examples in which they can be involved, and they like group work and peer feedback. The instructor is considered as a coach or helper. In comparison, reflective observation learners like to observe carefully before taking any action. They prefer that all the information be available for learning from the instructor instead of other peer learners. Abstract conceptualization learners like to work more with things and symbols and less with people. They like to work with theory and to conduct systematic analyses. Active experimentation learners prefer to learn by doing practical projects and participating in group discussions. They prefer active learning methods and interact with peers for feedback and information. They tend to establish their own criteria for evaluating situations. Ally and Fahy found that students with different learning styles have different preferences for support. For example, the assimilator learning style prefers high instructor presence, while the accommodator learning style prefers low instructor presence.

2.3 Assessment

Assessment could be one major challenge for online learning and home schooling. The common way is to use quiz or other tests in the online modules at the end of learning, which is convenient and provides instant feedback to the learner. However, quite a few disadvantages exist for the quiz. Firstly, to facilitate the generation of scores, most questions in a quiz are monotonous that only require user to make a choice between a few options. The lack of free-form questions has limited the capability and scale of assessment to a great extent. Secondly, students may take the shortcuts to pass the course rather than to learn the knowledge. It is often observed, for an online course, that the student checks the final questions first before start learning, and afterward seeks answers to the questions directly. Although it could be an efficient way to pass the exam, the student barely learns anything during this course. Thirdly, the assessment could be non-objective, and this disadvantage also exists for the traditional ways of assessment based on exams. Consider one student spending an hour exploring the related literature to gain in-depth understanding of the answer to a question, but another student just remembering the answer in half a minute. They may provide the same answer to the same question, although the first student should be accredited with the effort and exploration. Finally, very limited customized assessment method is available, which should take into account the different characteristics, learning profile, progress and interest of the students.

Although very limited literature has been identified on direct assessment of student learning progress using signal processing and multimodal analytics techniques, a few relevant research on the learning strategies have been spotted. Hu et al. investigated information-processing strategies in solving two types of complex problems [15].

They collected eye activities using the Tobii T120 eye tracker and found that different eye movement patterns exist between high and low performance students. Similarly, Khedher et al. proposed a twofold approach to assess students' reasoning process using static fixation and scan path with Tobii Tx300 eye tracker [16]. Their results revealed associations between eye movement metrics and students' reasoning capabilities. However, the challenge still exists that the expensive and specialized eye tracking devices prevent the technique from being deployed in a large scale in practice.

3 Method

In this chapter, we investigate the issue of measuring engagement in the setting of online learning. The challenge is to obtain a dynamic measure which can accurately reflect the learner's engagement level during learning. Conventional uni-modal approaches are limited in their delayed feedback and interaction data. As such, we adopted a multimodal approach and designed a case study for measuring engagement via computer usage behaviors.

We have designed and implemented an online learning analytic system in the Predator Lab, University of Technology, to examine the learners' progress and learning outcome via multimodal signals including mouse movements, keyboard tapping, together with eye gaze from the webcam. Those signals were sourced from related computer peripherals in a non-intrusive way. Our system can identify in real time what the learners are working on and where they are looking at, infer their engagement levels, and assist in student learning assessment as well as learning material development.

We designed an online course about food variety and healthy diets, with a quiz at the end. We collected the user behavior data during the course of learning, together with the learners' scores in the quiz as an objective criterion of learning outcome.

3.1 Participants

Twenty-two volunteers, including eight females, from the University of Technology Sydney participated in the study, with an age range of 20–42 years old. All the subjects had good computer skills as they were from School of Computer Science or undertaking related courses, but very few of them had taken courses on health and food before, which was the reason that we utilized food and health material for the study. Ethics approval was obtained for this research, and all the subjects confirmed their consent and understanding of the nature of the study before the experiment. They were unpaid but the best performer who answered all the questions in the quiz correctly with the shortest time would get a movie voucher as an award.

3.2 Learning Material and Procedure

The learning material was focused on food and health, the content of which was adapted from the nutrition Australia online information [17]. We used the learning material to design a short online course, including the following key elements: user registration (the first page), information for learning (eight pages), and a quiz (the last page). This short course was implemented with Google Forms. Images were shown in two out of the eight information pages, and the rest of the information pages was purely text based. Eight single selection questions were asked in the quiz, each corresponding to one information page. A correct answer to one question gained one point, so the highest score would be eight points.

Examples of the learning materials are shown in Figs. 1 and 2.

The subjects were required to register with a valid email at the onset of the study, and afterward they were asked to finish the online course aiming to achieve the highest score with the shortest time. All the subjects spent less than 20 min to finish the designed course.

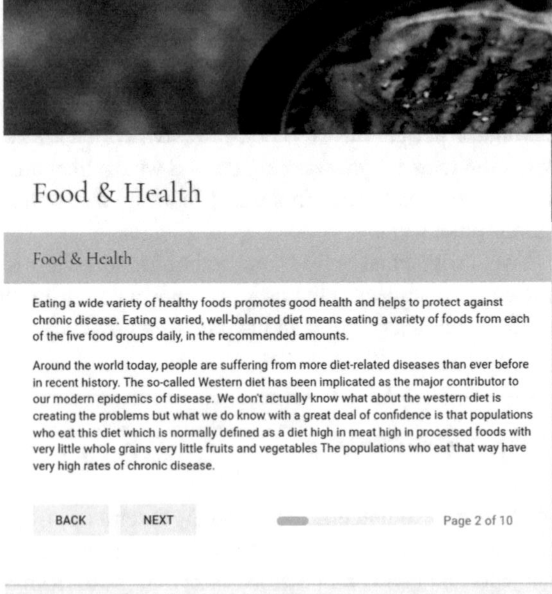

Fig. 1 Examples of the learning information pages, with text

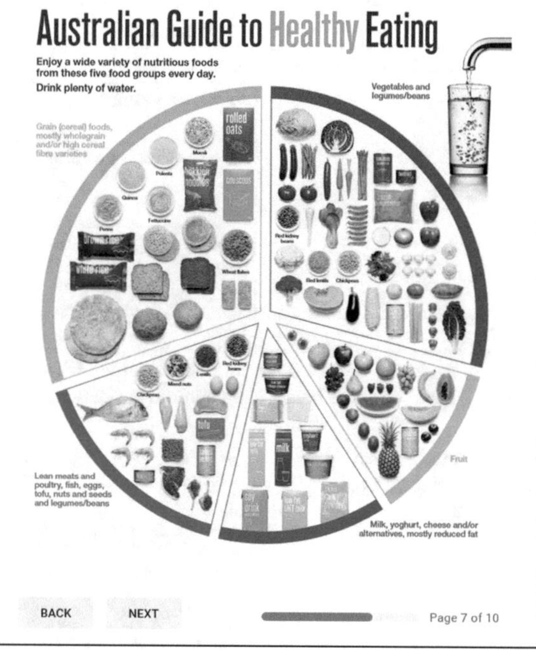

Fig. 2 Examples of the learning information pages, with image

3.3 Data Collection

We developed a web service server and a client-side application to collect user behavior data. Both are deployed on Acer Spin 5 laptop computers with embedded 720p webcams. The client-side application was responsible for collecting data including keyboard and mouse usage, as well as the face images of the subject. Every single user activity, including keyboard typing, mouse clicking and cursor movement while the left mouse button was pressed, would trigger a data recording event, i.e., the system would log the user activity with a time stamp, together with the screenshot of the screen. In comparison, face data was collected at a fixed rate of one sample per second. Detailed data collected was illustrated in Table 1.

On the other hand, the learning outcome is evaluated via the quiz following the learning material as introduced in the previous section. It can be quantified as the number of correct answers out of the eight questions in the quiz.

3.4 Face and Eye Gaze Detection

We applied the face detection algorithm to determine the existence of subjects' faces in the captured webcam images. The approach is based on Adaboost [18], with a

Table 1 Data collected by the system with time stamps

	Data category	Data attributes
Triggered by user behaviors	Keyboard typing	Key pressed
	Mouse clicking	Button clicked, cursor coordinates (x, y)
	Mouse wheel scrolling	Rotation direction, rotation speed, and cursor coordinates (x, y)
	Mouse dragging while button pressed	Cursor coordinates (x, y)
	Screenshot	Contents on the screen
Fixed rate	Face	Face images

The data triggered by user behaviors was recorded whenever a corresponding user behavior was detected, while one face image was captured per second

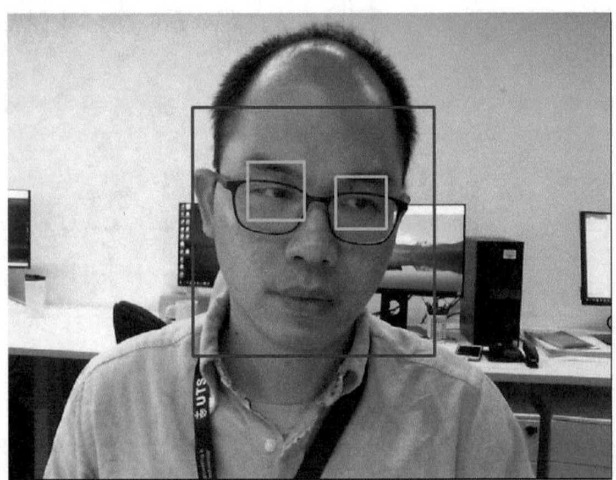

Fig. 3 Detected face (blue box) and detected eyes (green boxes)

cascade structure to boost the speed of face detection by focusing on more face like sub-windows on the image. Further details of this method can be found in the work of Viola and Jones [19]. This machine learning approach was adopted because it is capable of processing images rapidly with high detection rates. Based on the detected face, we could further locate the eyes in the image and infer their eye gaze. We employed the implementation of OpenCV [20] for our experiments, and an example of face and eye detection is shown in Fig. 3.

Based on the eye detection results, we derived the variable R_e, which indicates the relative level of engagement when reading the learning materials in one page:

$$R_e = \frac{T_e}{T_p}, \tag{1}$$

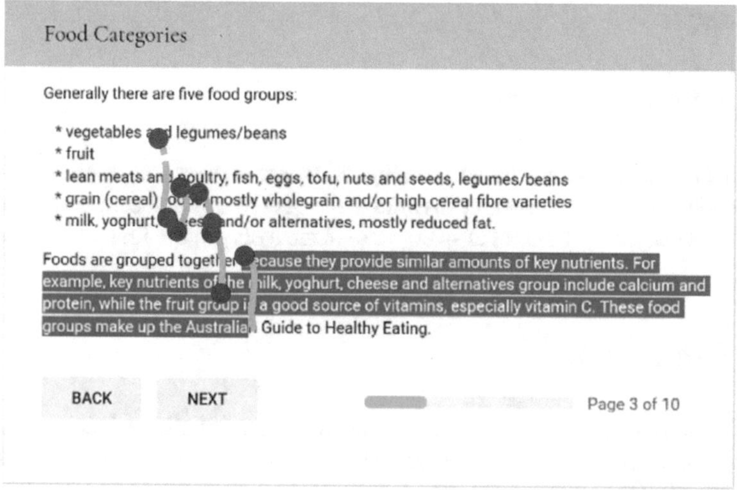

Fig. 4 Mouse behaviors from a typical subject: the red dots indicate that the left button of the mouse was pressed, and the green traces indicate mouse dragging while the left button was pressed. The text in blue resulted from the last selection action of the mouse

where T_p indicates the time spent on a specific page of the learning material, while T_e indicates the total time that the subject's eye gaze was detected with a focus on the screen.

3.5 *Mouse and Keyboard*

Based on the collected mouse usage data, we were able to retrieve the mouse behaviors of subjects and identify interesting mouse usage patterns. In the example shown in Fig. 4, a typical subject dragged the mouse to select a block of text while reading, which was followed by a quick single click to cancel the selection. This mouse operation was repeated during the whole course of reading and learning. However, for other subjects who rarely used the mouse clicks or such behaviors to assist the learning, the information we could gather was very limited. Similar to the eye gaze analytics, a variable R_m was derived with

$$R_m = \frac{T_m}{T_p}, \tag{2}$$

Due to the nature of the study, very few subjects used the keyboard when they were working on the course, so the keyboard data was insufficient for further examination, and hence our focus of examination was on the mouse usage.

4 Results

4.1 Learning Outcome

The final learning outcome is shown in Fig. 5. Except for three subjects, all the others have made one or more incorrect answers to the questions. On the other hand, except for the last question, incorrect answers were made to any of the first seven questions.

4.2 Engagement

As discussed earlier, this study focuses on the relationship between learning outcome and engagement characterized by learning behaviors. The learning outcome is characterized by whether a specific question is answered correctly, while the engagement of subjects was examined via the eye gaze detection result R_e and mouse usage ratio R_m.

For the 19 subjects who made wrong answers to the questions in the quiz, R_e and R_m were calculated as the indicators of engagement level, for all the information pages of the learning material. A paired t-test was used to compare R_e and R_m between correct answers and incorrect answers. For the mouse behaviors R_m, there was significant difference identified ($t(18) = 1.87$, $p < 0.05$), suggesting that the engagement level represented by mouse usage accounts for the learning differences between correct and incorrect answers: the higher the engagement on the information page reflected by mouse usage, the higher the chance that the subject answered the questions correctly. Examining the eye gaze detection results R_e, significant difference was found as well ($t(18) = 1.91$, $p < 0.05$). This implies engagement levels, as suggested by the eye fixation time on the screen, can be used to infer the learning outcome. A further examination for R_e and R_m across all the 22 subjects showed that there was a positive correlation between the two variables ($r = 0.46$, $p = 0.05$), which further confirmed that data from both channels could be used for engagement examination.

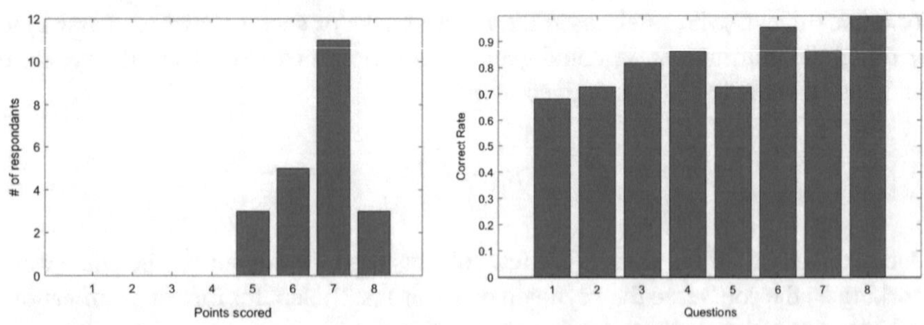

Fig. 5 Learning outcome of the subjects: (left) points scored from individuals and (right) correct answer rate of each question

5 Discussion

In this work, we utilized a multimodal approach to examine the engagement of learners and link the observations to the learning outcome. The developed system may assist teachers to understand the learning engagement under online learning settings. This will help the teacher to ensure teaching quality.

As a preliminary study, our results suggest that the eye fixation and mouse usage patterns are feasible indicators of engagement and can be used to infer the learning outcome, in particular, to diagnose when a learning issue might occur. As all the signals we have captured are naturally available from most e-learning systems, the learning process can be tracked in a non-intrusive way. We also identified the correlation between the gaze and mouse behaviors, which suggests that this technique is still applicable if only one modality is available in certain learning context.

Some interesting behavior patterns were observed during the course of the study, which we believe will bring insights into other researchers as well as improve our future work to refine the engagement measurement:

- We have found that some subjects had the habit of resting hands on their cheeks while thinking, resulting in inaccurate face detection and poor eye detection. Also the webcam might be placed at a different angles toward the face, which captured face partially, and hence brought new challenges for eye location detection.
- We captured mouse behaviors only when a button was pressed or when the scroll wheel was used; however, the mouse cursor movements without any button pressed were not recorded, which could be another potential indicator that the learner is highly engaged in learning.
- Some subjects used the mouse to direct and assist their reading but others did not use mouse as much.

The findings may be incorporated into more advanced computer vision modules, e.g., face expression recognition systems to better measure the learning engagement.

Starting from the onset of 2020, online learning has suddenly become the only option for many students, due to the pandemic of COVID-19. Its implication to the education is dramatic: The nationwide school closures are impacting over 91% of the world's student population. To increase physical distancing across the population and slow down the spread of the virus, remote and flexible learning has been adopted in many countries. In a short term, we will see the booming of online education and learning as a necessary means to replace traditional classroom education. The method introduced in this study will be able to assist the teachers and students in different learning setting: Using non-intrusive and automatic behavior data analytic methods, the learning progress, outcome and potential means to improve the learning process could be conveniently shared between teachers and students.

Last but not least, the multimodal approach presented in this chapter will benefit the broad e-learning domain and more general human learning performance. For example, from this approach we may effectively learn the performance of learners with expression difficulties, as we can capture different signals for measurement.

6 Conclusions

We present our study that utilizes user behaviors to characterize learning engagement and further identify their links to the learning outcome. The results indicate that analyzing the mouse usage and eye gaze information is a feasible means of diagnosing learning outcomes. We also discuss the challenges of using laptop webcam to capture human face and habits of mouse use from different individuals, which is essential for the development of techniques for tracking learners' engagement in real time. Our study adds to the general understanding of e-learning analytics and provides new ways to examine, understand and improve the learning process of different people. Our future research will take different factors mentioned in the discussion section into consideration, and new methods that are able to fuse the data from different modalities will be developed for a personalized engagement examination system.

Acknowledgements We would like to thank all the people who contributed their time, data, and helpful advice to this study. We would appreciate ACER Australia as well for their support and collaboration in the research project.

References

1. Juhaňák, L., Zounek, J., Rohlíková, L.: Using process mining to analyze students' quiz-taking behavior patterns in a learning management system. Computers in Human Behavior **92**, 496–506 (2019)
2. Carlsson, M., Simovska, V.: Exploring learning outcomes of school-based health promotion—a multiple case study. Health Education Research **27**(3), 437–447 (2012)
3. Norton, P., Hathaway, D.: Exploring two teacher education online learning designs: A classroom of one or many? Journal of Research on Technology in Education **40**(4), 475–495 (2008)
4. Lavy, V.: Expanding school resources and increasing time on task: Effects of a policy experiment in israel on student academic achievement and behavior. Tech. rep., National Bureau of Economic Research (2012)
5. Sinatra, G.M., Heddy, B.C., Lombardi, D.: The challenges of defining and measuring student engagement in science (2015)
6. D'Mello, S., Dieterle, E., Duckworth, A.: Advanced, analytic, automated (AAA) measurement of engagement during learning. Educational psychologist **52**(2), 104–123 (2017)
7. Henrie, C.R., Halverson, L.R., Graham, C.R.: Measuring student engagement in technology-mediated learning: A review. Computers & Education **90**, 36–53 (2015)
8. D'mello, S.K., Graesser, A.: Multimodal semi-automated affect detection from conversational cues, gross body language, and facial features. User Modeling and User-Adapted Interaction **20**(2), 147–187 (2010)
9. Aslan, S., Alyuz, N., Tanriover, C., Mete, S.E., Okur, E., D'Mello, S.K., Arslan Esme, A.: Investigating the impact of a real-time, multimodal student engagement analytics technology in authentic classrooms. In: Proceedings of the 2019 CHI Conference on Human Factors in Computing Systems, pp. 1–12 (2019)
10. Alyuz, N., Okur, E., Oktay, E., Genc, U., Aslan, S., Mete, S.E., Arnrich, B., Esme, A.A.: Semi-supervised model personalization for improved detection of learner's emotional engagement. In: Proceedings of the 18th ACM International Conference on Multimodal Interaction, pp. 100–107 (2016)

11. Salmeron-Majadas, S., Santos, O.C., Boticario, J.G.: An evaluation of mouse and keyboard interaction indicators towards non-intrusive and low cost affective modeling in an educational context. Procedia Computer Science **35**, 691–700 (2014)
12. Lim, Y.M., Ayesh, A., Stacey, M.: Using mouse and keyboard dynamics to detect cognitive stress during mental arithmetic. In: Science and Information Conference, pp. 335–350. Springer (2014)
13. Estrada, J., Buhia, J., Guevarra, A., Forcado, M.R.: Keyboard and mouse: tools in identifying emotions during computer activities. In: International Conference on Big Data Technologies and Applications, pp. 115–123. Springer (2017)
14. Ally, M.: Foundations of educational theory for online learning. Theory and practice of online learning **2**, 15–44 (2004)
15. Hu, Y., Wu, B., Gu, X.: An eye tracking study of high-and low-performing students in solving interactive and analytical problems. Journal of Educational Technology & Society **20**(4), 300–311 (2017)
16. Khedher, A.B., Jraidi, I., Frasson, C.: Static and dynamic eye movement metrics for students' performance assessment. Smart Learning Environments **5**(1), 1–12 (2018)
17. Nutrition Australia Fact Sheets, http://www.nutritionaustralia.org/national/resources (2019)
18. Freund, Y., Schapire, R.E.: A decision-theoretic generalization of on-line learning and an application to boosting. Journal of computer and system sciences **55**(1), 119–139 (1997)
19. Viola, P., Jones, M.: Rapid object detection using a boosted cascade of simple features. In: Proceedings of the 2001 IEEE computer society conference on computer vision and pattern recognition. CVPR 2001, vol. 1, pp. I–I. IEEE (2001)
20. Bradski, G., Kaehler, A.: Learning OpenCV: Computer vision with the OpenCV library. O'Reilly Media, Inc. (2008)

Virtual Teaching Assistants: Technologies, Applications and Challenges

Jun Liu, Lingling Zhang, Bifan Wei, and Qinghua Zheng

1 Introduction

AI brings surprising evolution in many industries, including transportation, health care, stocks, etc. In recent years, some educational tools enabled by artificial intelligence (AI), called virtual teaching assistants (VTAs), have emerged and attracted more attentions because of their great potential to improve education quality and enhance online learning efficiency [69].

VTAs are a special kind of online learning system with some intelligent components, which provide the intelligent interactive learning environment outside the lecture period for the learners. Previous online learning is a simple human–machine interaction mode that overcomes the geographical and time constraints, provides learners with abundant learning resources and realises basic functions such as attendance and homework checking. This is a virtualization of one-to-many teaching with the semi-separate state of students from their teachers. However, the teaching contents and assignments of one teacher cannot meet the requirements of multiple students due to their different knowledge levels, learning abilities and interests. And the teacher cannot always capture the gaps in their lectures that make students confused, with little communication between them. To solve these issues, VTAs are designed to simulate the process of one-to-one teaching, so as to provide special intelligent service in three aspects: personalised teaching, personalised guidance, and proficiency assessment. The goal of personalised teaching is to tailor learning materials, plans, paths and difficulties according to learners' learning progress and different require-

J. Liu (✉) · L. Zhang · Q. Zheng
School of Computer Science and Technology, Xi'an Jiaotong University, Xi'an, China
e-mail: liukeen@xjtu.edu.cn

L. Zhang
e-mail: zhanglling@xjtu.edu.cn

Q. Zheng
e-mail: qhzheng@xjtu.edu.cn

B. Wei
School of Continuing Education, Xi'an Jiaotong University, Xi'an, China
e-mail: weibifan@xjtu.edu.cn

F. Chen and J. Zhou (eds.), *Humanity Driven AI*,
https://doi.org/10.1007/978-3-030-72188-6_13

ments [27]. For example, when the online learner submits a wrong answer to an assignment, VTAs will recommend related teaching materials and assignments for him to practise repeatedly. For personalised guidance, VTAs act as tutors who engage in dialogue, answer questions and provide feedback to online learners [53]. This type of service often occurs when learners are confused about a certain knowledge point or assignment. Proficiency assessment refers to understanding the learners' level of knowledge mastery based on their multi-channel learning records, such as the learned courses, class status and assignments [8]. The accurate proficiency assessment for online learners is helpful to provide higher-quality personalised teaching and guidance for them. The above three intelligent services are often integrated with each other in VTAs, and they fully reflect the humanised characteristics of VTAs.

The various products of VTAs have emerged under the support of many critical AI technologies. The navigation learning system[1] developed by Xi'an Jiaotong University integrates the graph-data mining and natural language processing (NLP) to construct a novel education knowledge graph. Given a learning goal, this product exploits a personalised learning path for the online learner to avoid the problem of learning lost [86]. The typical chatting robot Xiaomu[2] proposed by Tsinghua University and XuetangX understands the learners' questions about the difficult knowledge concepts and answers them in the form of texts, images and videos [81]. Except for NLP, Xiaomu involves the hot AI techniques such as learning analytics, question answering, image and video understanding. Many well-known companies including Knewton,[3] DreamBox,[4] Cerego,[5] also specialise in the development of virtual teaching products. Further improvement on humanised service of VTAs needs to overcome more intractable AI challenges, such as knowledge tracing, diagram understanding, interpretable visual reasoning and the extraction of logic rules.

VTAs are in a stage of rapid development and will create high value for education. On the one hand, VTAs improve the education quality. Personalised teaching develops individualised learning plans according to learners' different goals and effectively trains their independence and creation [16]. Personalised guidance further stimulates learners' interests and provides them with immediate feedback without waiting for the reply from teachers. On the other hand, VTAs are conductive to boost education efficiency. VTAs create a virtualized and intelligent learning environment for learners. They not only reduce the management cost of the school, but also save the communication time between teachers and learners, so that teachers can concentrate on better teaching resources. In summary, VTAs play an important role in the intellectualisation of education.

---

[1] http://zscl.xjtudlc.com:888/studytool/.

[2] https://www.xuetangx.com/learn/THU08091000247/THU08091000247/5430764/video/7472198.

[3] https://www.knewton.com.

[4] https://www.dreambox.com.

[5] https://www.cerego.com.

2 Key Technologies

Much attention has been paid to VTAs with the development of techniques in AI, and many proposed AI technologies support the humanised service of recent VTAs. In this section, some key technologies of VTAs that mimic the human thinking and behaviour are introduced, including the education knowledge graph, natural language question answering, visual question answering and learning analytics.

2.1 Education Knowledge Graph

A knowledge graph is a semantic knowledge base composed of nodes and edges, which was first proposed by Google [56] for optimising searching results of search engine. The nodes in knowledge graph represent entities in the real world, and the edges represent the semantic relations between entities. The knowledge graph is usually stored in the knowledge base as a resource description framework (RDF) form. For example, the RDF $\langle YaoMing, placeOfbrith, Shanghai\rangle$ expresses the fact "Yao Ming was born in Shanghai". The education knowledge graph (EKG) organises large-scale learning resources according to their cognitive relations. A node of EKG represents a knowledge unit from one course or subject [38]. The edge between knowledge units indicates the cognitive relation. For example, Fig. 1 is a partial view of an EKG of the course "data structure" proposed by Xi'an Jiaotong University [86]. This EKG consists of facet trees and learning dependencies for solving the knowledge fragmentization problem. The fact contained in Fig. 1 can be expressed as $\langle linearlist, learning\ dependency, binary\ tree\rangle$. Many popular massive open online course (MOOC) platforms such as Khan Academy and MOOC China use the technology of EKG to visualise course concepts for learners [12]. Two key points of EKG are construction and embedding, and they are described in the following subsections.

2.1.1 Construction of Education Knowledge Graph

The construction of EKG includes three parts: knowledge unit extraction, attribute extraction and cognitive relation extraction.

The extraction of knowledge units from structured or unstructured data is the basis of the EKG construction. In different courses and subjects, the meaning and granularity of knowledge units are not uniform. Therefore, this procedure needs to consider the characteristics of different domains. One of the main methods is based on conditional random field (CRF), which transforms the knowledge unit extraction task into a sequence labelling. For example, Tang et al. [60] defined three types of token features and integrated them into CRF model to identify knowledge units in researcher profiles. Another kind of method uses neural networks to automatically

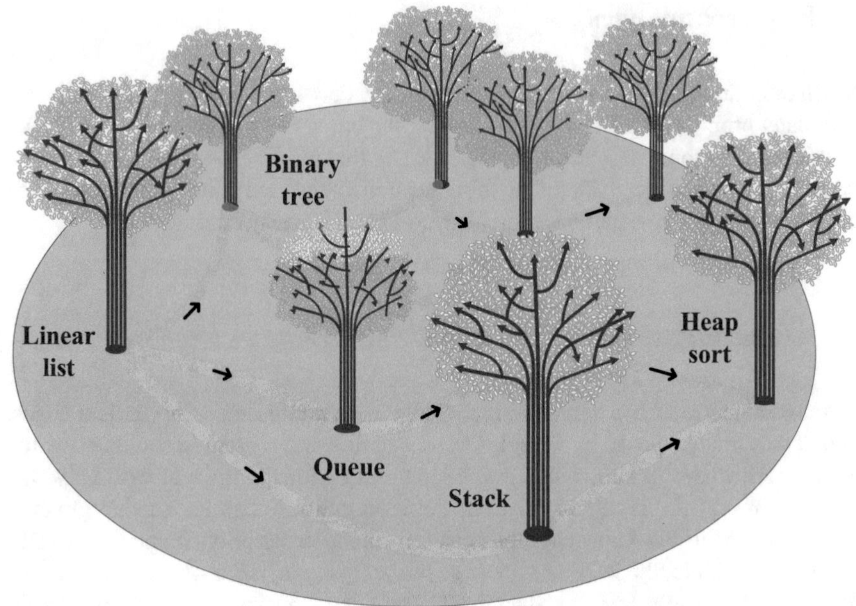

Fig. 1 Partial view of EKG of course "data structure", which includes many facet trees and learning dependencies between trees

discover the features of knowledge units in unstructured text. Chen et al. [12] defined three labels for knowledge unit extraction and applied neural sequence labelling technique to extract instructional concepts for a subject or course.

The attributes of one knowledge unit describe its characteristics from multiple perspectives. Yahya et al. [73] mined attributes by meta patterns, which first construct seed attributes, then mine the patterns between attributes and entities and finally obtain attributes by the generated patterns. Wei et al. [67] proposed DF-Miner to discover domain-specific attributes. DF-Miner first constructs a hyperlink graph from the Wikipedia article pages, then detects the motif feature of the digraph and finally groups the terms of a domain into multiple attributes based on community detection. Guo et al. [28] regarded attributes as the labels of entities, which extracts initial attributes set from *Content* sections of Wikipedia and runs a propagation algorithm based on an assumption that similar entities have similar attributes. Zhang et al. [85] proposed a joint model to extract entities and attributes simultaneously, which considers that there are relations between the qualities of entities and attributes. This method constructs a weighted bipartite graph firstly and then runs a mutually recursive algorithm to obtain the importance of entities and attributes iteratively.

Cognitive relation extraction refers to identifying cognitive relations between knowledge units from texts. Specifically, cognitive relations include hierarchical relations, prerequisite relations, hypernymy relations, etc. Wang et al. [63] captured the hierarchical relation based on the local relatedness and global coherence of the knowledge units from the texts. Talukar and Cohen [58] exploited graph-based features and content-based features on Wikipedia to explore prerequisite relation between concepts. Wang et al. [62] proposed an attention-based model that focuses on the difference between compound entities to extract the hypernymy relation between symptoms and diseases in medical areas. Among the various relations mentioned above, the prerequisite relation is the basis for teachers to specify the instructional design and teaching strategies, as well as the premise for the resource recommendation and navigation learning.

2.1.2 Embedding of Education Knowledge Graph

The embedding of EKG aims to map all nodes and edges into a low-dimensional continuous vector spaces while preserving the structure of the graph. The embedded nodes and edges can be applied to downstream tasks, such as link prediction [6] and node classification [45]. At far as we know, there is no research on specific embedding of EKG, and this task is achieved by the common embedding models of knowledge graph, including translational distance models and semantic matching models.

The translational distance measures the plausibility of each fact based on the distance between two entities. TransE [6] is the first translational distance measure, which is the most basic method of knowledge representation and has derived many variants. TransE considers that the offsets among entities with relations are similar and constructs positive and negative samples to train model. TransH [65] is proposed to alleviate the difficulty of modelling one-to-many, many-to-one and many-to-many relations in TransE. TransH projects the entities and relations onto the hyperplane and optimises it in the similar method as TransE on the hyperplane. TransH also designed a better negative sampling method to train model effectively. TransR [37] is a further promoted model of TransH. Different relations in TransR have different semantic spaces because they focus on different attributes of entities.

The semantic matching model uses similarity-based scoring functions to measure the plausibility of each fact. RESCAL [45] uses matrix factorization to decompose the graph matrix into entities embeddings and relation embeddings. The original graph can be refactored by multiplying the obtained embedding matrices. Although this method is effective, it is time-consuming to calculate. To overcome the time-consuming problem of RESCAL, DistMult [74] optimises the model by restricting the relation embedding matrix to a diagonal matrix. DistMult is a very effective method, but this method is oversimplified and cannot generalise to a normal knowledge graph. HolE [44] combines the effectiveness of RESCAL and the efficiency of DistMult, which uses the circular correlation operation to create compositional representations. By using the correlation as the compositional operator, HolE is effective, and it outperforms RESCAL and DistMult.

2.2 Natural Language Question Answering

Natural language question answering (QA) aims to automatically answer questions posed by humans in a natural language, which can be grouped into two paradigms: information retrieval (IR)-based QA and knowledge-based QA.

2.2.1 IR-based QA

IR-based QA systems refer to answering the questions depending on vast amount of text from Websites or documents. Figure 2a shows an example of IR-based QA in which the answers are given based on the questions and natural language articles. The answers "France" and "10th and 11th centuries" are results of retrieval from the articles, which are highlighted in red. The basic process of IR-based QA is divided into three parts, which are question analysis, information retrieval and answer generation. The question analysis intends to understand and represent the natural language questions for further extraction of corresponding answers. Basic strategies and some effective deep learning models for NLP are utilised in this process for textual representations. For example, Joulin et al. [30] proposed a FastText system for rapid processing on millions of question sentences, which incorporates additional statistics such as bags of N-grams to increase the accuracy of linear models by solving

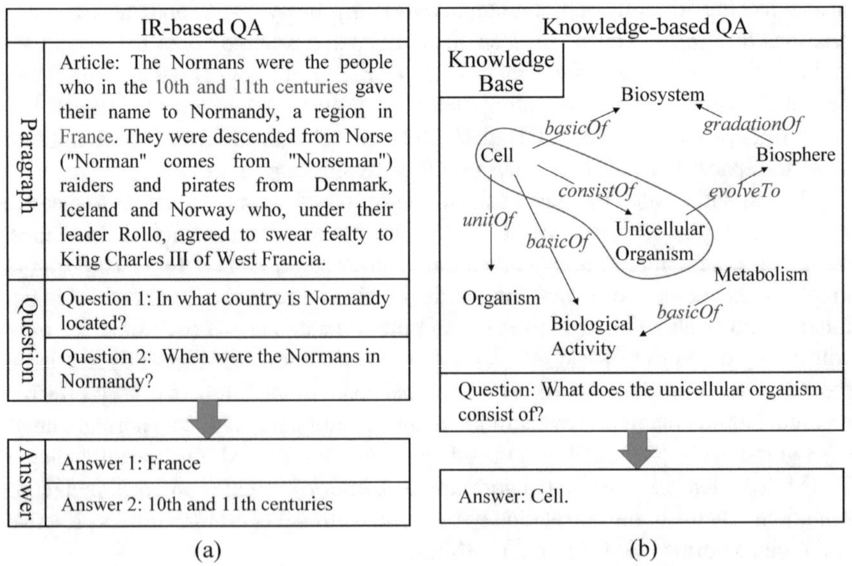

Fig. 2 Examples for two paradigms of QA: IR-based QA and knowledge-based QA. For the IR-based QA paradiagram, it refers to answering the questions depending on the text paragraph. For the Knowledge-based QA paradiagram, the answer lies in the knowledge base

the issue that linear classifiers do not share parameters between features and classes. Yang et al. [78] employed the hierarchical attention network in representations of text, which utilises GRU to encode the words and sentences, and the two encoders own corresponding attention models to increase the accuracy.

The information retrieval process intends to obtain relevant documents by the given queries from questions. For the QA from websites, the system could be easily transmitted to a search engine implementing the retrieval, but for the sets of documents, IR-based QA needs other approaches. For example, Chen et al. [11] employed a system named DrQA, helping compute TF-IDF over unigrams in the texts. When handling the information from corporate pages, like the documents from Wikipedia, the questions and articles are compared by the standard method, generally TF-IDF cosine matching. In addition, the unsupervised algorithms like TextRank [42] could extract topics from the set of documents, which utilises the relationship between local words by the co-occurrence window for subsequent keywords ranking.

The last phase of IR-based QA is the answer generation from the specific paragraphs. Some systems employ the features of the questions and answers in extraction process. For example, Tan et al. [59] built hybrid neural networks for better representations of both questions and answers. In the answer generation part, the answer candidates are ranked by the cosine similarity to the specific question. The QA system generally provides answers from the retrieved documents or passages by utilising reading comprehension algorithms in some studies. Devlin et al. [17] proposed BERT for the span-based QA, which adds two embeddings, span-start embedding and span-end embedding in the pretrained model. In the answer generation process, the system calculates the span-start and span-end possibilities of each output token and then sets the sum of the log-likelihoods of the correct start and end positions for each observation as the training objective for fine-tuning.

2.2.2 Knowledge-Based QA

For the tasks in natural language QA, the information could also exist in the structured forms and map the question in natural language to a query over a knowledge base as shown in Fig. 2b. The answer "Cell" is provided based on the question and knowledge base, especially the region within the red line. One of the methods to solve knowledge-based QA is by the symbolic representation, which is a traditional semantic parsing strategy. The system transforms natural language questions into the logical form to represent the semantics and obtain the answers by corresponding queries. Berant et al. [5] used a semantic parsing strategy to structure the logic form for the questions. The answers are obtained by corresponding queries with lambda-calculus searching in the knowledge base. Yih et al. [80] proposed a framework for knowledge-based QA, which defines query graphs similar to subgraphs in knowledge bases mapping to the logical forms. Then, the semantic parsing is treated as a search problem in the query graph representing a question, and it determines the core inference chain by calculating the similarity between the representations of the question and the candidate chains.

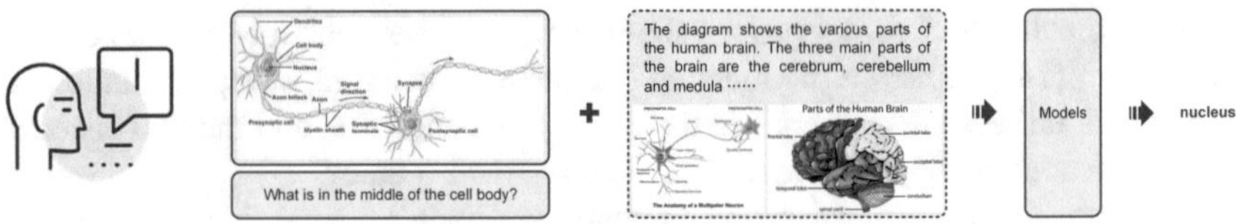

Fig. 3 Example of visual question answering. The second column denotes an/a image/diagram and a question about the image/diagram. The third column denotes the external knowledge. The fourth column denotes the answer

Another strategy for knowledge-based QA is by learning representation which considers the QA as a semantic matching process. The system obtains the embedding representations of knowledge bases and questions in natural language and finds the answer by calculating their similarities. Dong et al. [19] proposed the multi-column convolutional neural networks (CNNs) to understand questions from three different aspects (answer path, answer context and answer type) and compared the jointly learned vector representations of the question and the three features of candidate answers. Xu et al. [72] presented a model named SDP-LSTM to classify the relations via shortest dependency paths represented by the embedding vectors in increasing the accuracy of knowledge-based QA.

2.3 *Visual Question Answering*

Visual question answering (VQA) requires a machine to provide a natural language answer, given an image and a natural language question about the image [3], as shown in Fig. 3. It has extensive applications such as blind people assisting, young children education and intelligent drive and therefore has become a hot research topic in recent years. We present the VQA methods through three categories: joint embedding based, attention mechanism based and explainable.

2.3.1 Joint Embedding Based VQA

This kind of methods uses CNNs and recurrent neural networks (RNNs) to obtain image and question representations, respectively, and then projects them into a common space to perform inference. Deeper LSTM Q + Norm I [3] uses a two-layer LSTM, the last hidden layer of VGGNet [55] to encode questions and images, respectively. Then, it applies point-wise multiplication to fuse the features and projects the fusion features into the answer space by fully connected layers. Fukui et al. [25] assumed approaches to multi-modal pooling such as element-wise product, and sum and concatenation are not as expressive as outer product. This work first uses multi-modal compact bi-linear method to obtain the image features that fuse attended question features and then applies this method to obtain the features that fuse the image and question features. Finally, it projects the fusion features into the answer space to obtain the answer. Kim et al. [33] proposed a low-rank bi-linear pooling method with Hadamard product to replace multi-modal compact bi-linear pooling that has complex computations. Yu et al. [83] proposed a multi-modal factorised bi-linear pooling method to fuse the image features and question features effectively and efficiently based on the multi-modal low-rank bi-linear pooling. The principles of joint embedding-based approaches are straightforward, which are the basis of current VQA methods [70]. However, there still exist potential improvements in feature extraction and projection into the embedding space.

2.3.2 Attention Mechanism-Based VQA

This kind of methods uses attention mechanisms to assign different importance to features before information fusion. They aim at addressing the limitation caused by joint embedding-based methods, i.e. irrelevant or noisy information feeding during the prediction stage. Yang et al. [77] devised stacked attention networks, which first use the LSTM and VGGNet to obtain the question and image features and then apply the semantic representation of a question as a query to search for the attended regions in an image that are relevant to the answer. Lu et al. [39] proposed a co-attention model that jointly reasons on the answer space using the image-guided and question-guided attentions. However, the above methods have not considered how to determine the image regions or objects to be attended. To address this issue, Anderson et al. [2] first proposed a combined bottom-up and top-down attention mechanism that computes attention at the level of objects and other salient image regions, where the bottom-up attention is implemented by faster R-CNN [49]. Kim et al. [32] devised bi-linear attention networks that consider bi-linear interactions between regions of images and words of questions based on the low-rank bi-linear pooling architecture. Shrestha et al. [54] devised a recurrent aggregation of the multi-modal embeddings network that consists of three phases: early fusion of vision and language features, learning bimodal embeddings via shared projections and recurrent aggregation of the learned bimodal embeddings using a Bi-GRU [29]. Li et al. [35] proposed a relation-aware graph attention network that encodes image regions into a graph and models the inter-object relations via a graph attention mechanism to learn question-guided relation representations. Yu et al. [82] devised a deep modular co-attention network that not only uses the self-attention of questions and images, but also the question-guided attention of images to perform reasoning on the answer space based on transformers. Although attention mechanism-based methods play key roles in improving the VQA performance, they still need developing in explainability and complex reasoning.

2.3.3 Explainable VQA

This kind of methods gives learners the explainability with the help of specific means such as external knowledge and symbolic reasoning. Wang et al. [61] proposed a fact-based VQA dataset that requires much deeper reasoning. They also proposed a baseline consisting of four modules: unified knowledge base constructing, supporting fact finding using question-query mapping, fact retrieving and answer obtaining according to the retrieved fact. Yi et al. [79] proposed a neural-symbolic VQA method that first recovers a structural scene representation from the image and a natural programme from the question and executes the programme to obtain an answer. Based on this work, Mao et al. [41] proposed a neuro-symbolic concept learner that first learns the object-based scene representation and parses questions into executable, symbolic programmes and then performs reasoning on the scene representation to obtain the answer. However, these two methods need to design the domain-specific language manually. Ma et al. [40] devised a architecture towards span-level explanations of the textbook question answering. This method can give students not only the answer but also the evidences to choose them. We argue that explainable methods should consider the audience as a key aspect [4, 40], and this direction is worthy of further study.

2.4 Learning Analytics

Learning analytics (LA) is the measurement, collection, analysis and reporting of massive, diverse and heterogeneous data generated by learners in their learning process. The purpose of LA is to promote the understanding of the learning process and to optimise learning as well as the learning environment.[6] LA provides a new model for university administrators and teachers to improve teaching, learning and to predict teaching effects. It also plays an important role in the reform of the education systems, which is helpful to optimise educational decision-making, educational assessment and curriculum setting.

As shown in Fig. 4, an LA cycle includes four phases: understanding learners, collecting data, defining metrics and deriving interventions to optimise education [20]. Using the LA technology, the VTAs can obtain the learning state, learning progress and other data of learners and provide personalised guidance to online learners through the analysis of these data.

---

[6] https://tekri.athabascau.ca/analytics/.

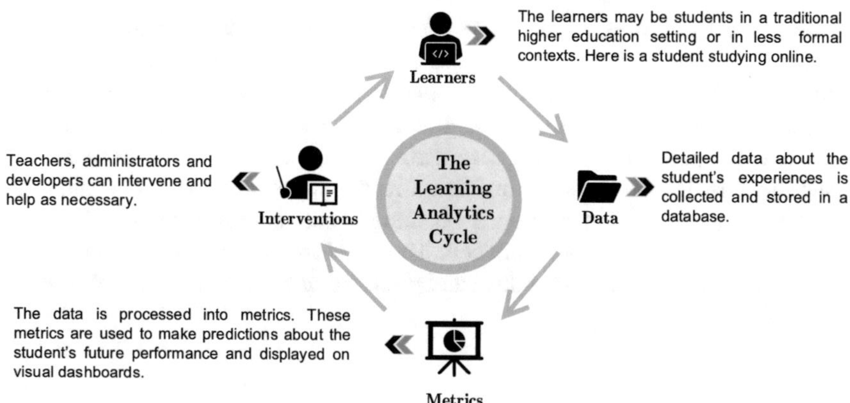

Fig. 4 Learning analytics cycle, which includes four phases: understanding learners, collecting data, defining metrics and deriving interventions to optimise education

2.4.1 Learning Analytics Methods

LA can extract implicit and potential information from massive data and provide intelligent and personalised learning guidance for learners. According to the different data sources, we divide the methods of LA into three categories.

Social Learning Analytics (SLA). SLA is an important sub-domain of LA because learners acquire knowledge and thinking through social interaction. SLA includes social network analytics, discourse analytics and content analytics. Ouyang et al. [24] used social network analytics to examine the attributes and development processes of the online learning community. The results show that all the participants formed a high frequency of interaction and reciprocity. Discourse analytics encompasses processing of open response questions in educational contexts, analysis of discussions occurring in discussion forums, blogs and even web pages [51]. Content analytics focuses on the analysis for different forms of educational contents. AlteredVista [34] is a collaborative system for discovering useful educational resources. It can recommend course notes and solutions to students based on their document browsing patterns and learning tasks, respectively.

Multimodal Learning Analytics (MLA). MLA focuses on extracting traces from the different modes of communication. Learning traces is combined from log-files, pen strokes, position tracking devices and any other modality that could be useful for understanding or measuring the learning process. Ochoa [46] used an array of cameras to record the head and eyes of the subjects, and then computer vision techniques are used to extract the gaze direction information and motion from the video recording. Oviatt et al. [47] used digital pens to capture the position, duration and pressure of writing and sketching with different people. By digitising these data, they explored the contribution that writing and sketching modes could have in the prediction of expertise.

Emotional Learning Analytics (ELA). Emotion is produced in the interaction between organism and environment, and its influence on learning is important and universal. D'Mello [18] studied the affective experience of students during their first programming session. All instructional activities including the videos of student' faces and computer screens were recorded. The authors examined how interaction events give rise to affective states and how affective states trigger various behaviours. Similarly, Yang et al. [75] developed a method to automatically identify discussion posts that indicate students' confusion. Their research shows that confusion will accelerate forgotten, but this status can be alleviated by providing clarification or other interventions.

2.4.2 Learning Analytics Tools

In terms of learning, learning analytics tools can provide learning paths according to individual needs by integrating background information and learning process data related to learners. In terms of teaching, learning analytics tools can evaluate and optimise the curriculum and provide a reliable basis for teachers and managers to carry out targeted teaching interventions. The learning analytics tools can be divided into three groups for different audiences [68]: teachers, students and school managers, so the design of learning analytics tools should follow different principles.

Teachers-oriented Tools (ToT). ToT can be used in the teaching activities to improve the teaching practise in a targeted manner. For example, the BoSCO browser tool [21] can be used by teachers to explore students' performance in different courses, assignments and semesters and analyse the correlation between them. Another exploratory learning analytics toolkit [22] can help teachers monitor and analyse teaching activities and explore, bore and evaluate teaching interventions based on their own interests.

Manager-oriented Tools (MoT). MoT conducts statistical analysis on school institution data, combines with predictive models and helps management behaviour through a visual system. Campbell et al. [7] studied the use of learning analytics tools for managers in several universities. Among them, the University of Alabama tried to predict and improve the retention rate of students from freshman to sophomore through learning analytics. Baylor University has created and perfected data analysis of potential applicants for its admission strategy. It has identified eight best predictive models that affect the final admission of the Texas group.

Student-oriented Tools (SoT). SoT can stimulate students' internal motivation and realise the function of students to understand their own learning-related data in real time. CanvesNet [9] is a learning analytics toolkit for students, which aims to promote students' online classroom discussions and transform the data from discussion forums into information for students to reflect on. Kiwi system [50] is a social network monitoring tool that collects social information from students and feeds back their interaction patterns.

3 Challenges

There are many technical challenges for the further development of humanised services provided by VTAs. In this section, we mainly analyse from four aspects: knowledge tracing, diagram understanding, explainable visual reasoning and extraction and representation of first-order logic.

3.1 Knowledge Tracing

Knowledge tracing (KT) models learners' knowledge states according to their historical response, so as to predict their performance on new questions. For the example shown in Fig. 5, if a learner can answer "$18 - 72 \div 12$" correctly, he might master the concept of both subtraction and division and have a high probability of providing right answer to "$6 \div 3 - 2$". KT is one of the essential tasks in personalised guidance, which helps VTAs provide assistance in accordance with learners' aptitude. Accurate and reliable knowledge tracing means suitable exercises can be recommended to learners based on their current knowledge states. But the learning process is complicated by both learners' knowledge and learning environment, which leads to many challenges in KT.

The Sparsity of Exercise Data. In online learning, learners' visiting to those platforms can be very infrequent, and they tend to take as few exercises as they can complete task. Therefore, for those huge question banks, only a few questions were answered, and for each questions, only few or no learners have attempted them.

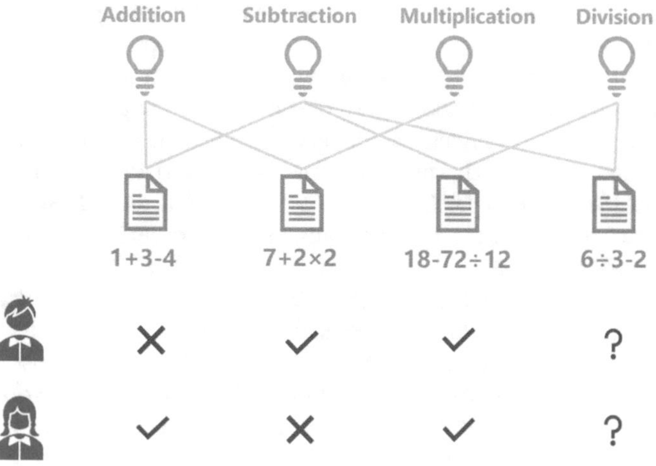

Fig. 5 Given a sequence of students' test results, KT predicates their performance on new questions. The green lines represent the concept requirements of each question

Those situations lead to data sparsity, which makes existing KT models based on deep neural networks suffer from under-fitting issue [48]. To handle these challenges, deep hierarchical KT models hierarchical information between items and concepts by embedding them and calculating their hinge loss of the inner product [64]. In addition, Chen et al. [13] proposed the hypothesis that learners master a concept after mastering its prerequisite concepts and then used prerequisites as constraints to relief data sparseness. Although the researchers have many attempts, the sparsity of exercise data is far from solved, which needs further research.

Heterogeneous Data in Learning Environment. Real environment of learning process generally contains different data forms. For example, there is text information, voice for listening and a small amount of pictures during English exams, and there are various types of interactive information between students and platforms in MOOC. These situations make the learning environment complex. Since learning effect is affected by many factors, the heterogeneous data should be considered by fusing multi-model information in the process of KT. Therefore, many knowledge fusion methods can be introduced to enhance KT. By embedding heterogeneous data into a common space, it is convenient to integrate multiple factors to track learners' knowledge. For example, exercise-enhanced RNNs [57] not only use exercising records as input but also introduce Bi-LSTM to encode the representation of topic information. Until now, researches on dealing heterogeneous data in KT are still scarce, and few data sources are considered.

3.2 Diagram Understanding

Diagrams are kinds of special images widely utilised in the teaching scene, which are existing in textbook and encyclopaedias. For example, the atmospheric circulation in geography and cellular structure in biology are usually represented with diagrams, which consist of simple lines and colour regions. Diagram understanding [31, 66] aims to fully understand the fine-grained objects and their relations in the diagrams, and this task has great significance in practical applications such as VQA, reading comprehension and so on. However, most researches focus on the nature images like in ImageNet [52] and MSCOCO [36] datasets to complete the image analysis tasks, and there are few researches on the diagrams because there exists two challenges for the diagram understanding.

The Lack of Annotated Data. Abundant annotations assist the deep models to achieve satisfactory results in image analysis, which are labour-intensive tasks. However, due to the lack of sufficient annotations for diagrams, it causes great difficulties to the diagram understanding. As shown in Fig. 6, non-professionals could only annotate coarse information of the *Animal cell*, which cannot convey the professional knowledge in diagrams. To fully understand the semantics of these diagrams, more fine-grained annotations are required by the professional annotators. See as the right of Fig. 6 [31], annotators with biological background can label the objects such as *centrioles*, *nucleolus* and *lysosome*, which are conducive for the accurately under-

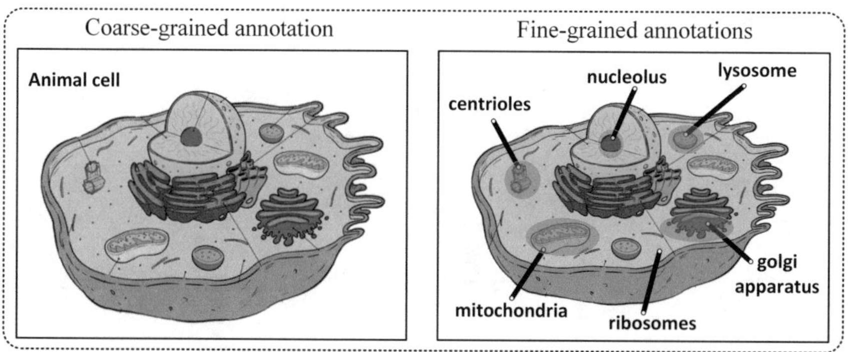

Fig. 6 Comparison of coarse- and fine-grained annotations for an *animal cell* diagram

standing of the diagrams and could improve the performance of downstream tasks. In addition, the diagrams are usually drawn by professional software, involving the domain knowledge of different subjects, and they are expensive to obtain, resulting in the more lack of training samples.

The Semantic Abstraction of Diagrams. Diagrams are kinds of highly abstract representations for knowledge. They are expressed as visual objects, arrows and lines, which bring two difficulties for diagram understanding. On the one hand, the same visual elements could represent different semantics, which may lead to the object confusion. As shown in Fig. 7a, understand the diagram from different perspectives, in which the orange and blue circles may express different semantics. Concretely, when this diagram shows the solar system, the orange circle represents the sun, while the surrounding blue circles indicate the planets in their respective orbits. If this diagram depicts an atom, the orange circle represents the nucleus, and the blue circles represent the electrons. On the other hand, the same semantics may have various forms of expression. The diagrams Fig. 7b and Fig. 7c depict the life cycle for a butterfly, and the arrows that represent the timeline are very different in visual sense [31]. Specifically, the arrows in Fig. 7b consist of dotted lines and arrow heads, while the red heads are in the middle of the whole arrows. The arrows in Fig. 7c are completely different forms, which are composed of green regions with certain width.

3.3 *Explainable Visual Reasoning*

Although these methods [40, 41, 79] make progress on the explainable visual reasoning, there still exist the following three challenges on the explainability.

The confusion of the definition and vocabulary. There is no agreement on the definition and vocabulary of the explainable visual reasoning [4]. For example, *feature importance/relevance* and *explainability/interpretability* are always referred to the same concept, respectively. This is more obvious for visualisation methods,

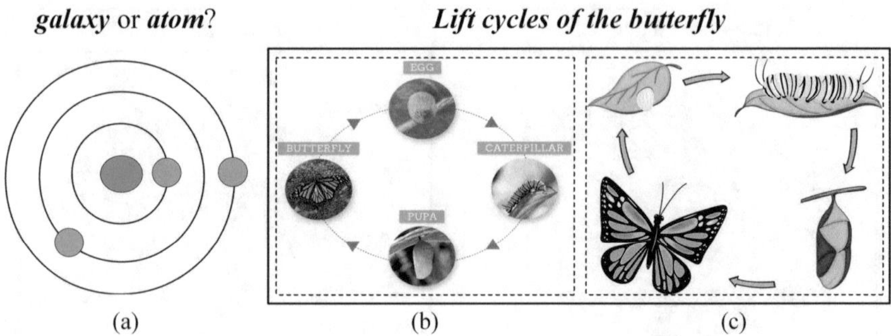

Fig. 7 Sample analysis of the semantic abstraction for diagrams. **a** shows the semantic confusion of the circles; **b** and **c** show the various expressions of arrows

in which the so-called saliency maps, salient masks, heat maps, neuron activations, attributions and other similar methods are completely inconsistent [4].

The Difference of the Study Object. There is no agreement on the objects focused by researchers. Some works [10, 84] use the post-hoc technologies such as visualising feature map and attention map to analyse the decision of models. However, some works [40, 41, 79] aim to give human observers explainability such as symbolic reasoning processes. The former focuses on the specific module of a model, and the latter focuses on giving reasons that make it easy for human observers to understand. We think that the explainable visual reasoning methods especially for the VTAs may place the students/human observers as a key aspect to be considered. In other words, these methods should give audiences the details and reasons to make their function clear or easy.

The Lack of the Evaluation Metric. There is no perfect evaluation metric for the explainable visual reasoning method. Generally speaking, the metrics should evaluate the goodness, usefulness and satisfaction of explanations, the improvement of the audience psychology induced by the explainable visual reasoning methods and the influence of these methods on the performance [4]. Miller et al. [43] argued that a good explanation should be constrictive, i.e. a prerequisite for the good explanation is that it shows not only why a model made decision X, but also why the model made decision X rather than Y. Regrettably, there is no convincing metric to evaluate the explainable visual reasoning methods, which may hinder the development of this direction. Therefore, it is important to design metrics for comprehensively evaluating explainable visual reasoning methods.

3.4 Extraction and Representation of First-Order Logic

First-order logic plays a foundational and significant role in education, as its highly expressive and well-structured nature for logical knowledge. By extracting and representing it efficiently, VTAs can realise interpretable process through reasoning to preferably assist learners. However, both extraction and representation of first-order logic are challengeable.

The Complexity of the Extraction Process. The logic of education field is composed of domain atomic formula, including special predicates and arguments transformed by different types of entities. For example, the logic of triangle postulate in Euclidean geometry is formalised as Eq. 1, which means that the sum of three inner angles of each triangle is 180°:

$$\forall X \text{ Triangle}(X) \Rightarrow \text{equal}(\text{add}(\angle X_1, \angle X_2, \angle X_3), 180°). \tag{1}$$

In this logic formula, $Triangle$, $equal$ and add are predicates. Meanwhile X, $\angle X_1$, $\angle X_2$, $\angle X_3$ and 180° are all arguments of atomic formulae. In general, the challenge of first-order logic extraction mainly lies in its complexity [15, 26]. Referring to Eq. 1, we further summarise the complexity challenge of the extraction process into two points: the diversity of predicates and arguments and the combination explosion in the formation of the logic. First, predicates and arguments in a discipline express multi-level and multi-granularity knowledge concepts, which are difficult to define and extract by unified standards. Such as the $Triangle$ versus add and X versus 180° in Eq. 1. Furthermore, the diversity is more obvious among different disciplines, leading to enormous difficulty of using unified neural networks for extraction. For example, there is a remarkable gap between $Triangle$ in geometry and $stack$ or $push$ in data structure. Second, there is the problem of combination explosion in the formation of logic from atomic formulae [76]. If the number of extracted atomic formulae is n, then the candidate logic increases exponentially with the increase of the length, reaching n^m with the maximum length m regardless of recursion or nesting. In conclusion, the above complexity makes the training and prediction process of extraction model cost huge space and time, causing it difficult to provide high-quality results for subsequent tasks efficiently.

The Semantic Intractability of Representation. The representation of first-order logic refers to embedding its logical formulae into a low-dimensional space, by which some calculation or reasoning tasks based on logic can be carried out through technologies of deep learning. Currently, representation methods of logic can be roughly divided into three categories: sequence-based [1], tree-based [14] and graph-based [71]. Although these methods have achieved some progress, they are all focusing on implementing discriminative representations at the syntactic level for logical formulae. There is a lack of research on semantic level. However, it is critical to the accuracy and intelligibility of downstream tasks to retain semantic information in representation of first-order logic. The semantics of logic equivalence theorems,[7] such as *distributive laws* and *De Morgan's laws*, should be reflected in logical representations. Meanwhile, as discussed by Evans et al. [23], the intrinsic semantics of logical knowledge is independent of arguments used in its formulae. Furthermore, Xie et al. [71] argued that small changes in syntax of logic formulae could lead to

[7] https://en.wikipedia.org/wiki/Logical_equivalence.

great changes in semantics. For example, comparing $\forall x\ (p(x) \wedge q(x)) \Rightarrow p(x)$ and $\forall x\ \neg(p(x) \wedge q(x)) \Rightarrow p(x)$, an extra negation symbol makes a great difference to intrinsic semantics. All these properties should be explicitly or implicitly embedded into representations as much as possible. But because of the large quantity and high complexity of them, it is intractable to design a unified framework for the semantic representation of first-order logic. As far as we know, there is no related research towards to this challenge.

4 Conclusion

VTAs enabled by AI technology create a novel learning pattern with personalised teaching and guidance, which play an important role in the development of intelligent education. In this chapter, we give a survey about the technologies and challenges of VTAs. We introduce four key technologies, namely education knowledge graph, natural language question answering, visual question answering and learning analytics for VTAs. VTAs have a good prospect for development, but they also face some challenges, such as knowledge tracing, diagram understanding, explainable visual reasoning and the extraction of logic rule.

Acknowledgements This work was supported by National Key Research and Development Program of China (2020AAA0108800), National Natural Science Foundation of China (62050194, 61937001 and 61877050), Innovative Research Group of the National Natural Science Foundation of China (61721002), Innovation Research Team of Ministry of Education (IRT_17R86), Project of China Knowledge Centre for Engineering Science and Technology, Consulting Research Project of Chinese Academy of Engineering "The Online and Offline Mixed Educational Service System for 'The Belt and Road' Training in MOOC China" and China Postdoctoral Science Found (2020M683493)

References

1. Allamanis, M., Chanthirasegaran, P., Kohli, P., Sutton, C.: Learning continuous semantic representations of symbolic expressions. In: Proceedings of the International Conference on Machine Learning (ICML), vol. 70, pp. 80–88. Sydney, Australia (2017)
2. Anderson, P., He, X., Buehler, C., Teney, D., Johnson, M., Gould, S., Zhang, L.: Bottom-up and top-down attention for image captioning and visual question answering. In: Proceedings of the IEEE Conference on Computer Vision and Pattern Recognition (CVPR), pp. 6077–6086. Salt Lake City, UT, USA (2018)
3. Antol, S., Agrawal, A., Lu, J., Mitchell, M., Batra, D., Lawrence Zitnick, C., Parikh, D.: Vqa: Visual question answering. In: Proceedings of the IEEE International Conference on Computer Vision (ICCV), pp. 2425–2433. Santiago, Chile (2015)
4. Arrieta, A.B., Díaz-Rodríguez, N., Del Ser, J., Bennetot, A., Tabik, S., Barbado, A., García, S., Gil-López, S., Molina, D., Benjamins, R., et al.: Explainable artificial intelligence (xai): Concepts, taxonomies, opportunities and challenges toward responsible ai. Information Fusion **58**, 82–115 (2020)

5. Berant, J., Chou, A., Frostig, R., Liang, P.: Semantic parsing on freebase from question-answer pairs. In: Proceedings of the Conference on Empirical Methods in Natural Language Processing (EMNLP), pp. 1533–1544. Seattle, USA (2013)
6. Bordes, A., Usunier, N., Garcia-Duran, A., Weston, J., Yakhnenko, O.: Translating embeddings for modeling multi-relational data. In: Proceedings of the Advances in neural information processing systems, pp. 2787–2795. Lake Tahoe, Nevada, United States (2013)
7. Campbell, J.P., DeBlois, P.B., Oblinger, D.G.: Academic Analytics: A New Tool for A New Era. Educause Review **42**(4), 40 (2007)
8. Chassignol, M., Khoroshavin, A., Klimova, A., Bilyatdinova, A.: Artificial intelligence trends in education: a narrative overview. Procedia Computer Science **136**, 16–24 (2018)
9. Chen, B., Chang, Y.H., Ouyang, F., Zhou, W.: Fostering Student Engagement in Online Discussion Through Social Learning Analytics. The Internet and Higher Education **37**, 21–30 (2018)
10. Chen, C., Li, O., Tao, D., Barnett, A., Rudin, C., Su, J.K.: This looks like that: Deep learning for interpretable image recognition. In: Advances in Neural Information Processing Systems (NeurIPS), pp. 8930–8941. Vancouver, BC, Canada (2019)
11. Chen, D., Fisch, A., Weston, J., Bordes, A.: Reading wikipedia to answer open-domain questions. In: Proceedings of the Annual Meeting of the Association for Computational Linguistics (ACL), pp. 1870–1879. Vancouver, Canada (2017)
12. Chen, P., Lu, Y., Zheng, V.W., Chen, X., Yang, B.: Knowedu: a system to construct knowledge graph for education. Ieee Access **6**, 31,553–31,563 (2018)
13. Chen, P., Lu, Y., zheng, V.W., Pian, Y.: Prerequisite-driven deep knowledge tracing. In: Proceedings of the IEEE International Conference on Data Mining (ICDM), pp. 39–48 (2018)
14. Chvalovský, K.: Top-down neural model for formulae. In: Proceedings of the International Conference on Learning Representations (ICLR). New Orleans, USA (2019)
15. Dai, W., Xu, Q., Yu, Y., Zhou, Z.: Bridging machine learning and logical reasoning by abductive learning. In: Proceedings of the Advances in Neural Information Processing Systems (NeurIPS), pp. 2811–2822. Vancouver, Canada (2019)
16. D'Anna, L.L.: Impact of individualized learning plans on educational completion among incarcerated youth. Walden Dissertations and Doctoral Studies (4918) (2018)
17. Devlin, J., Chang, M., Lee, K., Toutanova, K.: BERT: pre-training of deep bidirectional transformers for language understanding. In: Proceedings of the Conference of the North American Chapter of the Association for Computational Linguistics: Human Language Technologies (NAACL-HLT), pp. 4171–4186. Minneapolis, USA (2019)
18. D'Mello, S.: Emotional Learning Analytics. In: C. Lang, G. Siemens, A.F. Wise, D. Gaevic (eds.) The Handbook of Learning Analytics, pp. 115–127. Society for Learning Analytics Research (SoLAR) (2017)
19. Dong, L., Wei, F., Zhou, M., Xu, K.: Question answering over freebase with multi-column convolutional neural networks. In: Proceedings of the Annual Meeting of the Association for Computational Linguistics and the International Joint Conference on Natural Language Processing of the Asian Federation of Natural Language Processing (ACL), pp. 260–269. Beijing, China (2015)
20. Doug, C.: An Overview of Learning Analytics. Teaching in Higher Education **18**(6), 683–695 (2013)
21. Dunbar, R.L., Dingel, M.J., Prat-Resina, X.: Connecting Analytics and Curriculum Design: Process and Outcomes of Building A Tool to Browse Data Relevant to Course Designers. Journal of Learning Analytics **1**(3), 223–243 (2014)
22. Dyckhoff, A.L., Zielke, D., Bültmann, M., Chatti, M.A., Schroeder, U.: Design and Implementation of A Learning Analytics Toolkit for Teachers. Journal of Educational Technology & Society **15**(3), 58–76 (2012)
23. Evans, R., Saxton, D., Amos, D., Kohli, P., Grefenstette, E.: Can neural networks understand logical entailment? In: Proceedings of the International Conference on Learning Representations (ICLR). Vancouver, Canada (2018)

24. Fan, O., Cassandra, S.: The Influences of An Experienced Instructor's Discussion Design and Facilitation on An Online Learning Community Development:A Social Network Analysis Study. The Internet and Higher Education **35**, 34–47 (2017)
25. Fukui, A., Park, D.H., Yang, D., Rohrbach, A., Darrell, T., Rohrbach, M.: Multimodal compact bilinear pooling for visual question answering and visual grounding. In: Proceedings of the Conference on Empirical Methods in Natural Language Processing (EMNLP), pp. 457–468. Austin, Texas, USA (2016)
26. Galárraga, L., Teflioudi, C., Hose, K., Suchanek, F.M.: Fast rule mining in ontological knowledge bases with AMIE+. The VLDB Journal (VLDBJ) **24**(6), 707–730 (2015)
27. Goksel, N., Bozkurt, A.: Artificial intelligence in education: Current insights and future perspectives. In: Handbook of research on learning in the age of transhumanism, pp. 224–236. IGI Global (2019)
28. Guo, Z., Wei, B., Liu, J., Wu, B.: Tf-miner: Topic-specific facet mining by label propagation. In: Proceedings of the International Conference on Database Systems for Advanced Applications (DASFAA), pp. 457–460. Chiang Mai, Thailand (2019)
29. Hao, S., Miao, Z., Wang, J., Xu, W., Zhang, Q.: Labanotation generation based on bidirectional gated recurrent units with joint and line features. In: International Conference on Image Processing (ICIP), pp. 4265–4269. IEEE, Taipei, Taiwan (2019)
30. Joulin, A., Grave, E., Bojanowski, P., Mikolov, T.: Bag of tricks for efficient text classification. In: Proceedings of the Conference of the European Chapter of the Association for Computational Linguistics (EACL), pp. 427–431. Valencia, Spain (2017)
31. Kembhavi, A., Salvato, M., Kolve, E., Seo, M., Hajishirzi, H., Farhadi, A.: A diagram is worth a dozen images. In: Proceedings of the European Conference on Computer Vision (ECCV), pp. 235–251. Amsterdam, The Netherlands (2016)
32. Kim, J., Jun, J., Zhang, B.: Bilinear attention networks. In: Advances in Neural Information Processing Systems (NeurIPS), pp. 1571–1581. Montréal, Canada (2018)
33. Kim, J., On, K.W., Lim, W., Kim, J., Ha, J., Zhang, B.: Hadamard product for low-rank bilinear pooling. In: International Conference on Learning Representations (ICLR). Toulon, France (2017)
34. Kovanović, V., Joksimović, S., Gašević, D., Hatala, M., Siemens, G.: Content Analytics: The Definition, Scope, and An Overview of Published Research. In: C. Lang, G. Siemens, A.F. Wise, D. Gaševic (eds.) The Handbook of Learning Analytics, pp. 77–92. Society for Learning Analytics Research (SoLAR) (2017)
35. Li, L., Gan, Z., Cheng, Y., Liu, J.: Relation-aware graph attention network for visual question answering. In: Proceedings of the IEEE International Conference on Computer Vision (ICCV), pp. 10,313–10,322. Seoul, Korea (South) (2019)
36. Lin, T.Y., Maire, M., Belongie, S., Hays, J., Perona, P., Ramanan, D., Dollár, P., Zitnick, C.L.: Microsoft coco: Common objects in context. In: Proceedings of the European Conference on Computer Vision (ECCV), pp. 740–755. Zurich, Switzerland (2014)
37. Lin, Y., Liu, Z., Sun, M., Liu, Y., Zhu, X.: Learning entity and relation embeddings for knowledge graph completion. In: Proceedings of the AAAI Conference on Artificial Intelligence (AAAI), pp. 2181–2187. Austin, Texas, USA (2015)
38. Liu, J., Jiang, L., Wu, Z., Zheng, Q., Qian, Y.: Mining learning-dependency between knowledge units from text. The VLDB Journal **20**(3), 335–345 (2011)
39. Lu, J., Yang, J., Batra, D., Parikh, D.: Hierarchical question-image co-attention for visual question answering. In: Advances in Neural Information Processing Systems (NeurIPS), pp. 289–297. Barcelona, Spain (2016)
40. Ma, J., Liu, J., Li, J., Zheng, Q., Yin, Q., Zhou, J., Huang, Y.: Xtqa: Span-level explanations of the textbook question answering (2020)
41. Mao, J., Gan, C., Kohli, P., Tenenbaum, J.B., Wu, J.: the neuro-symbolic concept learner: Interpreting scenes, words, and sentences from natural supervision. In: International Conference on Learning Representations (ICLR). New Orleans, LA, USA (2019)
42. Mihalcea, R., Tarau, P.: Textrank: Bringing order into text. In: Proceedings of the Conference on Empirical Methods in Natural Language Processing (EMNLP), pp. 404–411. Barcelona, Spain (2004)

43. Miller, T.: Explanation in artificial intelligence: Insights from the social sciences. Artificial Intelligence (AI) **267**, 1–38 (2019)
44. Nickel, M., Rosasco, L., Poggio, T.: Holographic embeddings of knowledge graphs. In: Proceedings of the AAAI Conference on Artificial Intelligence (AAAI), pp. 1955–1961. Phoenix, Arizona (2015)
45. Nickel, M., Tresp, V., Kriegel, H.P.: A three-way model for collective learning on multi-relational data. In: Proceedings of the International Conference on Machine Learning (ICML), pp. 809–816. Bellevue, Washington, USA (2011)
46. Ochoa, X.: Multimodal Learning Analytics. In: C. Lang, G. Siemens, A.F. Wise, D. Gaševic (eds.) The Handbook of Learning Analytics, pp. 129–141. Society for Learning Analytics Research (SoLAR), Alberta, Canada (2017)
47. Oviatt, S., Cohen, A., Weibel, N.: Multimodal Learning Analytics: Description of Math Data Corpus for ICMI Grand Challenge Workshop. In: Proceedings of the International Conference on Multimodal Interaction(ICMI), pp. 563—-568. New York, USA (2013)
48. Piech, C., Bassen, J., Huang, J., Ganguli, S., Sahami, M., Guibas, L.J., Sohl-Dickstein, J.: Deep knowledge tracing. In: Proceedings of the Conference on Neural Information Processing Systems (NeurIPS), pp. 505–513 (2015)
49. Ren, S., He, K., Girshick, R., Sun, J.: Faster r-cnn: Towards real-time object detection with region proposal networks. In: Advances in Neural Information Processing Systems (NeurIPS), pp. 91–99. Salt Lake City, UT, USA (2015)
50. Rita, C., Carlos, F., Josep, M., Jordi, O., Joaquin, F.: Promoting Social Network Awareness: A Social Network Monitoring System. Computers & Education **54**(4), 1233–1240 (2010)
51. Rose, C.: Discourse Analytics. In: C. Lang, G. Siemens, A.F. Wise, D. Gaševic (eds.) The Handbook of Learning Analytics, pp. 105–114. Society for Learning Analytics Research (SoLAR) (2017)
52. Russakovsky, O., Deng, J., Su, H., Krause, J., Satheesh, S., Ma, S., Huang, Z., Karpathy, A., Khosla, A., Bernstein, M.: Imagenet large scale visual recognition challenge. International Journal of Computer Vision (IJCV) **115**(3), 211–252 (2015)
53. Sangapu, I.: Artificial intelligence in education-from a teacher and a student perspective. Available at SSRN 3372914 (2018)
54. Shrestha, R., Kafle, K., Kanan, C.: Answer them all! toward universal visual question answering models. In: Proceedings of the IEEE Conference on Computer Vision and Pattern Recognition (CVPR), pp. 10,472–10,481. Long Beach, CA, USA (2019)
55. Simonyan, K., Zisserman, A.: Very deep convolutional networks for large-scale image recognition. In: International Conference on Learning Representations (ICLR). San Diego, CA, USA (2015)
56. Singhal, A.: Introducing the knowledge graph: things, not strings. https://blog.google/products/search/introducing-knowledge-graph-things-not/ (2012)
57. Su, Y., Liu, Q., Liu, Q., Huang, Z., Yin, Y., Chen, E., Ding, C.H.Q., Wei, S., Hu, G.: Exercise-enhanced sequential modeling for student performance prediction. In: Proceedings of the AAAI Conference on Artificial Intelligence (AAAI), pp. 2435–2443 (2018)
58. Talukdar, P.P., Cohen, W.W.: Crowdsourced comprehension: Predicting prerequisite structure in wikipedia. In: Proceedings of the Building Educational Applications Using NLP, p. 307–315. Montreal, Canada (2012)
59. Tan, M., dos Santos, C.N., Xiang, B., Zhou, B.: Improved representation learning for question answer matching. In: Proceedings of the Annual Meeting of the Association for Computational Linguistics (ACL). Berlin, Germany (2016)
60. Tang, J., Zhang, J., Yao, L., Li, J., Zhang, L., Su, Z.: Arnetminer: Extraction and mining of academic social networks. In: Proceedings of the ACM SIGKDD International Conference on Knowledge Discovery and Data Mining (SIGKDD), p. 990–998. Las Vegas, Nevada, USA (2008)
61. Wang, P., Wu, Q., Shen, C., Dick, A., Van Den Hengel, A.: Fvqa: Fact-based visual question answering. IEEE Transactions on Pattern Analysis and Machine Intelligence (TPAMI) **40**(10), 2413–2427 (2017)

62. Wang, Q., Xu, C., Zhou, Y., Ruan, T., Gao, D., He, P.: An attention-based bi-gru-capsnet model for hypernymy detection between compound entities. In: Proceedings of the IEEE International Conference on Bioinformatics and Biomedicine (BIBM), pp. 1031–1035. Madrid, Spain (2018)
63. Wang, S., Liang, C., Wu, Z., Williams, K., Pursel, B., Brautigam, B., Saul, S., Williams, H., Bowen, K., Giles, C.L.: Concept hierarchy extraction from textbooks. In: Proceedings of the ACM Symposium on Document Engineering, p. 147–156. Lausanne, Switzerland (2015)
64. Wang, T., Ma, F., Gao, J.: Deep hierarchical knowledge tracing. In: Proceedings of the International Conference on Educational Data Mining (EDM) (2019)
65. Wang, Z., Zhang, J., Feng, J., Chen, Z.: Knowledge graph embedding by translating on hyperplanes. In: Proceedings of the AAAI Conference on Artificial Intelligence (AAAI), pp. 1112–1119. Québec City, Québec, Canada (2014)
66. Watanabe, Y., Nagao, M.: Diagram understanding using integration of layout information and textual information. In: Proceedings of the International Conference on Computational Linguistics (COLING). Montreal, Canada (1998)
67. Wei, B., Liu, J., Zheng, Q., Zhang, W., Wang, C., Wu, B.: Df-miner: Domain-specific facet mining by leveraging the hyperlink structure of wikipedia. Knowledge-Based Systems (KBS) **77**, 80–91 (2015)
68. Wise, A., Vytasek, J.: Learning Analytics Implementation Design. In: C. Lang, G. Siemens, A.F. Wise, D. Gaševic (eds.) The Handbook of Learning Analytics, pp. 151–160. Society for Learning Analytics Research (SoLAR) (2017)
69. Woolf, B.P., Lane, H.C., Chaudhri, V.K., Kolodner, J.L.: Ai grand challenges for education. AI magazine **34**(4), 66–84 (2013)
70. Wu, Q., Teney, D., Wang, P., Shen, C., Dick, A., van den Hengel, A.: Visual question answering: A survey of methods and datasets. Computer Vision and Image Understanding (CVIU) **163**, 21–40 (2017)
71. Xie, Y., Xu, Z., Kankanhalli, M.S., Meel, K.S., Soh, H.: Embedding symbolic knowledge into deep networks. In: Proceedings of the Advances in Neural Information Processing Systems (NeurIPS), pp. 4233–4243. Vancouver, Canada (2019)
72. Xu, Y., Mou, L., Li, G., Chen, Y., Peng, H., Jin, Z.: Classifying relations via long short term memory networks along shortest dependency paths. In: Proceedings of the Conference on Empirical Methods in Natural Language Processing (EMNLP), pp. 1785–1794. Lisbon, Portugal (2015)
73. Yahya, M., Whang, S., Gupta, R., Halevy, A.: Renoun: Fact extraction for nominal attributes. In: Proceedings of the Empirical Methods in Natural Language Processing (EMNLP), pp. 325–335. Doha, Qatar (2014)
74. Yang, B., Yih, W.t., He, X., Gao, J., Deng, L.: Embedding entities and relations for learning and inference in knowledge bases. In: Proceedings of International Conference on Learning Representations (ICLR). San Diego, CA, USA (2014)
75. Yang, D., Wen, M., Howley, I., Kraut, R., Rose, C.: Exploring the Effect of Confusion in Discussion Forums of Massive Open Online Courses. In: Proceedings of the ACM Conference on Learning @ Scale (L@S), pp. 121–130. New York, USA (2015)
76. Yang, F., Yang, Z., Cohen, W.W.: Differentiable learning of logical rules for knowledge base reasoning. In: Proceedings of the Advances in Neural Information Processing Systems (NeurIPS), pp. 2319–2328. Long Beach, USA (2017)
77. Yang, Z., He, X., Gao, J., Deng, L., Smola, A.: Stacked attention networks for image question answering. In: Proceedings of the IEEE Conference on Computer Vision and Pattern Recognition (CVPR), pp. 21–29. Las Vegas, NV, USA (2016)
78. Yang, Z., Yang, D., Dyer, C., He, X., Smola, A.J., Hovy, E.H.: Hierarchical attention networks for document classification. In: Proceedings of the Conference of the North American Chapter of the Association for Computational Linguistics: Human Language Technologies (NAACL-HLT), pp. 1480–1489. San Diego, USA (2016)
79. Yi, K., Wu, J., Gan, C., Torralba, A., Kohli, P., Tenenbaum, J.: Neural-symbolic VQA: disentangling reasoning from vision and language understanding. In: Advances in Neural Information Processing Systems (NeurIPS), pp. 1039–1050. Montréal, Canada (2018)

80. Yih, W., Chang, M., He, X., Gao, J.: Semantic parsing via staged query graph generation: Question answering with knowledge base. In: Proceedings of the Annual Meeting of the Association for Computational Linguistics and the International Joint Conference on Natural Language Processing of the Asian Federation of Natural Language Processing (ACL), pp. 1321–1331. Beijing, China (2015)
81. Yu, S.: Online education and blended learning practice at tsinghua university. In: European MOOCs Stakeholders Sumit (EMOOCs-WIP), pp. 224–229. Naples, Italy (2019)
82. Yu, Z., Yu, J., Cui, Y., Tao, D., Tian, Q.: Deep modular co-attention networks for visual question answering. In: Proceedings of the IEEE Conference on Computer Vision and Pattern Recognition (CVPR), pp. 6281–6290. Long Beach, CA, USA (2019)
83. Yu, Z., Yu, J., Fan, J., Tao, D.: Multi-modal factorized bilinear pooling with co-attention learning for visual question answering. In: Proceedings of the IEEE International Conference on Computer Vision (ICCV), pp. 1821–1830. Venice, Italy (2017)
84. Yuan, H., Tang, J., Hu, X., Ji, S.: Xgnn:towards model-level explanations of graph neural networks. In: The Conference on Knowledge Discovery and Data Mining (SIGKDD), pp. 430–438. Virtual Event, CA, USA (2020)
85. Zhang, Z., Sun, L., Han, X.: A joint model for entity set expansion and attribute extraction from web search queries. In: Proceedings of the AAAI Conference on Artificial Intelligence (AAAI), pp. 3101–3107. Phoenix, Arizona USA (2016)
86. Zheng, Q., Liu, J., Zeng, H., Guo, Z., Wu, B., Wei, B.: Knowledge forest: A novel model to organize knowledge fragments. Science China (Information Sciences) (2019)

Artificial Intelligence and People with Disabilities: a Reflection on Human–AI Partnerships

Jason J. G. White

1 Introduction

Having a disability gives rise to specific practical needs, related for example to mobility and transport, communication, learning, or access to information. It is an essential insight of the social model of disability [46] that the impairment of a person's capacity to function in a certain respect only becomes problematic in conjunction with specific physical or social environments. It is the combination of an impairment—for example, a sensory, physical, or cognitive limitation of the individual—with the demands of an environment that raises barriers to autonomy and social participation. Thus, by way of illustration, a physical disability that necessitates use of a wheelchair only creates difficulties if the built environment is not conducive to this mode of travel, for instance by requiring the use of stairs. Communication only poses inherent difficulties to a person who is deaf, for example, under circumstances in which the auditory mode is offered as the exclusive channel. Likewise, dyslexia only poses challenges in so far as reading is required to complete a task and suitable supports or alternatives are not available. Correspondingly, written text is problematic to a person who is blind only in the absence of a familiar, non-visual representation, such as braille or speech. Color blindness introduces challenges in so far as distinctions of color alone are used to convey information. This analysis, and the social model more generally have been criticized for offering an incomplete and inadequate conception of disability [45]. Nevertheless, its shifting of attention away from impairment as a problem of the individual that ought to be cured or alleviated as proposed by the medical model of disability, and toward the social determinants of inclusion and exclusion, is both historically and conceptually fundamental.

For this reason, much policy and advocacy in recent decades have focused on overcoming barriers to full participation in society by people with disabilities that

J. J. G. White (✉)
Educational Testing Service, Princeton, NJ, USA
e-mail: jjwhite@ets.org

F. Chen and J. Zhou (eds.), *Humanity Driven AI*,
https://doi.org/10.1007/978-3-030-72188-6_14

are the product of inadequacies in the design and construction of physical, social, and digital environments. The installation of ramps in buildings as alternatives to stairs and the use of braille and large print signage are among the most prominent accessibility features now increasingly found in public spaces.

Consistently with the insights derived from the social model,[1] article 1 of the *United Nations Convention on the Rights of Persons with Disabilities (CRPD)* [55] asserts that

> [p]ersons with disabilities include those who have long-term physical, mental, intellectual, or sensory impairments which in interaction with various barriers may hinder their full and effective participation in society on an equal basis with others.

As this characterization indicates, people with disabilities are highly diverse—an observation that will be of crucial importance in later discussion. According to the World Health Organization [59], more than one billion people, comprising approximately 15% of the global population, live with disability, and a continued increase is expected to result from the effects of aging as well as changes in the incidence of chronic health issues. Although the total population subject to disability is large, its great diversity with regard to the nature of impairments, capabilities, resources, experiences, and life circumstances undermines the reliability of naive generalizations or simplifying assumptions. Two people who appear to have a similar kind and degree of impairment may nevertheless differ greatly in their capabilities, needs, and experiences of disability. This heterogeneity is attributable to variation in the social conditions which have become the focus of critical attention by the disability rights movement and in disability studies scholarship. Indeed, the variability and complexity of the interactions between a person's impairment, development, and social conditions lie at the core of arguments against the received view that having a disability is in general bad for well-being [10].[2] Thus, for example, differences in educational opportunities can exercise a profound, long-term influence over the capacity of individuals not only to participate meaningfully in society, but also to address the practical needs that emerge from disability itself in such everyday contexts as employment, family life, and community activities. The quality of one's educational prospects depends significantly on socially determined conditions, including for example the availability of appropriate support, and the incidence of discriminatory treatment. The same is true in other domains of life activity.

Artificial intelligence has long served a valuable function in enhancing access for people with disabilities. Text-to-speech technology has been used as an alternative means of communication by those with speech-related disabilities. Speech recognition can function as an alternative to keyboard or pointer input, thus allowing those with certain physical disabilities to interact with software independently. From the 1970s onward, [30] people who are blind have benefited from the combination of optical character recognition with text to speech, enabling printed text to be read

[1] According to Degener [14], the CRPD acknowledges but then extends considerably beyond the conception of the human rights of people with disabilities recognized by the social model.

[2] The authors instead regard most forms of impairment as neutral traits that do not in themselves negatively affect quality of life.

aloud automatically. Each of these examples is an application that arguably engages capabilities that have traditionally required human intelligence. Consequently, they all amount to applications of AI, and indeed historically have constituted difficult computational problems. Each of these applications also stands to benefit greatly from recent advances in machine learning, notably deep neural networks.[3] It is reasonable to anticipate continued improvements in the accuracy of speech recognition and optical character recognition, as well as enhancements in the quality of text-to-speech synthesis. To this extent, the ongoing development of AI, including its shift toward machine learning, is likely further to improve the capabilities of long established applications valuable to people with disabilities.

These advances also open possibilities that have not been feasible with previous technologies. The World Institute on Disability [60] envisions automatic captioning for people who are deaf, autonomous vehicles for individuals who are unable to drive, image and facial recognition for those who are blind, language generation to support comprehension by people with cognitive disabilities, and technologies that support people with disabilities in pursuing and retaining employment. Desirable though these applications are in improving accessibility, each of them raises a variety of design challenges and ethical issues. Together, these and associated examples are taken up in Sect. 2 as suitable starting points for briefly considering some of the questions that emerge in the use of AI in overcoming barriers to access and participation. These areas of potential application focus on improving well-being by addressing challenges specifically arising from the needs and circumstances of people with disabilities.

AI presents a risk to people with disabilities in addition to opportunities. Although concerns about its potential role in discrimination have received sustained public and scholarly attention in recent years, the disability-related dimension of the problem is only beginning to be explored. Nevertheless, central issues have already been identified, and there is ample scope for further research. With this in mind, Sect. 3 offers an exploration of the problem and of some potential strategies for addressing it, emphasizing the role of the social and policy contexts. The scope of the discussion is here broadened to applications of AI in general, by which people with disabilities are affected, for example as users of a system or as individuals who are subject to decision-making processes that AI at least partly automates. Failing to address challenges of bias, discrimination, or exploitation of personal information can directly and negatively affect human well-being. There is thus a welfare-related dimension to the moral argument for establishing policies and for creating human-AI partnerships that address the potential of AI technologies to contribute to injustice. The discussion in this chapter also suggests that the concept of partnership should be understood in the current context as having social as well as technical aspects, as embracing the normative arrangements and practices in which the technology operates in addition to more narrowly conceived elements of its design and implementation.

[3] For an overview of these technical developments, see LeCun, Bengio and Hinton [31].

2 Use of AI to Enhance Accessibility and Inclusion

In this section, the potential of AI to contribute to the solution of practical problems arising in the lives of people with disabilities is explored. Ethical issues are raised that motivate consideration of the proper role of AI systems in given social contexts which affect design and development decisions. The general conclusions are informed by discussion of cases based on the domains of application noted by the World Institute on Disability [60]. Each of these examples is considered in turn (Sect. 2.1) to illuminate issues that it introduces. This analysis of the examples then leads in Sect. 2.2 to a reflection on the important contributions of design processes and policy incentives in influencing the fit between AI applications and the needs and values of users with disabilities.

2.1 Identification of Ethical and Design Issues Through Analysis of Examples

The examples considered here, which elaborate those put forward by the World Institute on Disability [60], serve multiple purposes. First, they are illustrative of applications of AI that have evident potential to solve practical problems which arise for people due to living with a disability. Second, considerations are introduced that demonstrate the contingency of these benefits on appropriate decisions in the design and deployment of the technologies. Such issues are the focus of the discussion in this section. Third, the examples motivate a more general treatment in Sect. 2.2 of approaches which can be taken to developing applications of AI that are genuinely and effectively responsive to the needs of people with disabilities.

2.1.1 Speech, Sound, and Image Recognition

Captions are a well-established means of providing access for people who are deaf or hard of hearing to information conveyed in the auditory content of online video and broadcast media. Although captions have traditionally been created manually and synchronized appropriately with the video content, speech recognition and natural language processing enable this work to be increasingly automated, as the example by the World Institute on Disability [60] acknowledges. Automatic caption generation is only useful in so far as the speech recognition system is sufficiently accurate, and the degree of accuracy that ought reasonably to be required varies according to context. Thus, speech recognition could be applied as the first step of adding captions to a video as part of the production process. In this scenario, a skilled human operator is responsible for editing the captions to correct speech recognition errors. The speech recognition system need only be sufficiently accurate that it is more efficient to correct its output than to write the captions manually. However, if the caption generation tool is used directly by a person who is deaf, for example in a live meeting, there may be inadequate opportunity to correct errors; and, plainly, the original audio is entirely inaccessible to the user. In such a situation, it is inequitable to impose the burden of dealing with the consequences of recognition errors solely on the person with a disability, except, perhaps, under conditions in which a high level of accuracy equivalent to that of human captioning can be assured. A better alternative would be to design the captioning application, or the context of its use, to facilitate manual, corrective intervention, for example by the producer of the communication or by a third party employed for the purpose, or to insist that captions be written manually by a skilled service provider. On the other hand, there may be circumstances in which a desire for privacy is best served by placing the speech recognizer under the control of the person with a disability. Whether this is the case additionally depends on privacy-related aspects of the system's design, as there is potential for disclosure of information both from the user who is deaf, and from other parties to communication. The user interface of the system could also provide notification of probable recognition errors, a capability that at least provides the user with means of judging its reliability and suitability for a given purpose in a specific context. Preliminary research investigating the styling of caption text to indicate the confidence level of the speech recognizer in the accuracy of each word suggests that this practice may be distracting to users who are deaf or hard of hearing, particularly the uninitiated [5]. It may also increase cognitive load, as the user is implicitly encouraged to interpret the confidence indicators in reading the content of the captions. There is also disagreement over whether captions should be given as full transcripts of the dialogue presented in the audio track or instead edited in the hope of reducing the required reading rate and facilitating comprehension by simplifying the vocabulary and syntax [51]. Text simplification combined with speech recognition would further increase the opportunities for error, while considerably complicating the design and development of an AI system. A decision to use automated captioning would thus tend to favor the use of full transcripts of the dialogue rather than the creation of simplified captions. In general, the appropriate course of action in deciding whether to offer automated captioning, and how the software should be designed, very much depends not just on the capabilities of the AI, but also on the social context of its proposed deployment.

The use of AI to recognize non-speech sounds and to report them via visual or tactile cues could also benefit people who are deaf or hard of hearing. However, it would evidently be inappropriate to rely on such an application in the circumstances of an emergency, for example as a substitute for providing an accessible alarm system in a building. Designing a general sound recognition tool also inherently involves making decisions about what sounds should be recognized, and what information about them should be presented to the user [18].

Similar observations apply to the use of object, face, and scene recognition by people who are blind. The question arises of under what circumstances it is appropriate to expect the person with a disability to use the technology without any effective opportunity for correction of errors, and in what conditions alternative solutions meeting the need for accessibility should be put in place. There is a risk that, unless image recognition systems become as reliable as human observers under a wide variety of conditions, their availability will be seen as an opportunity to reduce labor costs and to impose the responsibility for addressing the effects of their limitations directly on the ultimate beneficiaries. There are also circumstances in which deciding not to use image recognition is preferable to running the risk of being misled by it. Educating users in the limitations of the technology is clearly indispensable to informing decisions about its appropriate application, whether those users are people with disabilities themselves, or other parties responsible for ensuring equitable access and inclusion, such as educators or employers. For example, misidentification of people and objects could be at least embarrassing and at worst result in ill-advised decision making—as when a stranger at the door is mistaken for a friend [18]. As with speech recognition, questions of privacy emerge, not only for the person who has a disability, but potentially for others whose information is placed at risk of inappropriate disclosure. Analogously to the case of captions, there are applications of image recognition that do not raise all of the foregoing issues. For example, it could serve as a component in an authoring tool for the development of Web sites, in which the automatically generated descriptions are supposed to be manually reviewed and corrected.[4] Again, however, proper application of the AI technology depends on users' knowledge of its limitations, which can be reinforced through features of the application's user interface, for example by prompting document authors to verify textual descriptions produced by image recognition.

2.1.2 Text Simplification and User Interface Adaptation

AI-based text simplification and summary generation tools could be valuable to people with learning or cognitive disabilities that affect linguistic understanding. However, with every simplification or summarizing strategy, there is an associated risk of misinforming and misleading the recipient, or of producing information that is more rather than less difficult to comprehend. A twofold question arises: first, how best to control this risk in the design and use of such systems, and, second, in what contexts it is appropriate to deploy these language processing technologies. As in the previous examples, AI could here be used to empower people with disabilities and to promote individual autonomy, but it could also be relied on in circumstances to which it is unsuited. The task of system designers is further complicated by the observation that the objective should be not primarily to simplify natural language as such, but rather to ensure the simplicity of the tasks that users are expected to perform with the information to be provided. As Lewis [32] has argued, simplicity should be understood as a relation between the cognitive demands of using a system, and the cognitive capabilities of the user. Thus, a system that is simple for one individual may not be so for another whose cognitive abilities are relevantly different, as Lewis [32] illustrates by analyzing the trade-offs between breadth and depth of control

[4] For further discussion of issues raised by sound and image recognition systems designed for use by people with disabilities, including some of the concerns introduced here, see Findlater et al. [18].

presentation in graphical user interface design. A deeper hierarchy, for example in a menu structure, is simpler for users who are more easily distracted, for instance, but more complex for those who have difficulty holding attention throughout a long sequence of actions. The proper role of language simplification in designing tasks that are more cognitively tractable is thus likely to be highly dependent not only on the tasks themselves, but also on the user's capabilities and on the surrounding social context.

The diverse and sometimes conflicting needs of people with disabilities regarding what constitutes an accessible user interface, as illustrated by the preceding example, have motivated efforts to develop systems that can be configured appropriately according to each individual's personal needs and preferences. Significantly, the Global Public Inclusive Infrastructure (GPII) project [57] has created software that maintains a profile of the user's needs and preferences, on the basis of which any supported system that the individual with a disability wishes to access can be automatically configured to satisfy accessibility requirements. This is achieved by matching the profile with an appropriate set of configuration choices at the operating system, assistive technology, and application levels, and then setting those parameters accordingly. The benefits of AI can be seen in the 'matchmaking' process by which the user's profile, possibly also taking into account environmental conditions such as ambient light and noise characteristics, is used to infer a suitable system configuration [27]. Two approaches to matchmaking have been developed, the first of which is a system of rules based on knowledge representation [34], whereas the second employs statistical techniques to derive a configuration by analyzing the profiles and settings of other users who have similar needs. These rule-based and statistical techniques are not mutually exclusive, and may therefore be implemented in a complementary, hybrid solution [27]. So long as privacy is preserved, this application of AI has the potential greatly to simplify and to facilitate the adaptation of user interfaces to individual access needs.

2.1.3 Autonomous Vehicles

As the World Institute on Disability [60] recognizes, autonomous vehicles must be universally designed if they are to satisfy the needs of users with disabilities. The features needed for a vehicle to be accessible depend on the nature and extent of its autonomy. Notably, if human participation is required in aspects of driving, as is true of all but the most fully autonomous of systems, controls and sensory feedback arrangements need to be developed which can be used effectively by people with a wide variety of abilities. While a highly accessible autonomous vehicle does not appear to have yet been created, some aspects of the problem have been the subject of preliminary research. For example, the design of tactile and auditory interfaces to enable driving decisions to be made by a person who is blind or vision-impaired has been explored [9].

The prospect of a fully autonomous vehicle occupied by a person with a disability who cannot intervene in driving to override the decisions of an AI system, raises legal and moral concerns. Clearly, questions of safety are of paramount importance, both for the vehicle's occupant and for other road users, as are issues of ethical and legal responsibility in the event of accidents. As noted by Bradshaw-Martin and Easton [8], the use of autonomous vehicles by people with disabilities who are unable to take direct control departs from the long-standing legal assumption that a human being is responsible for driving decisions at all times. Bradshaw-Martin and Easton [8] suggest that such cases should be considered acceptable only if the operation of 'empty' autonomous vehicles (i.e., those without human occupants) on public roads is also acceptable. An alternative approach would be to enable the functioning of the autonomous vehicle to be overseen by a remote human observer who is able to assume manual control of the driving in potentially dangerous situations [8]. Although this solution introduces challenges of privacy and security, it could overcome risks to safety without greatly diminishing the independence of the person with a disability. If fully autonomous vehicles ultimately become commonplace, the skill and readiness of their human occupants to intervene can be expected to decline. Further, manual intervention is likely to be most difficult and risky in situations that pose the most danger. The problems of safety and accessibility are especially complex under conditions of mixed traffic, in which some vehicles are driven by humans and others are under the control of AI systems. In these circumstances, anticipating the actions of other 'drivers,' some of which are AI agents, can become difficult—and possibly more so for a person with a disability who is interacting with a vehicle via an assistive technology.[5] Fulfilling the promise of autonomous vehicles for people with disabilities thus necessitates the development of novel user interfaces, as well as a combination of technological and legal measures that can fairly allocate the risk of accidents, while reducing it to an acceptable level.

2.1.4 Employment and Education

The potential applications of AI that could enhance employment of people with disabilities are diverse, and capable of operating at all stages of the process from education and training to improving accessibility in the workplace.[6] Whether education is offered by educational institutions or directly in the work environment, there is the possibility of using AI to improve its efficacy. Intelligent tutoring systems, for example, are AI-based applications that can adapt the delivery of educational content to the learning needs of the individual. AI has also been introduced into the recruitment of employees, raising questions about the possibility of bias against candidates with disabilities. Employees may also take advantage of AI systems, including technologies supporting accessibility as considered elsewhere in this chapter, in performing their work. There are nevertheless issues of ethics and privacy to be taken into account in deciding what the capabilities of these applications should be, and in arriving at appropriate design decisions.

[5] Solutions to the general problem of mixed traffic are developed in Nyholm and Smids [38].

[6] See generally Employer Assistance and Resource Network on Disability Inclusion [16].

An 'intelligent' educational application could, in principle, adapt the presentation of material and its evaluations of the learner's responses according to needs arising from a disability. For example, it could offer additional explanations of geometric or spatial concepts to a student who is blind and whose knowledge of the relevant spatial relationships is found to be in need of consolidation. The possibility of individualizing the delivery of education based, in part, on a person's disability has genuine potential to improve learning, leading ultimately, in the present context, to greater success in a career. However, it also has the potential to perpetuate misconceptions about what people with disabilities can do and to entrench stereotypes. For example, whether a student who is blind would benefit from additional support in performing tasks requiring geometric knowledge ought not to be inferred from the disability category, but should instead be ascertained with respect to each person individually. Similarly, whether sign language interpretation should be provided for multimedia content (for instance, in a tutoring system) depends on the individual's knowledge of and preference for a sign language—factors that are not captured by the classification of the individual as a student who is deaf. There is thus a risk of drawing inappropriate generalizations from a disability classification, instead of attending to the specific needs of each learner. Adaptive AI systems developed as educational technologies could exacerbate this problem, unless suitable design choices are taken.

Further cause for concern emerges from the possibility of building educational systems that use AI-related techniques in an attempt to determine whether a person has a disability. For example, an arithmetic tutoring application might be equipped with the ability to flag a student as possibly having dyscalculia—a learning disability. The negative personal and social consequences that could result from a misclassification are considerable, including stigmatization and inappropriate educational interventions.[7] The same could also occur in the event of a correct classification, particularly in the absence of knowledgeable and skilled educators who understand the nature of the disability and the needs of the student. Depending on the design of the system and the conditions of its use, individual privacy rights could also be infringed in this scenario. In general, the design of AI systems to detect a disability—particularly a disability of which the individual may be unaware—is fraught with ethical difficulties, while also giving rise to legal issues. For example, the European Union's General Data Protection Regulation (GDPR) ([17], article 5(1) (b)) constrains the processing of personal information for purposes that are incompatible with the 'specified, explicit and legitimate' purposes for which the data are collected, and consent to which is among the permissible bases of authorization ([17], article 6(1) (a)).[8] In addition, the creation and disclosure of health-related information is a sensitive matter that is appropriately subject to legal safeguards which vary by jurisdiction.

[7] The risks of using AI as a tool of medical diagnosis in relation to people with disabilities is discussed in Trewin et al. [54].

[8] The limitation of data processing to specified, explicitly stated purposes is an aspect of European data protection law that raises difficulties for machine learning-based AI applications generally. See Marsch [37] for treatment of the relevant human rights obligations.

A further case which well illustrates the importance of preserving privacy is that of a hypothetical recommender system designed to match prospective employees with available employment opportunities. Under readily foreseeable conditions, voluntary disclosure of an individual's disability status to the system could be beneficial. For example, in some countries, there are policies in place which establish quotas to improve the employment rate of people with disabilities, who are expected to comprise a specified proportion of each employer's workforce [22]. A recommender system could take an individual's disability status into account, together with qualifications and experience, to suggest opportunities offered by employers who are likely to have unfilled quotas. Of course, this would require informed consent, as some people with disabilities may object to having their disability status operate as a factor in an employment decision. On the negative side, however, any disclosure of disability status to employers by such an AI system not only raises privacy issues, but also creates a risk of discrimination in the selection process. Such a case is thus illustrative of the value of statutory protection of privacy, and of requiring consent for the purposes for which data are collected. Controlling the disclosure of information—in this case, about a person's disability—thereby limits the opportunities for its misuse.

2.2 *Observations*

Drawing on a recent paper [47] that connects technological choices with social assumptions revealed by the contrasting models of disability introduced in Sect. 1, it is argued in Sect. 2.2.1 that a collaborative and participatory approach is necessary, which engages people with disabilities directly in the development of AI systems designed to meet their needs. This position is supported by further comments on examples considered in Sect. 2.1. Section 2.2.2 takes up the suggestion, advanced in a recent contribution to the literature on AI and people with disabilities [54], that theoretical and methodological traditions in design thinking have much to contribute to an elaboration of what constitutes appropriate participation. This scholarship also offers a framework—value-sensitive design—in which to address the moral questions raised by AI-related projects. In Sect. 2.2.3, it is maintained that such design-based approaches, though valuable, should also be complemented by supporting norms and incentives grounded in policy. The principal conceptual relations developed in this section are depicted in Fig. 1.

2.2.1 The Need for an Inclusive Collaboration

Each of the examples in Sect. 2.1 is a good illustration of the potential benefits that AI can bring to people with disabilities. It can serve a positive function by helping to overcome problems of access to information, communication, education, employment, and transport. Nevertheless, as has been shown in each case, there emerge important questions to be considered in deciding what AI applications should

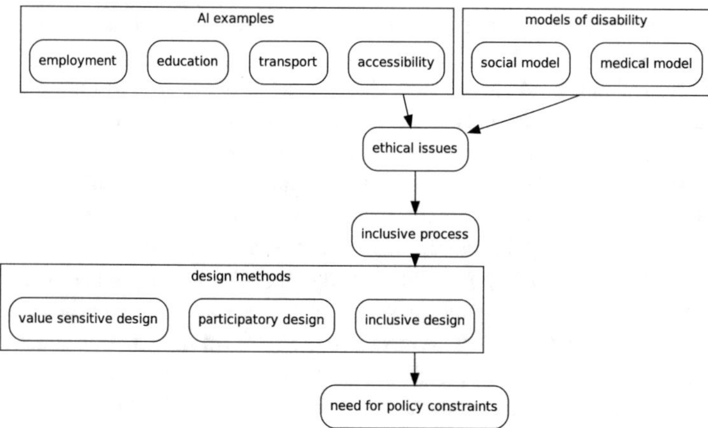

Fig. 1 Examples of AI applications intended to benefit people with disabilities (in accessibility, transport, education and employment), together with the medical and social models of disability, raise ethical issues. These issues give rise to the need for an inclusive development process, supported by design methods such as inclusive design, participatory design, and value-sensitive design. Consideration of these design methods illuminates the need for policy constraints

be built, and in arriving at appropriate design decisions. As has been emphasized in the discussion, these issues are concerned not only with the AI system as a technological artifact, but also with the wider social environment in which it is likely to be deployed and used. Choices about design and implementation should thus be made from a perspective that is informed by knowledge of how a proposed system would actually function in the specific life circumstances of people with disabilities.

In deciding what problems AI should be used to solve, and what constitute adequate solutions, there is a risk of introducing prejudiced assumptions about the lives of people with disabilities. Shew [47] warns of this danger, noting examples of technologies that perpetuate problematic assumptions about disability, particularly the notion central to the medical model that the shortcoming essentially resides in the bodily limitations of the individual, which must be 'treated' or minimized, rather than in the physical and social context. Narratives about the benefits of technology for people with disabilities are connected with notions of independence, which, Shew points out, downplay the extent to which people in general are interdependent in a multiplicity of respects. Thus, the promise of autonomous vehicles as enhancing independence for people with disabilities reinforces these narratives, situating the problem in the individual's inability to drive, rather than in a social responsibility to provide effective and accessible means of transport [47].[9] A more careful analysis would recognize that although autonomous vehicles would increase independence in some respects, they would also create a less obvious dependence on the developers

[9] Shew further develops the point in a brief discussion of additional examples, including the rationale for using companion robots, which may serve the interests of human care givers more than those of the person with a disability whose needs are to be met.

and maintainers of the technology—designers, implementers, trainers, and service personnel among them. Thus, the central question is concerned not with a greater or lesser degree of independence as such, but instead with the type of interdependence that is desired. An autonomous vehicle offers freedom to choose when and where to travel, without having to coordinate with other people (namely human drivers or public transport operators). However, it also requires the person with a disability to entrust his or her safety to the creators and maintainers of a complex AI system.

The discussion of speech, sound, and image recognition in Sect. 2.1.1 directs attention to issues of societal responsibility for making information and communication accessible, as well as associated questions of privacy and confidentiality. Clearly, imposing responsibility for using AI to solve problems of information access principally on the individual who is faced with accessibility barriers is consistent with an individualistic, medicalized concept of disability. Also, as has been noted, it shifts the burden of the technology's shortcomings onto the person who is least able to overcome them. This is not to suggest, however, that people with disabilities should be deprived of opportunities to gain the full benefit of such technologies and to use them independently. Rather, the point is to acknowledge the need for informed decision making about appropriate application, both at the individual level and in policy decisions regarding the overcoming of obstacles to access and inclusion.

Shew emphasizes the importance of ensuring the agency and autonomy of people with disabilities, and of fully recognizing their expertise in their own needs, lives, and experiences. This can be achieved, in part, by bringing the knowledge and experience of people with disabilities directly into the process of making decisions about the development and use of AI applications. User participation in design is thus of crucial value, as is educating decision-makers and developers about disability.

The concept of human–AI partnership can be extended to acknowledge the importance of social practices and institutions in shaping the creation and application of AI-based technologies. What is proposed here is that technological decision making ought to be sensitive to this social context, and, ideally, not isolated from choices about the social practices in which technologies are developed, maintained, and used. Questioning implicit presuppositions, as well as gaining a greater understanding of the lives, desires, and needs of people with disabilities are essential aspects of this approach. The slogan put forward by the disability rights movement, 'nothing about us without us', aptly conveys the importance of involving people with disabilities directly in making decisions that affect them, including choices about appropriate uses of AI technologies [58].

The considerations advanced so far build a case for engaging people with disabilities directly in problem identification and definition, as well as in determining what constitute appropriately designed solutions capable of meeting their practical needs effectively. To be clear, it is not argued here that only people with disabilities are appropriately qualified to conceive and to plan suitable AI-based solutions. Rather, the claim is that the design and development of these systems should be carried out in close collaboration with people who have disabilities and should preferably be undertaken by developers who are personally interacting with disability-related communities in non-trivial ways. Through a genuine and mutual understanding of the problems to be solved and of the design possibilities, informed decisions can be made which lead to AI projects that are successful in enhancing equity and life opportunities. The risks of perpetuating prejudiced assumptions, and of devising systems which attempt to solve the wrong problems, can thus be minimized by establishing an inclusive collaboration in which prospective users and beneficiaries play a crucial role. This collaboration should persist throughout a project, from its inception through to the evaluation and refinement of the delivered AI system.

2.2.2 The Role of Users in Application Design

As discussed by Trewin et al. [54] in connection with the development of AI systems that avoid algorithmic bias against people with disabilities, there are traditions of research and practice in which the users of a technology play a central role in the design process. Among these traditions, the authors emphasize the contributions of 'inclusive design,' 'participatory design,' and 'value-sensitive design' in particular. Such approaches are clearly germane not only to the design of AI applications generally, but also to the development of applications which, in their over-all purpose or via the inclusion of certain assistive technologies and accessibility-related features, aim to satisfy needs specific to certain users who have disabilities. In these cases, the potential users with disabilities who are intended to benefit from a proposed project (an automated captioning application, for example) can be identified, and efforts can then be made to engage representative individuals. Drawing on design methods that privilege the user's perspective in decision making or which make explicit the value judgments inherent in technical choices has the potential to improve the quality and suitability of the resulting AI systems. Nevertheless, the limitations of these methods should also be kept in mind in relation to the project at hand.

In participatory design, for example, the users are genuine partners in decision making. Participatory design approaches originated in the Scandinavian industrial democracy movement, and were substantially motivated by resistance to taylorism in the workplace.[10] There thus arose a tradition that recognizes the value of the tacit knowledge possessed by users (in the original context, industrial workers) in performing tasks and solving problems. Instead of seeking to analyze, formally describe and optimize this tacit, practical knowledge, participatory design develops and builds upon it in ways that are meant to empower the users and to preserve their autonomy. Moreover, participatory design methods are intended to be applied to the entire work process, not merely to the creation of technological artifacts. The emphasis placed on preserving and enhancing users' tacit knowledge gives rise to a tendency toward solutions that retain instead of radically reconfiguring established practices—a favoring of evolutionary over revolutionary change.[11] These aspects of the approach have

[10] For an overview of the history and the guiding ideas, see Ehn [15]. A more recent introduction to participatory design appears in Spinuzzi [49].

[11] This consequence of the value placed on preexisting tacit knowledge is acknowledged as a limitation of participatory design in Spinuzzi [49].

the potential to contribute to improving the design of AI systems intended for use by people with disabilities. However, they may also discourage more fundamentally innovative, long-term projects.

Development of an AI system to facilitate indoor navigation by people who are blind, for example, would begin with an understanding of existing, formal and informal practices of orientation and mobility. It would tend to favor extending established approaches, such as those centered on the white cane and the guide dog, instead of proposing the development of robots as substitutes. It would also seek to preserve existing mobility skills. This could be achieved, for instance, by further developing orientation applications suitable for use with mobile phones or wearable devices that could give information and directions to the user, especially in unfamiliar, indoor settings, and ideally without requiring the installation of specialized infrastructure such as radio beacons that enable precise locations to be identified. On the other hand, developing robots capable of navigating and of guiding their users in a wide variety of environments is arguably a valuable, long-term objective, notwithstanding the practical limitations of current prototypes. The state-of-the-art prototype described by Guerreiro et al. [23] is largely limited to flat, indoor environments in virtue of technical constraints, including weight and battery capacity. If these constraints could be overcome and the capabilities of the AI system responsible for navigation improved, the technology could manifestly be advantageous to users, at the risk of their placing too much reliance on a robotic guide to the detriment of existing skills. The shortfall in the user's orientation and mobility skills would then become problematic whenever robotic assistance was unreliable or unavailable. The principal benefits of robots—effective navigation in unfamiliar settings, and avoidance of hazards or obstacles that conventional mobility aids would miss—could be obtained by developing solutions that extend rather than supplant current tools and strategies. The robots, however, may in the long-term offer usability advantages that would not be achieved via more evolutionary approaches.

Respect for users' tacit knowledge in the design of new technological solutions is thus autonomy-preserving, enhancing the individual's control over the manner in which tasks are performed and capacity for decision making. It operates also as a constraint on more radical forms of innovation. Participatory design offers the advantage of making the practical knowledge and skills possessed by users conspicuous, and therefore of raising questions about the role it should continue to occupy in the application of new, AI-based systems. The fostering of user involvement in design decisions also provides practical means of negotiating these issues, among others, in arriving at appropriate technical solutions.

The design problems that have here been discussed all introduce questions of value, broadly construed. Value-sensitive design seeks to bring investigation of the values implicated by technological choices directly into the development process.[12] Importantly, value-sensitive design attends to the salient moral considerations that

[12] The approach is articulated and illustrated in Friedman, Kahn and Borning [20]. For a recent treatment of the underlying concepts and design methods, see Friedman and Hendry [19] (Chaps. 2 and 3).

may otherwise be overlooked or disregarded in technological projects. It accordingly has potential to serve as a useful tradition to draw upon in building AI systems for people with disabilities. Through 'conceptual,' 'empirical,' and 'technical' investigations, value-sensitive designers identify and engage direct and indirect stakeholders—people whose interests are affected by a project. The values of the stakeholders and of the designers themselves with respect to the design problem are investigated and incorporated into technical decisions. Of particular significance in relation to the role of AI in enhancing the lives of people with disabilities is the concept of 'value tensions' [19] (Chap. 2) among and even within stakeholders. Recognition of these value tensions can lead to creative solutions that reconcile apparently conflicting priorities. For instance, [19] (Chap. 2) an energy-efficient design may be agreed upon both by stakeholders who prioritize cost minimization and by those who favor environmental sustainability, without requiring resolution of their underlying moral disagreement. Of course, this is only possible if the proposal contains costs while also reducing energy consumption from sources that are ecologically harmful.

Opportunities for creatively overcoming value tensions can and indeed should be sought in cases such as those discussed in this chapter. As an illustration, the choice between providing captions that give a full transcript of the dialogue in a video, and providing captions as simplified summaries of the dialogue, can be understood as a value tension that may arise not only between users but even within a single individual. As is evident from the discussion in Szarkowska et al. [51], unsimplified captions offer the user full access to the dialogue, without interposing another person's interpretation of it, whereas simplified captions can improve readability and comprehension, which are also valuable to and valued by users, at the cost of precluding equal, unmediated access to the spoken content. If sufficiently reliable speech recognition and summary generation technologies were available, this value tension could be overcome simply by generating both types of caption. The user could then choose which type of caption to read in each particular situation. Though attractive, this solution also exacerbates a second value tension—that between the quality and availability of captions, on the one side, and the desirability of containing production costs by reducing the human labor associated with editing and verifying captions, on the other. Much of the appeal of automating caption creation derives from the desire for improved cost efficiency. Generating two sets of captions for video content obviously runs contrary to this objective. The resulting tension can be resolved by a technological solution if the automatic speech recognition and text simplification algorithms are sufficiently accurate to maintain labor costs that are acceptable to the producers. This places a heavy demand on AI researchers and software developers. In the absence of a technical solution, the value tension should instead be regarded as a value conflict. The wider question, then, is how to address such value conflicts if, as in the current example, the human rights of people with disabilities are at stake. In this case, the right of access to information and communication [55] (article 9) is implicated.

2.2.3 Commentary

Engaging users appropriately in the design process has genuine potential to encourage the development of technologies that are well aligned with the needs and values of people with disabilities. However, treating the resolution of value tensions largely as a design question for negotiation among designers and stakeholders in individual technical projects would risk the formation of compromises that undermine the rights and interests of those whom it is supposed to benefit. For this reason, policies, ultimately established by governments, have a necessary and important role. Indeed, the presence of deeply entrenched practices of social subordination operating against people with disabilities, manifested in technological choices as Shew has described, justifies skepticism toward the ability of designers and stakeholders to resolve value conflicts appropriately in the absence of incentives created by policy. In AI, as elsewhere, one can plausibly argue that regulation and oversight are indispensable elements of upholding a moral commitment to social equality for people with disabilities. Trewin et al. [54] do not suggest otherwise. Nevertheless, this conclusion is important in understanding the complementary role that design methods occupy to policy considerations in relevantly shaping the future of AI development.[13] Furthermore, design procedures centered on the participation of users and other stakeholders are expensive, raising doubts about whether organizations responsible for building AI-based technologies will deploy them sufficiently in the absence of externally imposed incentives. True power sharing among stakeholders in the design process challenges existing structures of authority in addition to creating participation costs. These factors suggest that its widespread application to AI development will require policy-based interventions. In evaluating current policies and planning future regulatory approaches, there also arises the challenge of promoting the rights of people with disabilities while allowing suitable flexibility for stakeholders to arrive at creative solutions to technological problems, including mutually advantageous responses to value tensions.

The development of human-AI partnerships that respect the rights and satisfy the needs of people with disabilities thus requires an interplay of technical and social choices. The social aspects of these choices bring to the fore issues of morality, including questions of justice and human rights. Adequate resolution of these considerations in technological projects depends on the nature of the design process, the motivations and skills of the participants, as well as the internal and external incentives that influence decisions. There is an important role for policy in establishing appropriate incentives. Traditions emerging from design research can also be applied and refined to support meaningful participation by direct and indirect stakeholders with disabilities. Addressing value tensions can be regarded as partly a function of the design process, and in large measure as lying in the domain of overarching policies.

[13] Interestingly, Friedman and Hendry [19] (Chap. 2) regard policy as a kind of technology for the purpose of applying value sensitive design methods.

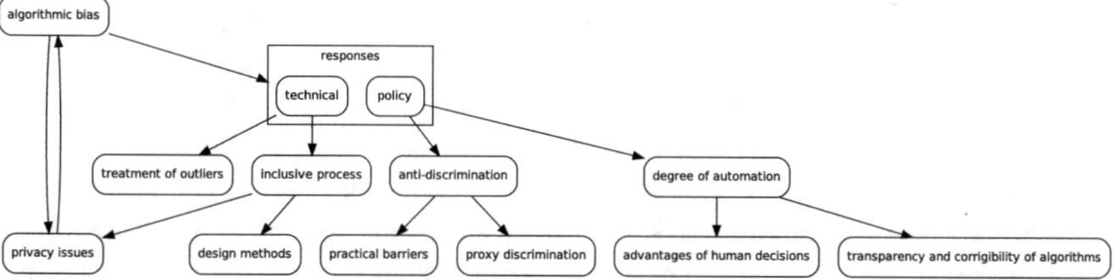

Fig. 2 Mutually related problems of bias and privacy give rise to technical and social responses. Technical responses concern treatment of outliers and inclusive development processes. Inclusive processes engage appropriate design methods (as described earlier in the chapter), while also interacting with privacy issues. Policy responses concern antidiscrimination (practical barriers as well as normative issues of proxy discrimination) and questions concerning the appropriate degree to which decisions should be automated. The latter questions, in turn, raise issues regarding the advantages of human decision making, and the transparency and auditability of machine learning algorithms

3 Disability as a Site of Algorithmic Bias

Whereas the previous section examined respects in which AI systems can be designed to benefit people with disabilities by solving specific, practical problems, the following discussion addresses the more general issue of the role of AI in perpetuating, and even amplifying, discrimination against them. The disability-related aspects of the problem of algorithmic bias are introduced (Sect. 3.1) and briefly illustrated by citing examples presented in recent literature (Sect. 3.1.1). Closely related issues of privacy are discussed in Sect. 3.1.2. The difficulties associated with technical, social, and policy-related remedies are then explored (Sect. 3.2), enabling the identification of open questions pertinent to research and practice. Even more so than in the preceding section, the purpose of this commentary is to pose questions rather than to recommend solutions and to offer a conceptual approach to thinking about the problems rather than to give concrete guidance. The accumulation of multidisciplinary research and evidence derived from actual cases of AI applications in subsequent years can be expected to clarify the issues, while strengthening the guidance available to practitioners. Figure 2 presents a conceptual overview of the issues considered.

3.1 Introduction to the Problem of Bias

It has long been established that software, including AI applications, can reinforce biases already present in the social context, while introducing new sources of bias of its own [21]. The growing utility and increasingly diverse applications of AI systems based on machine learning which have emerged in recent years greatly expand the potential for biases to be introduced and extend the range of possible harms that may result. As decision making becomes increasingly automated in a wide variety of domains, all the more opportunities arise for biased algorithms to contribute to social injustice,[14] including discrimination against people with disabilities. Questions concerning algorithmic bias with respect to disability are necessarily part of a larger discussion of the role of AI in discrimination generally. What distinguishes disability from other social categories subject to algorithmic bias, such as gender and national or ethnic origin, consists in the nature of the diversity that disability represents. As introduced in Sect. 1, impairments can affect a broad range of human functioning, including sensory, physical, psychological, and cognitive aspects. A given individual can have one or more impairments of different kinds and degrees, which may occur at different stages of life and vary over time. These impairments can then combine with highly variable, socially mediated conditions to constitute disabilities that present practical challenges to the individual. As with other social categories of interest in connection with algorithmic bias, societal practices of subordination and exclusion can have a large role in limiting a person's well-being and the life opportunities that can effectively be pursued. As has been recognized in recent literature, [53, 54, 58], the great diversity of impairments, social circumstances, resources, and experiences among people with disabilities creates an associated diversity in the ways in which they can be subjected to biases in AI systems.

3.1.1 Potential for Bias

Scholars and practitioners have reported on the findings of workshops that have identified a variety of AI applications in which such biases have real potential to occur [54, 58]. These examples are not exhaustive, as the range of AI applications is large and becoming more so. Nor are all of the examples reviewed here, as the discussion which follows can be sufficiently motivated by a brief overview.[15] It is clear from the actual and hypothetical cases discussed in the literature that the biases in question tend to operate against people with specific circumstances and types of disability, rather than against people with disabilities as a general category. Moreover, an AI system exhibiting bias may do so to different extents and in different ways to different individuals. This is a product of the many dimensions of diversity characteristic of people with disabilities. A clear illustration of the specificity and the danger of algorithmic bias is given by Treviranus, who presented machine learning models designed to control autonomous vehicles with images of a friend who 'propels herself backwards in her wheelchair' [52, 1]. The models would have directed the vehicle to run her over at an intersection, and, worse, they reached this decision with even greater confidence after having been trained with data depicting people in wheelchairs [52].

AI systems designed to draw inferences from the behavior or appearance of a person are problematic, since people with disabilities can differ in many respects from the relatively homogeneous populations likely to be used in training. Examples

[14] An informative overview of how discrimination can occur is presented in Barocas and Selbst [3].

[15] The cited references should be consulted for more detailed illustration and discussion of applications in which bias against people with disabilities can reasonably be foreseen.

of these applications, and the ways in which they may adversely classify people due to a disability, have been noted in domains such as partially automated job interview assessment, and public safety systems meant to detect suspect behavior [54, 58]. The monitoring of a person's interactions with a user interface, for example in an educational measurement application such as a test or an interactive learning tool, raises similar concerns [54, 58]. More generally, machine learning algorithms have been applied to various tasks in which people are ranked or categorized to determine their eligibility for an opportunity or benefit, or their liability for a sanction. In employment, for example, AI has been applied at every stage of the process from deciding whom to select for targeted advertising of open positions, to the screening of job applications, and ultimately the monitoring of the employee's work performance [7]. In such cases, biases could occur against people with disabilities for different reasons and to varying extents, depending on details of the interactions between disability-related circumstances and the factors taken into account by the machine learning algorithm. Such algorithmic bias may then be reflected in adverse decisions with discriminatory effects [54, 58]. For instance, an individual's job application may be automatically excluded from further consideration or an employee's work performance may be automatically flagged as likely to be inadequate.

As an additional example, AI systems have the potential to be used extensively by governments to determine eligibility for welfare benefits.[16] This prospect raises the possibility of algorithmic biases that could disadvantage people with disabilities, especially those who are in greatest need of public support. A formula used by software to calculate individualized budgets for government-funded services needed to support the independent living of adults with developmental disabilities has become the subject of litigation in the USA on grounds of due process [56]. Although this case does not appear to be an example of an AI technology, it is indicative of the types of welfare-related decisions that could be readily carried out by machine learning applications.

3.1.2 Privacy and Bias

There is also a complex relationship between privacy and the problem of bias in AI applications. Inclusion of data obtained from people with disabilities is often necessary to the construction and evaluation of machine learning systems that avoid or minimize bias. However, the acquisition of information that reveals a person's disability also introduces opportunities for exploitation, or for unintended but nonetheless substantive discrimination, whether carried out by the data collector or by third parties to whom details are disclosed. As noted in Trewin et al. [54], this problem is further complicated by diversity among people with disabilities. The exclusion of obviously identifying information from data collections may not be sufficient to anonymize them. Knowledge of the person's disability, combined with other attributes, may be enough to enable the individual to be uniquely identified, for example as the only

[16] See Alston [1] for an overview of human rights-related concerns about this practice.

wheelchair user who lives in a given locality [54]. Some individuals, such as those with cognitive disabilities that preclude the requisite understanding, may be unable to give informed consent to the acquisition and use of their data. Yet, these data could be highly valuable and indeed indispensable to the development of AI applications designed to enhance the well-being and to improve opportunities in life for such populations.

An additional risk of discriminatory treatment is created by what Marks [35] refers to as 'emergent medical data,' namely health-related information about an individual that is inferred at a high degree of probability from diverse sources of evidence. The distinctive characteristic of emergent medical data is that none of the sources of evidence is overtly health-related. Consequently, no voluntary disclosure of medical information is involved. For example, a person's purchasing history could be combined with indicators gleaned from online communications and interactions with social media applications to infer the nature of the individual's disability [36]. This disability classification, whether or not it is accurate, could then serve as a ground for unjustly denying a benefit or opportunity. Marks is essentially concerned with the deliberate inferring and later exploitation of disability-related information. However, as noted in Sect. 3.2.2, this process could also take place unintentionally. Whereas intentional derivation and misuse of medical data can be regulated by privacy laws as Marks [36] discusses, the possibility that a machine learning system could detect and respond adversely to disability in a completely autonomous fashion raises additional difficulties.

3.1.3 Summary and Comments

Thus, it is clear that the nature of the diversity manifest among people with disabilities opens the possibility of bias in a variety of AI applications, especially those built on machine learning. Being a statistical outlier–one who is significantly different in a relevant respect from most of the population—can readily lead to misrecognition or misclassification of a person by a machine learning model. For this reason, technical measures that have been proposed to address the problem of AI bias against people with disabilities focus largely on improving the ability of machine learning systems to treat outliers appropriately [53, 54]. The distinct but related problem of maintaining adequate privacy protection for information that reveals aspects of a person's disability also calls for technical and regulatory solutions. These solutions are necessary to support the acquisition of data enabling people with disabilities to be included in the development of machine learning systems, thereby alleviating bias and consequent discrimination. However, privacy controls can also reduce the risk of biases that result from the exploitation of emergent medical data.

3.2 *Responses to the Problem of Bias*

By reviewing some of the potential measures that can be taken to avoid or to mitigate bias in AI systems, it is possible to identify research problems of particular relevance in the context of disability. What follows is not therefore intended as a comprehensive survey of possible interventions, but rather as a discussion of starting points in this direction which illuminate issues worthy of further investigation.

Technical approaches to overcoming bias suitable for adoption in software development projects are briefly noted in Sect. 3.2.1. Attention is then turned in Sect. 3.2.2 to the limits of antidiscrimination law as a regulatory solution, emphasizing the challenges introduced by proxy discrimination and its relevance to decisions affecting people with disabilities. In determining which practical problems to solve by means of AI and in weighing the adequacy of proposed solutions, choices often need to be made concerning whether, how and to what extent decision making in the relevant domain of application should be automated. Issues concerning the strengths and weaknesses of human and algorithmic decision making are raised in Sect. 3.2.3 as they arise in relation to the automation of decisions involving a highly diverse population. Concluding remarks appear in Sect. 3.2.4.

3.2.1 Technical Measures

The advice for developers of AI systems put forward in Trewin et al. [54] is aligned with the typical process of building a machine learning application. Emphasis is placed on systematically identifying people with disabilities who constitute potential outliers for purposes of the application under development, and including them at all stages, beginning with the planning of the project and progressing through to testing of the delivered product. Once the application is deployed, monitoring of its outcomes and remediation of any discovered biases are recommended. Crucially, the inclusion of people with disabilities consists in both engaging them directly as part of the project and incorporating their data into the design and training of machine learning models. Attention is paid to questions of privacy, noting standardization efforts toward developing technical controls that can be implemented to enable users to specify their privacy-related preferences. As was discussed in Sect. 2.2, the authors recommend drawing on traditions of design practice in which the involvement of users and other stakeholders is accorded a central role. The guidance offered in Trewin et al. [54] serves as a valuable point of reference for anyone who is concerned with the practical challenge of designing machine learning applications which are inclusive of people with disabilities.

There are practical limits to the number and therefore the diversity of users or other stakeholders who have disabilities that can be meaningfully included in a software project. The people with disabilities who are introduced into the process should therefore be regarded as having a representative function. Their contributions of data and insight derive from their own personal circumstances and experiences of disability. They may also be able to deploy personally or professionally acquired knowledge concerning others who have disabilities and whose backgrounds differ relevantly from their own. The knowledge possessed collectively by participants in a project, including people with disabilities themselves, can thus vary substantially, even if systematic efforts are made to include appropriate stakeholders. How well this knowledge represents the actual diversity of the population who will ultimately be subject to the AI system may be decisive in determining the extent to which biases are avoided or minimized. For example, it is entirely plausible that an autonomous vehicle development project which effectively and meaningfully engaged wheelchair users at every stage could nonetheless overlook individuals such as the friend described by Treviranus [52]. The diversity among people with disabilities thus creates a challenge of representativeness and of collective expertise in AI-related software projects, even under favorable conditions in which inclusive development practices are followed. To what extent and under what circumstances engagement of suitable stakeholders with disabilities can effectively mitigate bias in machine learning systems should hence be regarded as an open research problem. It is also a strategy that holds considerable promise. The recognition that it raises unresolved research questions by no means diminishes its practical importance.

3.2.2 The Role and Limits of Antidiscrimination Law

Technical approaches can thus be taken to avoid the introduction of bias and to remediate it if it is detected in operational applications. Of course, these technical solutions are only likely to be implemented if appropriate social conditions are established, including incentives to undertake the necessary design and development work, and to do so competently. Antidiscrimination law is a major source of this incentive. However, there are also grounds for skepticism about the ability of antidiscrimination law effectively to regulate algorithmic bias against people with disabilities. The first consideration is practical: antidiscrimination laws are typically enforced only in response to proceedings brought by people who claim to have been subjected to unlawful discrimination. Bringing such a complaint requires one to engage considerable expertise and resources in challenging decisions made by or with the support of an AI system. Such advocacy may be problematic due to an individual's circumstances—for example, socioeconomic disadvantage and shortfalls in the availability of free or low-cost legal representation. Disability, including past practices of discrimination, can readily exacerbate difficulties that operate against bringing an antidiscrimination claim. In addition, individuals who, due to the nature of their disability, cannot participate directly in bringing a claim depend completely on others to assert their rights and to represent their interests. A public authority empowered to monitor potentially discriminatory AI systems, to investigate their operation, to respond to complaints, and to require adherence to legal standards of non-discrimination, could overcome the limitations of relying entirely on individual claims as an enforcement mechanism. Indeed, such a regulator—a 'neutral data arbiter'—has been proposed to address privacy-related harms associated with the use of data analytics [12, § III]. Its role could readily be extended to questions of non-discrimination, including those associated with disability.

The second consideration is that machine learning can be biased in ways that raise difficulties for regulation by antidiscrimination law. These difficulties also create practical challenges for designers and developers of AI applications in avoiding bias.[17] According to Prince and Schwarcz [41], machine learning applications that combine data from a variety of sources have a propensity to lead to proxy discrimination. Proxy discrimination occurs under circumstances in which a protected characteristic such as race, gender, or disability status is actually predictive of the legitimate outcome of interest to the discriminator, in ways in which other variables are not. The authors argue that, since the goal of machine learning is to optimize predictive accuracy with respect to the target variable based on the input data,[18] it can be expected to 'discover' unobvious correlates of protected characteristics even if those characteristics and their obvious correlates are excluded from the data in an attempt to prevent bias. Thus, they suggest, [41, § I] a person's membership in an online forum devoted to a particular genetic medical condition could lead a machine learning algorithm to recommend a higher insurance premium. In this case, membership in the forum is predictive of the target variable, namely insurance risk. There is a causal connection that runs from having the medical condition or a close relative who does, to both joining the online forum and having an elevated risk of disease. These correlations are of course far from perfect, but the point is that they are causal and sufficiently significant to be predictive. Forum membership is thus an unobvious proxy for sensitive health information that is excluded from the data supplied to the machine learning algorithm. One may further suppose that the medical condition could in turn be predictive of acquiring a disability.[19]

The fact that proxy discrimination is taking place may be entirely unknown to the discriminator and indeed to all the developers and users of the machine learning system [41]. Furthermore, due to the great diversity among people with disabilities and the unobvious correlates of disability-related information that may be present in data used by machine learning algorithms, the problem presented by proxy discrimination has the potential to be particularly difficult in this context. Identifying and excluding or otherwise addressing unobvious proxies for disability-related information that is genuinely predictive of the target variable stands as a technical challenge. Unlike Marks's concern with emergent medical data (Sect. 3.1.2), which are derived and used intentionally, the probabilistic inferences that lead to proxy discrimination arise internally to and as the product of the 'normal' operation of machine learning systems. They may be unintended, and they may also be difficult to detect. There is

[17] Trewin et al. [54] acknowledge the practical dimension of the problem, and recommend consultation with stakeholders as part of the development process.

[18] The target variable is that which the machine learning model is designed to predict. It is assumed here to be in the legitimate interest of the discriminator, such as the probability that a person would be an effective employee.

[19] Hoffman [24] argues that anti-discrimination law should be extended to address decisions based on predictions of a person's likelihood of developing a disability, and to require disclosure of the use of data in making such decisions.

thus an open research problem concerning the extent to which and the respects in which proxy discrimination is a particular difficulty in machine learning applications affecting people with disabilities, as well as what measures can be taken to control it. The diversity of impairments and the variable social conditions that affect the lives of people with disabilities provide a good ground for hypothesizing that proxy discrimination could here pose a substantial challenge. This challenge is further complicated by intersectional considerations that result from the multiplicity of legally protected social categories to which a single individual may belong. To extend the example, suppose not only that a person's online forum membership is a proxy for having a given medical condition associated with a disability, but also that there are linguistic indicators in her or his contributions to social media which function as proxies for belonging to a marginalized ethnic minority in the country in which he or she lives. Suppose further that, due to discrimination in the provision of early diagnosis and treatment services, the conjunction of having the medical condition and belonging to the ethnic minority is strongly predictive of adverse health effects of interest to the insurer, whereas neither circumstance is significant alone. Under such conditions, the disability is an essential factor in the proxy discrimination, but it only operates in combination with other category memberships. Apart from the technical and practical difficulties that such possibilities raise, there may also be legal obstacles, for example if the law requires one to choose which ground of discrimination to assert. In the current example, a choice may need to be made between alleging disability and racial discrimination, neither of which is well suited to the case.[20]

The legal difficulty which proxy discrimination creates is not confined to the empirical issue of establishing sufficient evidence of discrimination. Proxy discrimination also entails that eliminating variables which explicitly represent disability-related information as well as obvious proxies for them from the input data is inadequate to prevent bias [41]. Alleged discriminators can also seek to justify their practice by arguing that, since the proxies relied on by the machine learning model are truly predictive of the outcome of interest, and the model has been optimized for predictive success, no less discriminatory alternative is available that would be equally effective in achieving the defendant's legitimate objective. As Prince and Schwarcz [41](§ IV.A.2) argue in relation to disparate impact doctrine in the USA, this reasoning, if it is found to hold according to the facts of a particular case, can serve as an adequate defense against a claim of unlawful discrimination. Clearly, whether this is so depends on the details of the antidiscrimination law applicable in each jurisdiction.[21] There thus arises a research question with respect to disability

[20] An insightful discussion of intersectionality, noting the risk of over-simplifying its effects in responding to problems of injustice that result from machine learning technologies, appears in Hoffmann [25].

[21] The law concerning liability for disparate impact (often referred to outside the USA as indirect discrimination) has evolved differently between common law countries. See Khaitan [28] for a discussion.

discrimination in different legal and jurisdictional contexts regarding the implications of proxy discrimination, and what reforms, if any, should be introduced.[22]

At the core of the policy question raised by proxy discrimination is an ethical issue: under what circumstances is it morally permissible to discriminate against people based on a protected characteristic such as disability, if this characteristic is genuinely predictive of an outcome which is legitimately in the interests of the discriminator? This is a problem concerning the ethics of statistical discrimination [43]. Assuming that the costs of avoiding the discrimination by opting for a fairer but less predictively accurate AI solution are more than negligible, is the discriminator morally obligated to bear the costs and to choose the less discriminatory alternative? Depending on one's preferred normative analysis, the answer may be sensitive to details of the case at hand, for example whether the statistical relationships which purportedly justify the discrimination are in turn attributable to underlying social patterns of discriminatory practice [33].[23] In deciding what policy the law should reflect, and what choices should be made by developers and users of potentially discriminatory AI technologies, these moral issues are of central importance.

3.2.3 Human and Automated Decision-Making

Technical and policy measures that aim to reduce the discriminatory effect of a machine learning system are valuable, but they also presuppose a choice to develop the system for a specific purpose in the first place. This prior decision to use AI in a given context and the determination of what its role should be, if constructed, should also be examined in relation to the potential for discrimination against people with disabilities. It might on balance be preferable not to build the system at all, or to envision its role differently, thus shaping the character of the human–AI partnership.[24] Evidently, AI technology can be designed partly or completely to substitute for human judgment in making a specific kind of decision. What role, if any, the AI should have in a particular social situation is a choice that ought to be both well

[22] Prince and Schwarcz [41](§ IV.B) consider potential reforms, such as restricting the variables that may be used by AI systems in making certain kinds of decisions to a prescribed list of permitted factors.

[23] Selbst and Barocas [44](§ III.B) insightfully discuss difficulties resulting from the role of intuition in the reasoning required for the application of norms of non-discrimination. If the relations among variables apparently revealed by a machine learning system manifestly treat people with disabilities unfavorably, for example, but there is no coherent or plausible explanation of why this is the case, then evaluation of the grounds of these unequal outcomes becomes problematic. In some instances, techniques of 'interpretable' or 'explainable' machine learning may facilitate the emergence of a suitable explanation. On the other hand, and as the authors recognize, it would be naive to presuppose that social and natural phenomena are always amenable to explanations that cohere with human intuitions.

[24] An interesting further possibility is for a machine learning system to give an 'explanation' of its output that would enable an adversely affected person to change his or her situation sufficiently to achieve a more favorable classification. The difficulties of two promising approaches to such explanation are considered in Barocas, Selbst and Raghavan [4].

informed, and sensitive to the circumstances of the people involved as well as the rights and interests affected. It also raises issues that, if better understood, would allow for more effective policies and practices in deciding what part AI should play in different decision-making situations.

Competent and well-informed human decision-makers have capabilities of practical and moral reasoning that far surpass what is achievable by any AI technology yet devised. Human judgment can weigh and interpret the applicable ethical or legal norms, then apply them to the facts of a case to arrive at a just decision. The considerations taken into account need not be prescribed exhaustively in advance. General arguments have been developed in support of the view that, in the application of legal rules, each person has a moral claim for her or his case to be decided individually by the exercise of human judgment rather than to be determined algorithmically [6].[25] This position is supported by a number of independent philosophical arguments, for example regarding limitations on prior knowledge of uncertainties in the application of rules, the value of exercising discretion in decision making, and respect for each person's individuality [6](§ 3).[26]

An interesting further question suggested by this broader claim is whether a high degree of diversity present in a population, coupled with the need to make decisions based on disparate facts and norms that affect rights and interests, should be regarded as an additional ground for limiting the role of AI, even excluding it altogether, in reaching decisions. To develop the point more specifically, one may consider a hypothetical proposal to construct an AI system for determining, based on supplied data, whether specified support services requested by a person with a disability are likely to meet her or his needs. Such a system could be used either alone or, more probably, in combination with human review, by a government welfare program or in an educational setting. Arguably, the diverse nature of the population which would be subject to the proposed AI application, and the uniqueness of individual needs and circumstances, establishes a case for exercising human judgment that extends beyond the general arguments already cited. In a population that can reasonably be expected to contain many outliers, there is ample reason to be skeptical of efforts to formalize the decision-making problem and to develop algorithms capable of reaching just outcomes in most, let alone all cases. The diverse needs and circumstances of the people whose entitlements are to be determined establish a condition in which uncertainty in the interpretation and application of the relevant rules calls for modes of reasoning and consideration of unanticipated factors that only human decision making can provide. Justice may foreseeably require a degree of individual treatment of cases that current technology is unable to automate.

[25] Article 22 of the GDPR [17] establishes a limited right not to be subject to legally significant, fully automated decisions. For an argument against recognizing such a right to human involvement in individual decisions, which does not entirely address the philosophical grounds summarized in Binns [6], see Huq [26].

[26] Citron [11](§ III A and B) discusses the tendency of automation to substitute precise rules for more general legal standards that allow for the exercise of human discretion. This trend, Citron argues, prioritizes cost efficiency over justice.

Human judgment, however, is known to be fallible and prone to biases. Beyond intentional discrimination, which at least is under conscious control, prejudices against out-groups such as people with disabilities can be held and may influence behavior unconsciously [13]. Decision making can also be distorted by cognitive biases. If AI is combined with human involvement to reach decisions, automation bias [48] can limit the vigilance and effectiveness of the human decision-maker in identifying and compensating for erroneous findings of the AI technology. Invoking evidence from cognitive science and social psychology, Kleinberg et al. [29](§ 3) argue that human decisions are not only open to social and cognitive biases, but also that the true motivations are often not transparent to the agent.[27] Machine learning algorithms, they argue, can on the contrary be rigorously audited to ascertain the sources and extent of bias [29](§ 5). An appropriately designed algorithm can also be demonstrably less discriminatory than human judges, for example in criminal risk assessment [29](§ 6.2). They accordingly maintain that algorithmic decision making has distinctive equity-promoting advantages, noting [29](§ 6.1) the difficulty of determining the effectiveness of efforts to train humans to overcome biases.[28]

3.2.4 General Comments

Having regard to the unparalleled advantages of human judgment in making decisions in novel cases, and the potential of algorithms for auditability and bias mitigation, there is a need to develop a greater understanding of how best to gain the benefits of both in the service of social equality. Whereas technical measures can be taken to reduce biases in machine learning algorithms, social interventions can be made in an effort to overcome the more fundamental problem of human biases. The extent to which algorithmic bias can be detected and corrected in the face of a very diverse population of people with disabilities is an important question on which the potential of AI as a force for greater equality depends. If auditing is to be relied on as the principal mechanism, as proposed recently in Rambachan et al. [42](§ 1),[29] much depends on developing effective strategies for identifying and overcoming potentially context-specific manifestations of bias. Intersectional effects involving disability together with other protected characteristics, and the occurrence of proxy discrimination against possibly small subsets of the population, present two sources of difficulty. More generally, the many facets of diversity characteristic of disability constitute a challenge for overcoming the problem of algorithmic bias.

---

[27] A clear summary of the authors' position appears in Sunstein [50].

[28] A much discussed strategy for seeking to overcome human biases against social out-groups is the contact hypothesis. See, for example, Pettigrew and Tropp [39] and Pettigrew et al. [40].

[29] Under this proposal, the auditing is to be carried out by a regulator with the authority to compel changes that address discrimination. A more skeptical view of transparency as a means to greater accountability of machine learning systems is elaborated in Ananny and Crawford [2].

4 Conclusion

Developing AI technologies that facilitate equality while furthering the well-being and aspirations of people with disabilities is at least as much a social as it is a technical challenge. The concept of partnership between human beings and AI systems is useful in characterizing what ought to be built—a mutual interplay of social arrangements and software-based systems that promote morally good human ends through meeting practical needs. Devising meaningful approaches to including stakeholders who have disabilities (whether they be users or indirectly affected parties) in AI development projects is clearly a necessity. This participation should extend from the initial identification and clarification of the problem that is to be solved, through to the ultimate design, development, implementation, and maintenance of an AI-based solution. Further research and practical experience are vital to creating more specific guidance as to how this should be done, and as to what comprises an inclusive AI software development process. Promising approaches to design have emerged which empower potential users of the technology as well as indirect stakeholders whose interests are affected by its implementation, and which encourage reflection upon the value-dependent judgments associated with technical decisions. Such design-related scholarship offers valuable insights and methods, but treating the relationship of AI to people with disabilities as purely a design problem is not sufficient. Equally vital is the shaping of norms and policies associated with the development and use of AI.

The challenge of algorithmic bias raises technical, social, legal, and moral questions of importance in overcoming disability-based forms of discrimination that AI systems risk reinforcing. Many of these questions also apply to the problem of bias in machine learning generally, but there are disability-specific aspects and implications of these issues that have been emphasized here. Although technical means of mitigating or preventing bias have been proposed in recent literature, the perspective taken in this chapter suggests that any such measures should be applied in the context of a larger, policy-oriented approach to the problem. To a considerable degree, developing appropriate policy responses to issues of bias depends upon answering as yet unresolved research questions, some of which are identified in the preceding discussion.

Antidiscrimination law, at least in its predominant, adversarial and complaint-oriented form, seems inadequate, by itself, to redress harms resulting from algorithmic bias. There may thus need to emerge a complementary role, alongside antidiscrimination law, for proactive regulatory mechanisms which do not rely on people with disabilities who claim to have been adversely affected by algorithmic decisions to furnish the resources to sustain litigation. Proxy discrimination not only introduces practical difficulties for the removal or prevention of bias. It also raises moral and, depending on the applicable antidiscrimination regime, potentially also legal arguments purporting to justify discriminatory decision-making practices on the basis that an unbiased algorithm would be less effective in accomplishing a legitimate purpose, and, to that extent, more costly to the discriminator. The multiple social categories to which individuals belong may have unobvious intersectional consequences, involving disability together with other factors, which create additional sources of bias. Developing a deeper understanding of whether and to what extent this issue complicates efforts toward non-discrimination in the design and use of AI applications seems justified. Although acquiring data from people with disabilities is necessary to mitigate bias and to design AI applications that meet their needs effectively, it also risks compromising privacy and thus opens opportunities to exploit knowledge of an individual's disability. This is especially problematic for those who have limited capacity to give voluntary and informed consent to the use of their information, and under conditions in which the law allows data to be processed for the purpose of drawing inferences about a person's disability without the individual's knowledge or agreement.

The problem of bias also raises important research and policy questions concerning the appropriate roles to be accorded, respectively, to algorithmic and human decision making, particularly in application to the highly diverse circumstances of people with disabilities. Greater understanding is needed of how best to forge human-AI partnerships that overcome tendencies toward prejudice, biases, and discrimination as they manifest themselves in human decisions generally, as well as in the development and use of machine learning systems. Combining uniquely human capacities for practical reasoning and moral judgment appropriately with insights that can be derived from the operation of machine learning algorithms on large and diverse collections of data remains a challenge both in principle and in practice. An adequate response would proceed from an understanding of how biases occur in human judgment and in AI systems, while seeking to develop solutions that shape the social and policy-related aspects of the environments in which the technologies are developed and deployed, in addition to the technical design of the applications themselves.

Addressing these issues adequately in connection with disability can most effectively be pursued as part of a broader response to the potential for bias introduced by AI, and in particular by applications of machine learning. Devising appropriate human–AI partnerships should be regarded as a problem of putting in place effective policies, practices, technical expertise, and participatory processes throughout the development and maintenance of software projects. This is a large and complex undertaking, involving regulators, researchers, developers of AI technology, and, in the context at hand, people with disabilities.

Acknowledgements The author gratefully acknowledges Mark Hakkinen, Klaus Zechner, and Cary Supalo of Educational Testing Service for reviewing the manuscript. Mark Hakkinen and Kris Anne Kinney of Educational Testing Service offered valuable advice concerning creation of the diagrams. Anonymous reviewers contributed thoughtful suggestions for improving the chapter. This work has also been influenced by various seminars and workshops on the ethics of artificial intelligence that the author has attended.

References

1. Alston, P.: Report of the special rapporteur on extreme poverty and human rights. Tech. rep., United Nations (2019). https://www.ohchr.org/Documents/Issues/Poverty/A_74_48037_AdvanceUneditedVersion.docx
2. Ananny, M., Crawford, K.: Seeing without knowing: Limitations of the transparency ideal and its application to algorithmic accountability. new media & society **20**(3), 973–989 (2018)
3. Barocas, S., Selbst, A.D.: Big data's disparate impact. Calif. L. Rev. **104**, 671 (2016)
4. Barocas, S., Selbst, A.D., Raghavan, M.: The hidden assumptions behind counterfactual explanations and principal reasons. In: Proceedings of the 2020 Conference on Fairness, Accountability, and Transparency, pp. 80–89 (2020)
5. Berke, L., Caulfield, C., Huenerfauth, M.: Deaf and hard-of-hearing perspectives on imperfect automatic speech recognition for captioning one-on-one meetings. In: Proceedings of the 19th International ACM SIGACCESS Conference on Computers and Accessibility, pp. 155–164 (2017)
6. Binns, R.: Human judgment in algorithmic loops: Individual justice and automated decision-making. Regulation & Governance (2020). DOI https://doi.org/10.1111/rego.12358. https://onlinelibrary.wiley.com/doi/abs/10.1111/rego.12358
7. Bogen, M., Rieke, A.: Help wanted: An examination of hiring algorithms, equity, and bias. Tech. rep., Upturn (2018). https://www.upturn.org/reports/2018/hiring-algorithms/
8. Bradshaw-Martin, H., Easton, C.: Autonomous or 'driverless' cars and disability: a legal and ethical analysis. European Journal of Current Legal Issues **20**(3) (2014)
9. Brewer, R.N., Kameswaran, V.: Understanding the power of control in autonomous vehicles for people with vision impairment. In: Proceedings of the 20th International ACM SIGACCESS Conference on Computers and Accessibility, pp. 185–197 (2018)
10. Campbell, S.M., Stramondo, J.A.: The complicated relationship of disability and well-being. Kennedy Institute of Ethics Journal **27**(2), 151–184 (2017)
11. Citron, D.K.: Technological due process. Wash. UL Rev. **85**, 1249 (2007)
12. Crawford, K., Schultz, J.: Big data and due process: Toward a framework to redress predictive privacy harms. BCL Rev. **55**, 93 (2014)
13. Dasgupta, N.: Implicit ingroup favoritism, outgroup favoritism, and their behavioral manifestations. Social justice research **17**(2), 143–169 (2004)
14. Degener, T.: A new human rights model of disability. In: V. Della Fina, R. Cera, G. Palmisano (eds.) The United Nations convention on the rights of persons with disabilities, pp. 41–59. Springer (2017)
15. Ehn, P.: Scandinavian design: On participation and skill. In: Participatory design: Principles and practices, p. 77. CRC Press (1993)
16. Employer Assistance and Resource Network on Disability Inclusion: Use of artificial intelligence to facilitate employment opportunities for people with disabilities (2019). https://askearn.org/wp-content/uploads/2019/06/AI_PolicyBrief-A.pdf
17. European Union: Regulation (eu) 2016/679 of the european parliament and of the council of 27 april 2016 on the protection of natural persons with regard to the processing of personal data and on the free movement of such data, and repealing directive 95/46/ec (general data protection regulation). Official Journal of the European Union **L 119**, 1 (2016)
18. Findlater, L., Goodman, S., Zhao, Y., Azenkot, S., Hanley, M.: Fairness issues in ai systems that augment sensory abilities. ACM SIGACCESS Accessibility and Computing (125) (2020)
19. Friedman, B., Hendry, D.G.: Value sensitive design: Shaping technology with moral imagination. Mit Press (2019)
20. Friedman, B., Kahn, P.H., Borning, A.: Value sensitive design and information systems. In: K.E. Himma, H.T. Tavani (eds.) The handbook of information and computer ethics, pp. 69–101. John Wiley & Sons (2008)
21. Friedman, B., Nissenbaum, H.: Bias in computer systems. ACM Transactions on Information Systems (TOIS) **14**(3), 330–347 (1996)

22. Giermanowska, E., Racław, M., Szawarska, D.: Employing People with Disabilities: Good Organisational Practices and Socio-cultural Conditions, chap. 2, pp. 9–36. Springer (2020)
23. Guerreiro, J., Sato, D., Asakawa, S., Dong, H., Kitani, K.M., Asakawa, C.: Cabot: Designing and evaluating an autonomous navigation robot for blind people. In: The 21st International ACM SIGACCESS Conference on Computers and Accessibility, pp. 68–82 (2019)
24. Hoffman, S.: Big data's new discrimination threats: Amending the americans with disabilities act to cover discrimination based on data-driven predictions of future disease. In: I.G. Cohen, H.F. Lynch, E. Vayena, U. Gasser (eds.) Big Data, Health Law, and Bioethics. Cambridge University Press (2018)
25. Hoffmann, A.L.: Where fairness fails: data, algorithms, and the limits of antidiscrimination discourse. Information, Communication & Society **22**(7), 900–915 (2019)
26. Huq, A.Z.: A right to a human decision. Va. L. Rev. **106**, 611 (2020)
27. Iglesias-Pérez, A., Loitsch, C., Kaklanis, N., Votis, K., Stiegler, A., Kalogirou, K., Serra-Autonell, G., Tzovaras, D., Weber, G.: Accessibility through preferences: context-aware recommender of settings. In: International Conference on Universal Access in Human-Computer Interaction, pp. 224–235. Springer (2014)
28. Khaitan, T.: Indirect discrimination. In: K. Lippert-Rasmussen (ed.) The Routledge handbook of the ethics of discrimination, pp. 30–41. Routledge (2017)
29. Kleinberg, J., Ludwig, J., Mullainathan, S., Sunstein, C.R.: Discrimination in the age of algorithms. Journal of Legal Analysis **10** (2018)
30. Kleiner, A., Kurzweil, R.C.: A description of the kurzweil reading machine and a status report on its testing and dissemination. Bull Prosthet Res **10**(27), 72–81 (1977)
31. LeCun, Y., Bengio, Y., Hinton, G.: Deep learning. Nature **521**(7553), 436–444 (2015)
32. Lewis, C.: Simplicity in cognitive assistive technology: a framework and agenda for research. Universal Access in the Information Society **5**(4), 351–361 (2007)
33. Lippert-Rasmussen, K.: Nothing personal: On statistical discrimination. Journal of Political Philosophy **15**(4), 385–403 (2007)
34. Loitsch, C., Weber, G., Kaklanis, N., Votis, K., Tzovaras, D.: A knowledge-based approach to user interface adaptation from preferences and for special needs. User Modeling and User-Adapted Interaction **27**(3-5), 445–491 (2017)
35. Marks, M.: Emergent medical data (2017). https://blog.petrieflom.law.harvard.edu/2017/10/11/emergent-medical-data/
36. Marks, M.: Algorithmic disability discrimination. In: I.G. Cohen, C. Shachar, A. Silvers, M.A. Stein (eds.) Disability, Health, Law, and Bioethics. Cambridge University Press (2020)
37. Marsch, N.: Artificial intelligence and the fundamental right to data protection: Opening the door for technological innovation and innovative protection. In: Regulating Artificial Intelligence, pp. 33–52. Springer (2020)
38. Nyholm, S., Smids, J.: Automated cars meet human drivers: Responsible human-robot coordination and the ethics of mixed traffic. Ethics and Information Technology pp. 1–10 (2018)
39. Pettigrew, T.F., Tropp, L.R.: A meta-analytic test of intergroup contact theory. Journal of personality and social psychology **90**(5), 751 (2006)
40. Pettigrew, T.F., Tropp, L.R., Wagner, U., Christ, O.: Recent advances in intergroup contact theory. International journal of intercultural relations **35**(3), 271–280 (2011)
41. Prince, A.E., Schwarcz, D.: Proxy discrimination in the age of artificial intelligence and big data. Iowa L. Rev. **105**, 1257 (2019)
42. Rambachan, A., Kleinberg, J., Mullainathan, S., Ludwig, J.: An economic approach to regulating algorithms. Tech. Rep. w27111, National Bureau of Economic Research (2020)
43. Schauer, F.: Statistical (and non-statistical) discrimination. In: K. Lippert-Rasmussen (ed.) The Routledge Handbook of the Ethics of Discrimination, pp. 42–53. Routledge (2017)
44. Selbst, A.D., Barocas, S.: The intuitive appeal of explainable machines. Fordham L. Rev. **87**, 1085 (2018)
45. Shakespeare, T.: Critiquing the social model. In: A. Lawson (ed.) Disability and equality law, pp. 67–94. Routledge London (2017)

46. Shakespeare, T.: The social model of disability. In: L.J. Davis (ed.) The disability studies reader, 5 edn. Routledge (2017)
47. Shew, A.: Ableism, technoableism, and future ai. IEEE Technology and Society Magazine **39**(1), 40–85 (2020)
48. Skitka, L.J., Mosier, K., Burdick, M.D.: Accountability and automation bias. International Journal of Human-Computer Studies **52**(4), 701–717 (2000)
49. Spinuzzi, C.: The methodology of participatory design. Technical communication **52**(2), 163–174 (2005)
50. Sunstein, C.R.: Algorithms, correcting biases. Social Research: An International Quarterly **86**(2), 499–511 (2019)
51. Szarkowska, A., Krejtz, I., Klyszejko, Z., Wieczorek, A.: Verbatim, standard, or edited? reading patterns of different captioning styles among deaf, hard of hearing, and hearing viewers. American annals of the deaf **156**(4), 363–378 (2011)
52. Treviranus, J.: The value of being different. In: Proceedings of the 16th web for all 2019 conference—personalization-personalizing the web, pp. 1–7 (2019)
53. Trewin, S.: Ai fairness for people with disabilities: Point of view. arXiv preprint arXiv:1811.10670 (2018)
54. Trewin, S., Basson, S., Muller, M., Branham, S., Treviranus, J., Gruen, D., Hebert, D., Lyckowski, N., Manser, E.: Considerations for ai fairness for people with disabilities. AI Matters **5**(3), 40–63 (2019)
55. UN: Convention on the rights of persons with disabilities. United Nations Treaty Series **2515**, 3 (2006)
56. United States: *K. w. v. Armstrong*, no. 14-35296 (9th cir. 2015)
57. Vanderheiden, G.C., Treviranus, J., Gemou, M., Bekiaris, E., Markus, K., Clark, C., Basman, A.: The evolving global public inclusive infrastructure (gpii). In: International Conference on Universal Access in Human-Computer Interaction, pp. 107–116. Springer (2013)
58. Whittaker, M., Alper, M., Bennett, C.L., Hendren, S., Kaziunas, L., Mills, M., Morris, M.R., Rankin, J., Rogers, E., Salas, M., et al.: Disability, bias, and ai. Tech. rep., AI Now Institute (2019). https://ainowinstitute.org/disabilitybiasai-2019.pdf
59. World Health Organization: Disability and health (2020). https://www.who.int/news-room/fact-sheets/detail/disability-and-health
60. World Institute on Disability: Ai and accessibility (2019). https://wid.org/2019/06/12/ai-and-accessibility/

Towards a Taxonomy for Explainable AI in Computational Pathology

Heimo Müller, Michaela Kargl, Markus Plass, Bettina Kipperer, Luka Brcic, Peter Regitnig, Christian Geißler, Tobias Küster, Norman Zerbe, and Andreas Holzinger

1 Introduction

AI technology is boosting personalized healthcare services and significantly improving the quality of services and accessibility of information for patients. The application of AI in medicine covers a wide area, including AI robots assisting critical

H. Müller (✉) · M. Kargl · M. Plass · B. Kipperer · L. Brcic · P. Regitnig · A. Holzinger
Medical University Graz, Graz, ST, Austria
e-mail: heimo.mueller@medunigraz.at

M. Kargl
e-mail: michaela.kargl@medunigraz.at

M. Plass
e-mail: markus.plass@medunigraz.at

B. Kipperer
e-mail: bettina.kipperer@medunigraz.at

L. Brcic
e-mail: luka.brcic@medunigraz.at

P. Regitnig
e-mail: peter.regitnig@medunigraz.at

A. Holzinger
e-mail: andreas.holzinger@medunigraz.at

C. Geißler · T. Küster
DAI-Labor, Technical University Berlin, Berlin, Germany
e-mail: christian.geissler@dai-labor.de

T. Küster
e-mail: tobias.kuester@dai-labor.de

N. Zerbe
Charité Universitätsmedizin Berlin, Berlin, Germany
e-mail: norman.zerbe@charite.de

F. Chen and J. Zhou (eds.), *Humanity Driven AI*,
https://doi.org/10.1007/978-3-030-72188-6_15

microsurgeries, chatbots in patient care, AI-assisted health monitoring with wearables to public health studies and different life science research areas such as computational biology and drug development. In precision medicine and companion diagnostics, AI-based clinical decision support systems (CDDS) and deep learning in medical image processing will be a big game changer in various fields such as the detection of skin cancer [2], AI support for "perception" and "reasoning" in radiology [25], ophthalmologic diagnosis of diabetes-associated changes [21], and in assisting pathologists in the detection and grading of cancer [30], finding small tumour deposits within lymph nodes, quantification of immunohistochemistry reactions and prescreening of Papanicolaou-stained gynaecological cytology in cervical cancer screening, just to name some of the most recent AI solutions in computational pathology [28].

However, AI solutions in medicine and in particular in computational pathology face also a number of challenges [8]. One of them is the fact that machine learning (ML) and specifically deep learning solutions are hard to interpret, to understand and to explain [6], which is a central issue for trustworthiness, validation and acceptance [32]. There is some work addressing user interface solutions for digital pathology [1] and explainable AI topics on computational pathology [26]. However, a systematic taxonomy for the whole chain from algorithmic development to validation and usage of AI solutions is still missing. We, therefore, aim to define a taxonomy for

- Stakeholders of AI solutions in computational pathology (Sect. 2)
- Types of AI solutions (Sect. 3)
- The interface between the stakeholders and the AI solutions (Sect. 4)
- Varieties of explanations (Sect. 5), and finally
- Methods to measure the quality of explanations (Sect. 6).

Such a comprehensive taxonomy is necessary, because (as depicted in Fig. 1) only if we know *who* used *which* type of AI solution for *what* purpose and *how* the human–AI interface was designed, we can judge the efficiency and effectiveness of an explanation component.

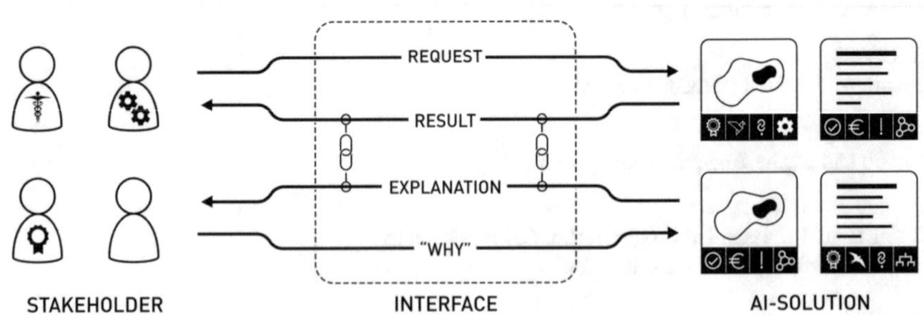

Fig. 1 Integration of AI solutions in computational pathology

2 Stakeholders in Computational Pathology

Pathologists working in clinical diagnostics are probably the most obvious users for AI solutions in computational pathology. However, the list of stakeholders for AI solutions in computational pathology is much longer and comprises:

- Pathologists in diagnostics
- AI laboratory technician
- Quality managers at pathology institutes
- Researchers in medicine/molecular biology
- Researchers in data science/AI
- AI solution providers' staff responsible for requirement analysis, software development, quality assurance, sales, marketing or technical support
- Staff of organizations assessing market conformity of medical software solutions, such as for example notified bodies designated under the EU In-Vitro Devices Regulation (IVDR) [24].

Depending on the status of an AI solution in computational pathology, different stakeholder groups are relevant, as shown in Fig. 2.

These stakeholder groups have different levels of domain knowledge and expertise in the field of medicine or molecular biology, as well as different levels of computer literacy, as shown in Fig. 3. Specific knowledge levels and expertise of a user group are important aspects that must be taken into account when looking at interfaces

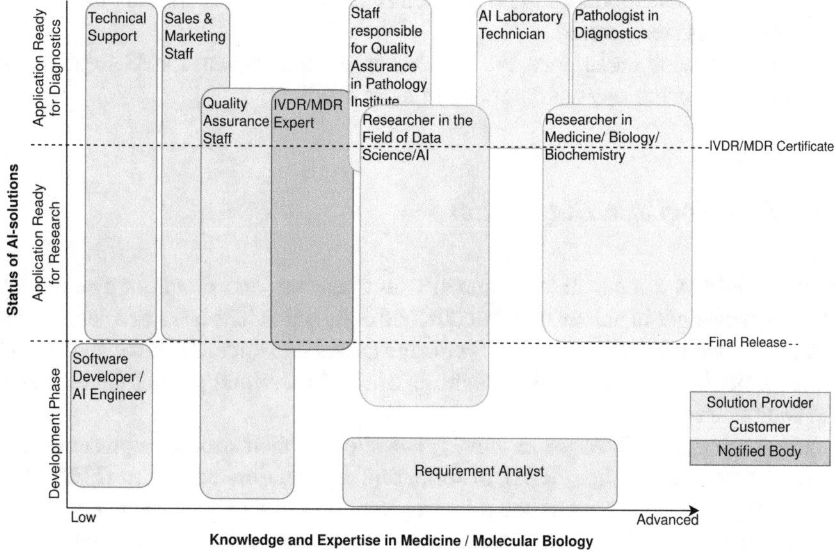

Fig. 2 Relevant stakeholders in different states of an AI solution for computational pathology and their level of expertise in medicine/molecular biology

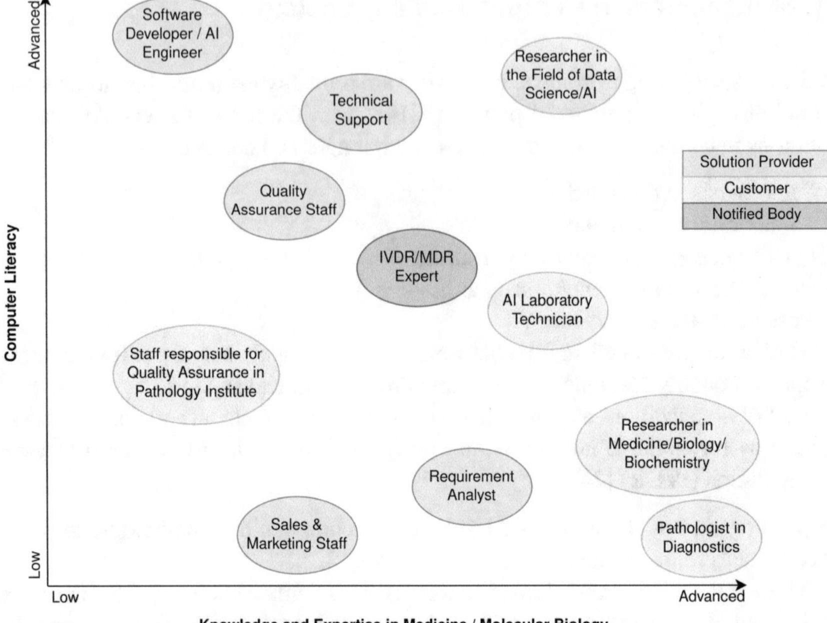

Fig. 3 Schematic overview of the expertise of stakeholders in computational pathology

between these stakeholders and AI solutions (see Sect. 4) and assessing the quality of explanations (see Sect. 6).

In the following paragraphs, the stakeholder groups relevant for AI solutions in computational pathology are described in more detail.

2.1 *Pathologist in Diagnostics*

A pathologist is a medical practitioner, who diagnoses and monitors diseases by looking at changes in human tissues, cells, and body fluids. The tasks of a pathologist are, on the one hand, to make an exact diagnosis and classification of the lesion, and on the other hand, to assess the prognosis of the disease and predict the expected outcome of a specific therapy.

In pathology, a pathologist examines glass slides or their scanned representations called whole-slide images (WSI), of formalin-fixed paraffin-embedded (FFPE) tissues or frozen sections, under the microscope or on the screen, respectively. These tissue samples have been pre-processed in the histopathology, immunohistochemistry or molecular-pathology laboratory with different staining/marker techniques for detecting cellular components and molecules. However, to come up with a diagnosis, a pathologist does not only take into account the findings from microscopic examination of the specimen, but applies a holistic view and considers also the case history and the results of other laboratory tests such as for example molecular pathology.

Therefore, a pathologist needs a fundamental medical education followed by a discipline-specific education/training. Furthermore, a pathologist has got a comprehensive understanding of laboratory medicine, including management, safety and quality issues for the laboratory, as well as knowledge on how to interpret complex patterns of test results and what further testing may be appropriate to help making correct diagnoses. A pathologist works in close cooperation with other staff in the laboratory (technicians, scientists) and communicates with other pathologists and clinical specialists to seek and provide referral opinion on difficult cases.

The expectations of a pathologist towards computational methods in general and in particular AI algorithms include increasing quality and accuracy, time savings and getting new insights in unexplored fields. Examples for these general principles are AI support in finding small tumour deposits within lymph nodes, detection and grading of cancer, quantification of cells (e.g. in immunohistochemistry) and several prescreening algorithms for the detection of atypical cells and architectural structures.

2.2 AI Laboratory Technician

An AI laboratory technician is the main applicant of the AI solution for diagnostics within the pathology institute/medical institution. The AI laboratory technician applies the algorithm on the samples, prepares a first analysis and evaluation of the findings, adjusts, if needed, the parameters in a preconfigured AI solution environment and transfers the results from a technical language to a more understandable way to and for the pathologists. These tasks require intermediate IT knowledge and medical know-how.

2.3 Quality Manager at a Pathology Institute

The quality manager at the pathology institute usually comes from the medical area or has gained experience in quality management or economics. The main task of the quality manager is to have insight into the local workflows and medical processes of the medical institution. The quality manager ensures the quality management system is established, implemented and maintained. The quality manager's responsibilities include development and monitoring of key quality indicators, key performance indicators, audit schedules, contingency plans, assessing risks and risk mitigation, as well as ensuring compliance with relevant legislation, standards and guidance.

2.4 Researcher in Medicine, Molecular Biology

Beside its diagnostic work, a medical expert usually works on research tasks as well. This is in particular the case in a research hospital, which is often connected to a medical university. Research work differs in several aspects from routine diagnostics: (1) it is multidisciplinary bringing together experts from medicine, biology, pharmacy, biochemistry and bioinformatics; (2) it aims to go beyond current medical state of the art and introduces new approaches; and (3) it can spend more time and resources on a single case and/or question compared to routine diagnostics. Researchers with a university degree in medicine, biology, biochemistry or pharmacy either work in a (medical) university, a public institution (e.g. the World Health Organization (WHO)), or in the research department of a company (e.g. in the pharmaceutical industry).

Medical researchers are usually not trained IT experts, so they need either AI solutions that are easily accessible (available and affordable) and easily adaptable/extendable to fit their specific research question or have to work in an interdisciplinary environment. A pathologist in research naturally has different requirements for AI solutions than a pathologist in their role as a diagnostician. The explanatory information for this stakeholder group should be much more comprehensive in order to allow the generation and validation of new hypothesis.

2.5 Researcher in Data Science/AI

Researchers in data science/AI often have a background in software engineering, mathematics or computer science and are skilled in translating real world into machine learning problems and design of complete AI solutions. They are, therefore, involved in the developmental part of AI solutions from the early stages on. Data science researchers are supposed to have specific knowledge in configuring and adjusting the AI solution and attempting to discover patterns in data. A researcher in data science/AI is on the developmental side but also a user on the application/customer side of AI solutions.

2.6 Provider of an AI Solution

Within the provider of an AI solution, typically a commercial company, we can identify several stakeholder roles with different technical skills and needs towards explainability.

The Requirement Analyst performs market analyses (needs and demands), combines them with the company policy and thus defines requirements for the to-be developed software. A basis for these tasks is a profound background in economics and medical knowledge in the particular field, but only little IT skills.

The AI Engineer has in-depth knowledge in IT and computer science, based on an education in informatics or software engineering. However, software developers/AI engineers usually have only little know-how in medicine. Being involved in the process of developing AI solution tools from the beginning, software developers/AI engineers implement software based on needs and requirements of the end-users, which were collected by the requirement analyst.

The Sales & Marketing Division brings the product to the market and finally to the end-user/customer. They are the first contact for the (potential) applicants of the software. The people working in sales & marketing usually do not have a lot of knowledge in IT and the medical domain. However, they have a marketing and sales background and the skill of persuasiveness to present the AI solution to the end-user/applicant.

The Technical Support staff of the provider of an AI solution normally has an education in informatics or computer science in order to solve first- and second-level problems. The technical support is in direct contact with the customer/end-user of the AI solution and usually does not need to have medical knowledge at all.

Quality Assurance Manager of the provider of an AI solution have either a background in software engineering or quality management/economics which gives them insight into the development processes and a high awareness of quality standards [17]. According to the EU IVDR, manufacturers of medical AI solutions, which shall be used in diagnostics, must have a so-called Person Responsible for Regulatory Compliance (PRRC), with a degree in law/medicine/pharmacy/engineering or another relevant scientific discipline or four years of experience in regulatory affairs or quality management systems relating to medical devices [24]. It is the task of the PRRC to establish, document, implement and maintain a quality management system that ensures compliance with the EU IVDR.

2.7 IVDR/MDR Expert/Staff of Notified Body

The IVDR/MDR expert is an independent auditor from a notified body who is restricted by regulations and norms. The IVDR/MDR expert probably has knowledge of the solution provider's processes and work flows but mainly should have expertise in the markets current demands and knowledge of other state-of-the-art AI solutions. An IVDR/MDR expert will use the explanatory components in the evaluation of the scientific validity, analytical performance (together with the AI solution provider) and clinical performance (together with the pathologist and quality managers).

3 AI Solutions

This section briefly explains what we understand by the term AI solution, and how they are developed in computational pathology. As described by Regitnig et al. [22], there exists a large variety of applications for the analysis of histopathological images, comprising a wide range of methods and tasks including image-enhancing, measuring and quantification, highlighting/preselection of regions of interest (RoI) and fully automated assessments, but there are a lot of expectations to digital pathology. Currently, there is a lot of ongoing research in this area [15, 23, 29], which will presumably lead to a plethora of new applications for histopathological imaging in the near future.

In order to facilitate establishing a common understanding of histopathological imaging applications, we propose a set of aspects constituting the minimum information, which can be used to profile, compare and categorize applications in histopathological imaging. Furthermore, this minimum information can act as a basis for developing explainability interfaces for different categories of applications and different types of users. In the next section, we introduce such a taxonomy.

The proposed set of aspects, which can be used to profile, compare and categorize applications in histopathological imaging, comprises administrative and technical aspects as well as aspects related to the application field, as shown in Fig. 4. This template can help to describe any such application in a nutshell.

In the following paragraphs, each of these aspects listed in Fig. 4 is described briefly.

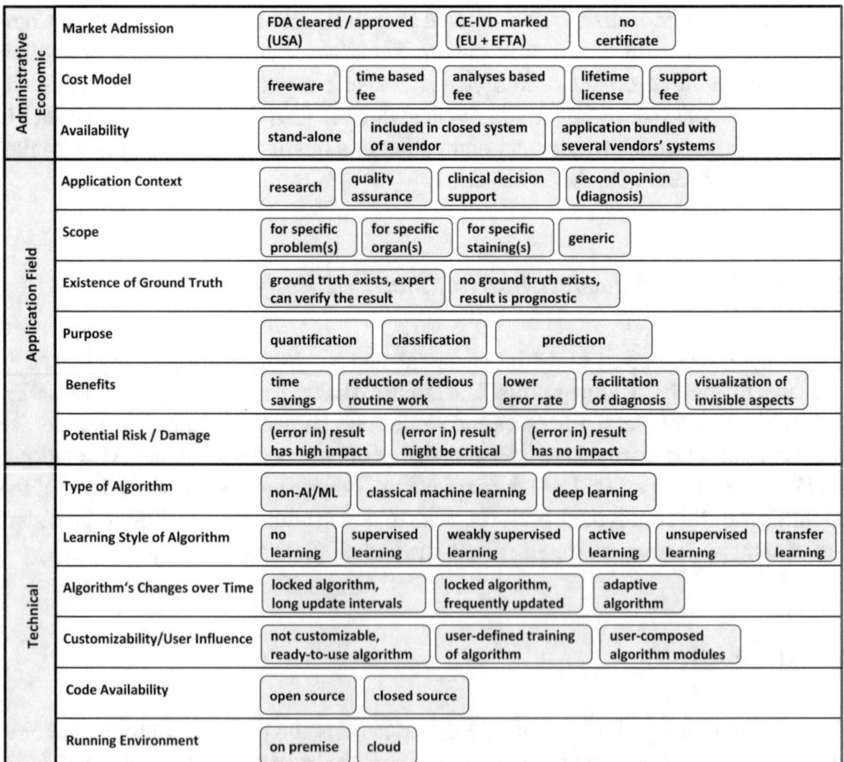

Fig. 4 Template for categorization of histopathological imaging applications

3.1 Administrative/Economic Aspects

Market Admission—Any software intended to be used for In-Vitro Diagnostics in the EU/EFTA must bear the *CE marking* to indicate its conformity with the regulation 2017/746 of the European Parliament and of the Council on In-Vitro Diagnostic medical devices (CE-IVDR) [24]. Similar regulations are in place in other countries. For example, before a medical device product (including software as a medical device) may be legally sold in the USA, it must gain approval by the US Food and Drug Administration (FDA).

Cost Model—A histopathological imaging application may be available as so-called *freeware* without monetary cost, or it may be sold as a commercial product with a *time-based fee, analyses-based fee* or *lifetime license*. Furthermore, users may have to pay a *fee for support*.

Availability—A histopathological imaging application may be a *stand-alone* application, it may be *included in a closed system of a vendor*, or the application may be *bundled with several vendors' systems*.

3.2 Aspects Related to the Application Field

Application Context—Histopathological imaging applications are mainly used in three distinct fields: in biological/pharmaceutical/medical *research*, in clinical *quality assurance* and in routine diagnostics, where they can be applied for *clinical decision support* or provision of a *second opinion*.

Scope—Histopathological imaging applications may be dedicated to *a specific problem* (e.g. PD-L1 scoring in lung cancer…), *specific organ(s)* (e.g. prostate, breast…) or *specific staining(s)* (e.g. H&E, HER2 IHC…), or may be applied in a *generic* scope (e.g. solutions for image pre-processing).

Existence of Ground Truth for the Result—When we look at the result of histopathological imaging applications, we can distinguish two cases: either *ground truth exists* and the result can be verified by experts or the result is prognostic and *no ground truth exists*.

Purpose—A histopathological imaging application may be used for a variety of histopathological tasks such as *quantification*, *classification* or *prediction*.

Benefits—The histopathological imaging application may bring about different benefits for the user: *time saving*, *reduction of tedious routine work*, *lower error rates*, *facilitation of diagnoses* (e.g. by better visualization of important aspects) or *new insights* (e.g. by visualization of (otherwise) invisible aspects).

Potential Risk/Possible Damage—When assessing the risks associated with a histopathological imaging application, we must look at the impact an erroneous result of the application would have on the diagnosis. We may find that an erroneous result has a *high impact on the diagnosis*, *might be critical for the diagnosis* or has *no impact on the diagnosis*.

3.3 Technical Aspects

Type of Algorithm—A histopathological imaging application includes one or more algorithms, which may be of different types: conventional *non-AI/ML* algorithms, *classical machine learning* algorithms (such as decision trees, support vector machines, k-nearest neighbours…) and *deep learning* algorithms utilizing neural networks.

Learning Style of Algorithm—While conventional algorithms need *no learning* to function, AI algorithms that use machine learning models must be trained. There are different learning styles: in *supervised learning* a large amount of training data with labels indicating the desired outcome is used, in *weakly supervised learning* the training data comes with only incomplete or coarse-grained labels, in *unsupervised learning* training data without annotations are used and in *transfer learning* the training of the model is split into two stages so that the training of a pretrained model can be finished with a low amount of training data. In *active learning*, the algorithm decides which examples from the training data should be labelled (by the user) next.

Algorithm's Changes over Time—On the one hand, a histopathological imaging application may be based on *locked* algorithms, which always provide the same output for a given input. Such algorithms, may be *updated frequently* (i.e. several updates per year) or have *longer update intervals* (i.e. one update per year or less). On the other hand, a histopathological imaging application may be based on *adaptive* algorithms, such as for example continuously learning algorithms, which change their behaviour by using a defined learning process on new or additional input data [27].

Customizability/User Influence—This aspect describes the ability of the application to be changed by the user, but at the same time it gives an indication of the need of the application to be customized by the user in order to become fully functional. A histopathological imaging application may be based on ready-to-use algorithms, without any customization options/obligations by the user. The application may need a user-defined training of the algorithm to be customized for the specific problem and work properly. Apart from that, the application may be a modular system, where users must compose the modules according to their needs in order to build a working algorithm.

Code Availability—Histopathological imaging applications may be *open source* software, with publicly available and modifiable code or *closed source* software, where the code is not published and owned by the vendor. Note that open source does not automatically imply that the code can be modified.

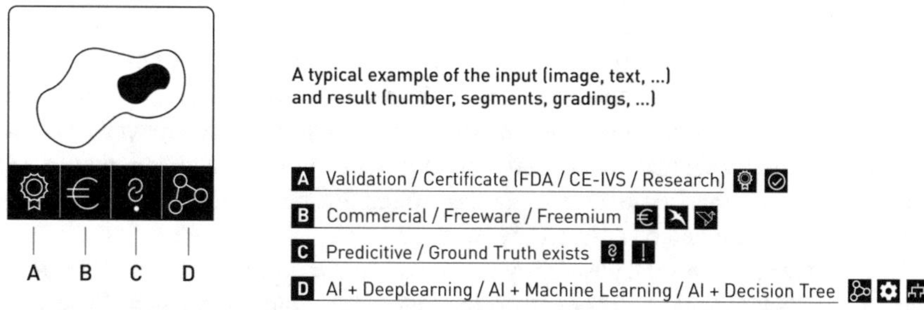

Fig. 5 Icon visualization of an AI solution

Running Environment—A histopathological imaging application may be run *on premise* or it may be run (partially or completely) *in the cloud.*
The set of all attributes describing an AI solution is quite comprehensive. In order to give an overview, an iconic representation of the most important aspects (see Fig. 5), based on the visual summary approach as developed in [16], is used:

- **Icon/Image** illustrating a typical example of the input data (image, text, etc.) and the result (segment, classification, number, etc.) of the AI solution.
- **4 main attributes** of the AI solution. The selection of these attributes should be community based.

4 Human–AI Interface

The interface between stakeholders and the AI solution usually consists of a management and viewer part and specific user interface components of an AI solution. These in turn can be divided into a visualization and an interaction component for the primary result and an optional display of the explanatory information. The basic component of the user interface is (ideally) the same for all AI solutions and should offer, in addition to the viewer functionality, a dynamic possibility (plugins) for the presentation of the AI solution's results. We will, therefore, describe the functional classes for the base component and the AI solutions interface separately below.

4.1 Case- and Slide Viewer

The "Case Viewer" and the "Slide Viewer" are two software parts that are playing a major role in the human–AI interface. They can be implemented as a combined software or as stand-alone products, both as Web application or as locally running instance.

Those software parts can be divided into three categories: *(1) vendor-specific solutions*: solutions that only offer access to WSI that are digitized with a specific WSI-scanner, perhaps with the possibility of importing/converting scans from other vendors. *(2) Proprietary vendor neutral solutions*: providing a commercial environment for viewing WSI that are created from different sources (scanner vendors). *(3) Open-source solutions*: non-commercial environments, which provide full access to the source code and can be adjusted by the user.

A "**Case Viewer**" offers the possibility to access and view a complete set of slides. In diagnoses, it acts as the layer between the laboratory information management system (LIMS) and the actual Slide Viewer, often the entry point to digital pathology for the pathologist and in research, to manage and organize WSIs for projects. In diagnostics for example, a single case can consist of up to 100 slides. The main aim of the "Case Viewer" is to present those slides in a structured way to the pathologist/researcher as shown in Fig. 6.

The main functionalities of a "Case Viewer" are related to the organization of whole cases' WSIs and metadata enrichment of these cases:

Organization of Whole Cases and Slide Images

- *Grouping of slides in cases and blocks*—Display of the hierarchical structure of slides
- *Access management to cases*—Possibility to define who has access to which cases
- *Reordering of slides*—Manual and/or automatic reordering of slides
- *Prioritization of cases*—Task and worklist creation for pathologists
- *Report creation*—A "Case Viewer" can provide an interface for report creation on a case-level.

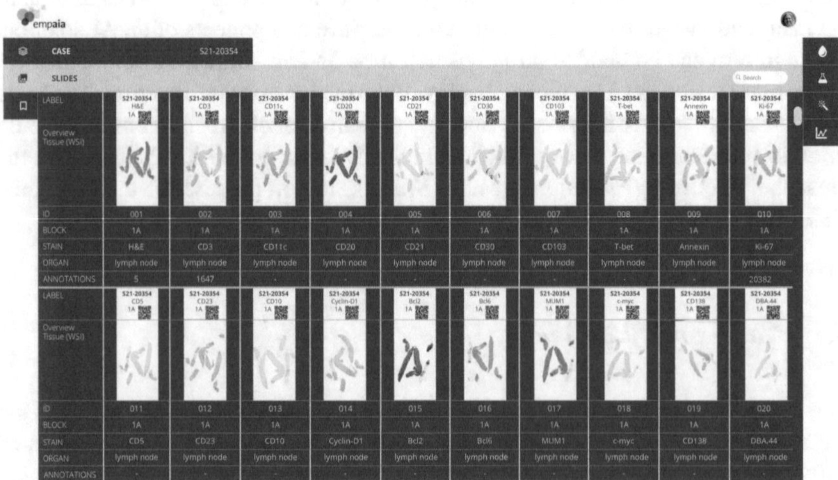

Fig. 6 Example of a "Case Viewer".

Metadata Enrichment

- *Connection to LIMS*—Gathering of information from the LIMS system to show case relevant metadata
- *Connection to AI Solutions*—Triggering of AI Solutions to perform analysis of slides and displaying the high-level results
- *Plugin Integration*—Possibility to add different additional functionalities, i.e. WSI pre-possessing to the “Case Viewer”.

On the next level in the stack the so-called **Slide Viewer** (see Fig. 7) is positioned. The “Slide Viewer” provides an interface to view the whole-slide images with the following basic and/or additional functionalities:

- *Display of WSI*—Visualization of the WSI files (vendor specific or vendor independent) in different magnifications
- *User annotations*—Possibility for user annotations, for example marking of RoIs (circle, rectangle, polygon, text) and displaying them
- *External annotations*—Visualization of annotations generated by an AI solution (RoIs, classifications, quantification, …)
- *Z-stacking*—Possibility to scroll across different focus-layers of a slide
- *Overlay and multislide view*—Allows the view of 2 or more slides (e.g. for immunohistochemistry) at once as overlayed images or in a grid layout
- *Autoalignment*—Automated translation and transformation to align different WSIs
- *Image correction*—Functionality to perform colour correction and channel adjustment of the displayed image
- *Tracking*—Marking of the viewed areas
- *Plugin integration*—Opportunity to extend the existing tools with additional third-party applications such as quantification tools or annotations.

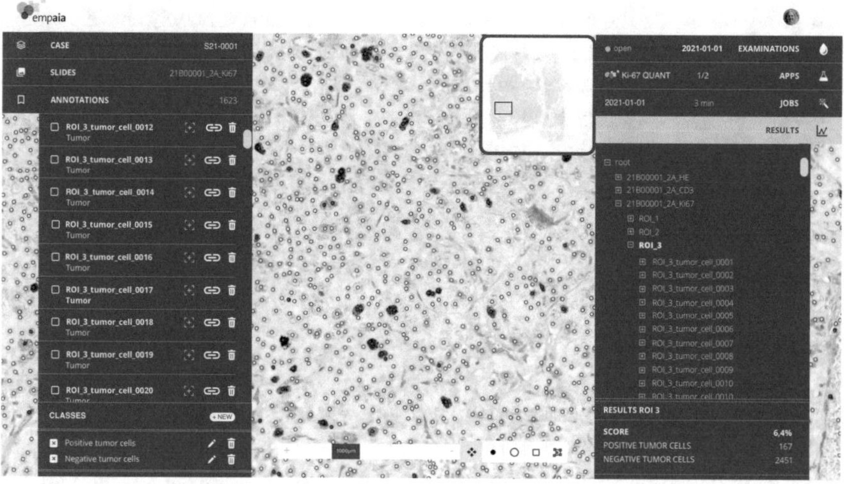

Fig. 7 Example of a “Slide Viewer” displaying the WSI and annotations as well as analysis results generated by an AI solution

4.2 User Interface Components of an AI Solution

The human–AI user interface can be divided into two parts: first, the interaction and visualization functionality supporting the primary research question and second the user interface and communication functionality dedicated to the question "Why", the explanatory component. We analysed existing workflows in pathology [11] and developed methods to visualize the process how a pathologist makes a specific diagnosis [19, 20] as a starting point to define functionality for the user interface components of AI solutions. Besides the visualization of the whole-slide image and the appropriate interaction techniques for gigapixel images the following visualization and interaction techniques are well known:

- Pixel, RoI-based annotations and visualizations
- Heat maps, saliency maps
- Representative tiles
- Statistical values, related to regions
- Textual output (using domain concepts).

Pathologist is trained to look at images and interpret image information, consequently, we should use both for the result and for the explanation whenever possible as overlays/ heat map/salience map at the source image. If results of an AI solution are directly related to the whole-slide image, for example by an image segmentation, there is a natural way to combine the results and explanatory information. Principles which should be harmonized across different AI solutions are:

- Different AI solutions should use the same visual language (symbols, colour codes) to visualize the results and explanatory information
- The explanatory component should be optimized for different stakeholder groups. This is especially true for the algorithm developers, who want to understand what is going on inside the model, as well as for quality managers, who have to judge an AI solution according to its analytical and overall clinical performance.
- Even if the same visualization methods (heatmaps, saliency maps, …) are applied, they have to be carefully adapted and optimized to the needs and prior knowledge of the different stakeholder groups.

5 Varieties of Explanations

Explaining is a form of purpose driven communication. It requires a recipient (stakeholder), information about a subject, a way (modality, representation) to convey it and a context in which it takes place. A good explanation supports the purpose and goals of the task the recipient is confronted with. This is typically achieved by considering the context, the recipient's need for information, the recipient's background knowledge and capability to interpret and understand the explanation (more on this in the following section). Since explanations require to be specific with respect to a stakeholder, a context and a task, a large variety of different explanation approaches exists.

To determine which subject of information can provide an appropriate explanation for the stakeholder, a good start is to analyse the specific task and context in which the stakeholder requires an explanation. For pathologists, a common task is examining WSIs (or their analogues form) and finally, based on their findings and medical criteria, deriving a diagnosis from it. Since this is a visual task, explanations for AI solutions on images often use visual modalities (geometrical shapes or coloured overlays such as heatmaps) to represent information. One example for the purpose of verifying the correctness of an AI-calculated cell ratio is highlighting recognized cells or RoI. A second example would be highlighting the most relevant parts of the image that led to a certain outcome of an algorithm (sensitivity/saliency maps). While the first example uses concepts that are within the medical domain or common knowledge (e.g. how to calculate a ratio) and therefore are probably easier to understand for pathologists, the second example is different: first, in this context, it does not help the pathologist to determine if the calculated ratio is correct; second, interpreting the coloured areas requires domain knowledge about the inner workings of the AI solution and probably, about convolutional neural networks. But while this second explanation is not appropriate for this medical context, within another context and for another recipient, it might be. Considering a developer who wants to detect "Clever Hans" (for the Clever-Hans effect see the original source [18]) predictors [12], a saliency map can be a valuable Explainable Artificial Intelligence (XAI) tool.

While most of the research on explainable AI in the recent years focused on explaining the behaviour of machine-learned models, embedding explainability into practical AI applications requires a much broader approach, as typically not just a single model needs to be explained but also the connections and inner workings of such AI solutions. We, therefore, suggest the following categories (including examples, non-exhaustive) when analysing or describing explainability methods and techniques in the context of AI solutions for pathology:

- **Stakeholders**—End-users, certifiers/validators, AI developers
- **Background Knowledge**—Medical, statistical, machine learning, neural architectures
- **Task**—Development, validation (scientific validity, analytical performance, clinical performance), certification, application (diagnosis, exploratory research), quality monitoring
- **Subject**—Complete AI solution, single learned model, training process, application
- **Scope**—Local (a single decision/single instance), global (general behaviour, over many instances)
- **Source of Information**—Intermediate results, intrinsic model, direct post-hoc derivation (Layerwise relevance propagation (LRP)), post-hoc approximation (local interpretable model-agnostic explanations (LIME), surrogates), scientific validation (benchmarks)
- **Modality/Representation**—Visual overlay (shape, heatmap), text label, interactive dialogue system, figure/chart, example images (counterfactuals).

6 What Makes an Explanation a Good Explanation?

For an explanation given for an AI solution, we aim to measure effectiveness (does an explanation describe a statement with an adequate level of detail), efficiency (is this done with a minimum of time and effort) and user satisfaction (how satisfactory was the explanation for the decision making process). When looking at the explanation component of an AI solution, we distinguish between

- Explainability, which in a technical sense highlights decision relevant parts of machine representations and machine models, i.e. parts that contributed to model accuracy in training, or to a specific prediction. It does not refer to a human model of the problem domain.
- Causability [9] similar to usability as the extent to which an explanation of a statement to a user achieves a specified level of causal understanding with effectiveness, efficiency and satisfaction in a specified context of use. This does refer to a human model.

In order to measure causability, one can use different approaches [31], via user surveys and questionnaires, and/or using the System Causability Scale (see next section).

6.1 System Causability Scale (SCS)

With the help of the System Causability Scale (SCS) [7], we can determine whether and to what extent an explainable component of an AI solution, its human–AI interface, and the explanation process itself is suitable for the intended purpose. Based on the Likert attitude method [14], as a standard psychometric scale to measure human responses, we are examining the following ten statements:

1. I found that the data included all relevant known causal factors with sufficient precision and granularity.
2. I understood the explanations within the context of my work.
3. I could change the level of detail on demand.
4. I did not need support to understand the explanations.
5. I found the explanations helped me to understand causality.
6. I was able to use the explanations with my knowledge base.
7. I did not find inconsistencies between explanations.
8. I think that most people would learn to understand the explanations very quickly.
9. I did not need more references as medical guidelines and regulations.
10. I received the explanations in a timely and efficient manner.

When applying the SCS, the recipients of the explanation (e.g. pathologists) are asked to score ten items with one of five responses that range from "strongly agree" to "strongly disagree". According to the Framingham model (for a discussion of the Framingham model refer to [5]), the following numerical values are used: 1 = strongly disagree, 2 = disagree, 3 = neutral, 4 = agree and 5 = strongly agree. The final SCS value is then computed by the sum of all ratings divided by 50. In accordance with the original System Usability Scale (SUS) [13], a score above 68 is considered to be above average, however, here further studies are in preparation.

6.2 Causability Laboratory

In such a laboratory, we investigate how pathologists make judgements and decisions with the goal of finding out how AI can support them in their daily work—towards an "augmented pathologist" [10]. Key questions include: How do pathologists make causal judgements? What role, if any, do counterfactual approaches play in this process? We know from theory that counterfactual theories of causal judgements predict that people compare what actually happened with what would have happened if the possible cause had not been present [3]. Common theories say that people focus only on what actually happened to judge the mechanism linking the cause and the outcome. To this end, for example, it is important to record pathologists' eye movements and compare them with other evidence relevant to the decision. Here it is important to analyse in real time the satisfaction of a pathologist when using the AI solution. This can be done with different methods, e.g. to analyse eye movements, facial expressions and micromovements such as nodding the head. We combine and analyse all these sensor parameters and thus get insights in both, the usability and the mental load of the overall interface and causability, i.e. level of causal understanding. Ideally, this would need a prototyping laboratory (BYOD, Bring Your Own Data), a demo space and a human-centred AI testing laboratory to test human–AI interaction to inspire the design, development and testing of novel human–AI interfaces and to carry out tests ensuring ethical AI.

7 Conclusion

AI solutions using machine learning and deep learning methods are able to find correlations in complex data, but there is no guarantee that these correlations are meaningful and correspond to actual causal relationships. Another problem is that the complexity of black box models is preventing the inspection and the control by human operators. We conclude with a quote for the JRC technical report on *Robustness and Explainability of Artificial Intelligence* [4], which states three important topics for the right deployment of human-centred AI:

1. **Transparency of models**: it relates to the documentation of the AI processing chain, including the technical principles of the model, and the description of the data used for the conception of the model. This also encompasses elements that provide a good understanding of the model and related to the interpretability and explainability of models;

2. **Reliability of models**: it concerns the capacity of the models to avoid failures or malfunction, either because of edge cases or because of malicious intentions. The main vulnerabilities of AI models have to be identified, and technical solutions have to be implemented to make sure that autonomous systems will not fail or be manipulated by an adversary;
3. **Protection of data in models**: The security of data used in AI models needs to be preserved. In the case of sensitive data, for instance personal data, the risks should be managed by the application of proper organizational and technical controls [4].

All the above-mentioned aspects support the hypothesis that explainability is one of the most important points to establish trustworthiness to AI. This taxonomy of explainable AI in the field of computational pathology is an important contribution for building future human–AI interfaces generally and paving the way for a clearer and better understanding for working in human-centred AI specifically.

Acknowledgements Parts of this work have received funding from the European Union's Horizon 2020 research and innovation programme under grant agreement No. 857122 (CY-Biobank), No. 824087 (EOSC-Life) and No. 874662 (HEAP). This publication reflects only the authors' view and the European Commission is not responsible for any use that may be made of the information it contains. Parts of this work have received funding from the Austrian Research Promotion Agency (FFG) under grant agreement No. 879881 (EMPAIA) and by the Austrian Science Fund (FWF), Project: P-32554 explainable Artificial Intelligence.

References

1. Alcaraz-Mateos, E., Turic, I., Nieto-Olivares, A., Perez-Ramos, M., Poblet, E.: Head-tracking as an interface device for image control in digital pathology: a comparative study. Revista Espanola de Patologia **53**(4), 213–217 (2020). DOI https://doi.org/10.1016/j.patol.2020.05.007
2. Esteva, A., Kuprel, B., Novoa, R.A., Ko, J., Swetter, S.M., Blau, H.M., Thrun, S.: Dermatologist-level classification of skin cancer with deep neural networks. Nature **542**(7639), 115–118 (2017). DOI https://doi.org/10.1038/nature21056
3. Gerstenberg, T., Peterson, M.F., Goodman, N.D., Lagnado, D.A., Tenenbaum, J.B.: Eye-tracking causality. Psychological science **28**(12), 1731–1744 (2017). DOI https://doi.org/10.1177/0956797617713053
4. Hamon, R., Junklewitz, H., Sanchez, I.: European Commission JRC Technical Report: Robustness and Explainability of Artificial Intelligence (2020). DOI https://doi.org/10.2760/5749
5. Hemann, B.A., Bimson, W.F., Taylor, A.J.: The Framingham risk score: an appraisal of its benefits and limitations. American Heart Hospital Journal **5**(2), 91–96 (2007). DOI https://doi.org/10.1111/j.1541-9215.2007.06350.x
6. Holzinger, A., Biemann, C., Pattichis, C.S., Kell, D.B.: What do we need to build explainable ai systems for the medical domain? arXiv:1712.09923 (2017)
7. Holzinger, A., Carrington, A., Müller, H.: Measuring the quality of explanations: The system casuability scale (scs). comparing human and machine explanations. KI - Künstliche Intelligenz (German Journal of Artificial intelligence), Special Issue on Interactive Machine Learning, Edited by Kristian Kersting, TU Darmstadt **34**(2), 193–198 (2020). DOI https://doi.org/10.1007/s13218-020-00636-z
8. Holzinger, A., Goebel, R., Mengel, M., Müller, H.: Artificial Intelligence and Machine Learning for Digital Pathology: State-of-the-Art and Future Challenges. Springer, Cham (2020). DOI https://doi.org/10.1007/978-3-030-50402-1

9. Holzinger, A., Langs, G., Denk, H., Zatloukal, K., Müller, H.: Causability and explainability of artificial intelligence in medicine. Wiley Interdisciplinary Reviews: Data Mining and Knowledge Discovery **9**(4) (2019). DOI https://doi.org/10.1002/widm.1312
10. Holzinger, A., Malle, B., Kieseberg, P., Roth, P.M., Müller, H., Reihs, R., Zatloukal, K.: Machine learning and knowledge extraction in digital pathology needs an integrative approach. In: Towards Integrative Machine Learning and Knowledge Extraction, Springer Lecture Notes in Artificial Intelligence Volume LNAI 10344, pp. 13–50. Springer, Cham (2017). DOI https://doi.org/10.1007/978-3-319-69775-8-2
11. Kargl, M., Regitnig, P., Müller, H., Holzinger, A.: Towards a better understanding of the workflows: Modeling pathology processes in view of future AI integration. In: Artificial Intelligence and Machine Learning for Digital Pathology, pp. 102–117. Springer, Cham (2020)
12. Lapuschkin, S., Wäldchen, S., Binder, A., Montavon, G., Samek, W., Müller, K.R.: Unmasking clever Hans predictors and assessing what machines really learn. Nature communications **10**(1), 1–8 (2019)
13. Lewis, J.R.: The system usability scale: past, present, and future. International Journal of Human–Computer Interaction **34**(7), 577–590 (2018). DOI https://doi.org/10.1080/10447318.2018.1455307
14. Likert, R.: A technique for the measurement of attitudes. Archives of Psychology **140**, 1–55 (1932)
15. Litjens, G., Kooi, T., Bejnordi, B., Setio, A.A.A., et.al: A survey on deep learning in medical image analysis. Medical Image Analysis **42**, 60–88 (2017). DOI https://doi.org/10.1016/j.media.2017.07.005
16. Müller, H., Sauer, S., Zatloukal, K., Bauernhofer, T.: Interactive patient records. In: 2010 14th International Conference Information Visualisation, pp. 252–257. IEEE (2010)
17. O'Sullivan, S., et al.: Legal, regulatory, and ethical frameworks for development of standards in artificial intelligence (ai) and autonomous robotic surgery. The International Journal of Medical Robotics and Computer Assisted Surgery **15**(1), e1968 (2019)
18. Pfungst, O.: Clever Hans:(the horse of Mr. Von Osten.) a contribution to experimental animal and human psychology. Holt, Rinehart and Winston, London (1911)
19. Pohn, B., Kargl, M., Reihs, R., Holzinger, A., Zatloukal, K., Müller, H.: Towards a deeper understanding of how a pathologist makes a diagnosis: Visualization of the diagnostic process in histopathology. In: 2019 IEEE Symposium on Computers and Communications (ISCC), pp. 1081–1086. IEEE (2019)
20. Pohn, B., Mayer, M.C., Reihs, R., Holzinger, A., Zatloukal, K., Müller, H.: Visualization of histopathological decision making using a roadbook metaphor. In: 2019 23rd International Conference Information Visualisation (IV), pp. 392–397. IEEE (2019)
21. Rahim, S.S., Palade, V., Almakky, I., Holzinger, A.: Detection of diabetic retinopathy and maculopathy in eye fundus images using deep learning and image augmentation. In: International Cross-Domain Conference for Machine Learning and Knowledge Extraction, pp. 114–127. Springer (2019). DOI https://doi.org/10.1007/978-3-030-29726-8-8
22. Regitnig, P., Mueller, H., Holzinger, A.: Expectations of artificial intelligence in pathology. In: Springer Lecture Notes in Artificial Intelligence LNAI 12090, pp. 1–15. Springer, Cham (2020). DOI https://doi.org/10.1007/978-3-030-50402-1-1
23. Srinidhi, C.L., Ciga, O., Martel, A.L.: Deep neural network models for computational histopathology: A survey. Medical Image Analysis **67** (2021). DOI https://doi.org/10.1016/j.media.2020.101813
24. The European Parliament, The Council of the European Union: Regulation (EU) 2017/ 746 of the European Parliament and of the Council - of 5 April 2017 - on in vitro diagnostic medical devices. Official Journal of the European Union **L117**, 176–332 (2017). https://eur-lex.europa.eu/legal-content/EN/TXT/PDF/?uri=CELEX:32017R0746&rid=6
25. Thrall, J.H., Li, X., Li, Q., Cruz, C., Do, S., Dreyer, K., Brink, J.: Artificial intelligence and machine learning in radiology: opportunities, challenges, pitfalls, and criteria for success. Journal of the American College of Radiology **15**(3), 504–508 (2018)

26. Tosun, A.B., Pullara, F., Becich, M.J., Taylor, D.L., Chennubhotla, S.C., Fine, J.L.: Histomapr: An explainable ai (xai) platform for computational pathology solutions. In: Artificial Intelligence and Machine Learning for Digital Pathology, pp. 204–227. Springer (2020)
27. U.S. Food and Drug Administration: Proposed regulatory framework for modifications to artificial intelligence/machine learning (AI/ML)-based software as a medical device (samd)-discussion paper and request for feedback (2019). https://www.fda.gov/media/122535/download
28. Wulczyn, E., Nagpal, K., Symonds, M., Moran, M., Plass, M., Reihs, R., Nader, F., Tan, F., Cai, Y., Brown, T., Flament-Auvigne, I., Amin, M.B., Stumpe, M.C., Mueller, H., Regitnig, P., Holzinger, A., Corrado, G.S., Peng, L.H., Chen, P.H.C., Steiner, D.F., Zatloukal, K., Liu, Y., Mermel, C.H.: Predicting prostate cancer-specific mortality with ai-based gleason grading. arXiv:2012.05197 (2020)
29. Yi, X., Walia, E., Babyn, P.: Generative adversarial network in medical imaging: A review. Medical Image Analysis **58** (2019). DOI https://doi.org/10.1016/j.media.2020.101552
30. Zhang, Z., Chen, P., McGough, M., Xing, F., Wang, C., Bui, M., Xie, Y., Sapkota, M., Cui, L., Dhillon, J.: Pathologist-level interpretable whole-slide cancer diagnosis with deep learning. Nature Machine Intelligence **1**(5), 236–245 (2019). DOI https://doi.org/10.1038/s42256-019-0052-1
31. Zhou, J., Gandomi, A.H., Chen, F., Holzinger, A.: Evaluating the quality of machine learning explanations: A survey on methods and metrics. Electronics **10**(5), 593 (2021). DOI https://doi.org/10.3390/electronics10050593
32. Ziefle, M., Klack, L., Wilkowska, W., Holzinger, A.: Acceptance of telemedical treatments – a medical professional point of view. In: S. Yamamoto (ed.) Human Interface and the Management of Information. Lecture Notes in Computer Science LNCS 8017, pp. 325–334. Springer (2013). DOI https://doi.org/10.1007/978-3-642-39215-3-39

Printed in the United States
by Baker & Taylor Publisher Services